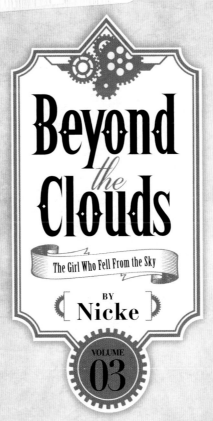

Beyond
the
Clouds

The Girl Who Fell From the Sky

BY
{ Nicke }

VOLUME
03

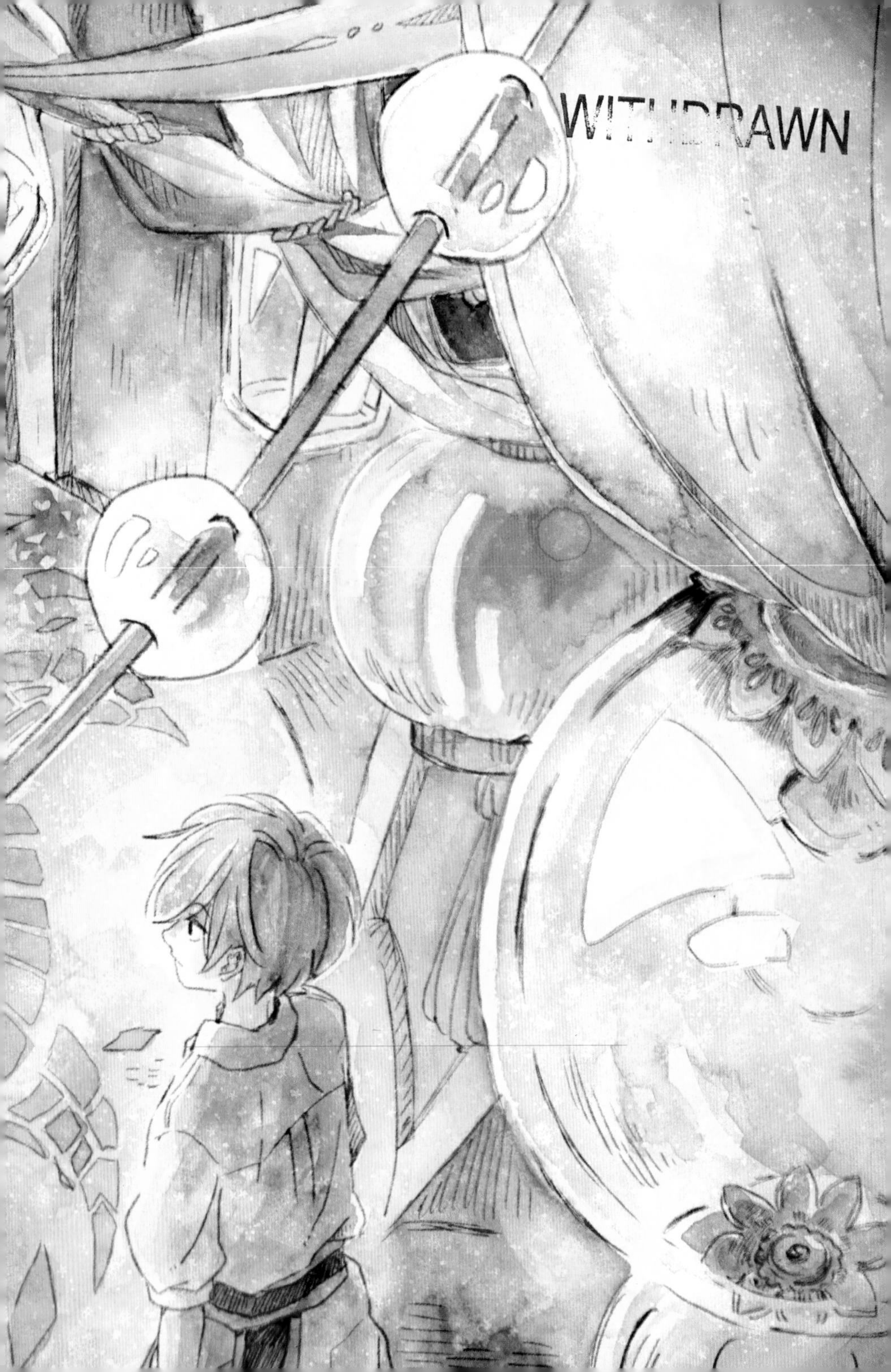

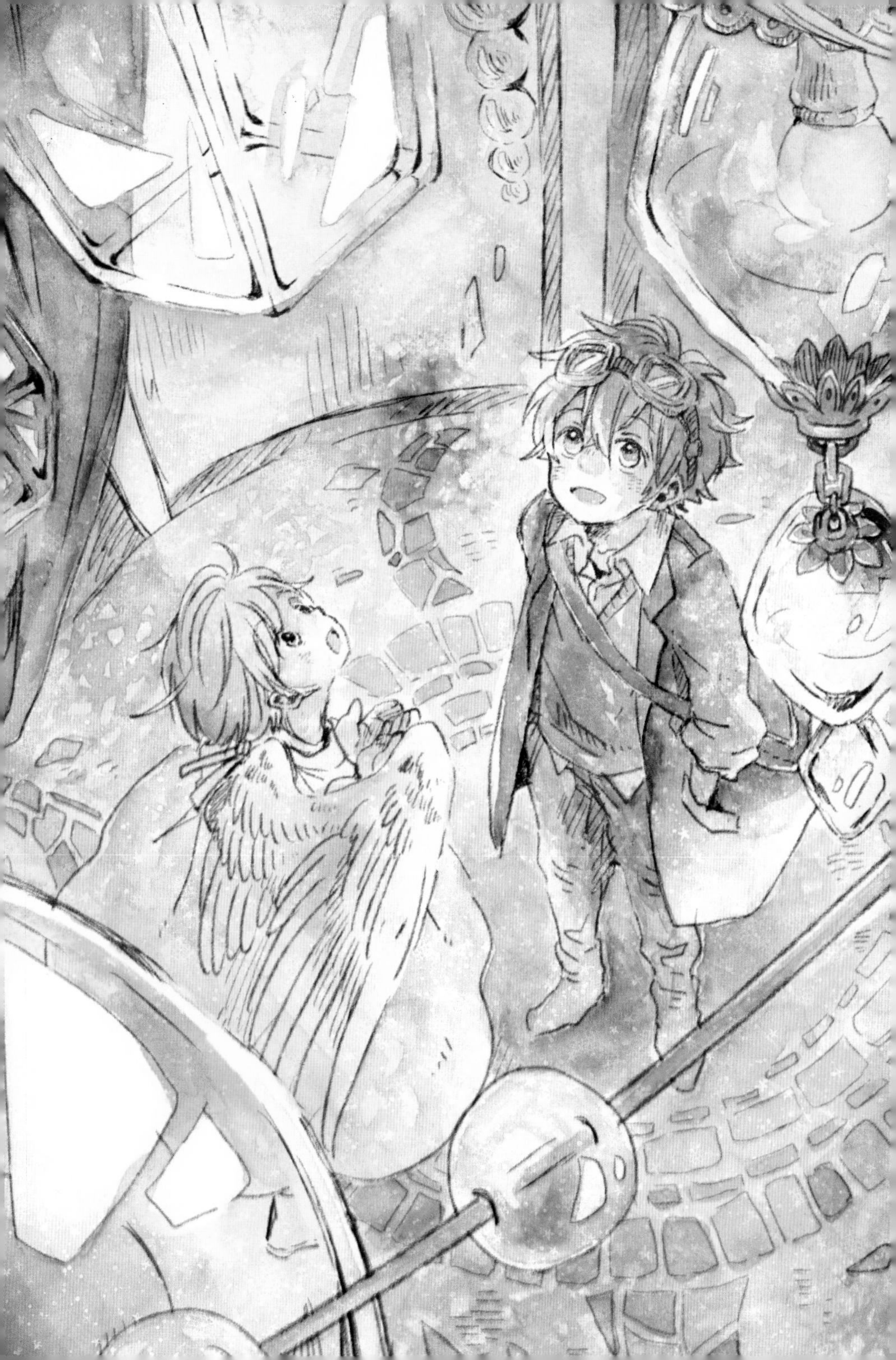

Table of Contents

Chapter 12: The Secret of the Seer

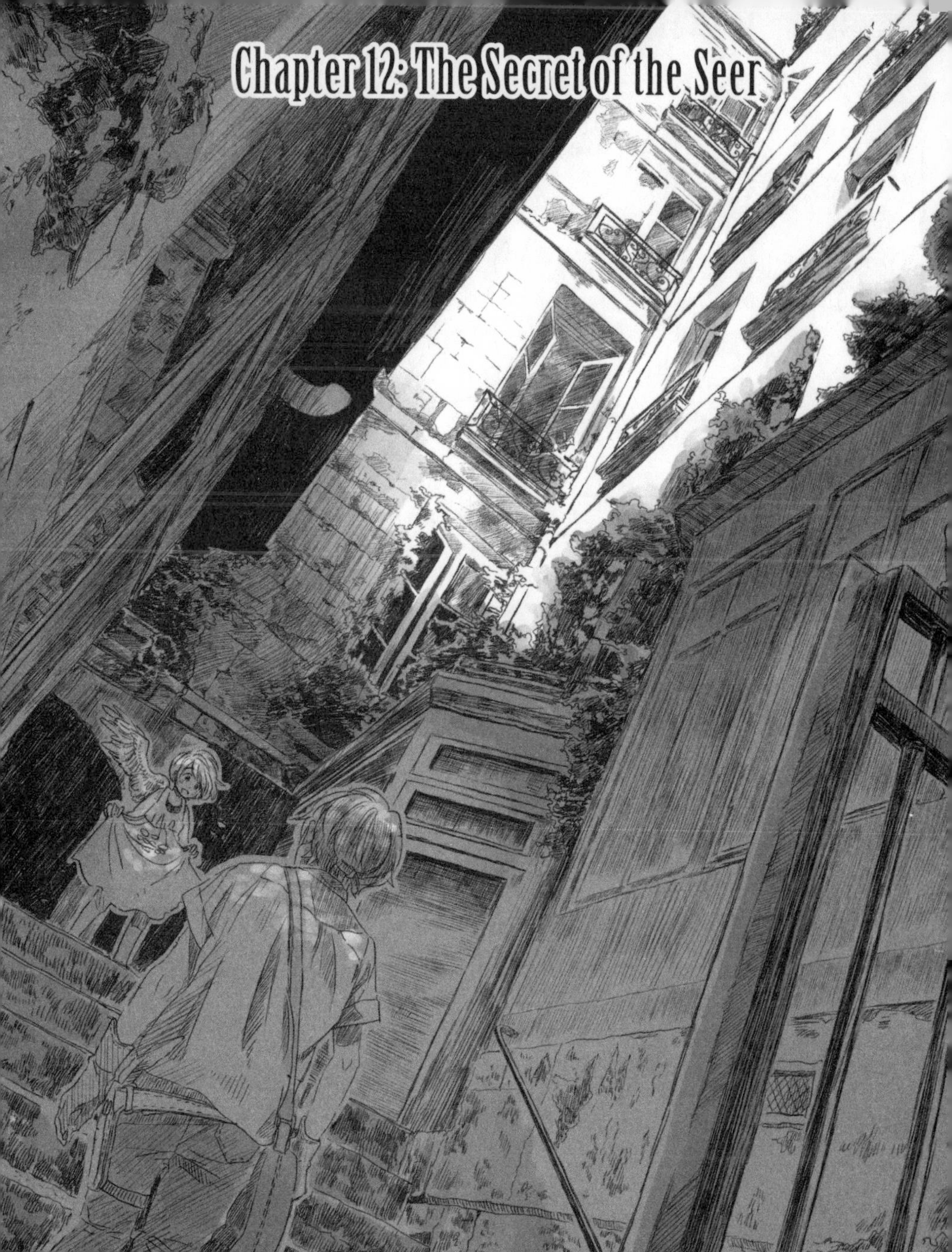

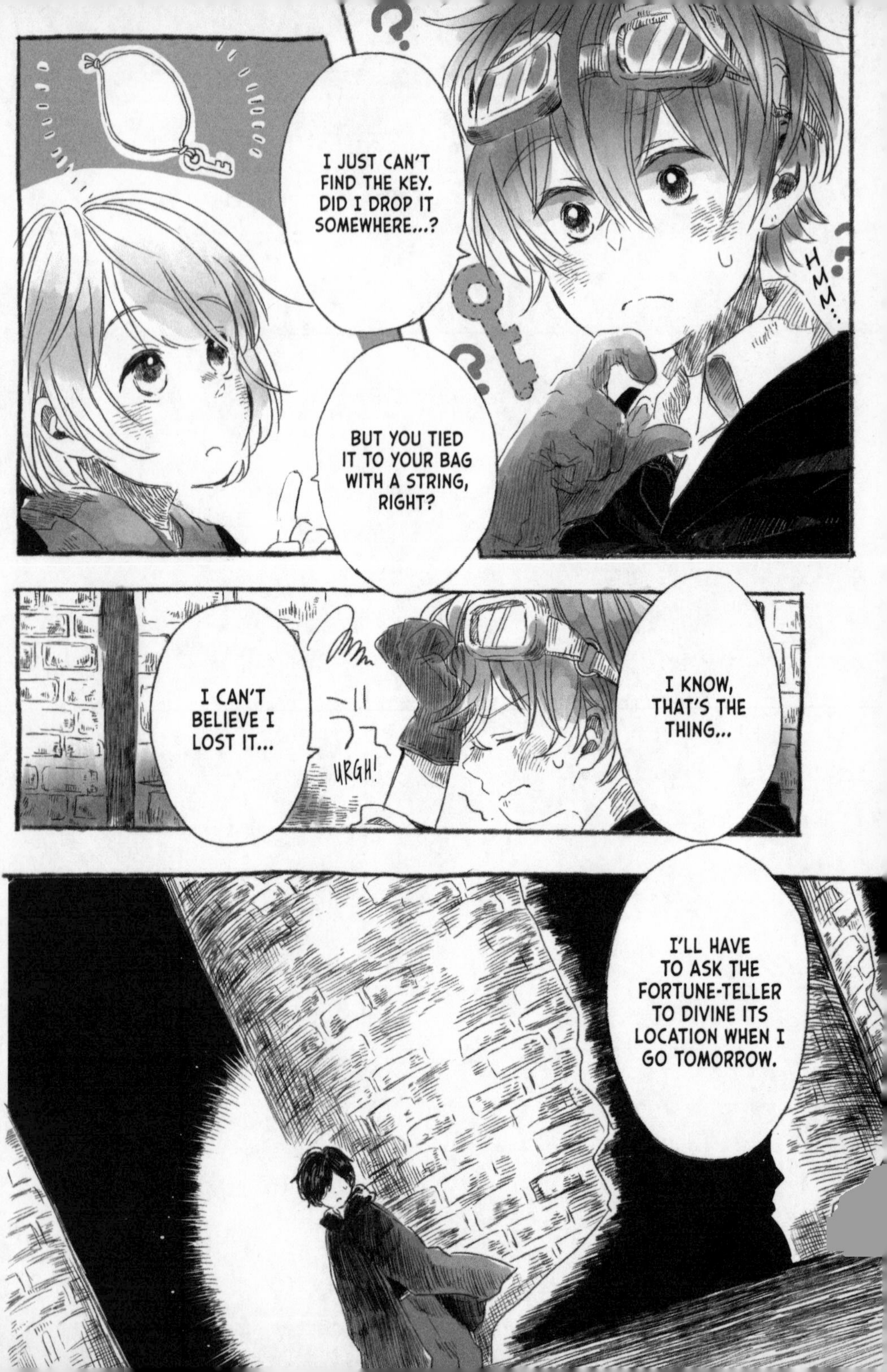
HMM...
I JUST CAN'T FIND THE KEY. DID I DROP IT SOMEWHERE...?
BUT YOU TIED IT TO YOUR BAG WITH A STRING, RIGHT?
I KNOW, THAT'S THE THING...
URGH!
I CAN'T BELIEVE I LOST IT...
I'LL HAVE TO ASK THE FORTUNE-TELLER TO DIVINE ITS LOCATION WHEN I GO TOMORROW.

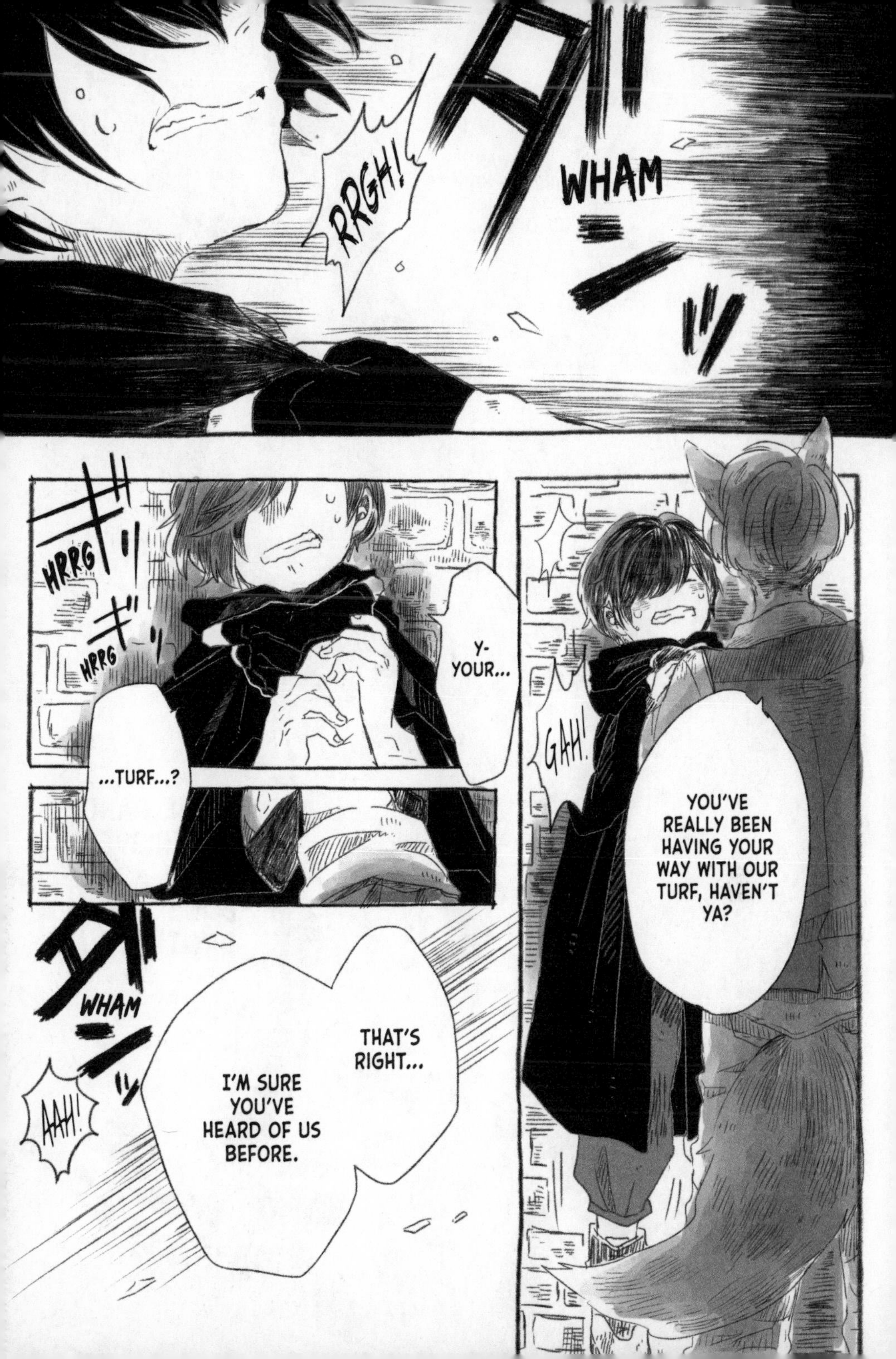
WHAM
RRGH!
YOU'VE REALLY BEEN HAVING YOUR WAY WITH OUR TURF, HAVEN'T YA?
GAH!
Y- YOUR...
HRRG
HRRG
...TURF...?
THAT'S RIGHT...
I'M SURE YOU'VE HEARD OF US BEFORE.
WHAM
AAH!

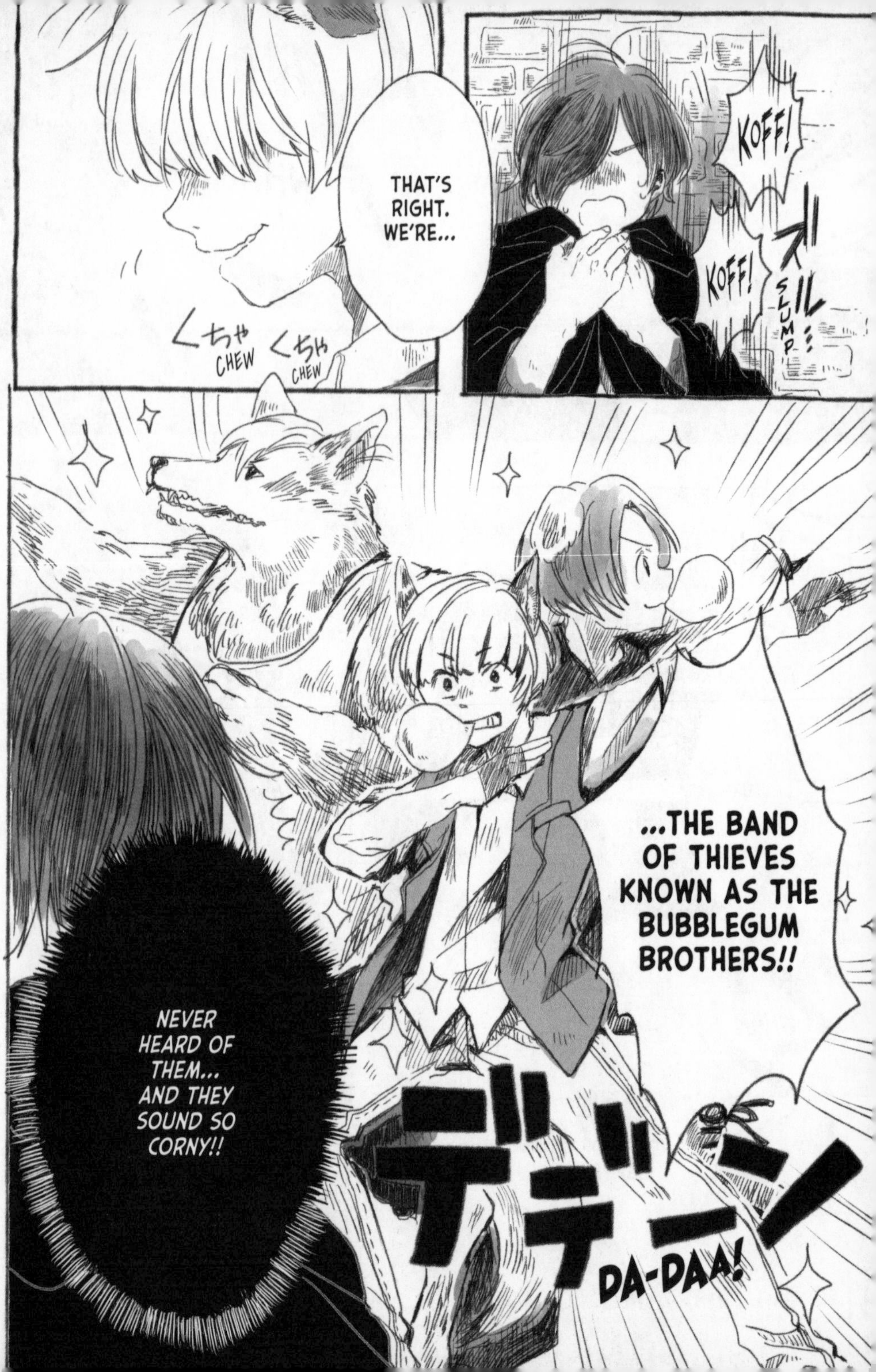
KOFF!
KOFF!
SLUMP
THAT'S RIGHT. WE'RE...
くちゃ
CHEW
くちゃ
CHEW
...THE BAND OF THIEVES KNOWN AS THE BUBBLEGUM BROTHERS!!
DA-DAA!
NEVER HEARD OF THEM... AND THEY SOUND SO CORNY!!

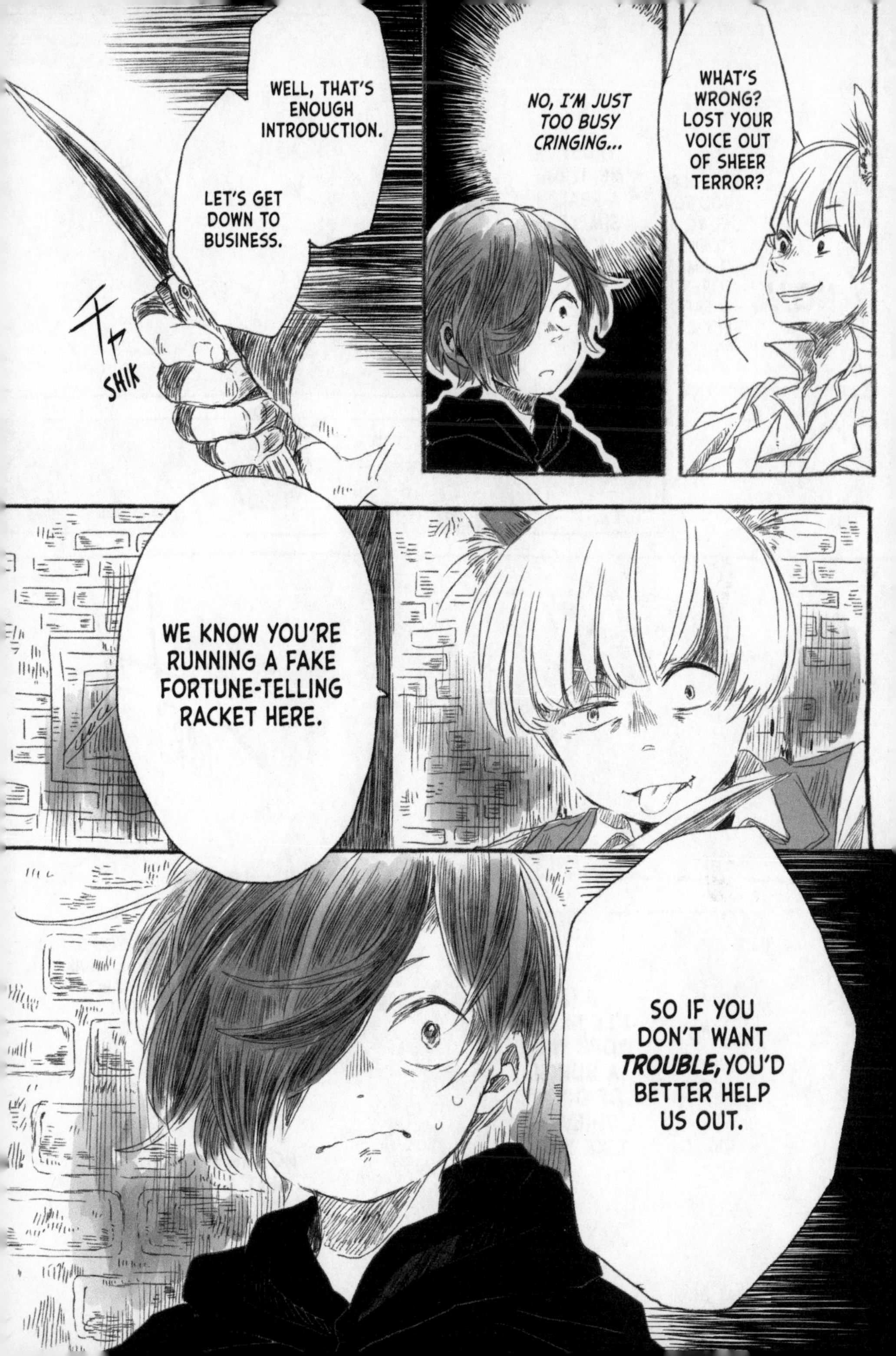
WHAT'S WRONG? LOST YOUR VOICE OUT OF SHEER TERROR?
NO, I'M JUST TOO BUSY CRINGING...
WELL, THAT'S ENOUGH INTRODUCTION.
LET'S GET DOWN TO BUSINESS.
チャ
SHIK
WE KNOW YOU'RE RUNNING A FAKE FORTUNE-TELLING RACKET HERE.
SO IF YOU DON'T WANT *TROUBLE,* YOU'D BETTER HELP US OUT.

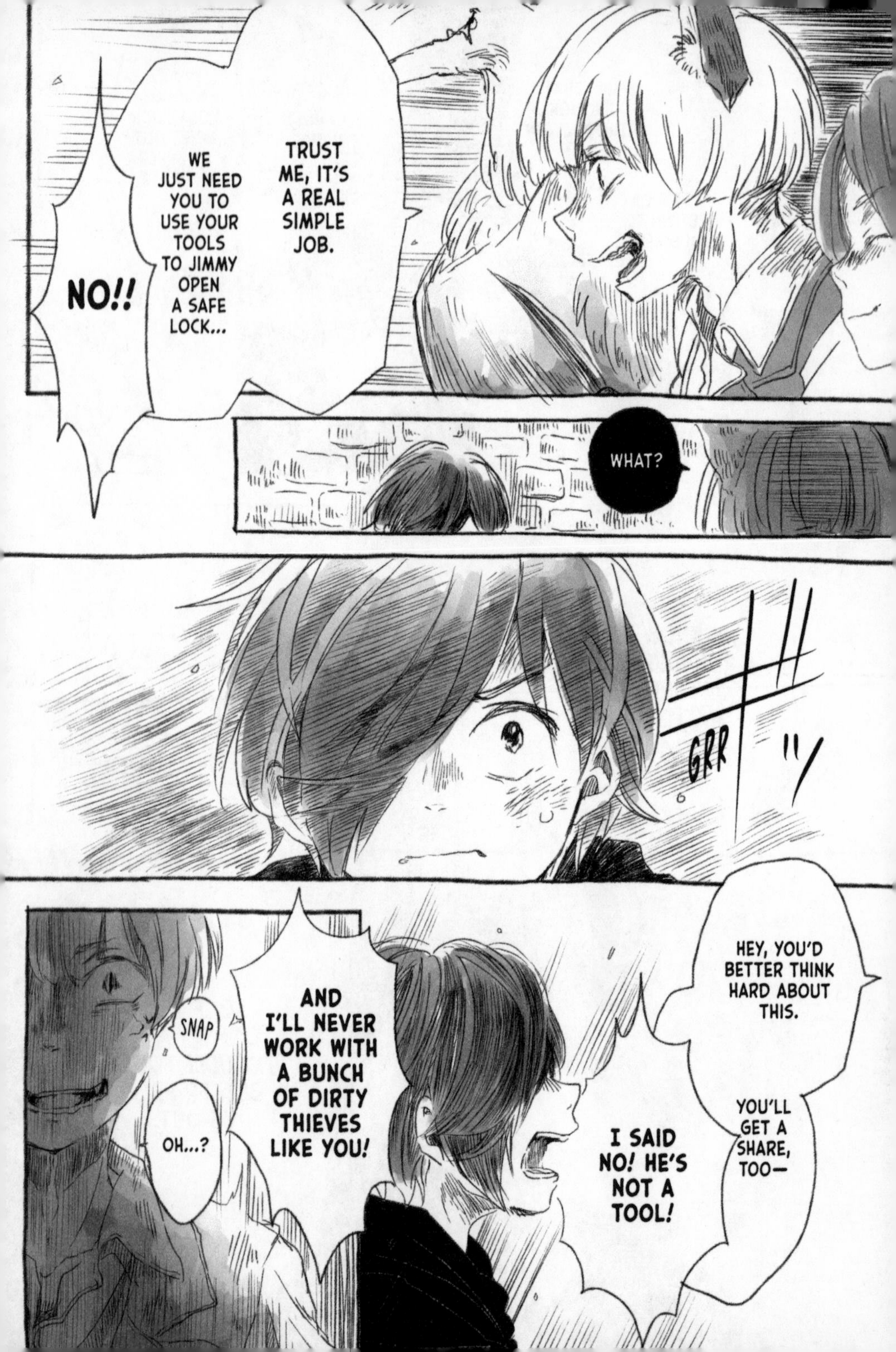
TRUST ME, IT'S A REAL SIMPLE JOB.
WE JUST NEED YOU TO USE YOUR TOOLS TO JIMMY OPEN A SAFE LOCK...
NO!!
WHAT?
GRR
HEY, YOU'D BETTER THINK HARD ABOUT THIS.
YOU'LL GET A SHARE, TOO—
I SAID NO! HE'S NOT A TOOL!
AND I'LL NEVER WORK WITH A BUNCH OF DIRTY THIEVES LIKE YOU!
SNAP
OH...?

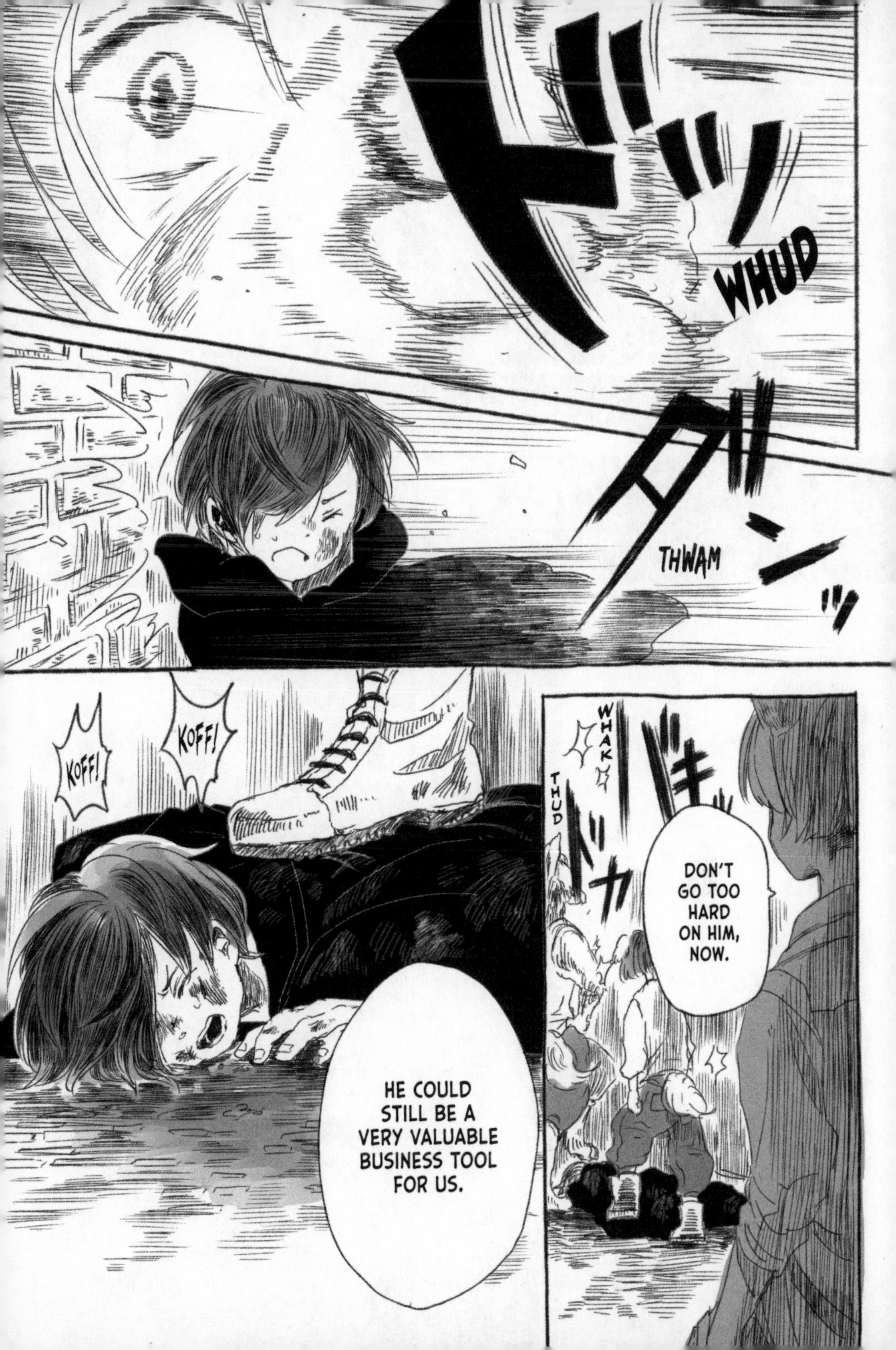
WHUD
THWAM
WHAK
THUD
DON'T GO TOO HARD ON HIM, NOW.
KOFF!
KOFF!
HE COULD STILL BE A VERY VALUABLE BUSINESS TOOL FOR US.

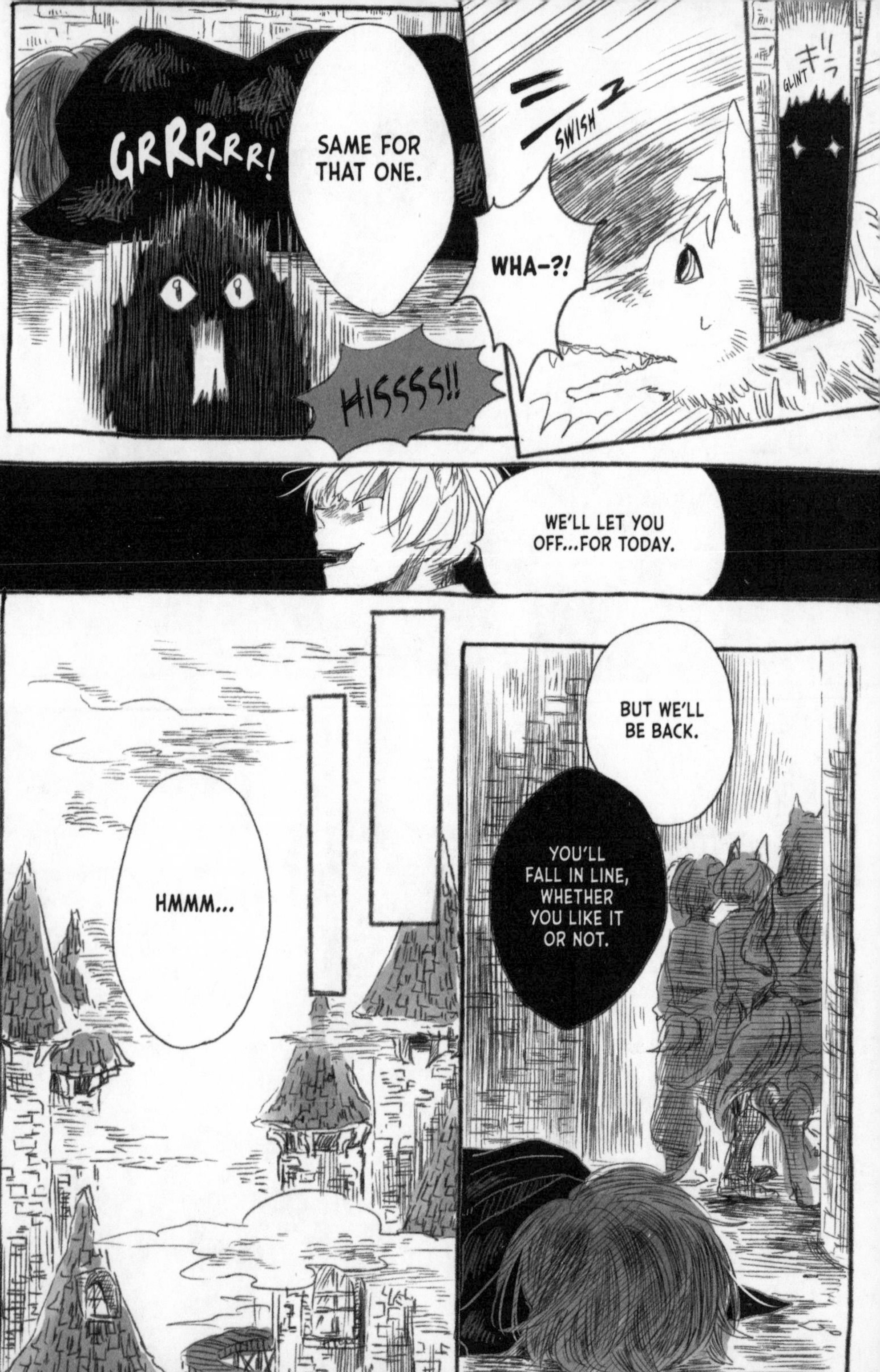
GLINT ギラ
SWISH
WHA-?!
SAME FOR THAT ONE.
GRRRRR!
HISSSS!!
WE'LL LET YOU OFF...FOR TODAY.
BUT WE'LL BE BACK.
YOU'LL FALL IN LINE, WHETHER YOU LIKE IT OR NOT.
HMMM...

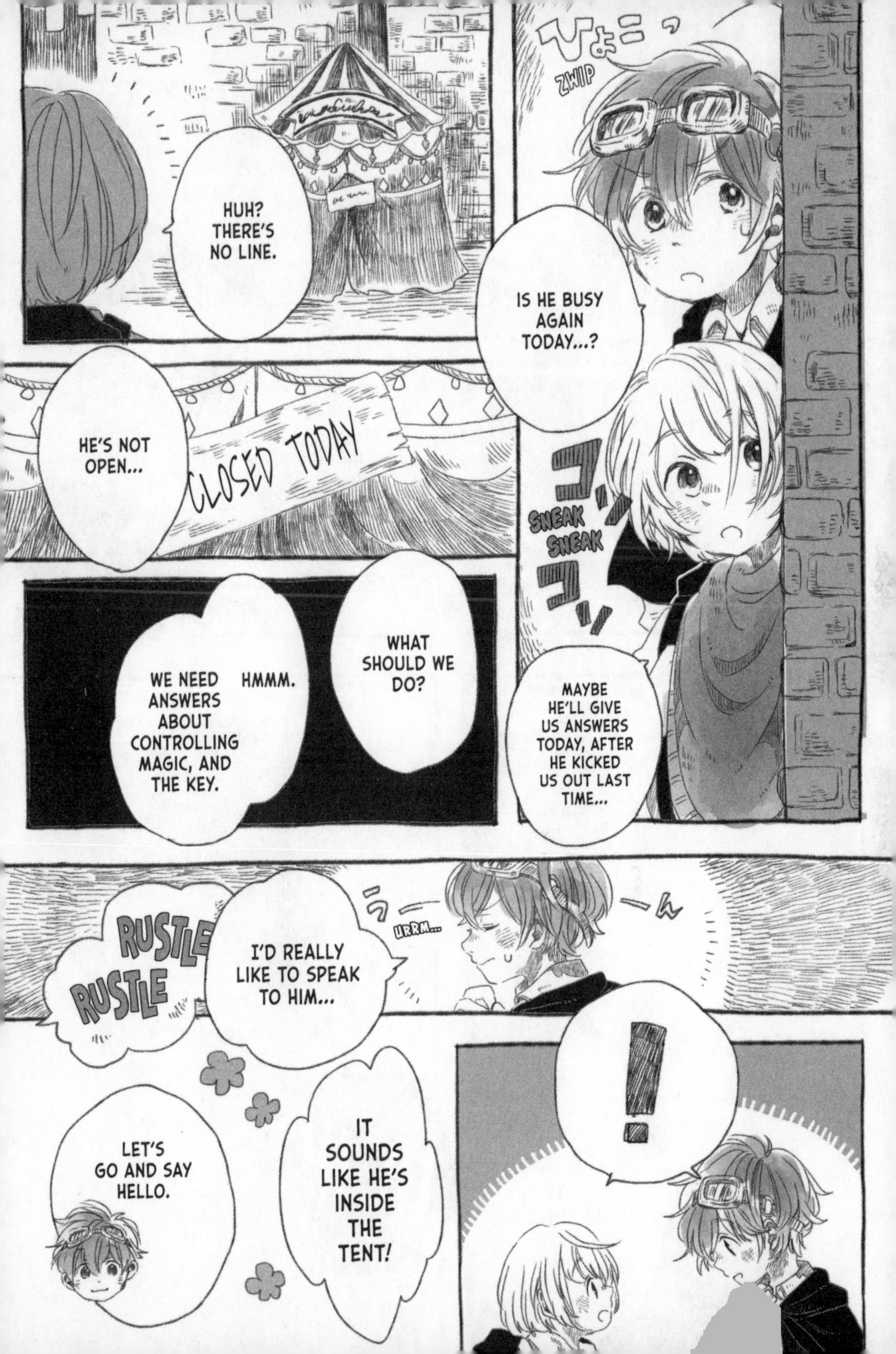

ひょこっ
ZWIP
IS HE BUSY AGAIN TODAY...?
コソコソ
SNEAK SNEAK
MAYBE HE'LL GIVE US ANSWERS TODAY, AFTER HE KICKED US OUT LAST TIME...
HUH? THERE'S NO LINE.
HE'S NOT OPEN...
CLOSED TODAY
WHAT SHOULD WE DO?
HMMM.
WE NEED ANSWERS ABOUT CONTROLLING MAGIC, AND THE KEY.
うーーん
URRM...
I'D REALLY LIKE TO SPEAK TO HIM...
RUSTLE RUSTLE
!
IT SOUNDS LIKE HE'S INSIDE THE TENT!
LET'S GO AND SAY HELLO.

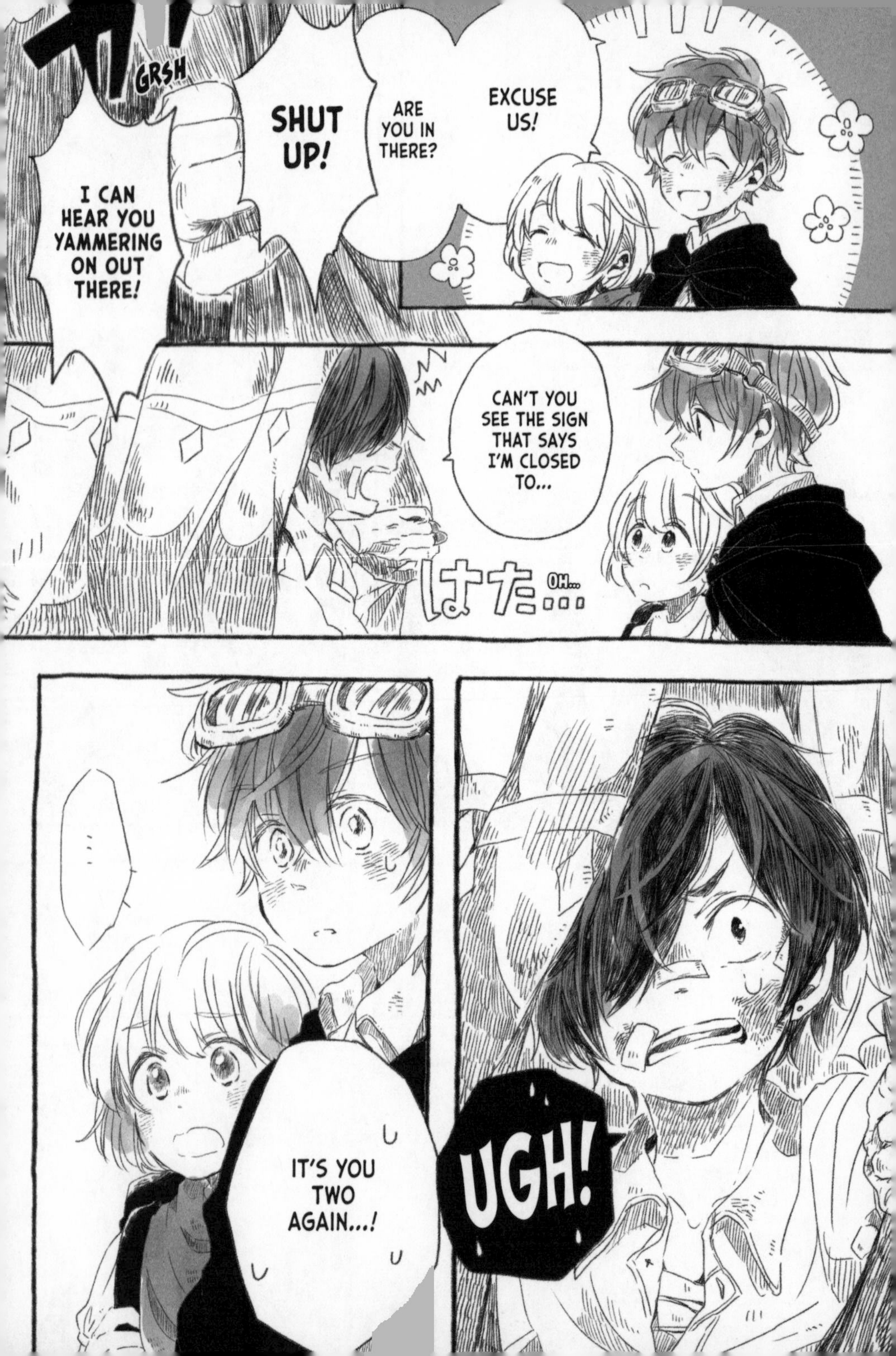
EXCUSE US!
ARE YOU IN THERE?
SHUT UP!
GRSH
I CAN HEAR YOU YAMMERING ON OUT THERE!
CAN'T YOU SEE THE SIGN THAT SAYS I'M CLOSED TO...
はた...
OH...
UGH!
...
IT'S YOU TWO AGAIN...!

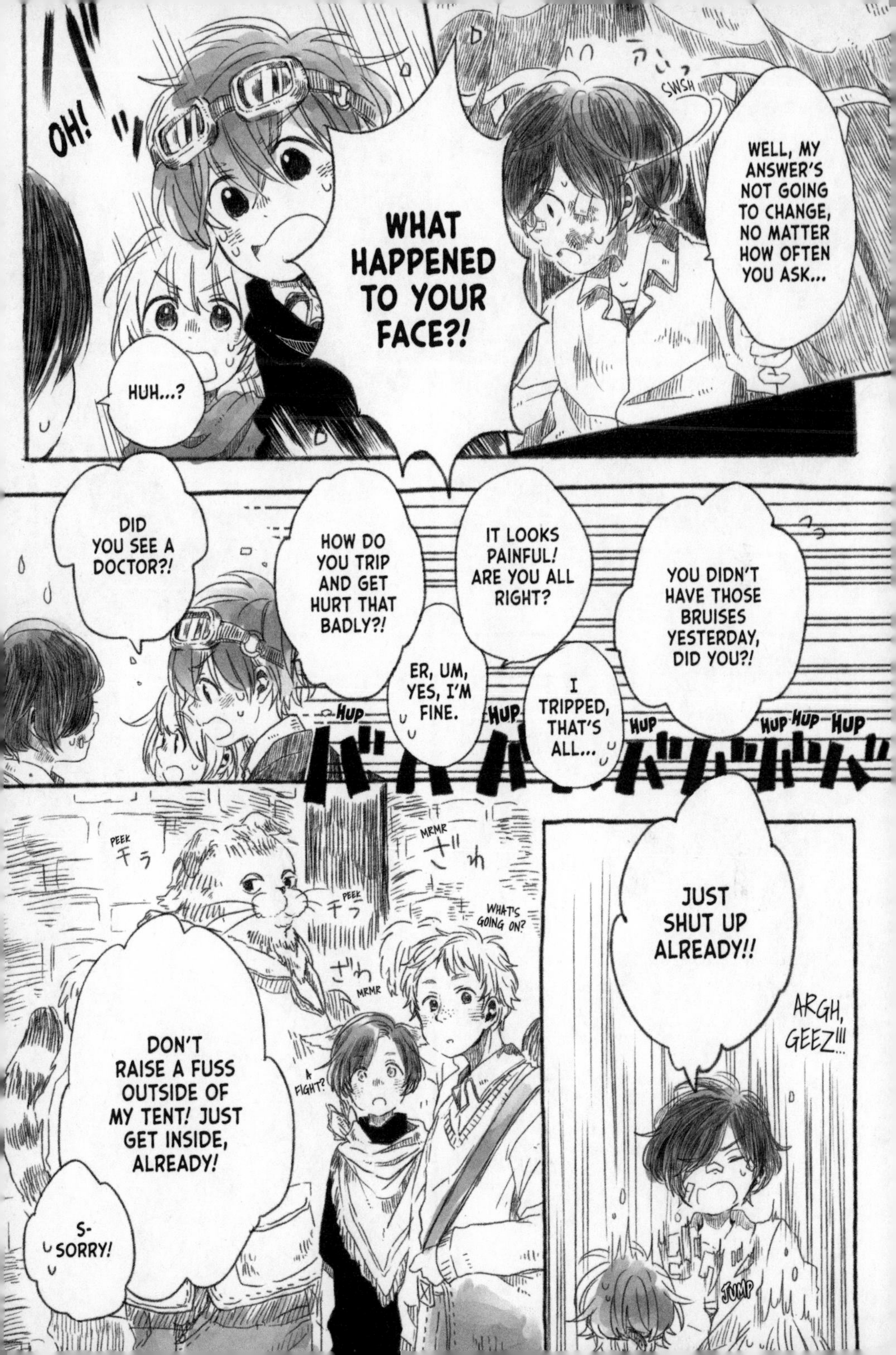
SWSH
WELL, MY ANSWER'S NOT GOING TO CHANGE, NO MATTER HOW OFTEN YOU ASK...
WHAT HAPPENED TO YOUR FACE?!
OH!
HUH...?
YOU DIDN'T HAVE THOSE BRUISES YESTERDAY, DID YOU?!
IT LOOKS PAINFUL! ARE YOU ALL RIGHT?
I TRIPPED, THAT'S ALL...
HOW DO YOU TRIP AND GET HURT THAT BADLY?!
ER, UM, YES, I'M FINE.
DID YOU SEE A DOCTOR?!
HUP HUP HUP HUP HUP HUP
JUST SHUT UP ALREADY!!
ARGH, GEEZ!!!
JUMP
MRMR
WHAT'S GOING ON?
PEEK
PEEK
MRMR
A FIGHT?
DON'T RAISE A FUSS OUTSIDE OF MY TENT! JUST GET INSIDE, ALREADY!
S-SORRY!

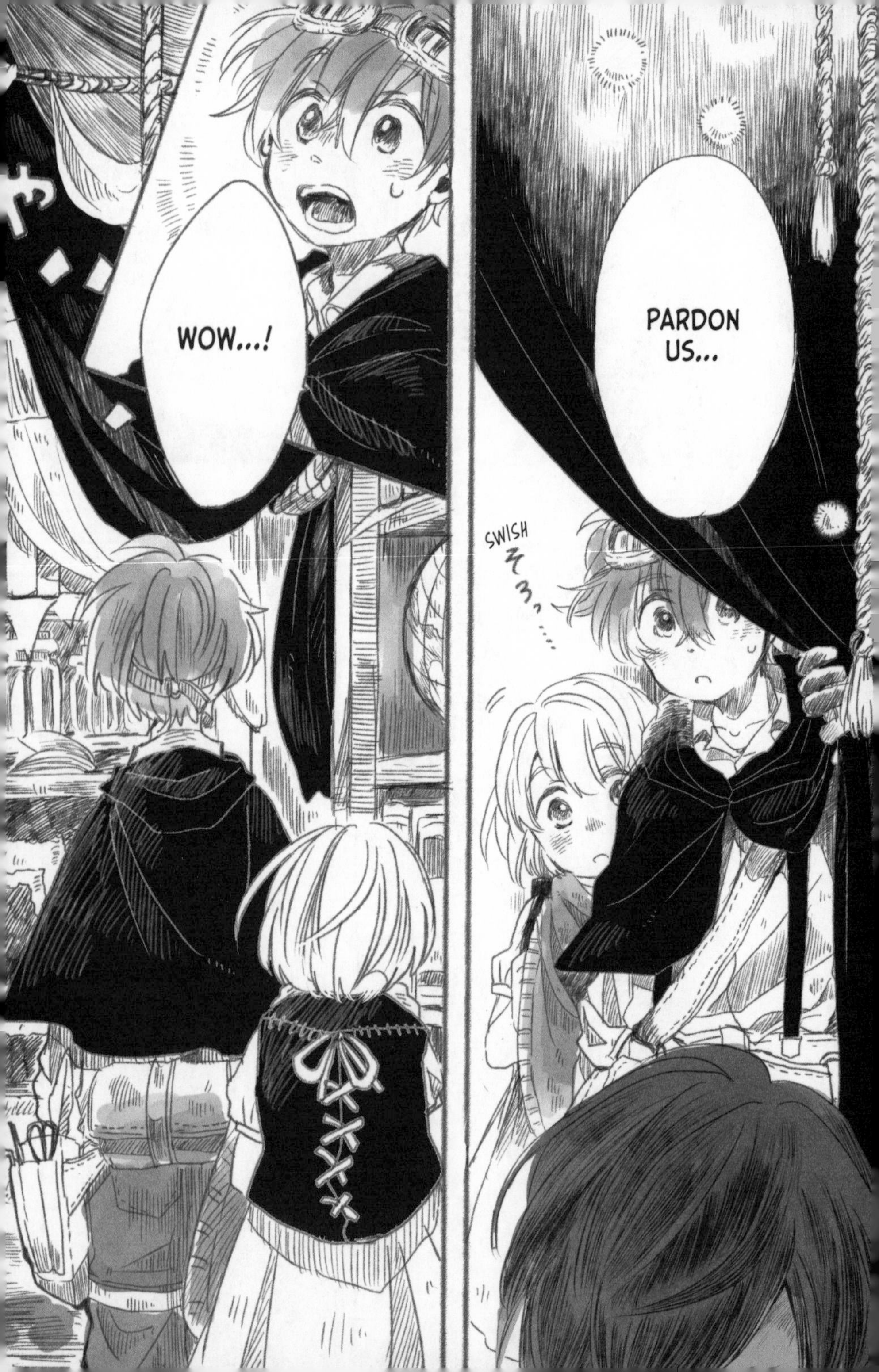
PARDON US...
SWISH
WOW...!

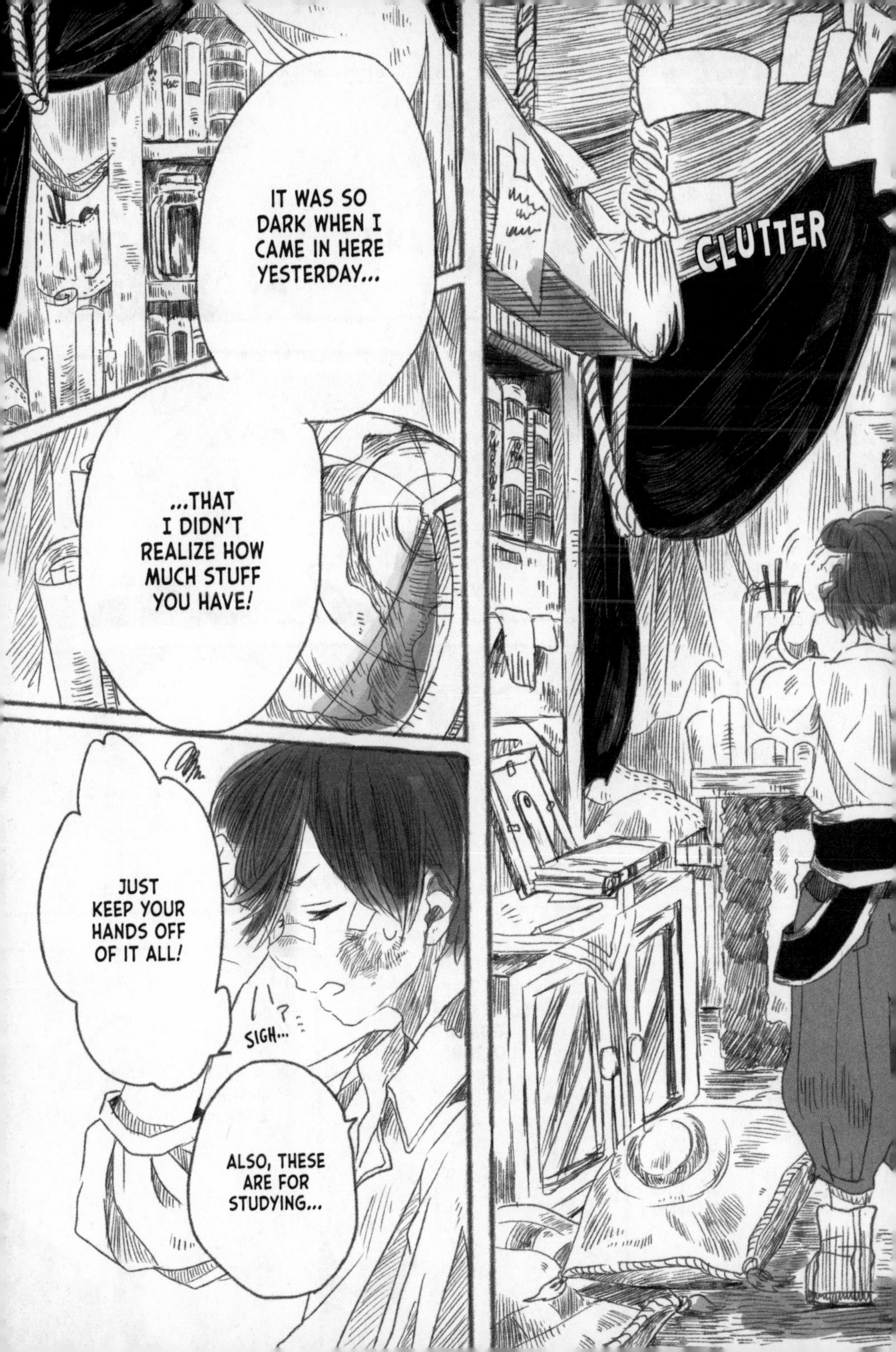
CLUTTER
IT WAS SO DARK WHEN I CAME IN HERE YESTERDAY...
...THAT I DIDN'T REALIZE HOW MUCH STUFF YOU HAVE!
JUST KEEP YOUR HANDS OFF OF IT ALL!
SIGH...
ALSO, THESE ARE FOR STUDYING...

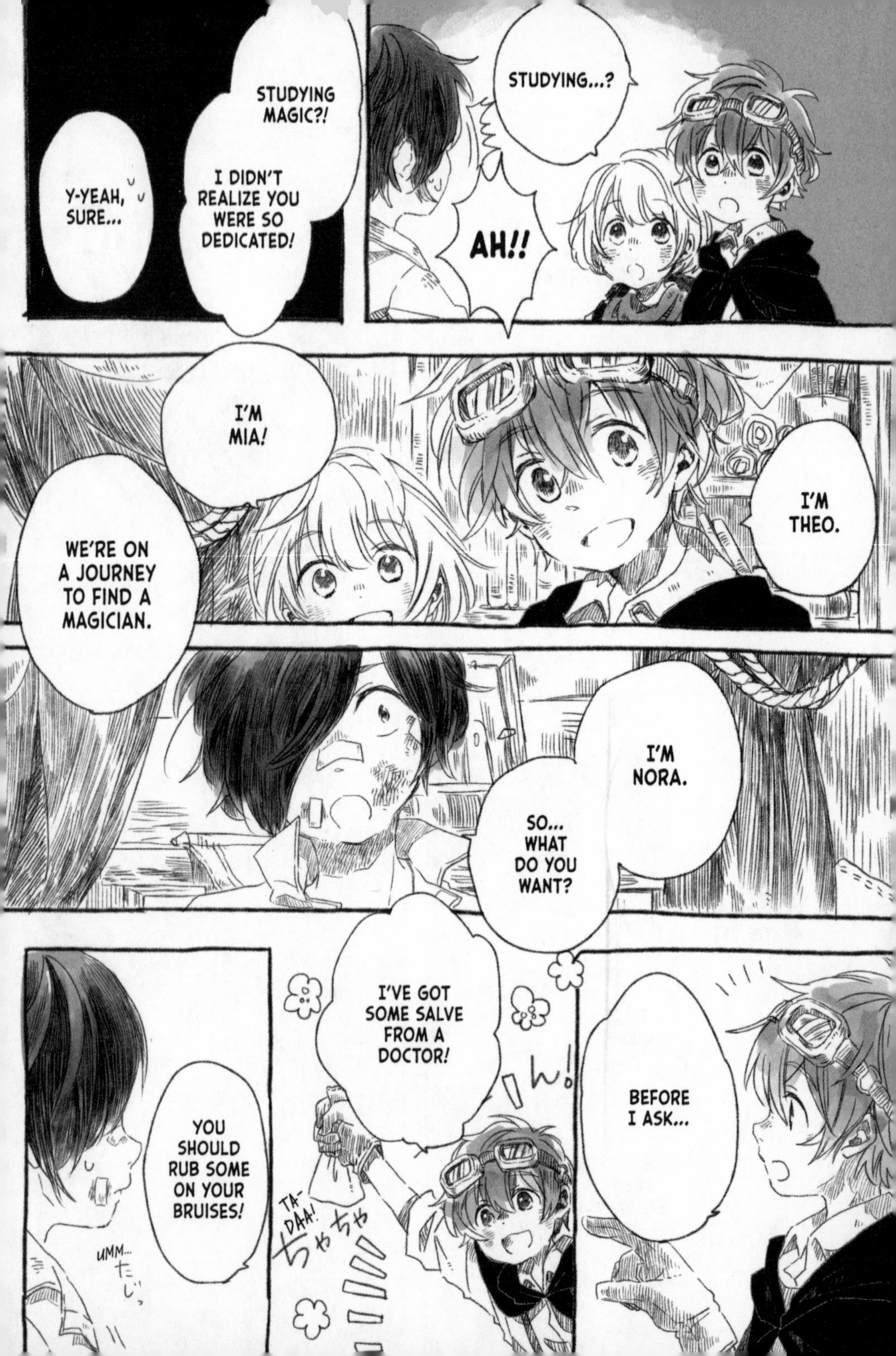

STUDYING...?
AH!!
STUDYING MAGIC?!
I DIDN'T REALIZE YOU WERE SO DEDICATED!
Y-YEAH, SURE...
I'M THEO.
I'M MIA!
WE'RE ON A JOURNEY TO FIND A MAGICIAN.
I'M NORA.
SO... WHAT DO YOU WANT?
BEFORE I ASK...
I'VE GOT SOME SALVE FROM A DOCTOR!
TA-DAA!
YOU SHOULD RUB SOME ON YOUR BRUISES!
UMM...

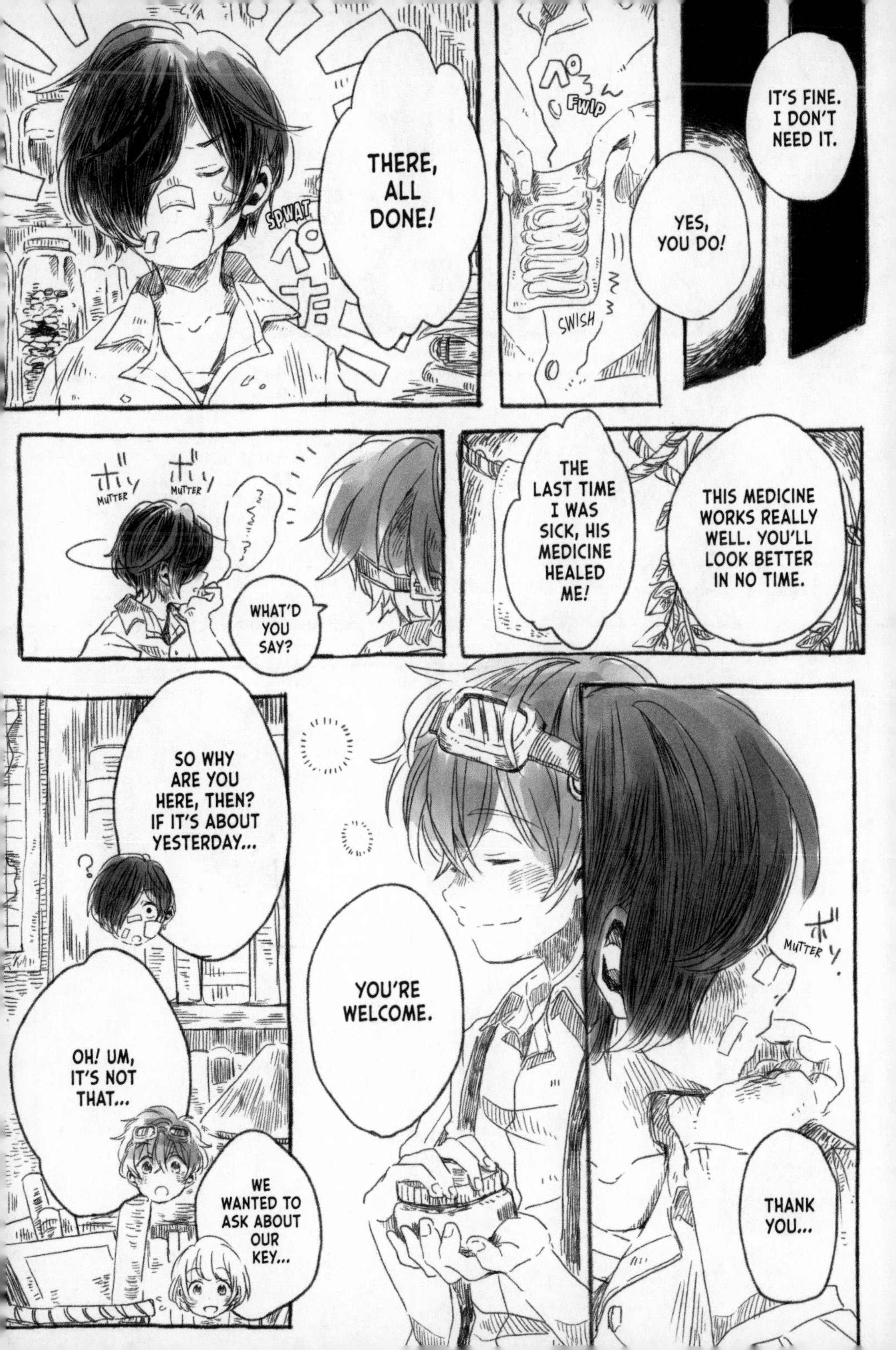
IT'S FINE. I DON'T NEED IT.
YES, YOU DO!
FWIP
SWISH
THERE, ALL DONE!
SPWAT
THIS MEDICINE WORKS REALLY WELL. YOU'LL LOOK BETTER IN NO TIME.
THE LAST TIME I WAS SICK, HIS MEDICINE HEALED ME!
MUTTER
MUTTER
WHAT'D YOU SAY?
MUTTER
THANK YOU...
YOU'RE WELCOME.
SO WHY ARE YOU HERE, THEN? IF IT'S ABOUT YESTERDAY...
OH! UM, IT'S NOT THAT...
WE WANTED TO ASK ABOUT OUR KEY...

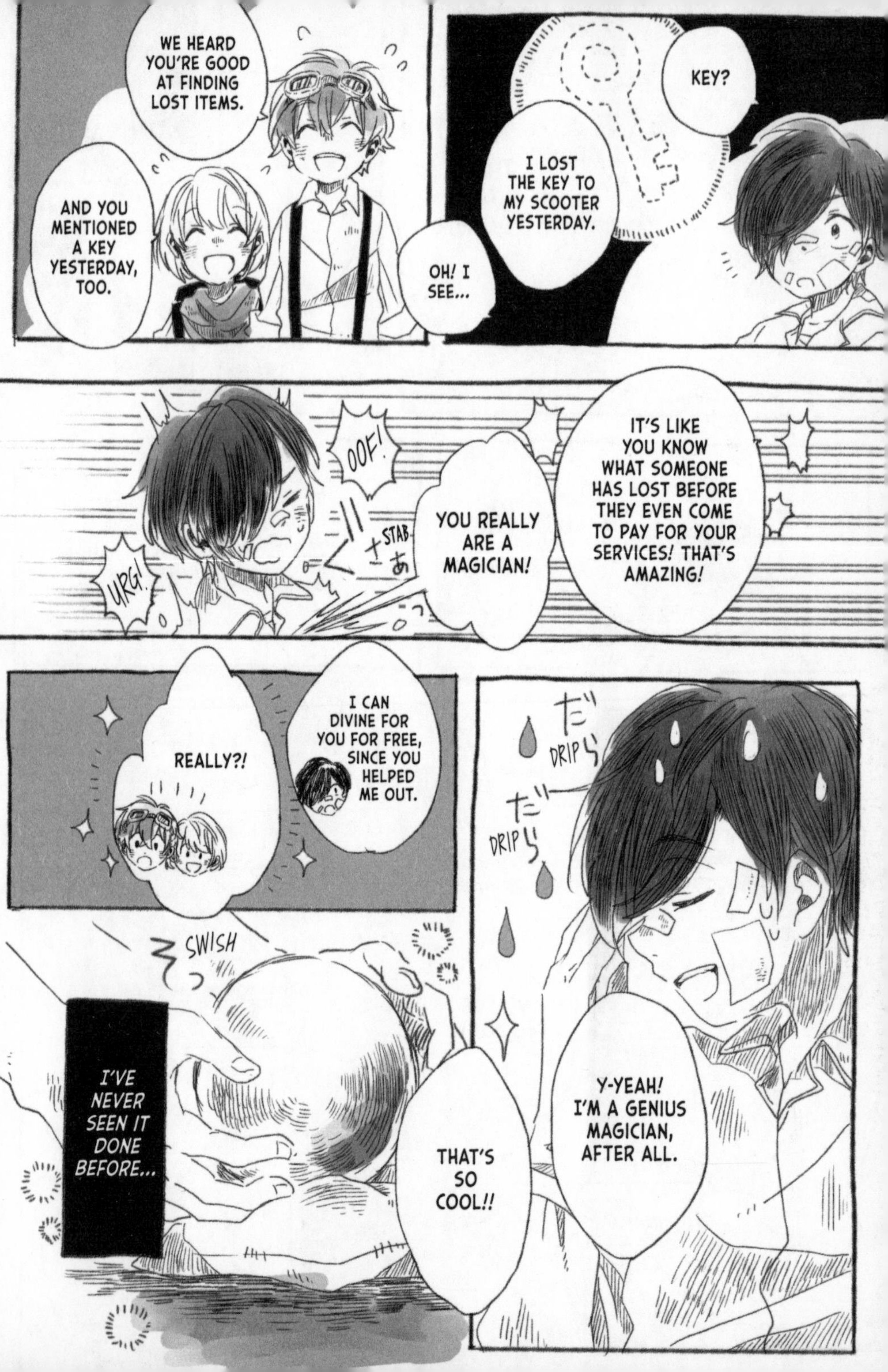
KEY?
I LOST THE KEY TO MY SCOOTER YESTERDAY.
OH! I SEE...
WE HEARD YOU'RE GOOD AT FINDING LOST ITEMS.
AND YOU MENTIONED A KEY YESTERDAY, TOO.
IT'S LIKE YOU KNOW WHAT SOMEONE HAS LOST BEFORE THEY EVEN COME TO PAY FOR YOUR SERVICES! THAT'S AMAZING!
YOU REALLY ARE A MAGICIAN!
STAB
OOF!
URG!
DRIP
DRIP
Y-YEAH! I'M A GENIUS MAGICIAN, AFTER ALL.
THAT'S SO COOL!!
I CAN DIVINE FOR YOU FOR FREE, SINCE YOU HELPED ME OUT.
REALLY?!
SWISH
I'VE NEVER SEEN IT DONE BEFORE...

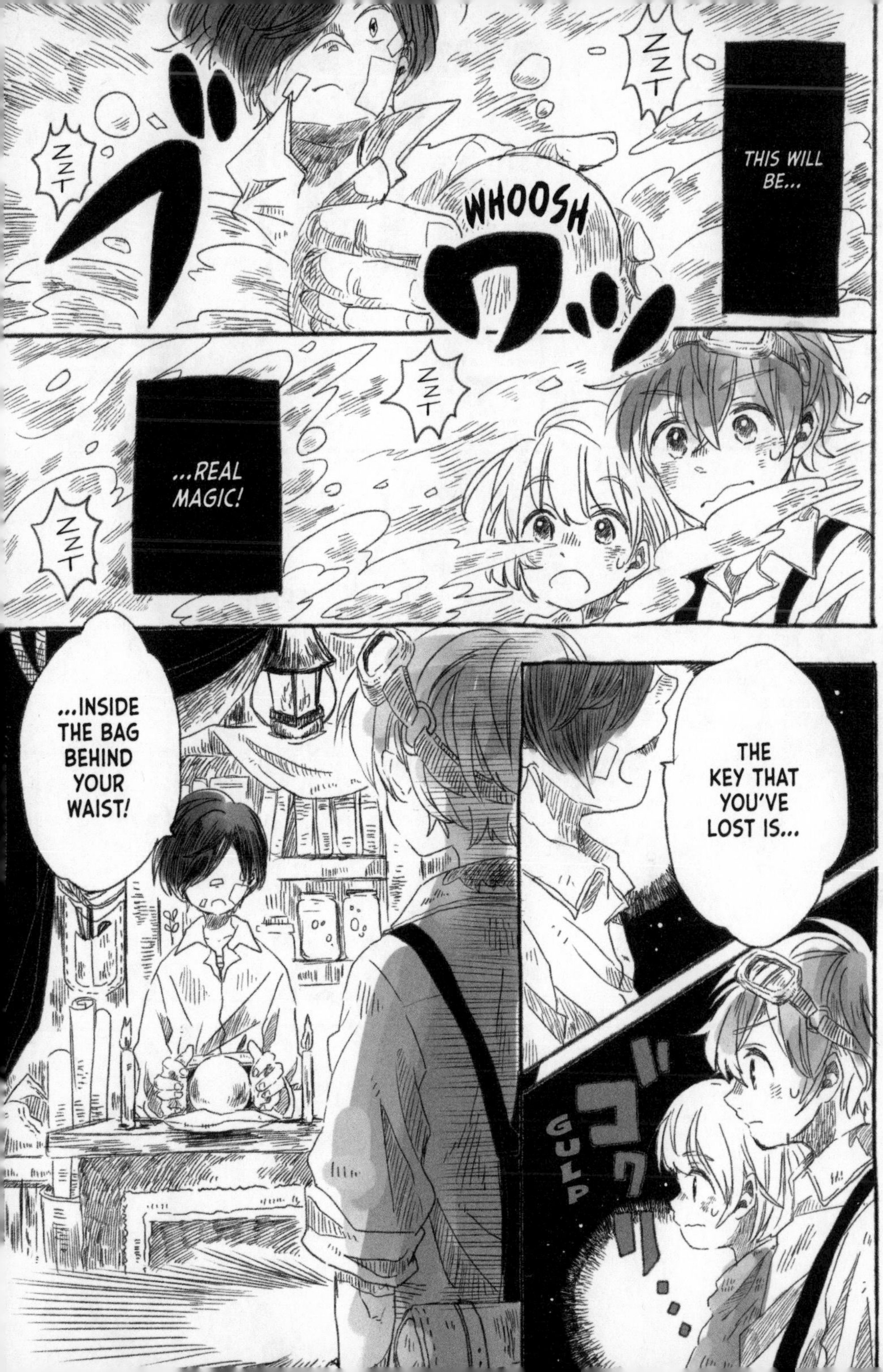
THIS WILL BE...
ZZZT
WHOOSH
ZZZT
ZZZT
...REAL MAGIC!
ZZZT
THE KEY THAT YOU'VE LOST IS...
GULP
...INSIDE THE BAG BEHIND YOUR WAIST!

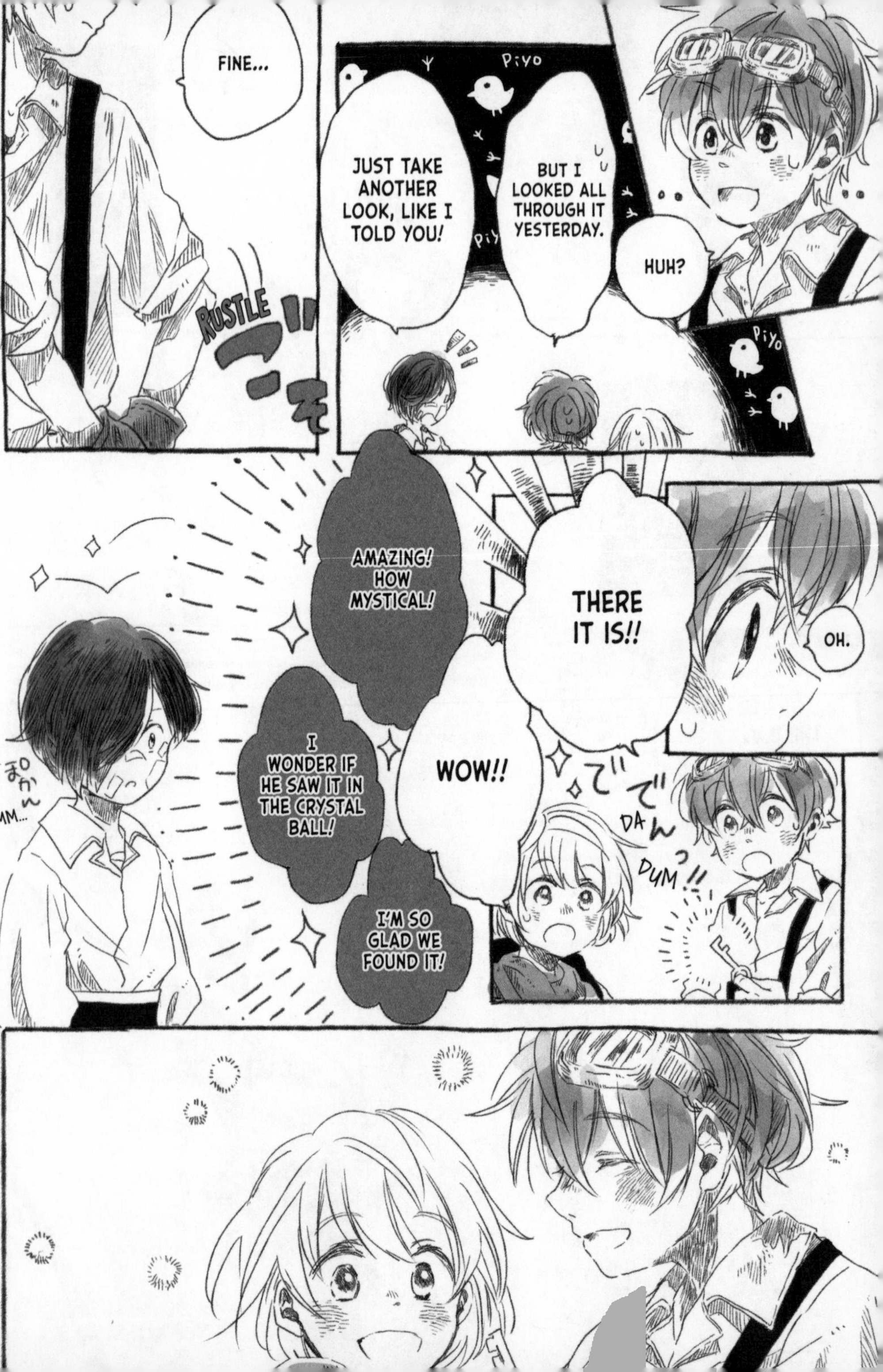
HUH?
PiYo
BUT I LOOKED ALL THROUGH IT YESTERDAY.
JUST TAKE ANOTHER LOOK, LIKE I TOLD YOU!
FINE...
RUSTLE
OH.
THERE IT IS!!
DA DUM!!
WOW!!
AMAZING! HOW MYSTICAL!
I WONDER IF HE SAW IT IN THE CRYSTAL BALL!
I'M SO GLAD WE FOUND IT!
UMM...

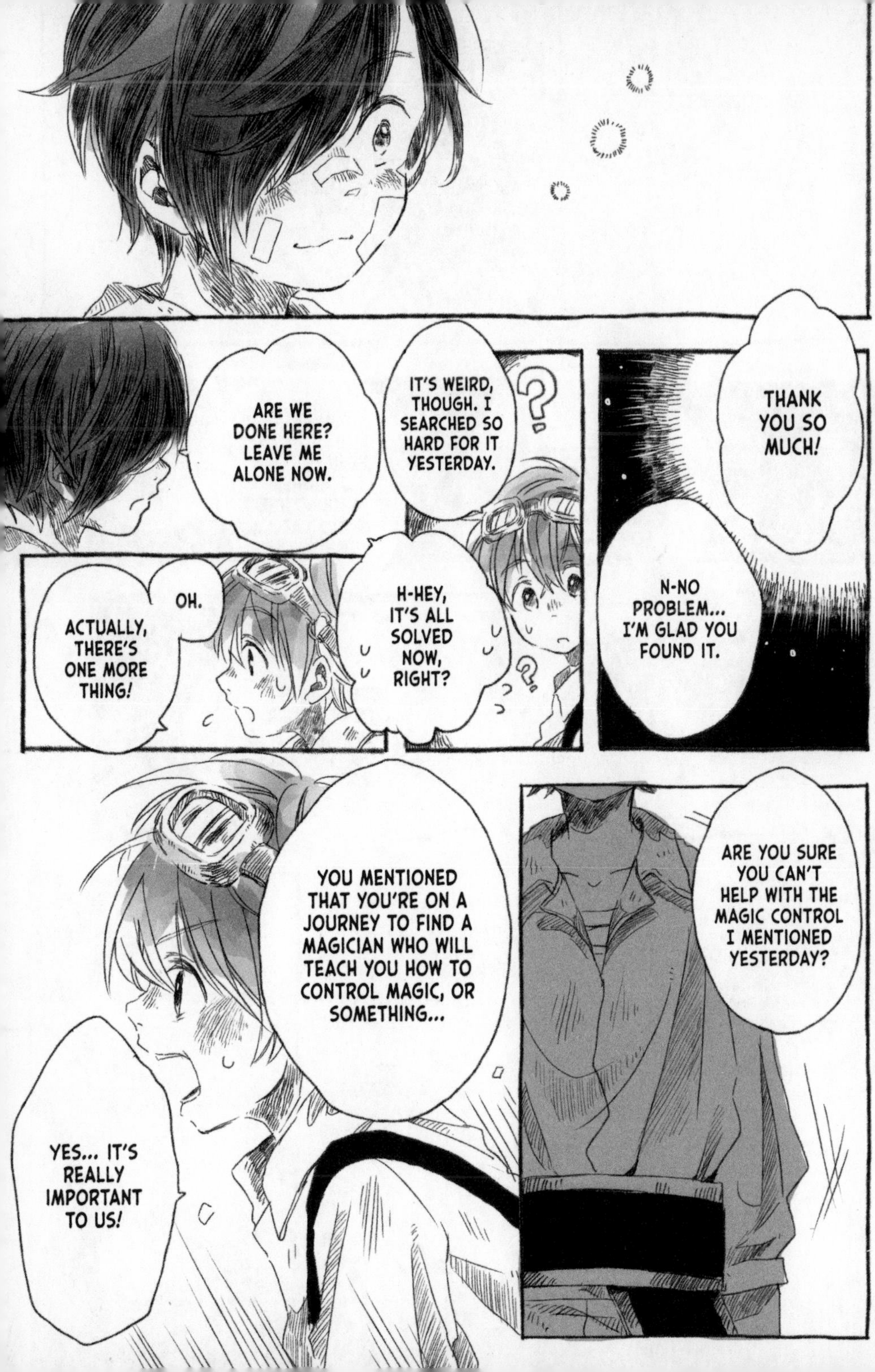
THANK YOU SO MUCH!
N-NO PROBLEM... I'M GLAD YOU FOUND IT.
IT'S WEIRD, THOUGH. I SEARCHED SO HARD FOR IT YESTERDAY.
H-HEY, IT'S ALL SOLVED NOW, RIGHT?
ARE WE DONE HERE? LEAVE ME ALONE NOW.
OH.
ACTUALLY, THERE'S ONE MORE THING!
ARE YOU SURE YOU CAN'T HELP WITH THE MAGIC CONTROL I MENTIONED YESTERDAY?
YOU MENTIONED THAT YOU'RE ON A JOURNEY TO FIND A MAGICIAN WHO WILL TEACH YOU HOW TO CONTROL MAGIC, OR SOMETHING...
YES... IT'S REALLY IMPORTANT TO US!

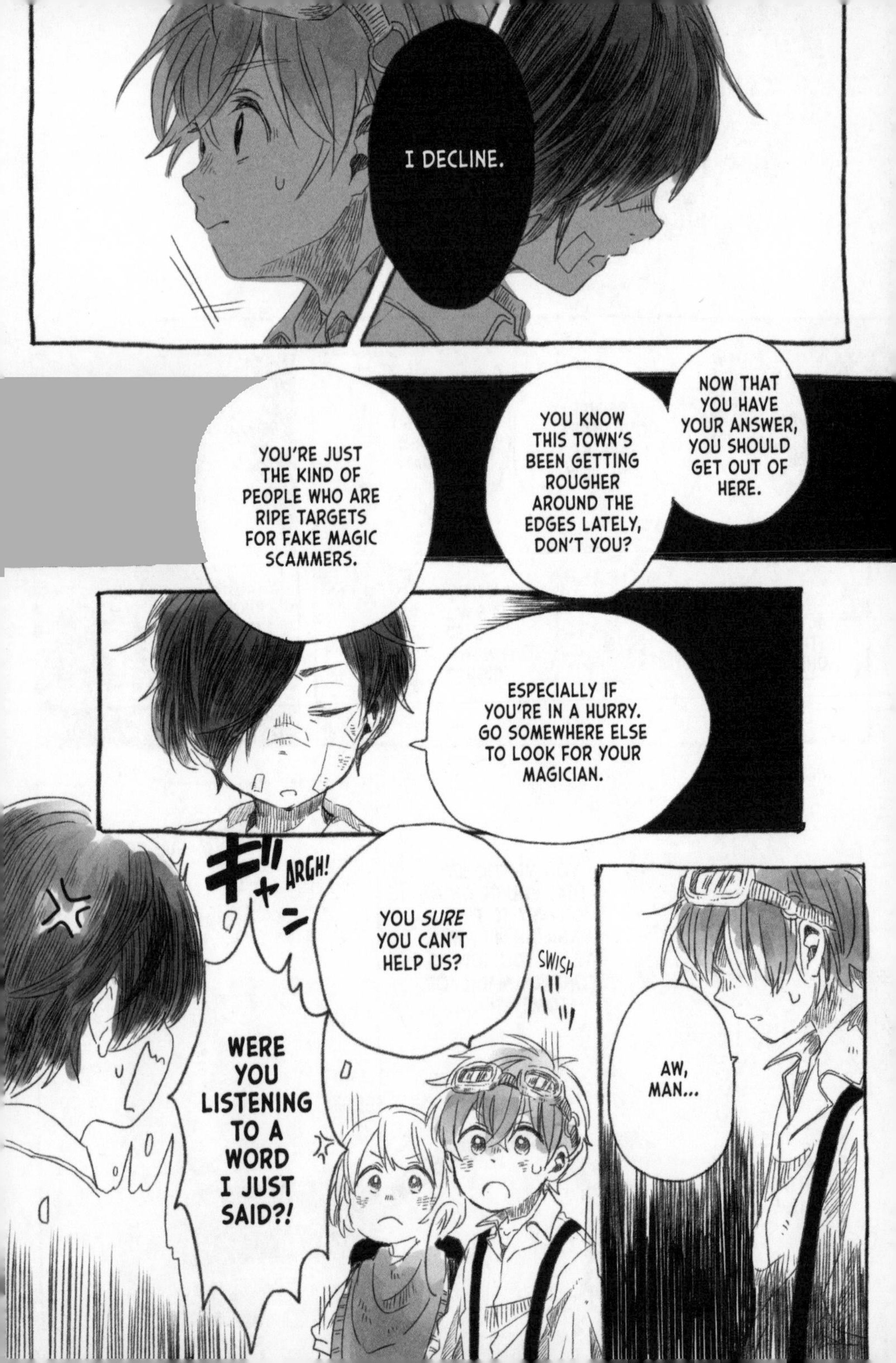
I DECLINE.
NOW THAT YOU HAVE YOUR ANSWER, YOU SHOULD GET OUT OF HERE.
YOU KNOW THIS TOWN'S BEEN GETTING ROUGHER AROUND THE EDGES LATELY, DON'T YOU?
YOU'RE JUST THE KIND OF PEOPLE WHO ARE RIPE TARGETS FOR FAKE MAGIC SCAMMERS.
ESPECIALLY IF YOU'RE IN A HURRY. GO SOMEWHERE ELSE TO LOOK FOR YOUR MAGICIAN.
AW, MAN...
SWISH
YOU *SURE* YOU CAN'T HELP US?
ARGH!
WERE YOU LISTENING TO A WORD I JUST SAID?!

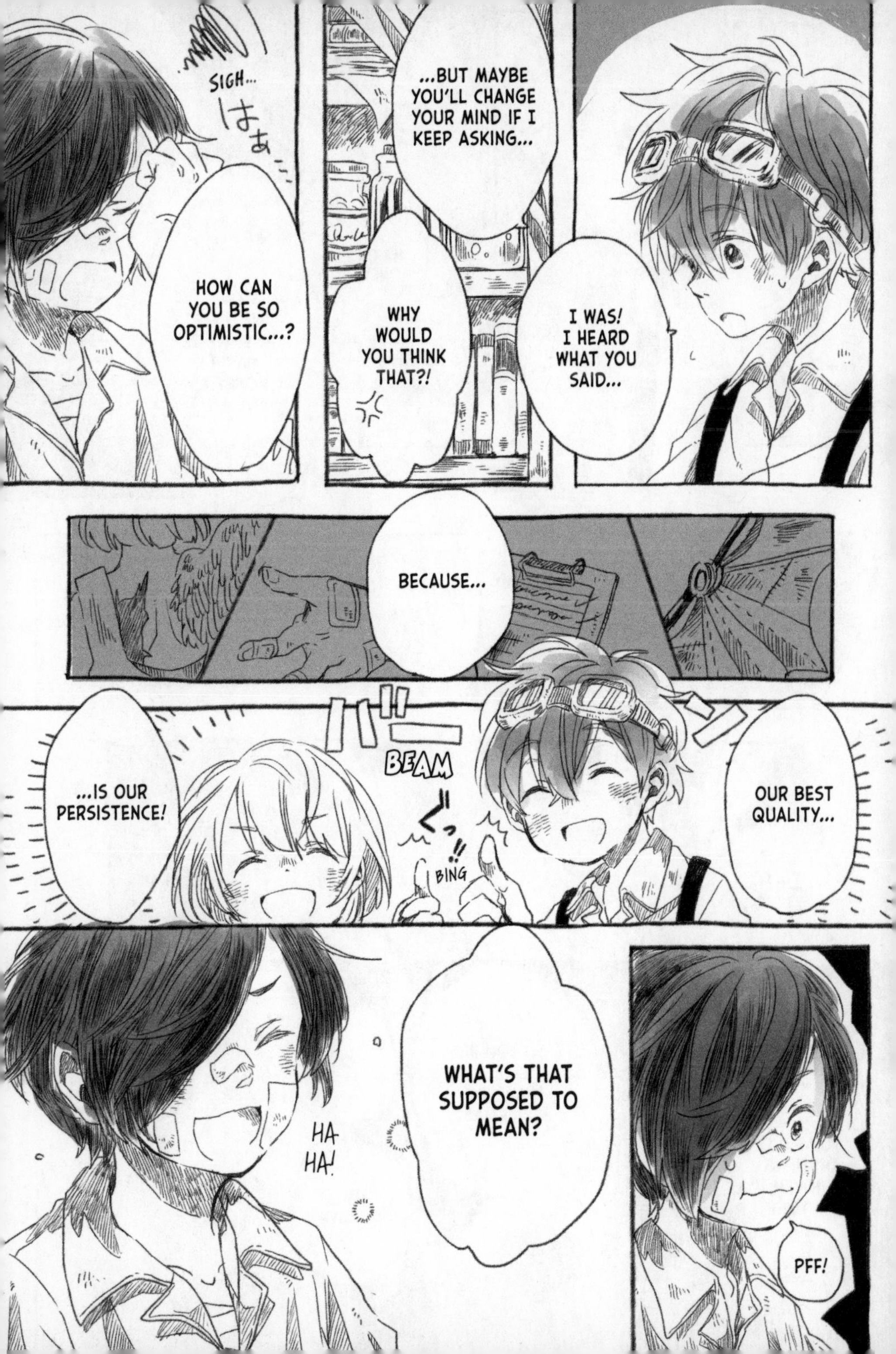
I WAS! I HEARD WHAT YOU SAID...
...BUT MAYBE YOU'LL CHANGE YOUR MIND IF I KEEP ASKING...
WHY WOULD YOU THINK THAT?!
SIGH...
はぁ
HOW CAN YOU BE SO OPTIMISTIC...?
BECAUSE...
OUR BEST QUALITY...
バー
BEAM
ぐっ!!
BING
...IS OUR PERSISTENCE!
PFF!
WHAT'S THAT SUPPOSED TO MEAN?
HA HA!

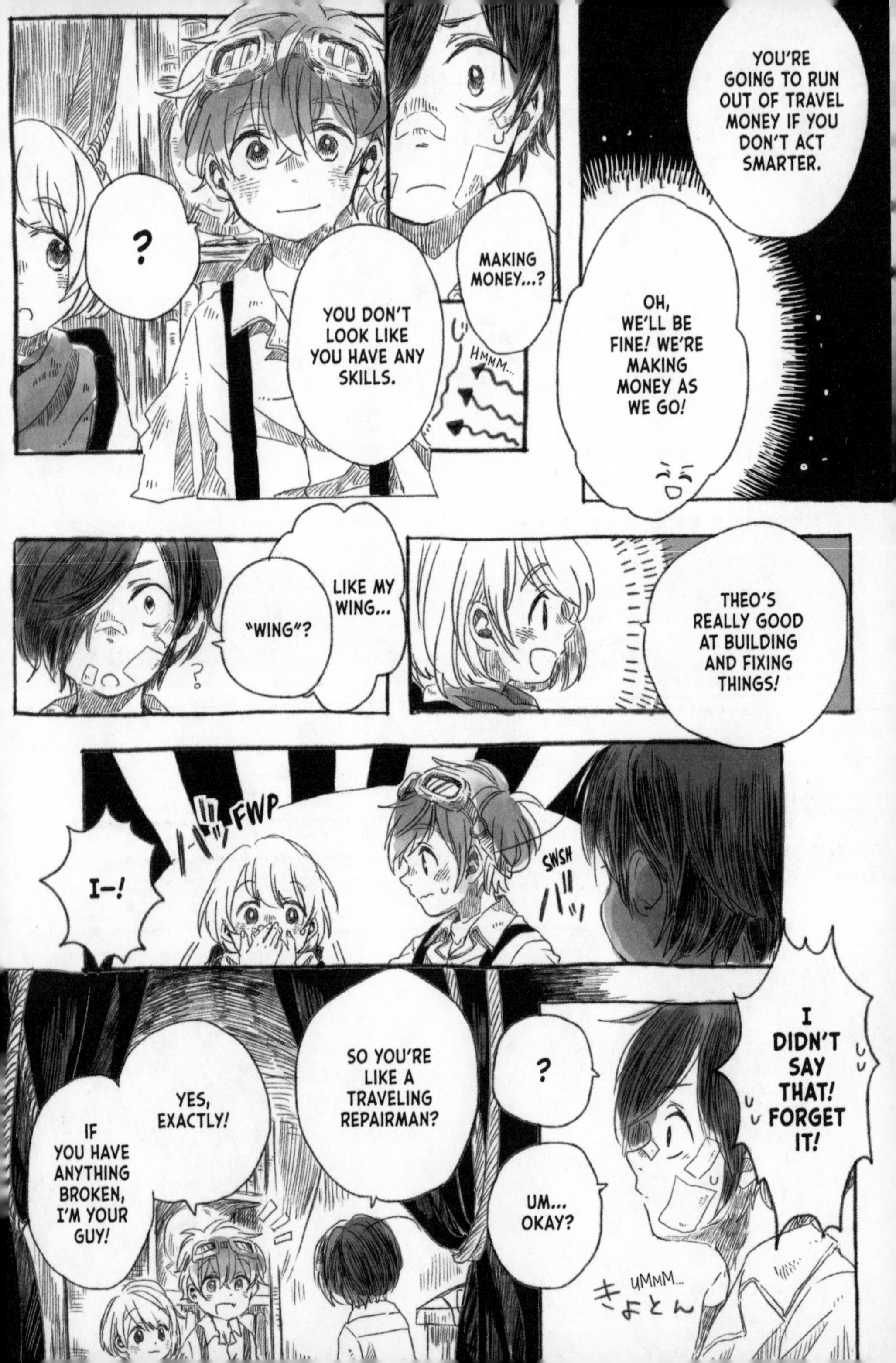
YOU'RE GOING TO RUN OUT OF TRAVEL MONEY IF YOU DON'T ACT SMARTER.
OH, WE'LL BE FINE! WE'RE MAKING MONEY AS WE GO!
MAKING MONEY...?
HMMM...
YOU DON'T LOOK LIKE YOU HAVE ANY SKILLS.
?
THEO'S REALLY GOOD AT BUILDING AND FIXING THINGS!
LIKE MY WING...
"WING"?
SWSH
FWP
I—!
I DIDN'T SAY THAT! FORGET IT!
UMMM...
?
UM... OKAY?
SO YOU'RE LIKE A TRAVELING REPAIRMAN?
YES, EXACTLY!
IF YOU HAVE ANYTHING BROKEN, I'M YOUR GUY!

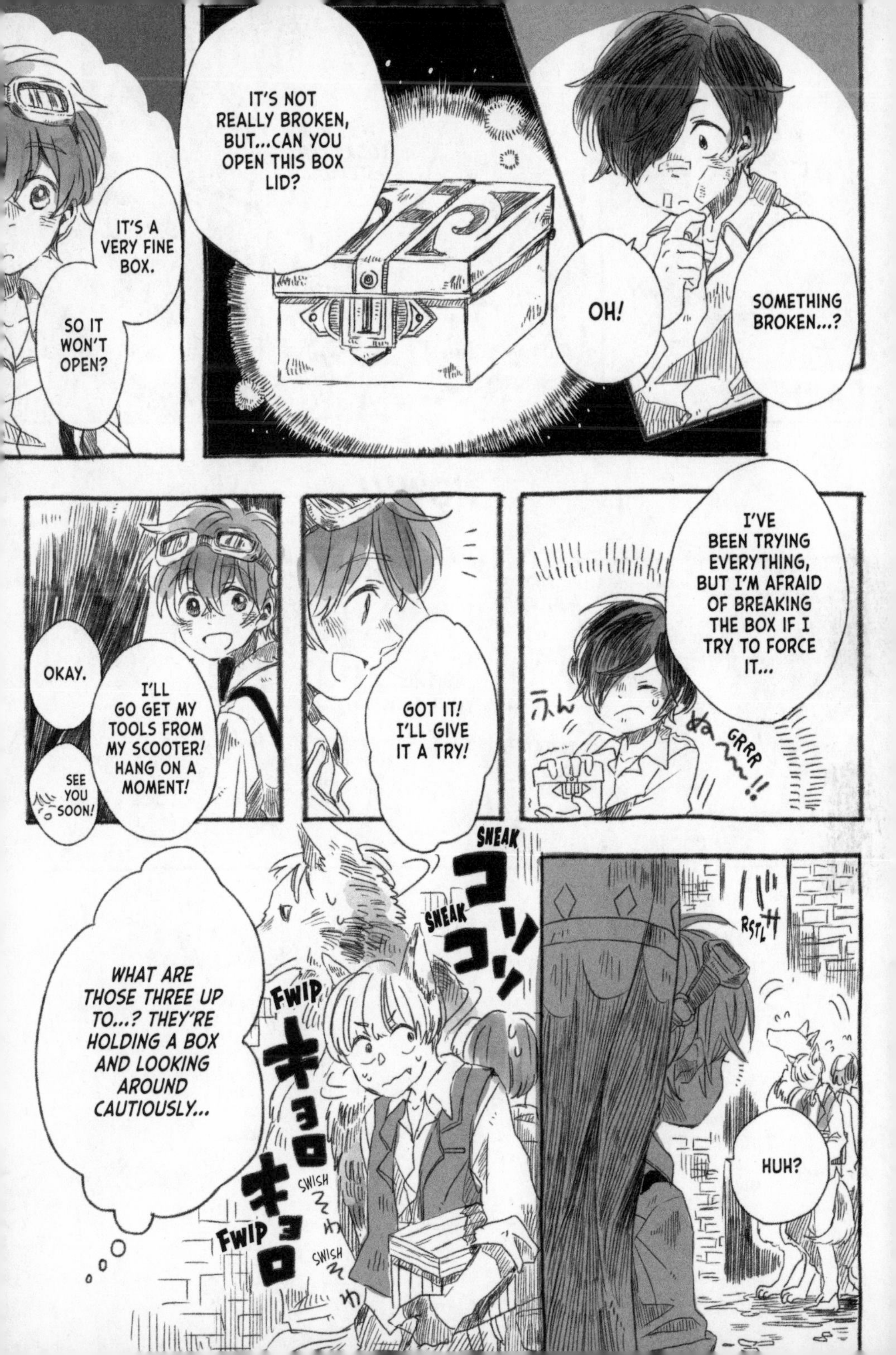
SOMETHING BROKEN...?
OH!
IT'S NOT REALLY BROKEN, BUT...CAN YOU OPEN THIS BOX LID?
IT'S A VERY FINE BOX.
SO IT WON'T OPEN?
I'VE BEEN TRYING EVERYTHING, BUT I'M AFRAID OF BREAKING THE BOX IF I TRY TO FORCE IT...
ふん
ぬ〜〜!!
GRRR
GOT IT! I'LL GIVE IT A TRY!
OKAY.
I'LL GO GET MY TOOLS FROM MY SCOOTER! HANG ON A MOMENT!
SEE YOU SOON!
バサ
RSTL
HUH?
SNEAK
コソコソ
SNEAK
WHAT ARE THOSE THREE UP TO...? THEY'RE HOLDING A BOX AND LOOKING AROUND CAUTIOUSLY...
FWIP
キョロキョロ
FWIP
SWISH
SWISH

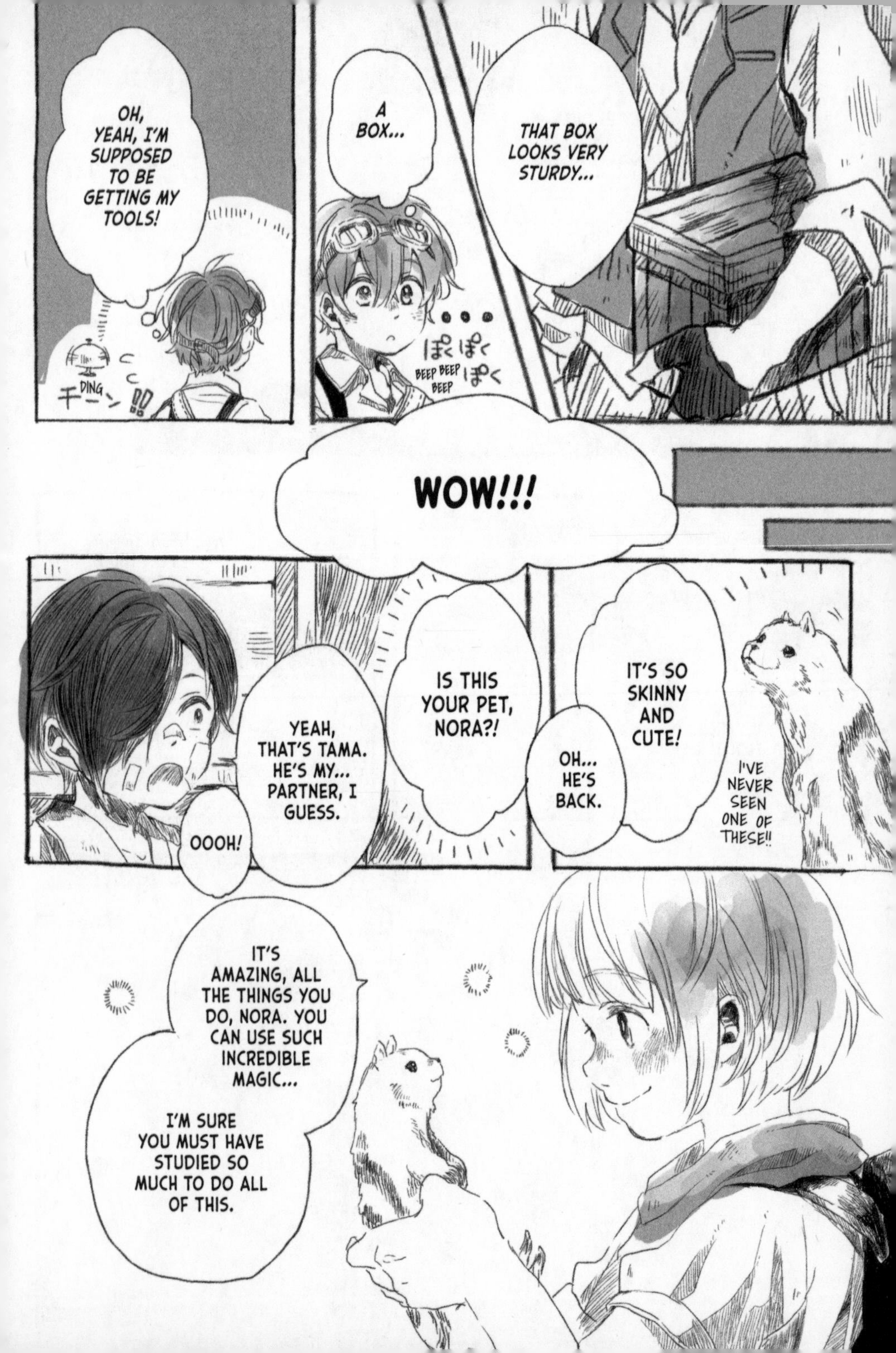
THAT BOX LOOKS VERY STURDY...
A BOX...
ぽくぽくぽく
BEEP BEEP BEEP
OH, YEAH, I'M SUPPOSED TO BE GETTING MY TOOLS!
チーン!!
DING
WOW!!!
IT'S SO SKINNY AND CUTE!
I'VE NEVER SEEN ONE OF THESE!!
OH... HE'S BACK.
IS THIS YOUR PET, NORA?!
YEAH, THAT'S TAMA. HE'S MY... PARTNER, I GUESS.
OOOH!
IT'S AMAZING, ALL THE THINGS YOU DO, NORA. YOU CAN USE SUCH INCREDIBLE MAGIC...
I'M SURE YOU MUST HAVE STUDIED SO MUCH TO DO ALL OF THIS.

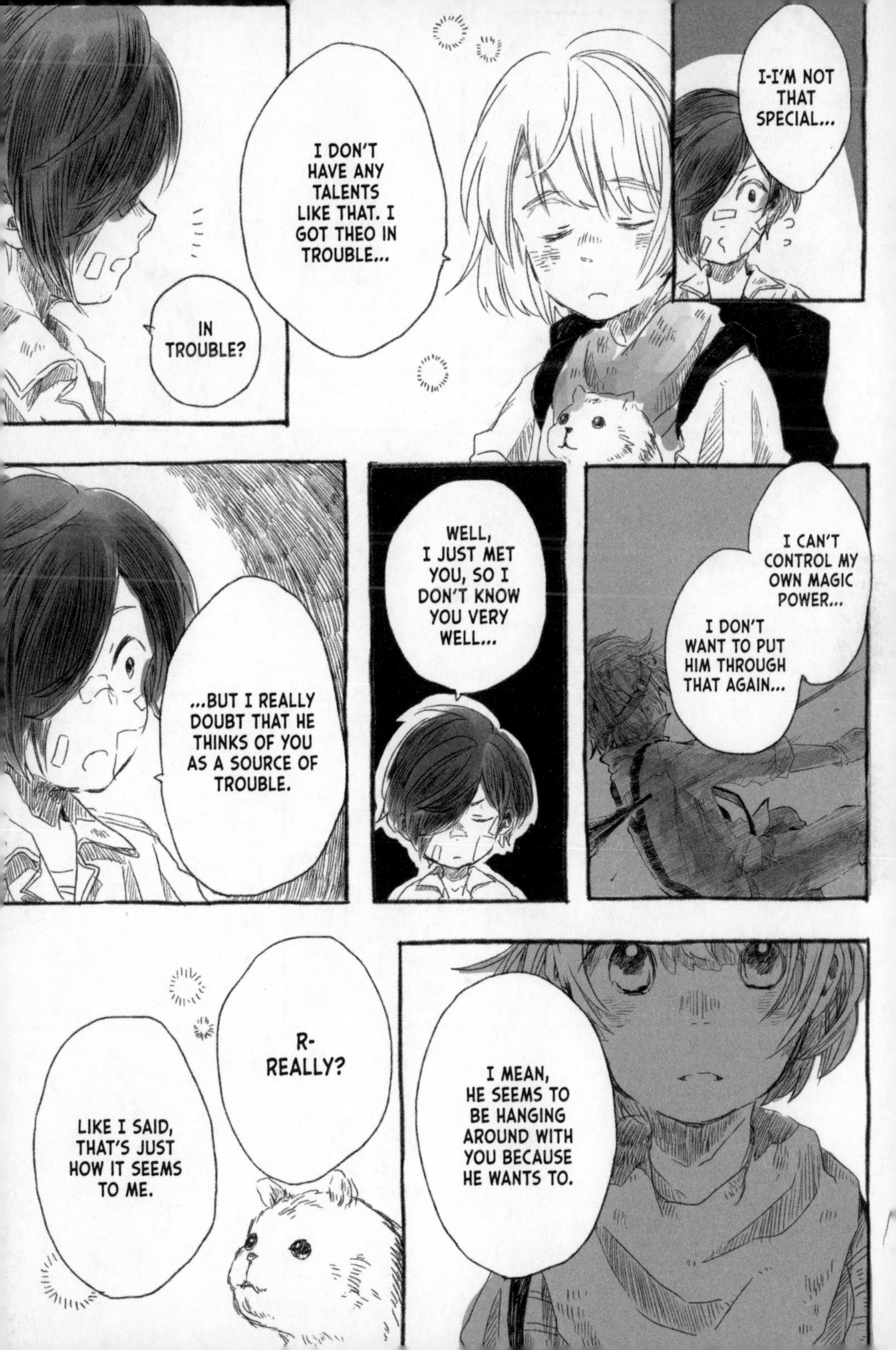
I-I'M NOT THAT SPECIAL...
I DON'T HAVE ANY TALENTS LIKE THAT. I GOT THEO IN TROUBLE...
IN TROUBLE?
I CAN'T CONTROL MY OWN MAGIC POWER...
I DON'T WANT TO PUT HIM THROUGH THAT AGAIN...
WELL, I JUST MET YOU, SO I DON'T KNOW YOU VERY WELL...
...BUT I REALLY DOUBT THAT HE THINKS OF YOU AS A SOURCE OF TROUBLE.
I MEAN, HE SEEMS TO BE HANGING AROUND WITH YOU BECAUSE HE WANTS TO.
R-REALLY?
LIKE I SAID, THAT'S JUST HOW IT SEEMS TO ME.

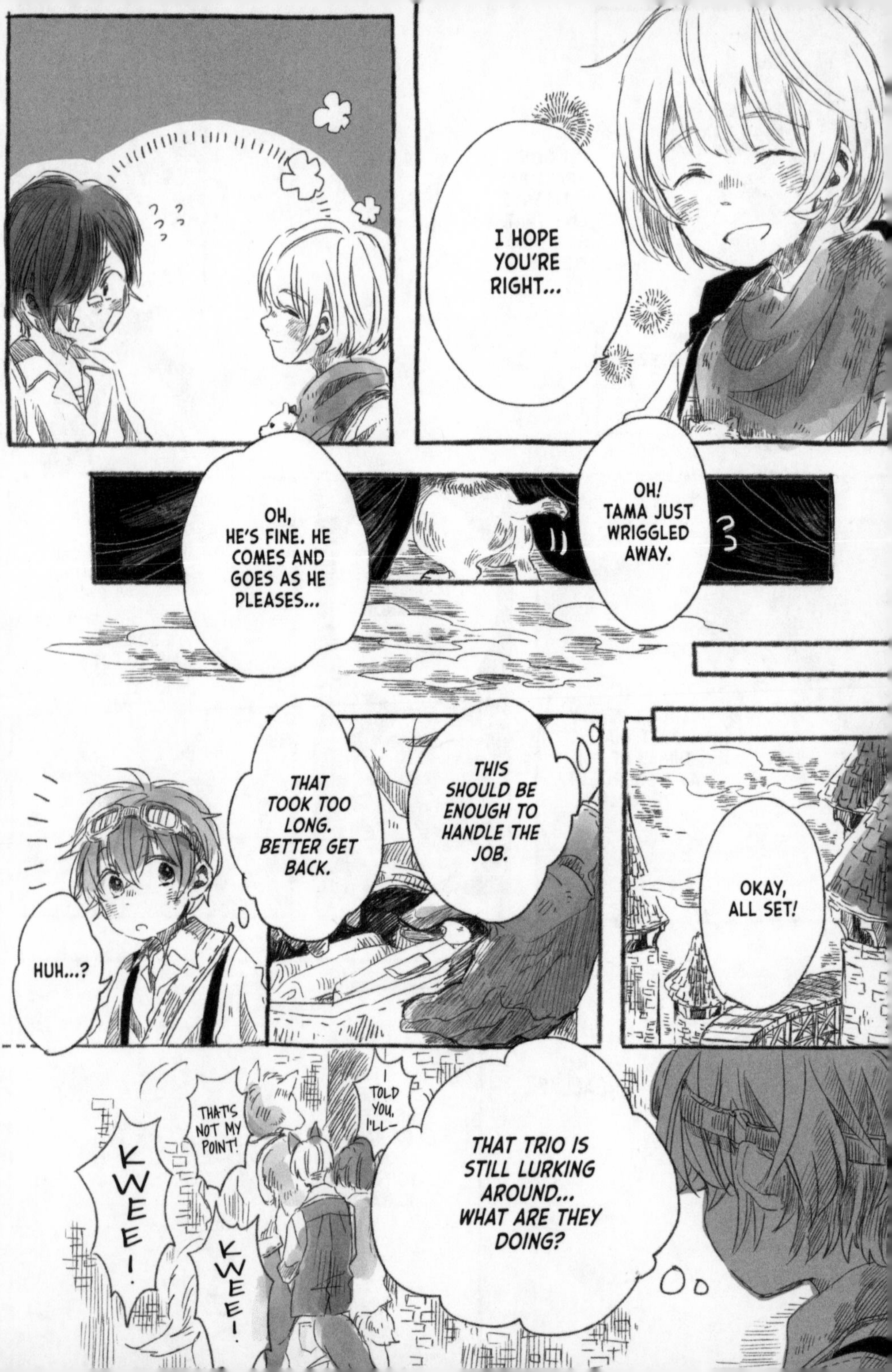
I HOPE YOU'RE RIGHT...
OH! TAMA JUST WRIGGLED AWAY.
OH, HE'S FINE. HE COMES AND GOES AS HE PLEASES...
OKAY, ALL SET!
THIS SHOULD BE ENOUGH TO HANDLE THE JOB.
THAT TOOK TOO LONG. BETTER GET BACK.
HUH...?
THAT TRIO IS STILL LURKING AROUND... WHAT ARE THEY DOING?
I TOLD YOU, I'LL—
THAT'S NOT MY POINT!
KWEE!
KWEE!

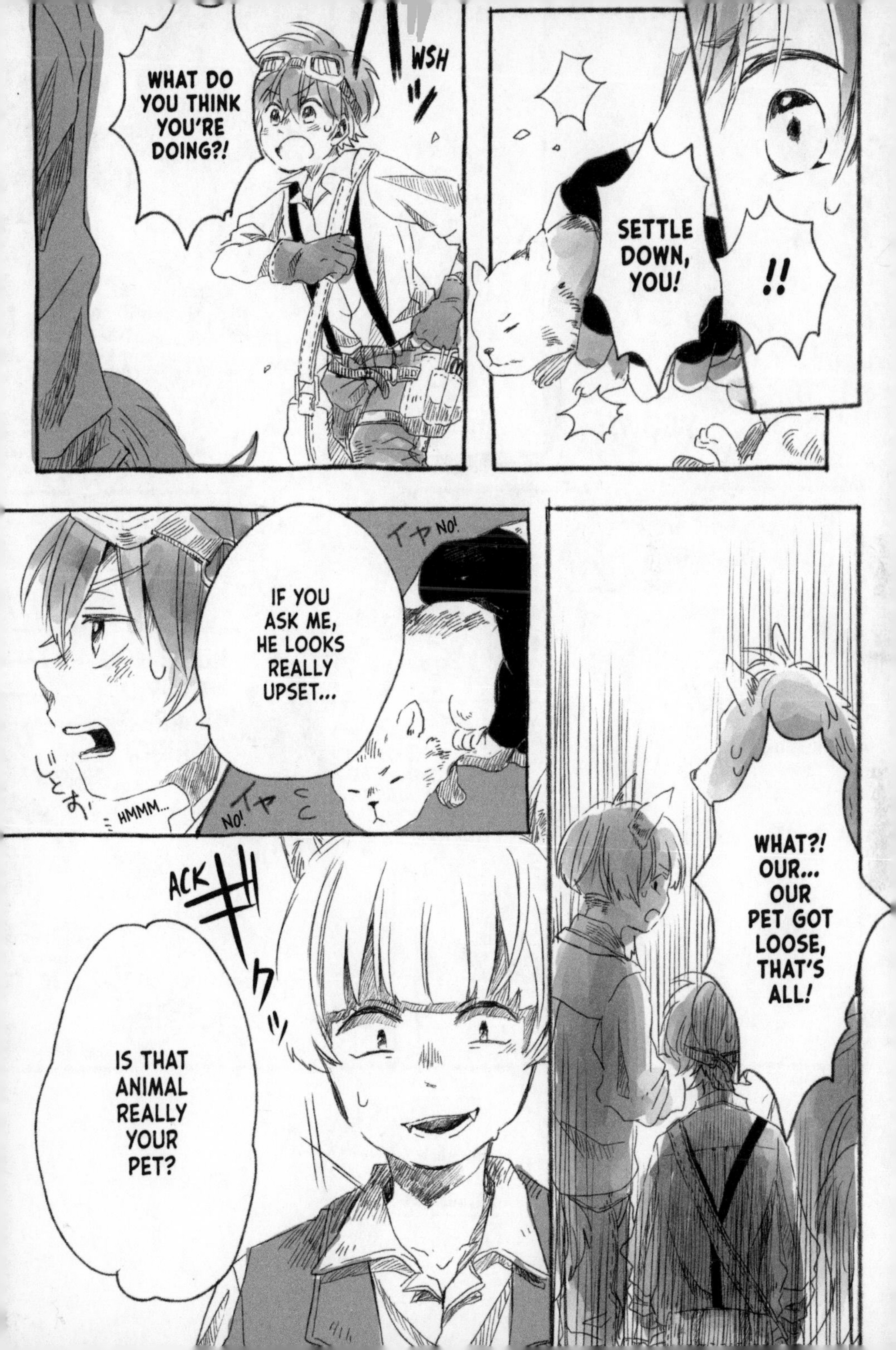
!!
SETTLE DOWN, YOU!
WSH
WHAT DO YOU THINK YOU'RE DOING?!
WHAT?! OUR... OUR PET GOT LOOSE, THAT'S ALL!
NO!
IF YOU ASK ME, HE LOOKS REALLY UPSET...
NO!
HMMM...
ACK
IS THAT ANIMAL REALLY YOUR PET?

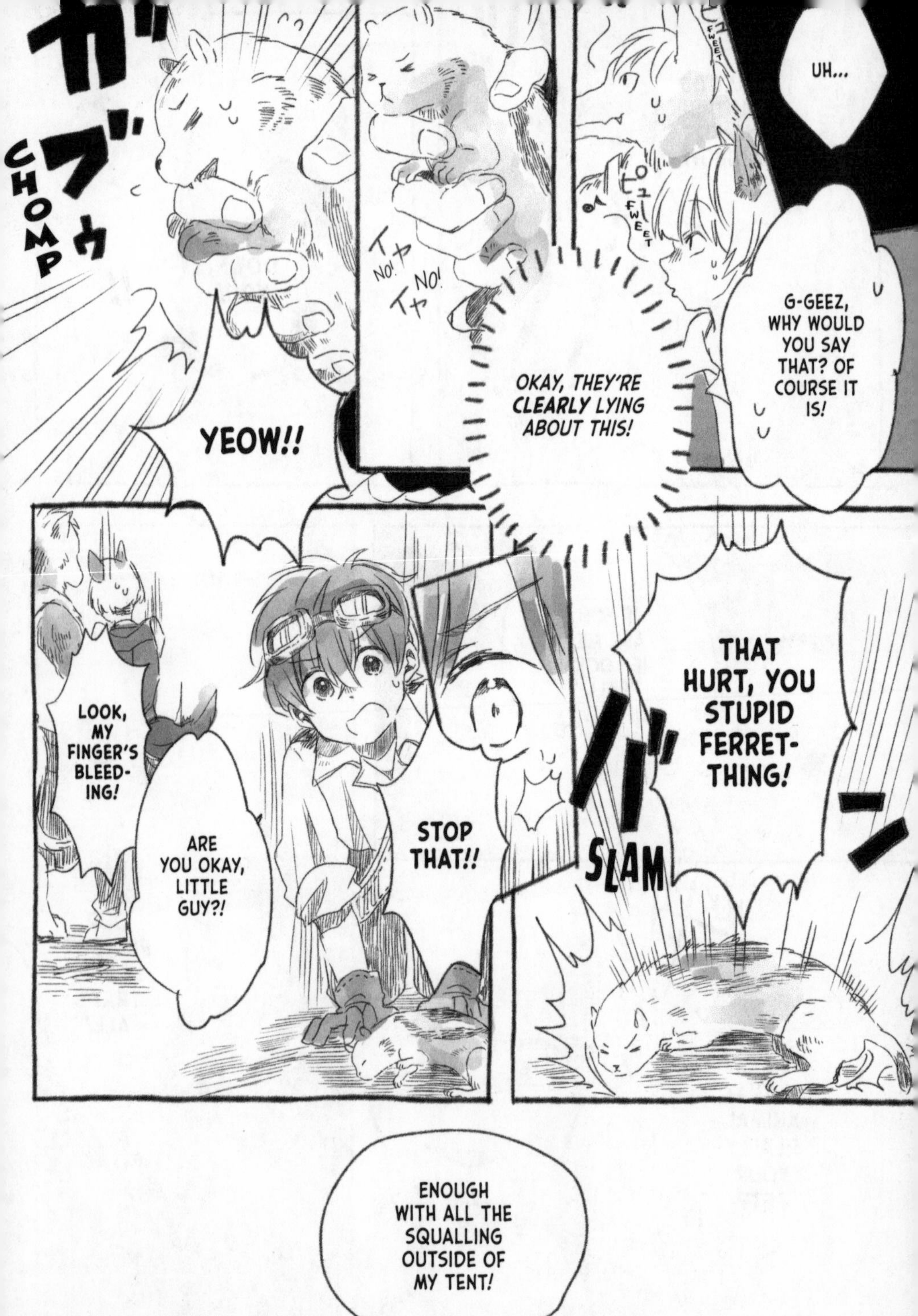
UH...
G-GEEZ, WHY WOULD YOU SAY THAT? OF COURSE IT IS!
FWEET
FWEET
OKAY, THEY'RE CLEARLY LYING ABOUT THIS!
NO!
NO!
CHOMP
YEOW!!
THAT HURT, YOU STUPID FERRET-THING!
SLAM
STOP THAT!!
ARE YOU OKAY, LITTLE GUY?!
LOOK, MY FINGER'S BLEED-ING!
ENOUGH WITH ALL THE SQUALLING OUTSIDE OF MY TENT!

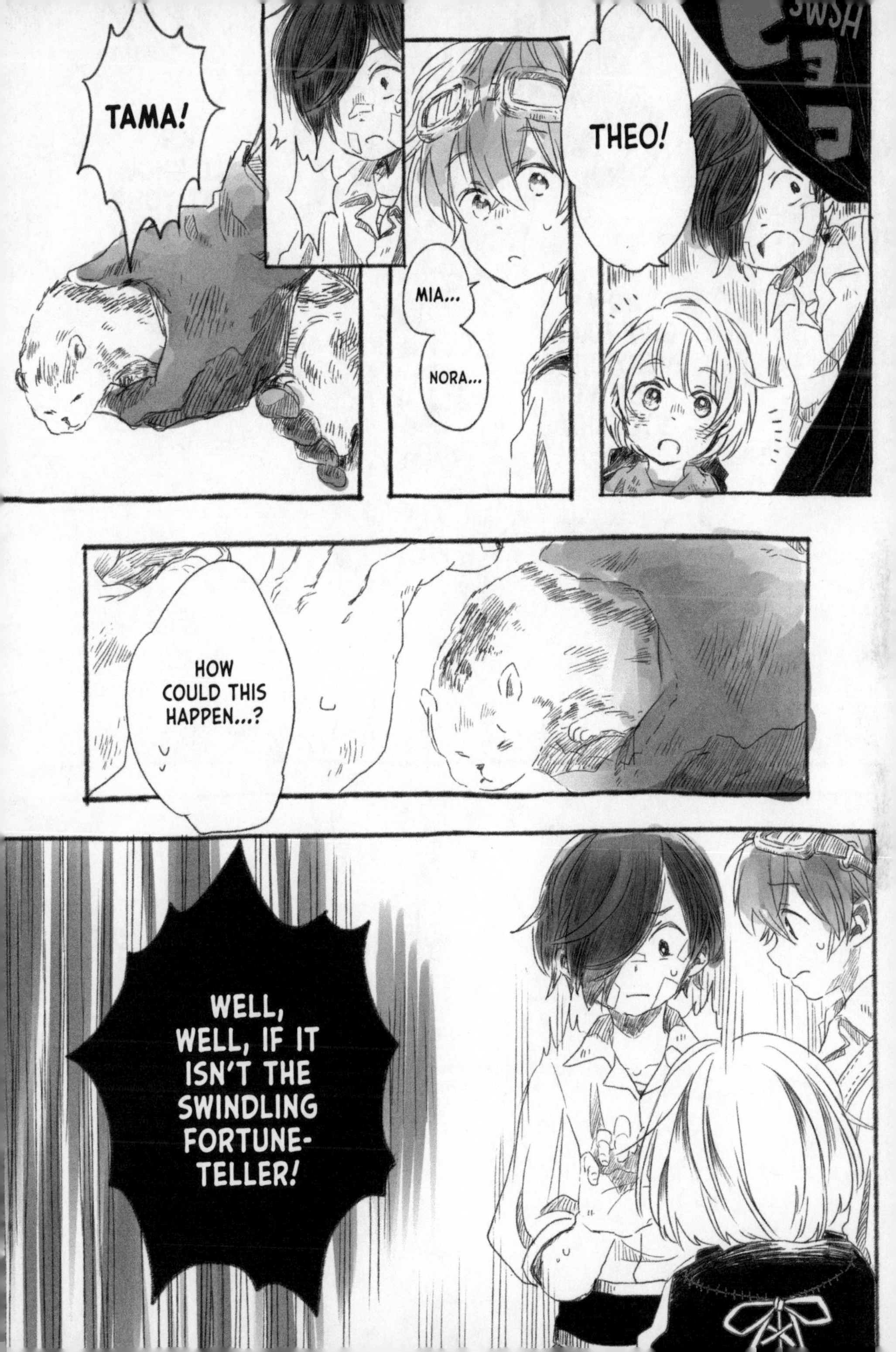
SWSH
THEO!
MIA...
NORA...
TAMA!
HOW COULD THIS HAPPEN...?
WELL, WELL, IF IT ISN'T THE SWINDLING FORTUNE-TELLER!

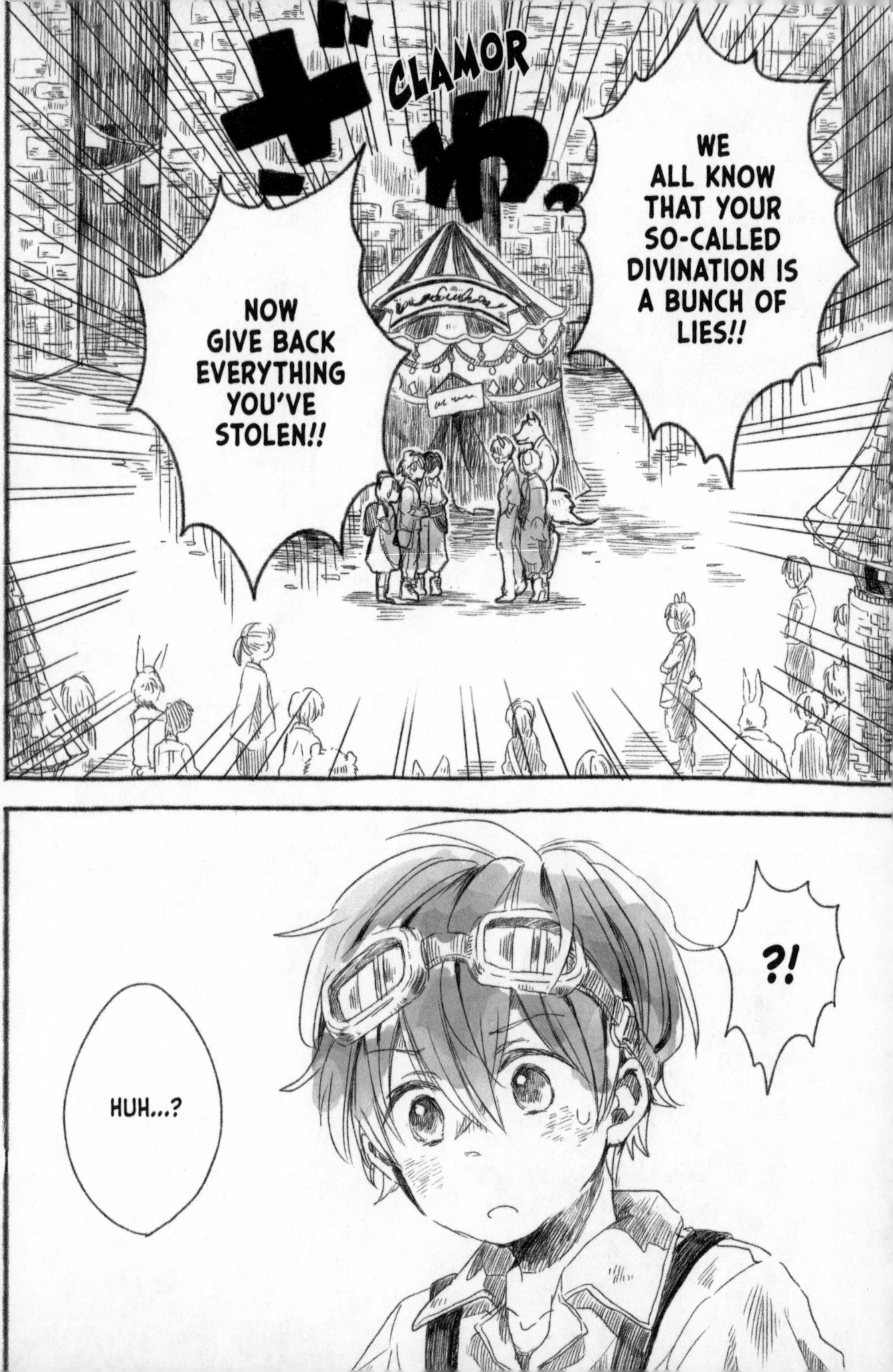
CLAMOR
WE ALL KNOW THAT YOUR SO-CALLED DIVINATION IS A BUNCH OF LIES!!
NOW GIVE BACK EVERYTHING YOU'VE STOLEN!!
?!
HUH...?

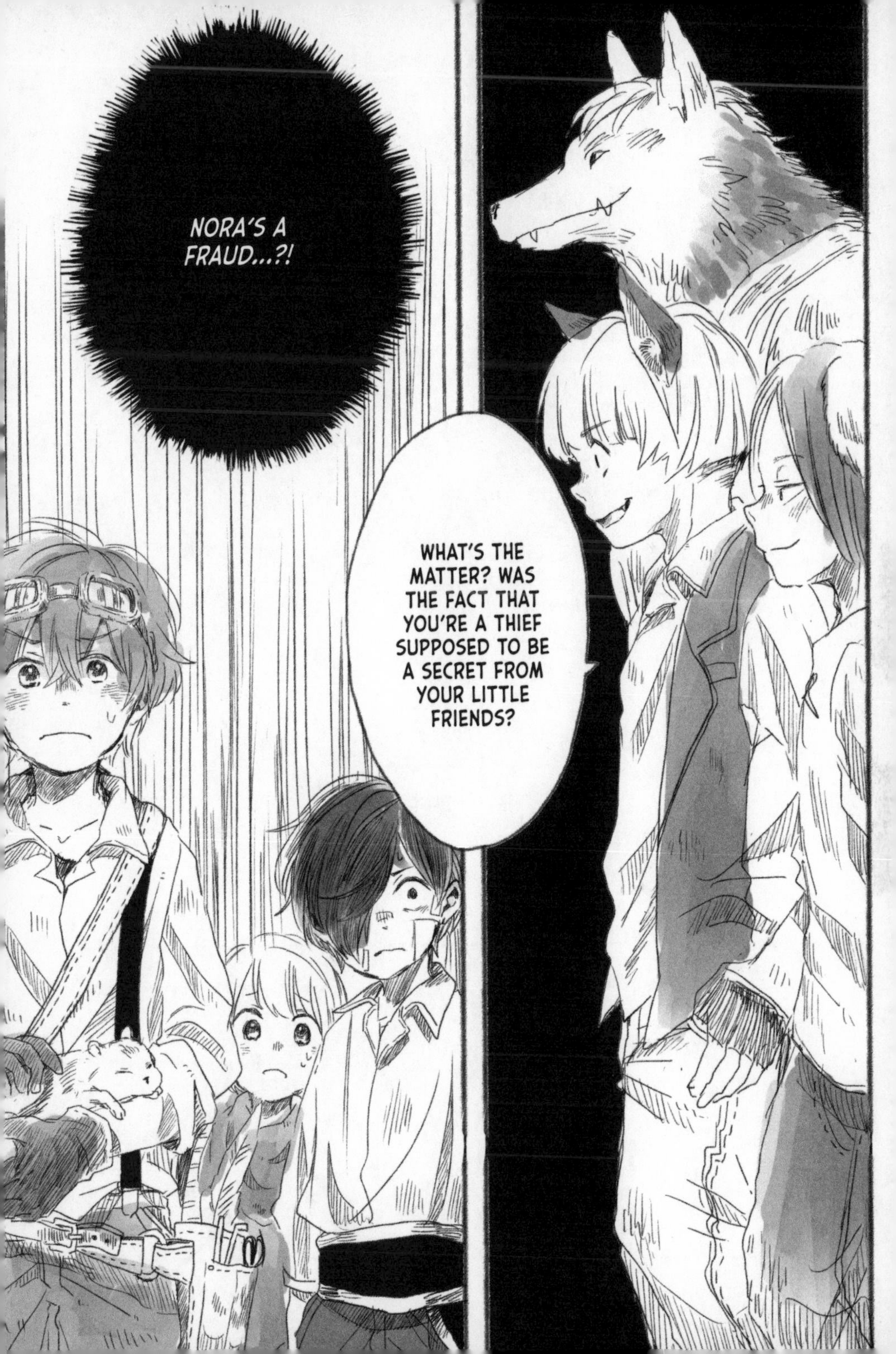
WHAT'S THE MATTER? WAS THE FACT THAT YOU'RE A THIEF SUPPOSED TO BE A SECRET FROM YOUR LITTLE FRIENDS?
NORA'S A FRAUD...?!

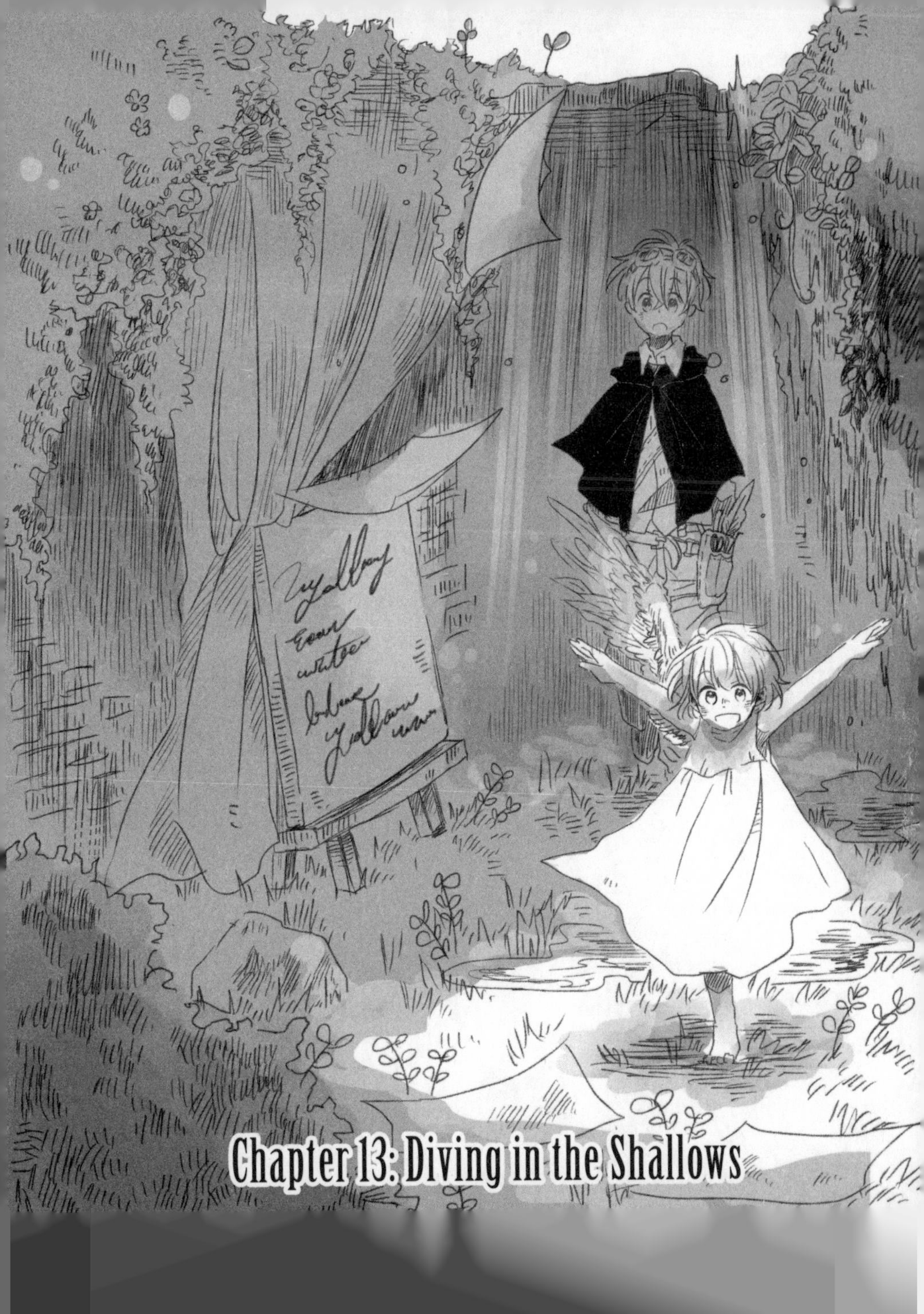

Chapter 13: Diving in the Shallows

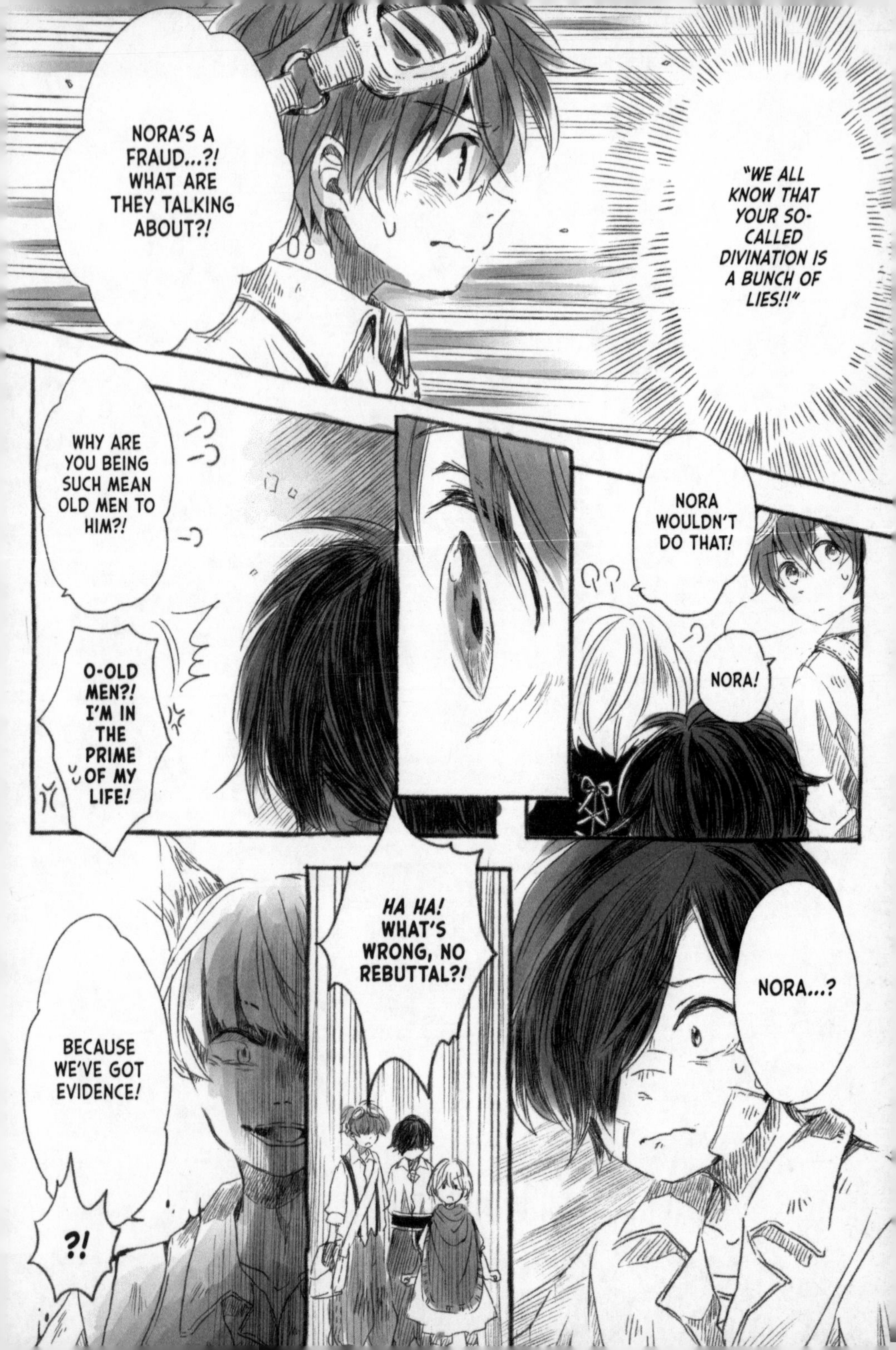
"WE ALL KNOW THAT YOUR SO-CALLED DIVINATION IS A BUNCH OF LIES!!"
NORA'S A FRAUD...?! WHAT ARE THEY TALKING ABOUT?!
NORA WOULDN'T DO THAT!
NORA!
WHY ARE YOU BEING SUCH MEAN OLD MEN TO HIM?!
O-OLD MEN?! I'M IN THE PRIME OF MY LIFE!
NORA...?
HA HA! WHAT'S WRONG, NO REBUTTAL?!
BECAUSE WE'VE GOT EVIDENCE!
?!

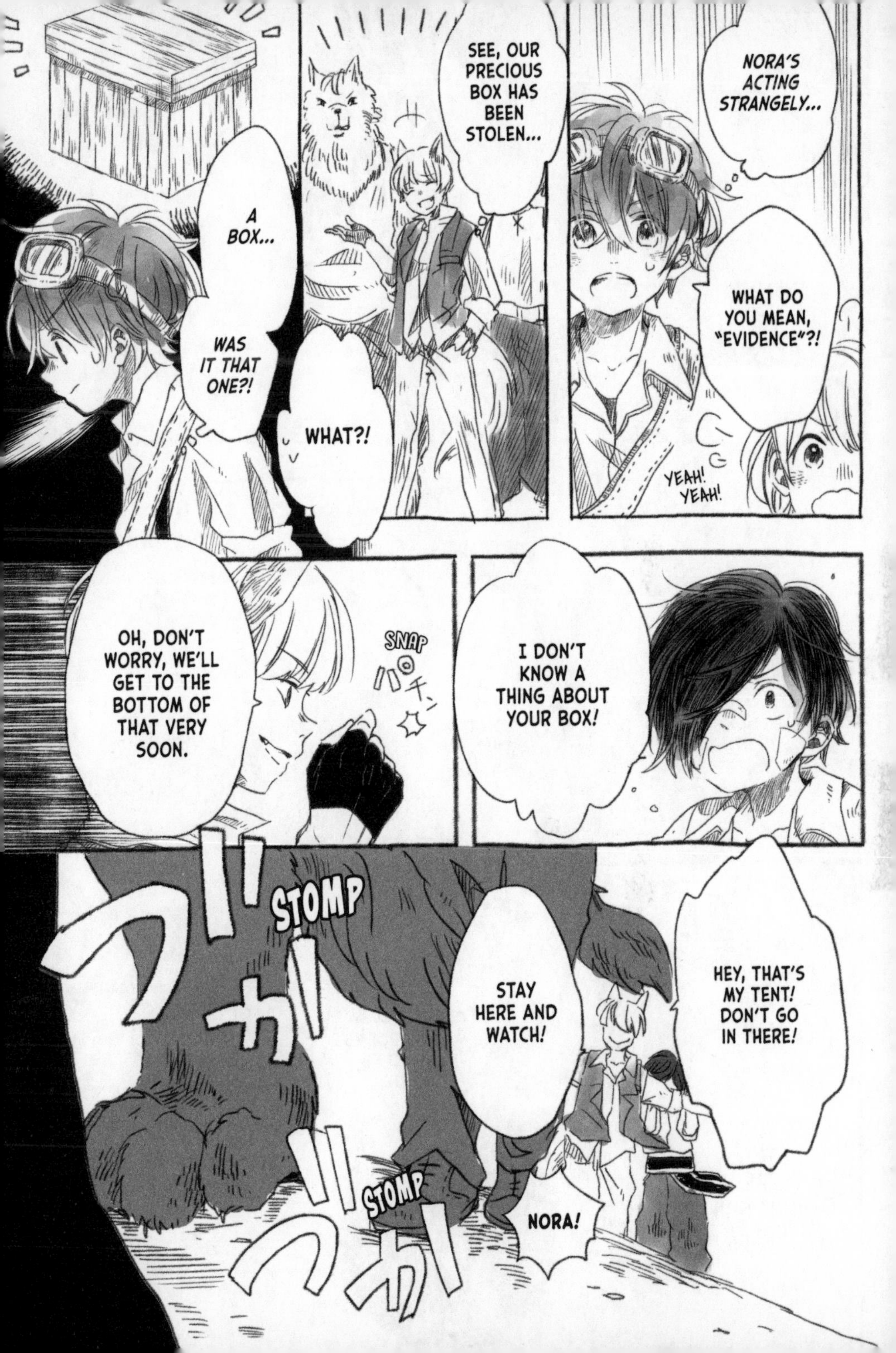
NORA'S ACTING STRANGELY...
WHAT DO YOU MEAN, "EVIDENCE"?!
YEAH! YEAH!
SEE, OUR PRECIOUS BOX HAS BEEN STOLEN...
WHAT?!
A BOX...
WAS IT THAT ONE?!
I DON'T KNOW A THING ABOUT YOUR BOX!
SNAP
OH, DON'T WORRY, WE'LL GET TO THE BOTTOM OF THAT VERY SOON.
HEY, THAT'S MY TENT! DON'T GO IN THERE!
STAY HERE AND WATCH!
NORA!
STOMP
STOMP

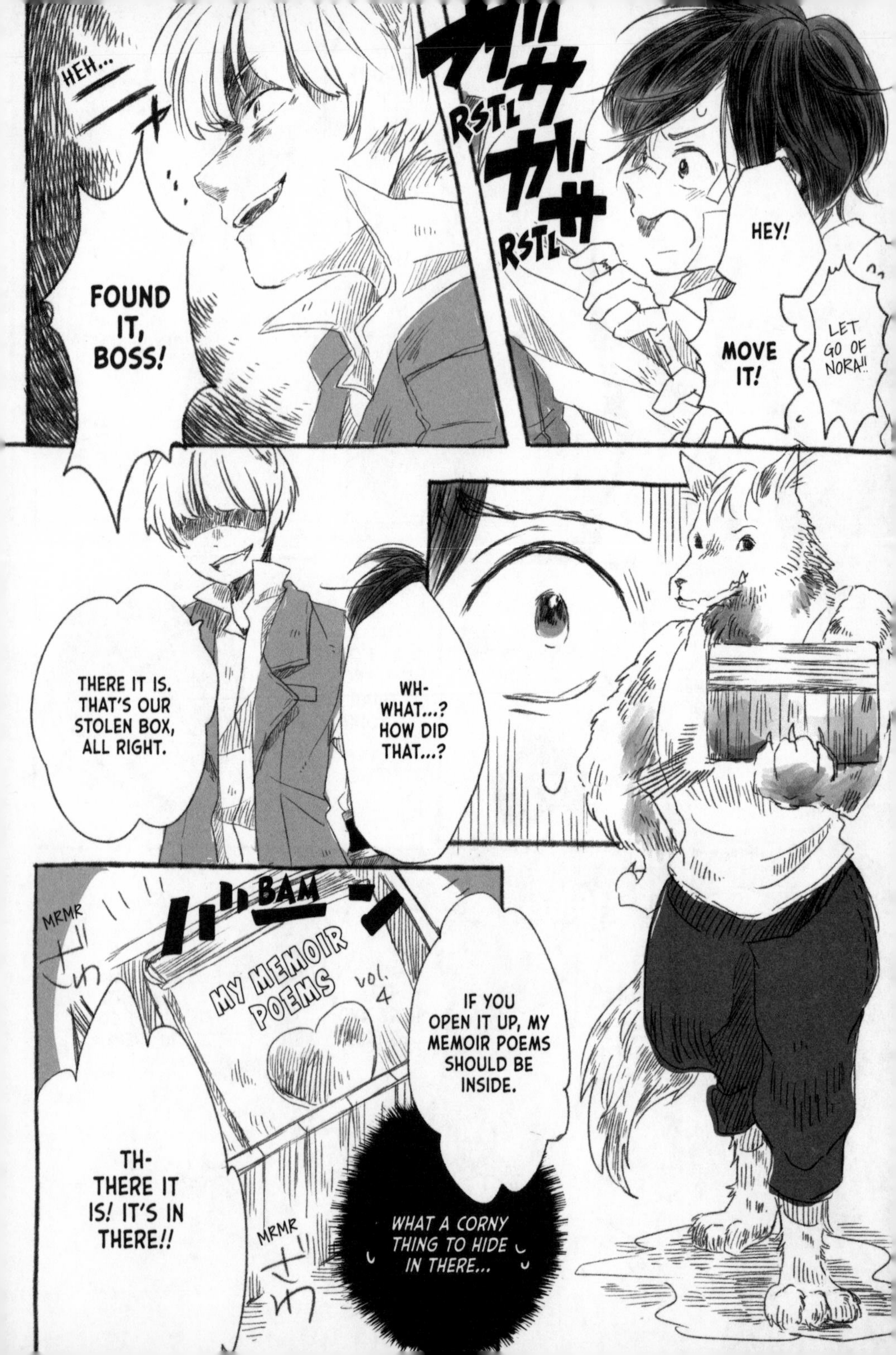
RSTL
RSTL
HEY!
LET GO OF NORA!!
MOVE IT!
HEH...
FOUND IT, BOSS!
WH- WHAT...? HOW DID THAT...?
THERE IT IS. THAT'S OUR STOLEN BOX, ALL RIGHT.
IF YOU OPEN IT UP, MY MEMOIR POEMS SHOULD BE INSIDE.
BAM
MY MEMOIR POEMS vol. 4
MRMR
TH- THERE IT IS! IT'S IN THERE!!
MRMR
WHAT A CORNY THING TO HIDE IN THERE...

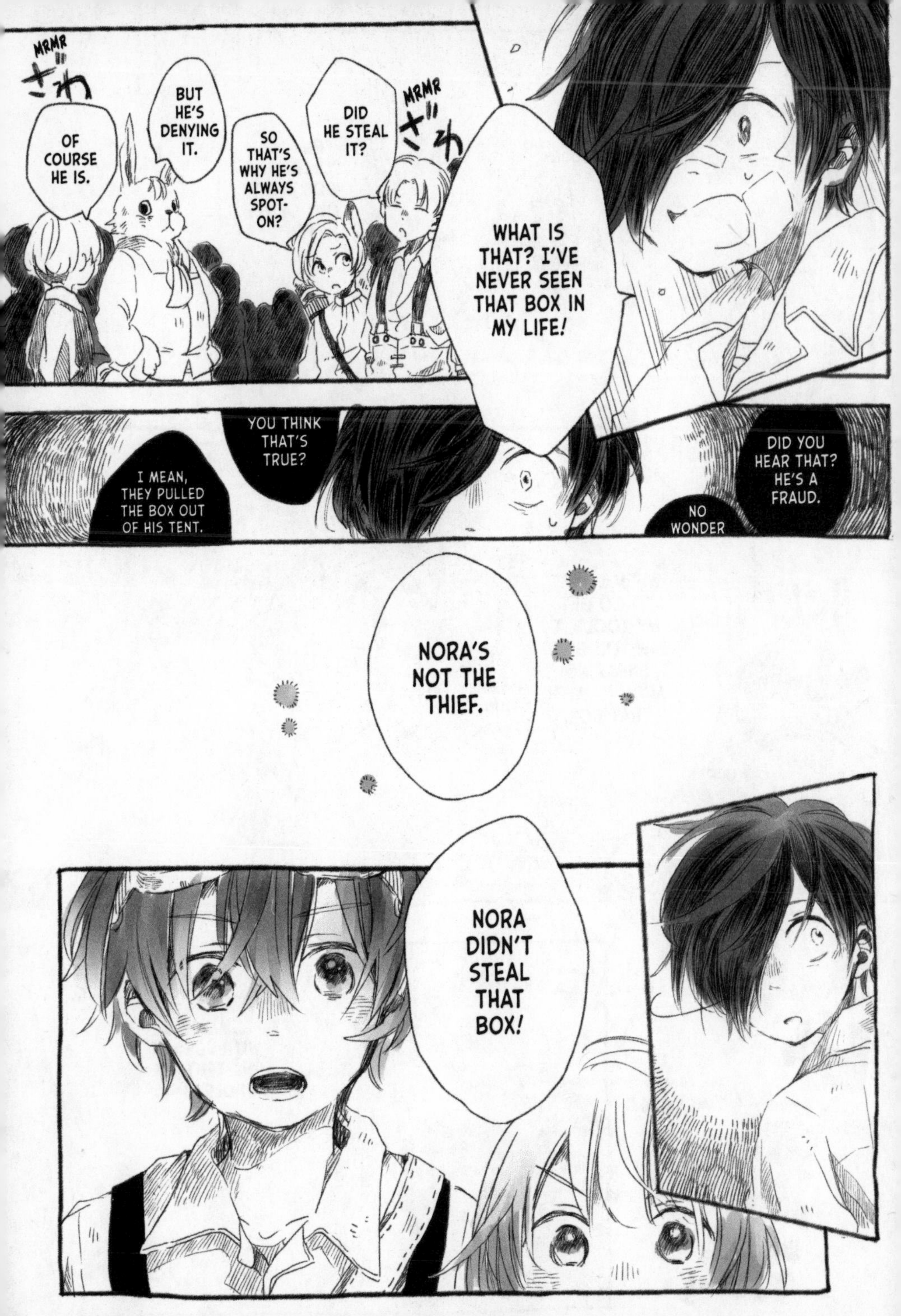
WHAT IS THAT? I'VE NEVER SEEN THAT BOX IN MY LIFE!
MRMR ざわ
DID HE STEAL IT?
SO THAT'S WHY HE'S ALWAYS SPOT-ON?
BUT HE'S DENYING IT.
OF COURSE HE IS.
MRMR ざわ
DID YOU HEAR THAT? HE'S A FRAUD.
NO WONDER
YOU THINK THAT'S TRUE?
I MEAN, THEY PULLED THE BOX OUT OF HIS TENT.
NORA'S NOT THE THIEF.
NORA DIDN'T STEAL THAT BOX!

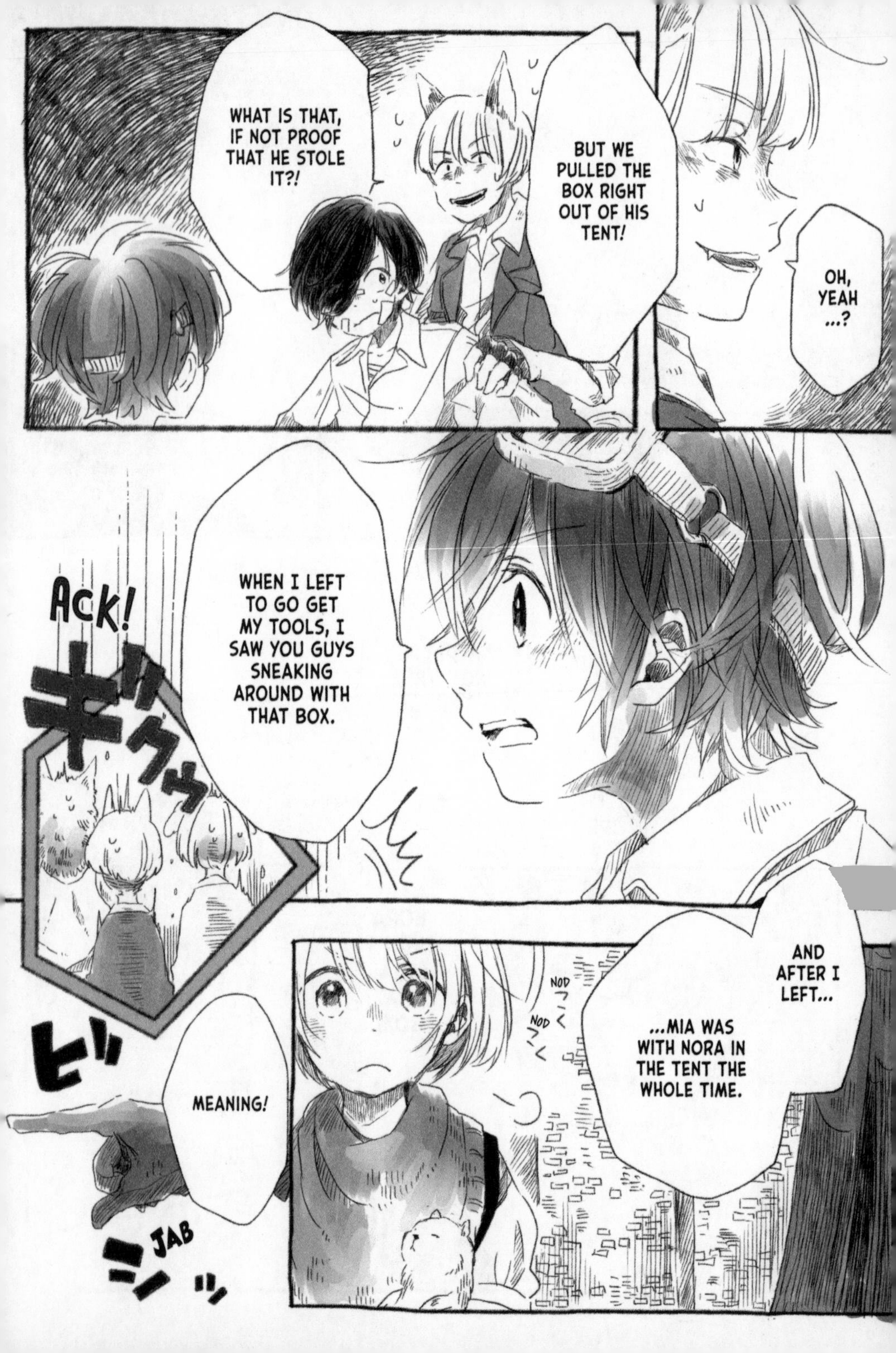

OH, YEAH ...?
BUT WE PULLED THE BOX RIGHT OUT OF HIS TENT!
WHAT IS THAT, IF NOT PROOF THAT HE STOLE IT?!
WHEN I LEFT TO GO GET MY TOOLS, I SAW YOU GUYS SNEAKING AROUND WITH THAT BOX.
ACK!
ギクゥ
AND AFTER I LEFT...
...MIA WAS WITH NORA IN THE TENT THE WHOLE TIME.
NOD
NOD
MEANING!
JAB

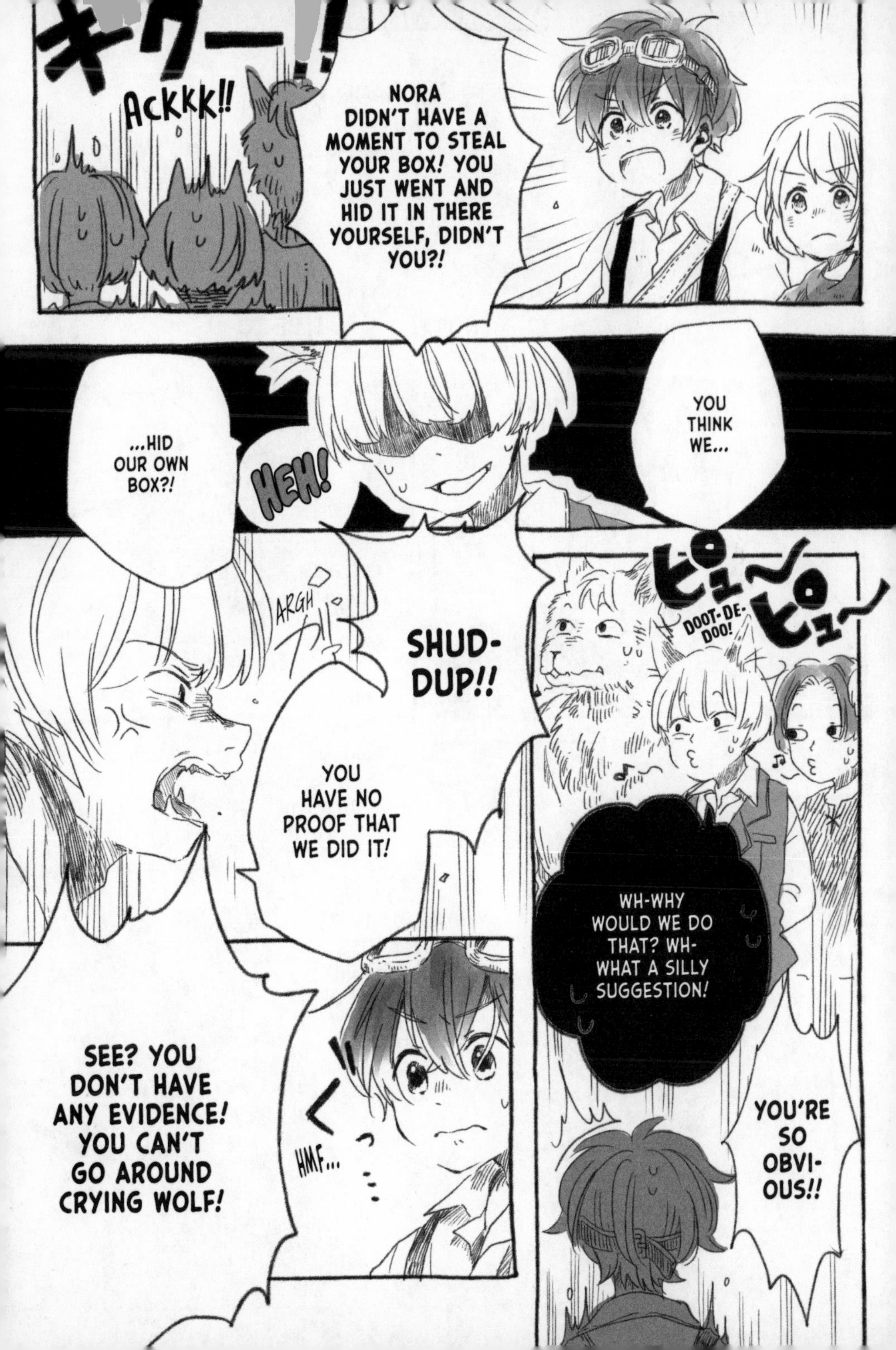
NORA DIDN'T HAVE A MOMENT TO STEAL YOUR BOX! YOU JUST WENT AND HID IT IN THERE YOURSELF, DIDN'T YOU?!
ACKKK!!
YOU THINK WE...
HEH!
...HID OUR OWN BOX?!
ピュ~ピュ~
DOOT-DE-DOO!
WH-WHY WOULD WE DO THAT? WH-WHAT A SILLY SUGGESTION!
YOU'RE SO OBVI-OUS!!
SHUD-DUP!!
ARGH
YOU HAVE NO PROOF THAT WE DID IT!
HMF...
SEE? YOU DON'T HAVE ANY EVIDENCE! YOU CAN'T GO AROUND CRYING WOLF!

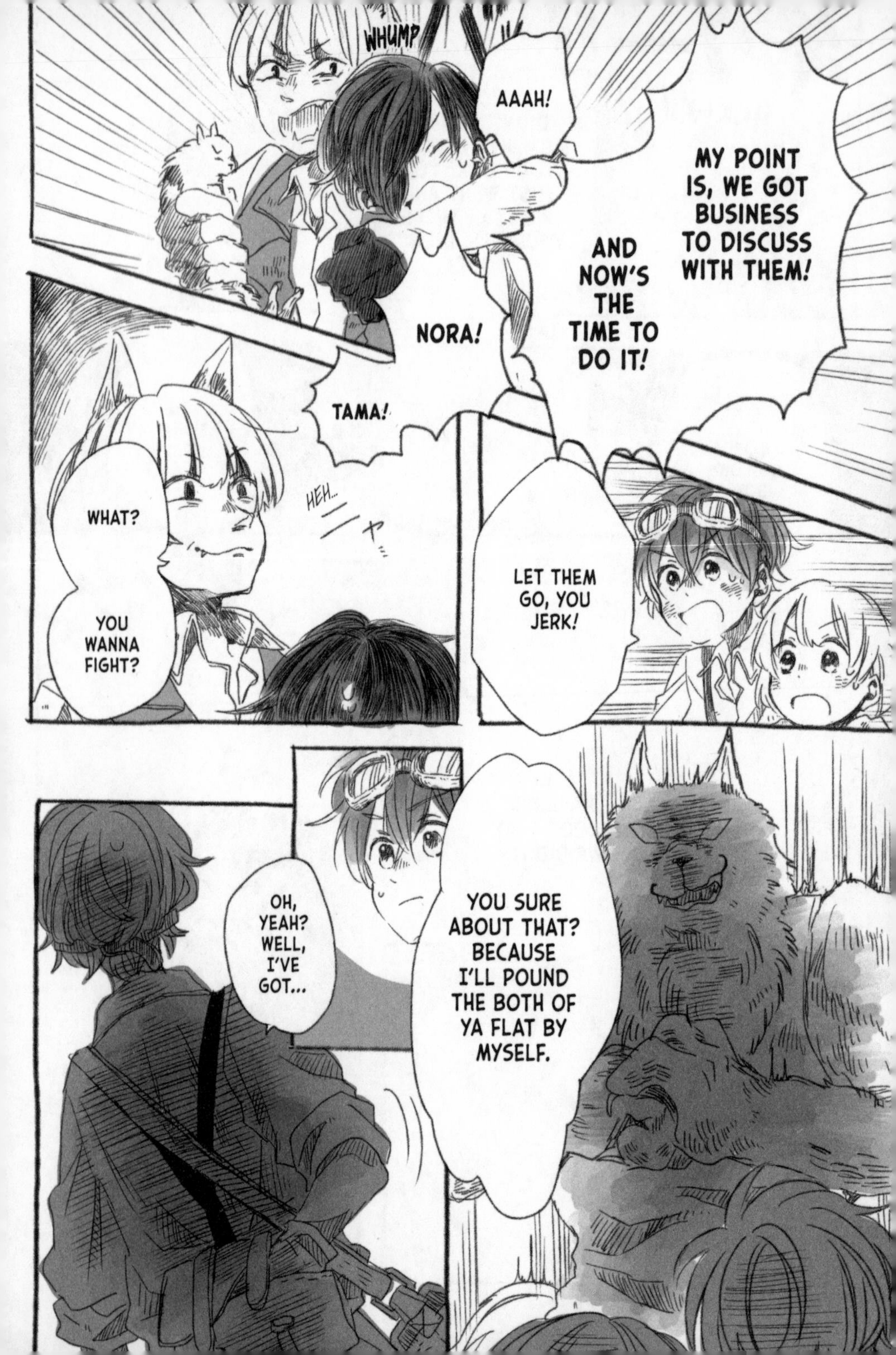

MY POINT IS, WE GOT BUSINESS TO DISCUSS WITH THEM!
AND NOW'S THE TIME TO DO IT!
WHUMP
AAAH!
NORA!
TAMA!
LET THEM GO, YOU JERK!
WHAT?
HEH...
YOU WANNA FIGHT?
YOU SURE ABOUT THAT? BECAUSE I'LL POUND THE BOTH OF YA FLAT BY MYSELF.
OH, YEAH? WELL, I'VE GOT...

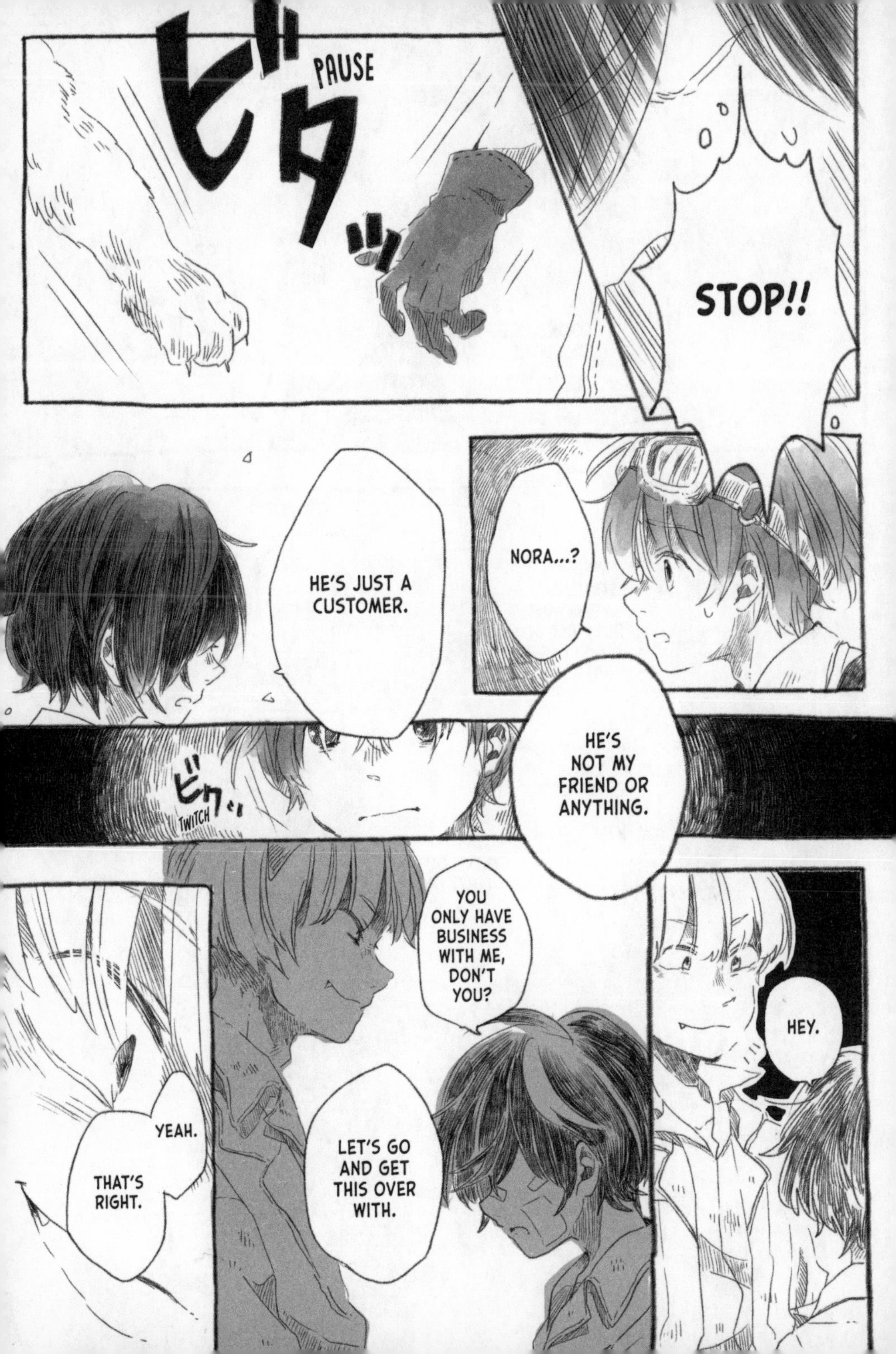
STOP!!
ビタッ
PAUSE
NORA...?
HE'S JUST A CUSTOMER.
HE'S NOT MY FRIEND OR ANYTHING.
ビクッ
TWITCH
HEY.
YOU ONLY HAVE BUSINESS WITH ME, DON'T YOU?
LET'S GO AND GET THIS OVER WITH.
YEAH.
THAT'S RIGHT.

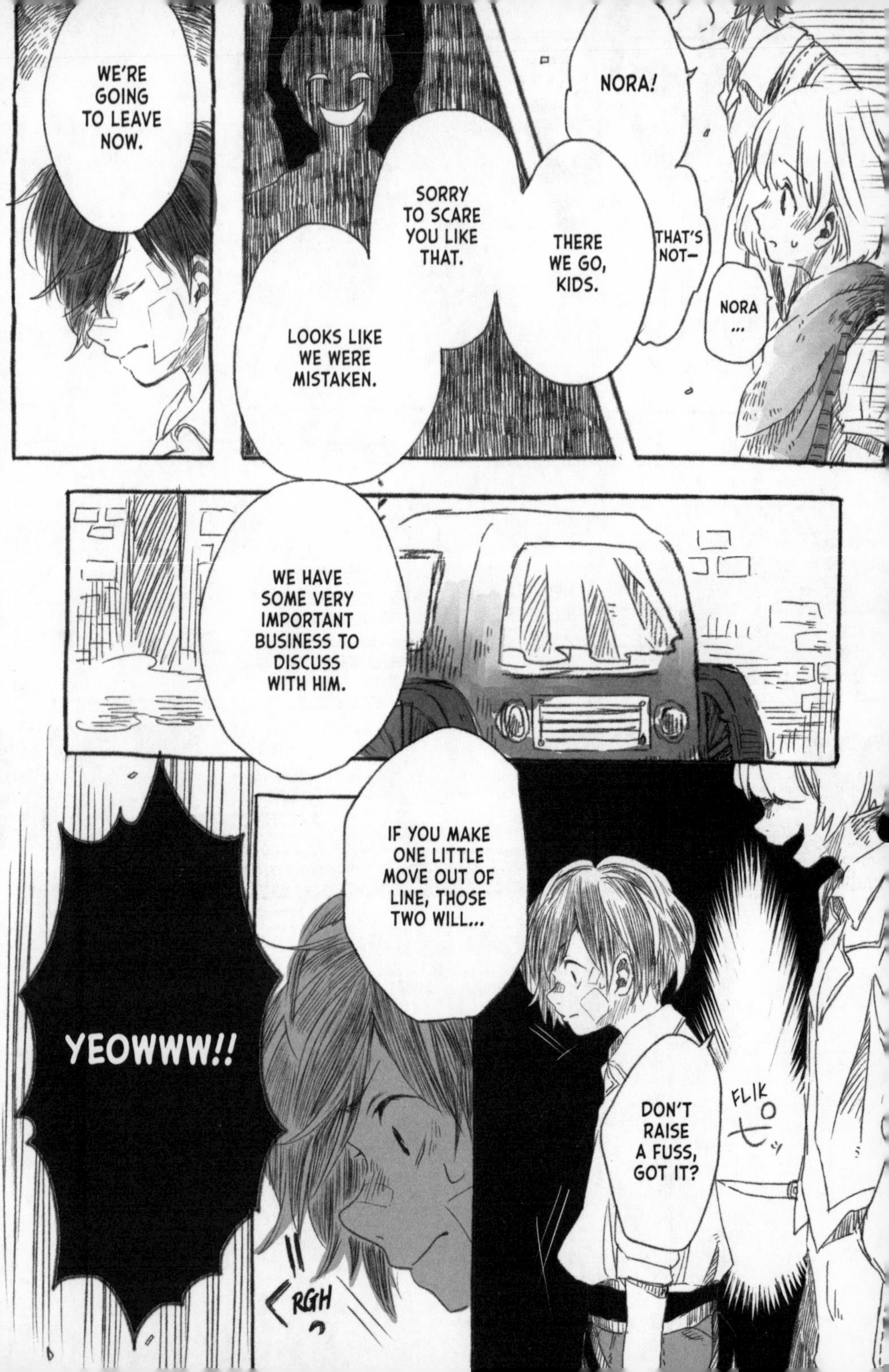
NORA!
THAT'S NOT—
NORA ...
THERE WE GO, KIDS.
SORRY TO SCARE YOU LIKE THAT.
LOOKS LIKE WE WERE MISTAKEN.
WE'RE GOING TO LEAVE NOW.
WE HAVE SOME VERY IMPORTANT BUSINESS TO DISCUSS WITH HIM.
IF YOU MAKE ONE LITTLE MOVE OUT OF LINE, THOSE TWO WILL...
FLIK
DON'T RAISE A FUSS, GOT IT?
RGH
YEOWWW!!

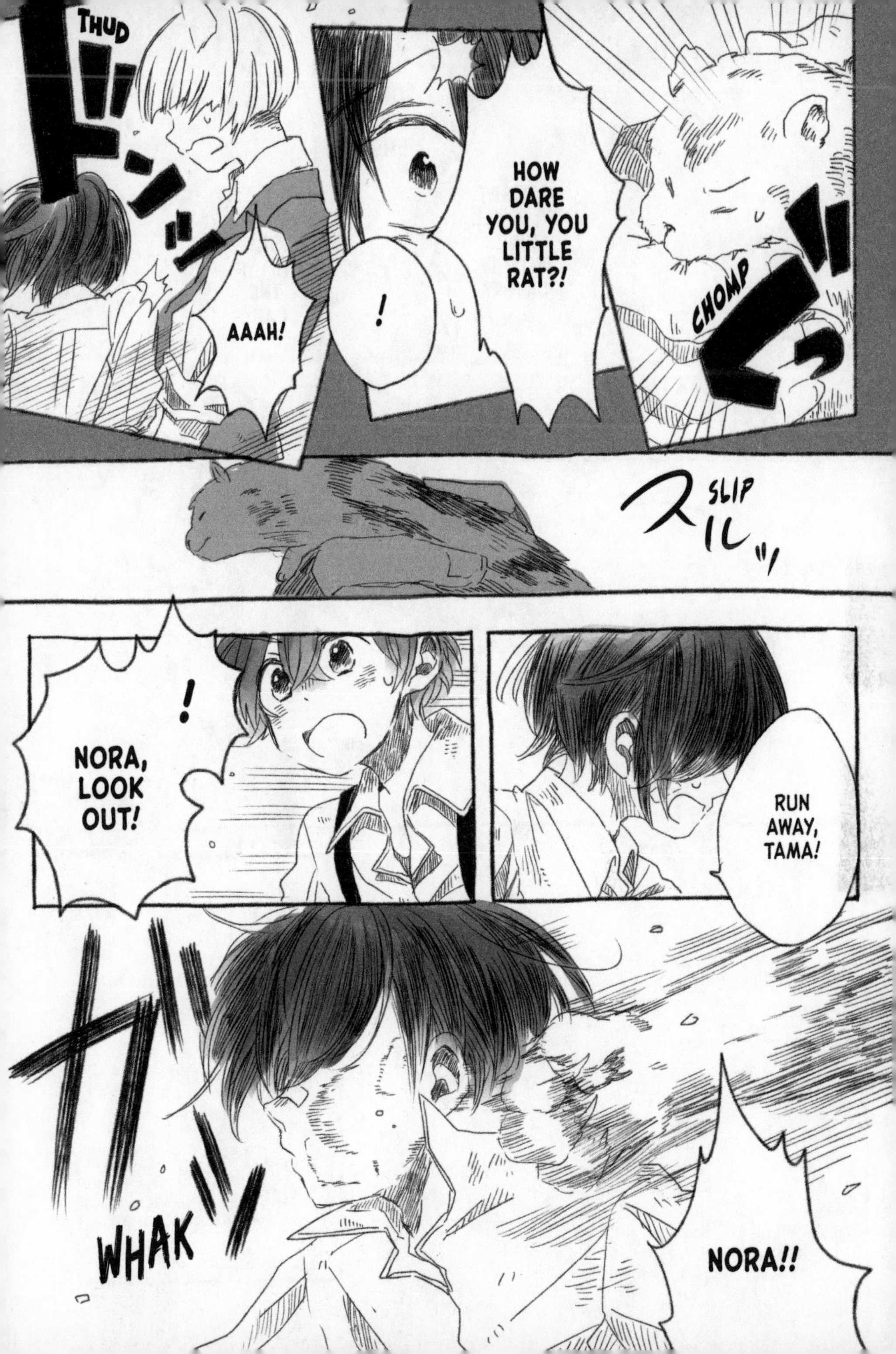
CHOMP
HOW DARE YOU, YOU LITTLE RAT?!
!
THUD
AAAH!
SLIP
スルッ
RUN AWAY, TAMA!
!
NORA, LOOK OUT!
NORA!!
WHAK

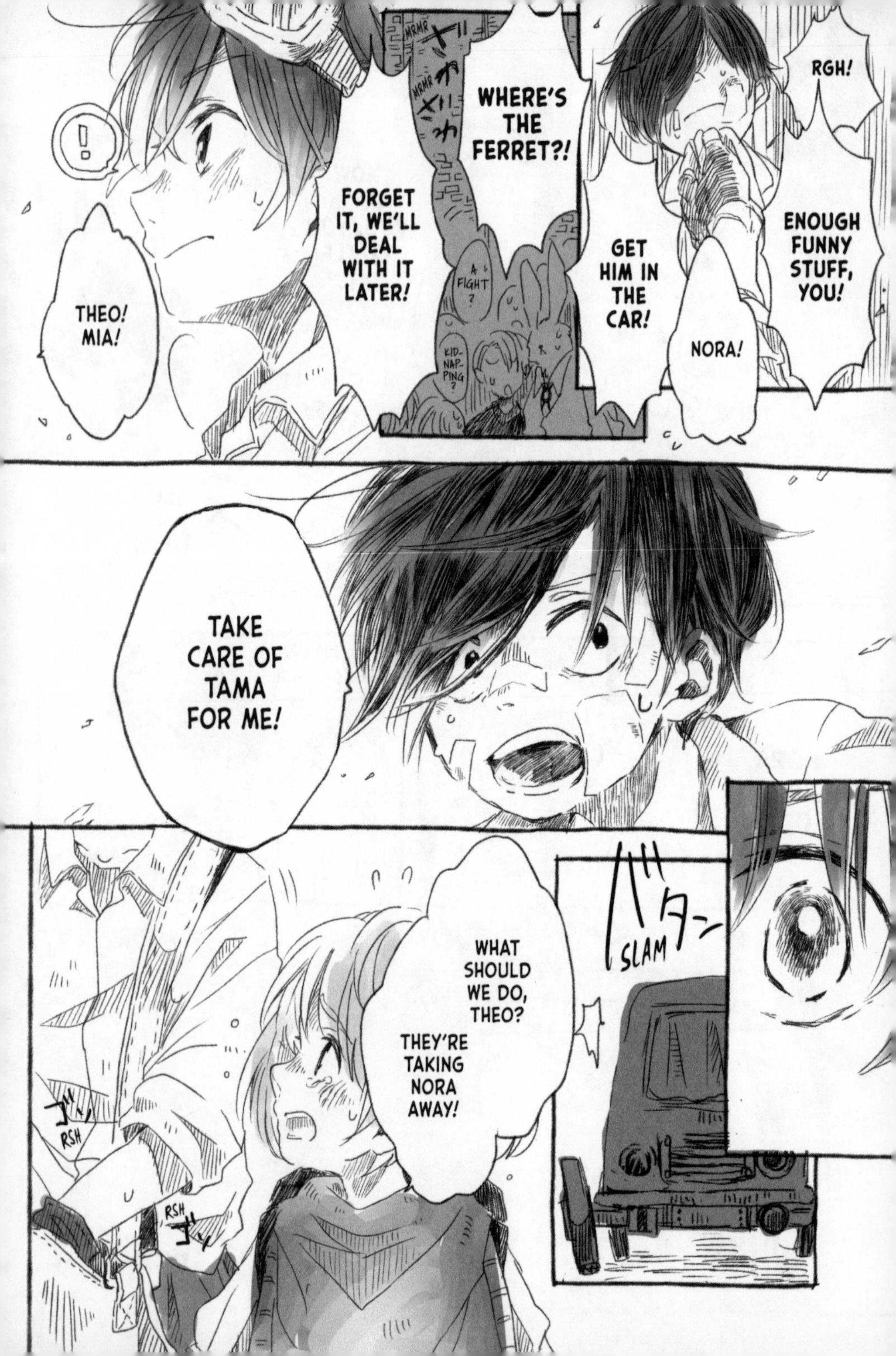
RGH!
ENOUGH FUNNY STUFF, YOU!
NORA!
GET HIM IN THE CAR!
WHERE'S THE FERRET?!
MRMR
MRMR
A FIGHT?
KID-NAPPING?
FORGET IT, WE'LL DEAL WITH IT LATER!
!
THEO! MIA!
TAKE CARE OF TAMA FOR ME!
SLAM
WHAT SHOULD WE DO, THEO?
THEY'RE TAKING NORA AWAY!
RSH
RSH

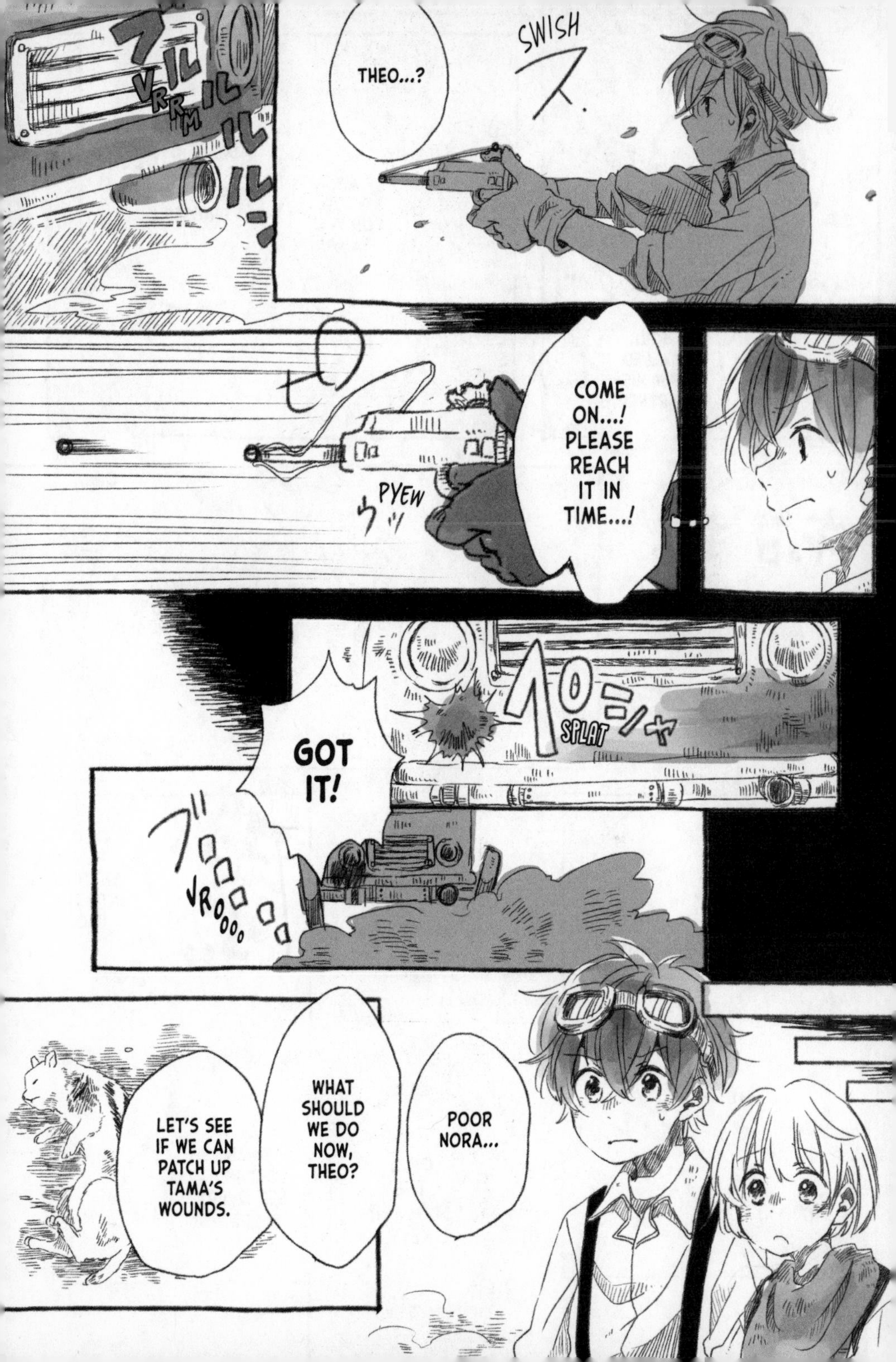
THEO...?
SWISH
VRRRM
COME ON...! PLEASE REACH IT IN TIME...!
PYEW
SPLAT
GOT IT!
VROOOO
POOR NORA...
WHAT SHOULD WE DO NOW, THEO?
LET'S SEE IF WE CAN PATCH UP TAMA'S WOUNDS.

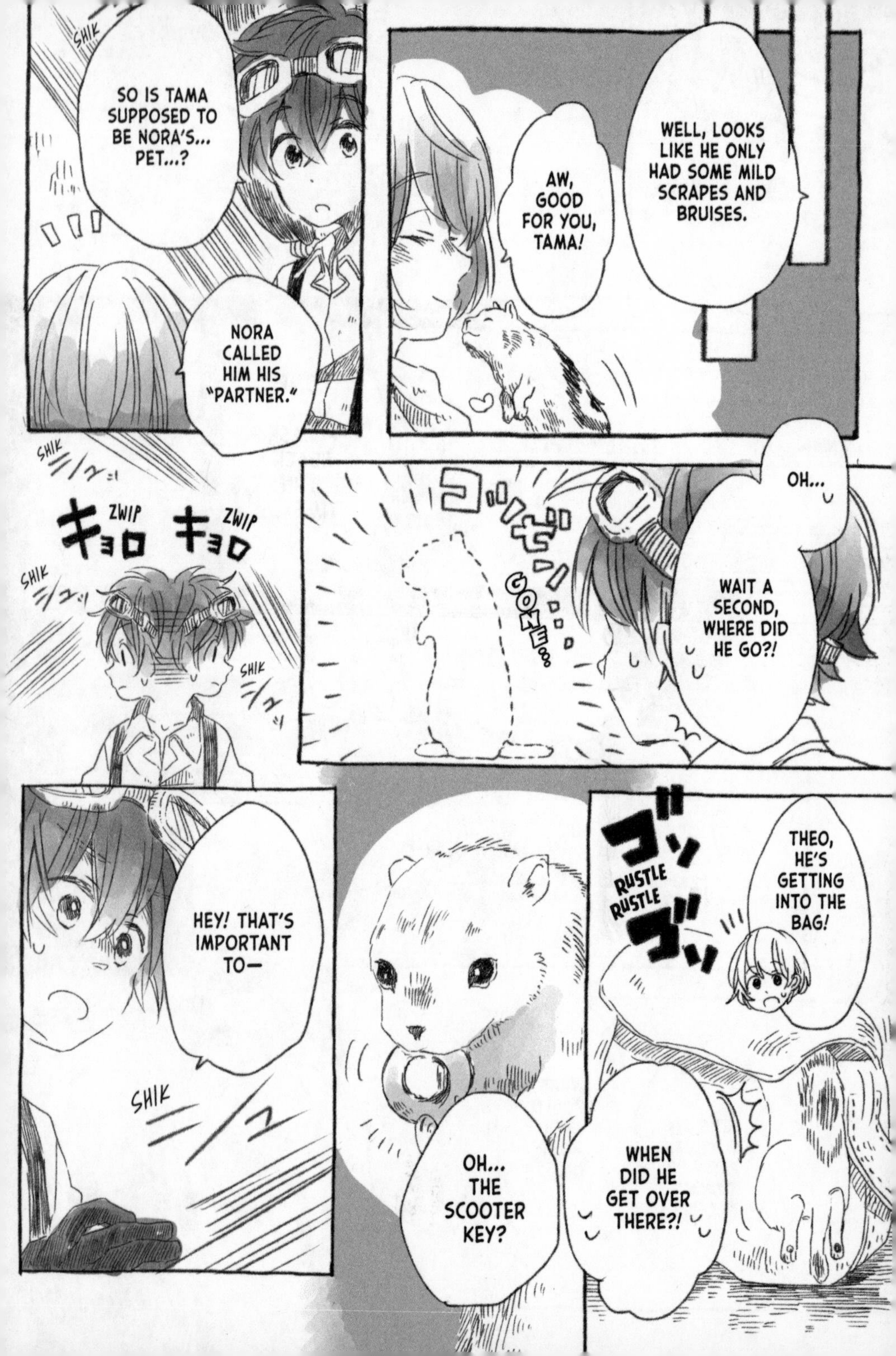
WELL, LOOKS LIKE HE ONLY HAD SOME MILD SCRAPES AND BRUISES.
AW, GOOD FOR YOU, TAMA!
SHIK
SO IS TAMA SUPPOSED TO BE NORA'S... PET...?
NORA CALLED HIM HIS "PARTNER."
OH...
WAIT A SECOND, WHERE DID HE GO?!
GONE...
SHIK
キョロ ZWIP キョロ ZWIP
SHIK
SHIK
RUSTLE RUSTLE
THEO, HE'S GETTING INTO THE BAG!
WHEN DID HE GET OVER THERE?!
OH... THE SCOOTER KEY?
HEY! THAT'S IMPORTANT TO—
SHIK

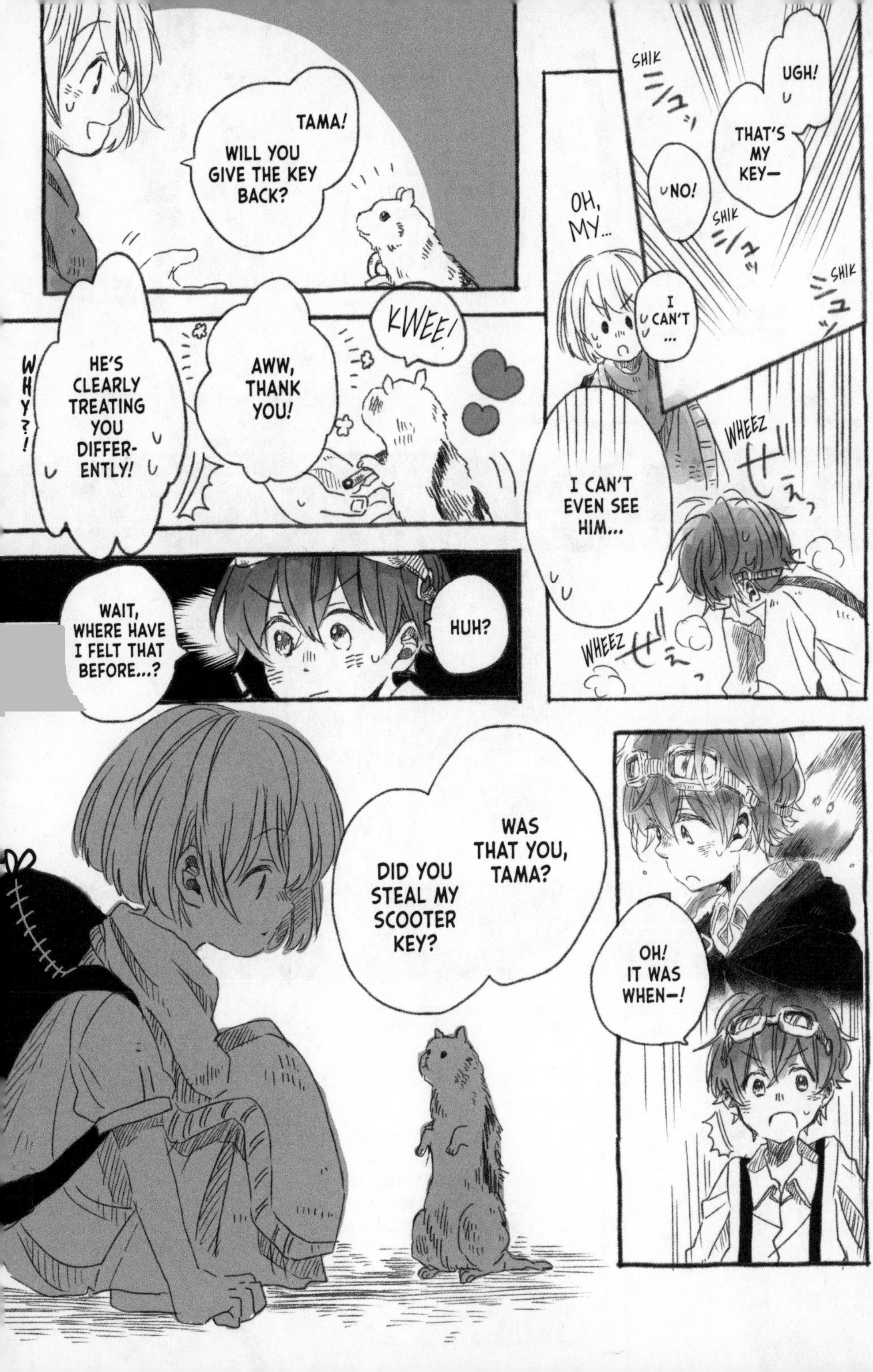
SHIK
UGH!
THAT'S MY KEY—
NO!
SHIK
SHIK
OH, MY...
I CAN'T ...
I CAN'T EVEN SEE HIM...
WHEEZ
WHEEZ
TAMA!
WILL YOU GIVE THE KEY BACK?
KWEE!
AWW, THANK YOU!
HE'S CLEARLY TREATING YOU DIFFER-ENTLY!
WHY?!
HUH?
WAIT, WHERE HAVE I FELT THAT BEFORE...?
OH! IT WAS WHEN—!
WAS THAT YOU, TAMA?
DID YOU STEAL MY SCOOTER KEY?

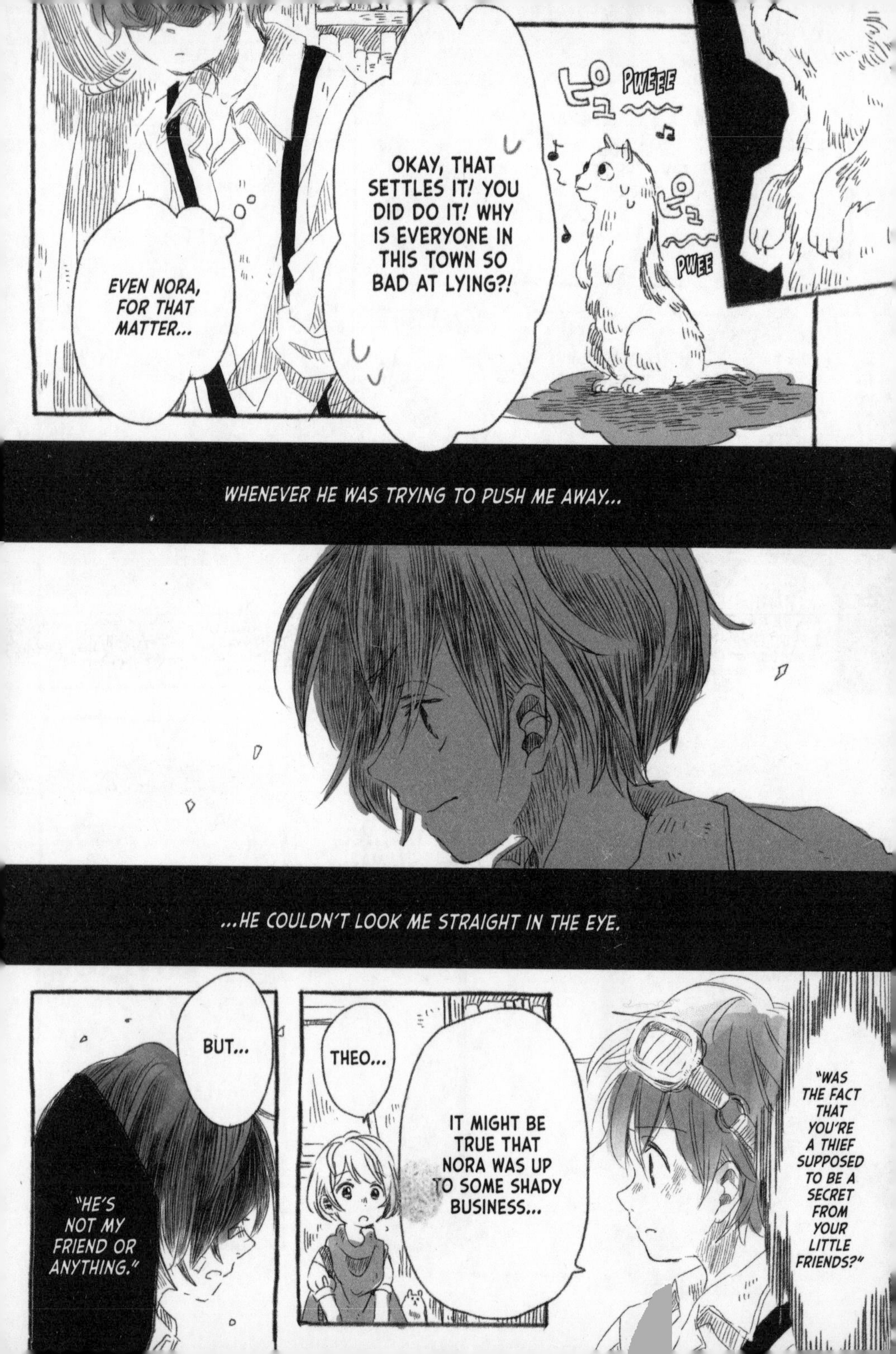
ピュ PWEEE
ピュ PWEE
OKAY, THAT SETTLES IT! YOU DID DO IT! WHY IS EVERYONE IN THIS TOWN SO BAD AT LYING?!
EVEN NORA, FOR THAT MATTER...
WHENEVER HE WAS TRYING TO PUSH ME AWAY...
...HE COULDN'T LOOK ME STRAIGHT IN THE EYE.
"WAS THE FACT THAT YOU'RE A THIEF SUPPOSED TO BE A SECRET FROM YOUR LITTLE FRIENDS?"
THEO...
IT MIGHT BE TRUE THAT NORA WAS UP TO SOME SHADY BUSINESS...
BUT...
"HE'S NOT MY FRIEND OR ANYTHING."

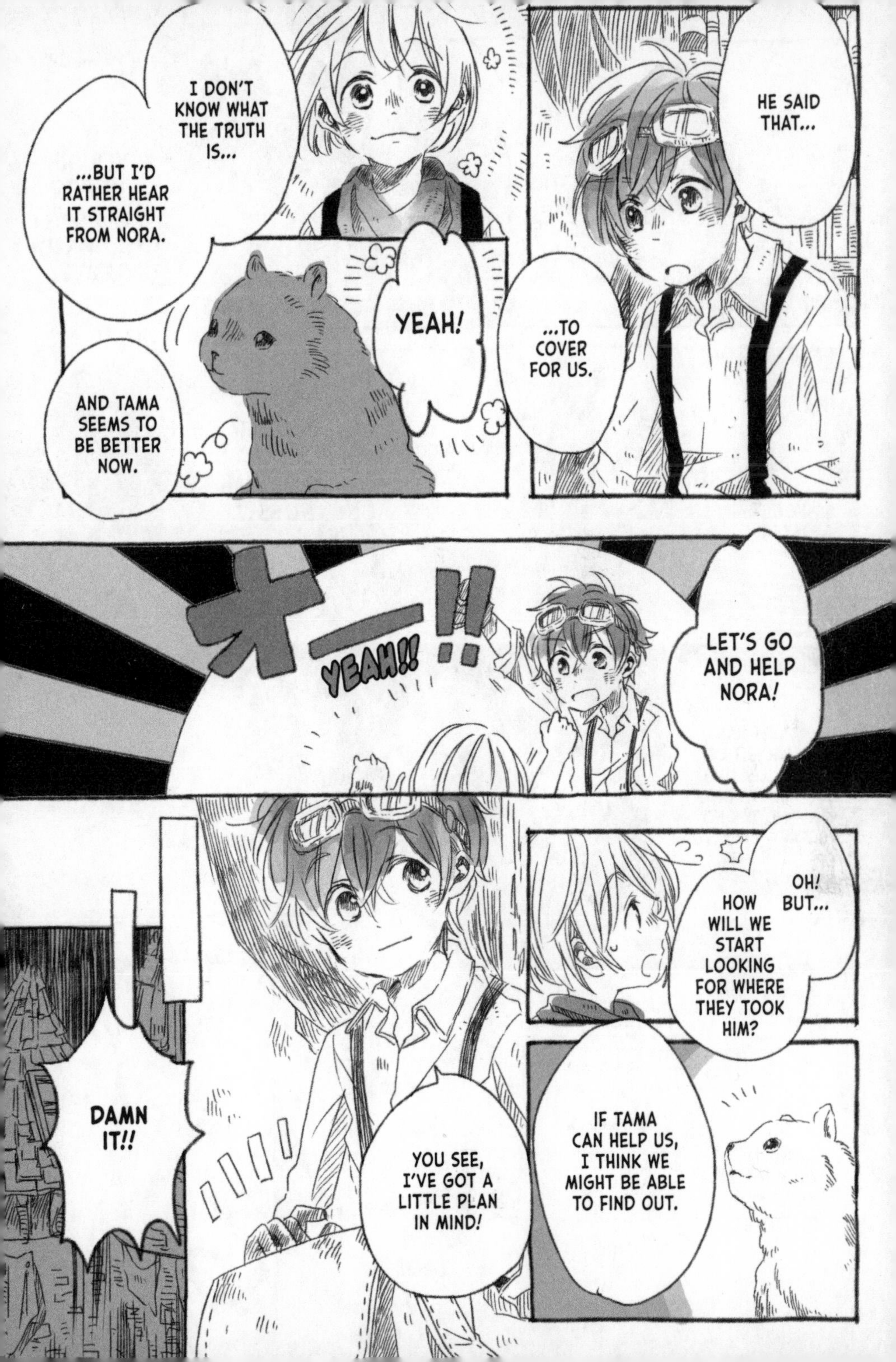
HE SAID THAT...
...TO COVER FOR US.
I DON'T KNOW WHAT THE TRUTH IS...
...BUT I'D RATHER HEAR IT STRAIGHT FROM NORA.
YEAH!
AND TAMA SEEMS TO BE BETTER NOW.
LET'S GO AND HELP NORA!
オー!!
YEAH!!
OH! BUT...
HOW WILL WE START LOOKING FOR WHERE THEY TOOK HIM?
IF TAMA CAN HELP US, I THINK WE MIGHT BE ABLE TO FIND OUT.
YOU SEE, I'VE GOT A LITTLE PLAN IN MIND!
DAMN IT!!

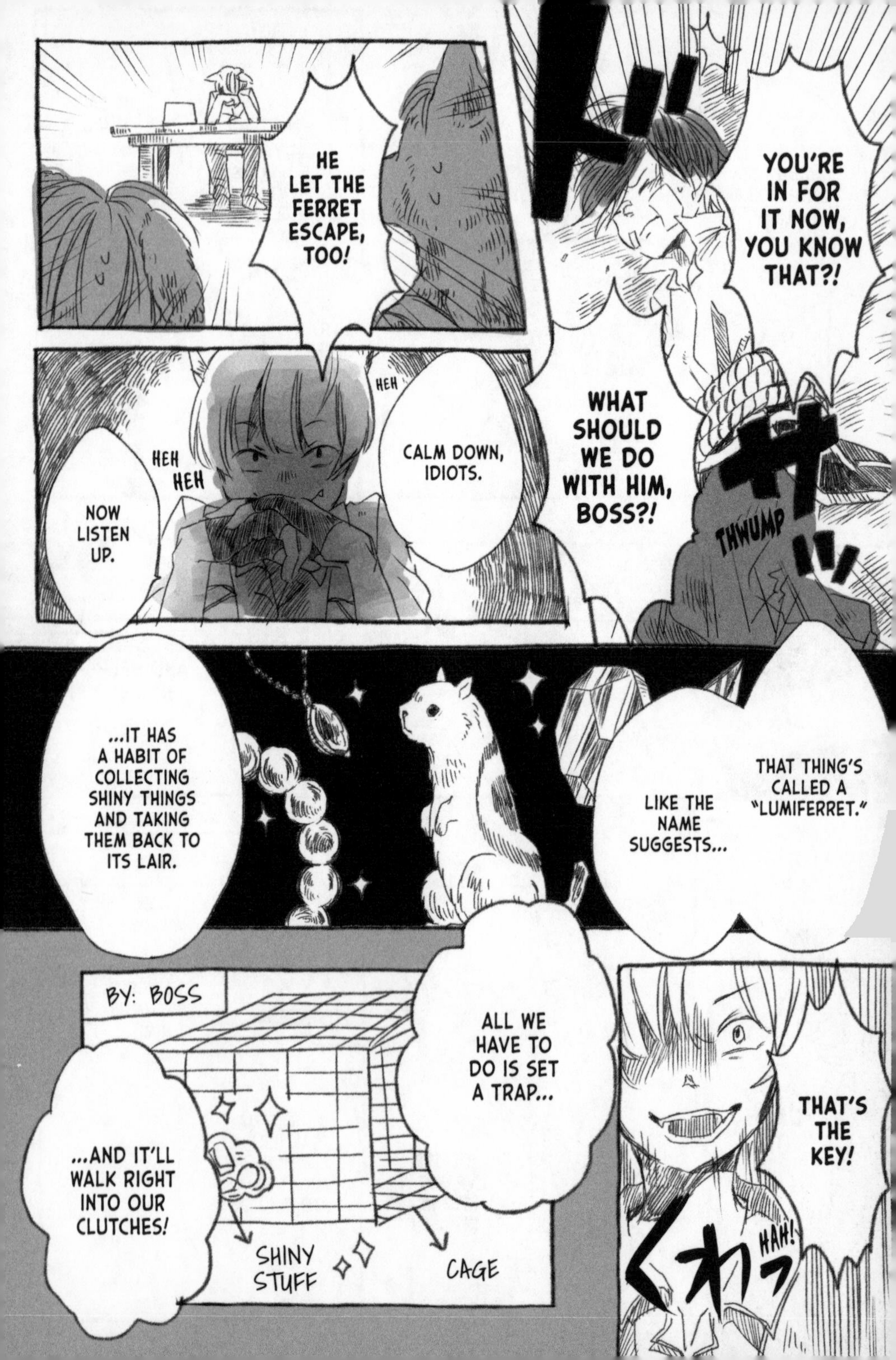
YOU'RE IN FOR IT NOW, YOU KNOW THAT?!
WHAT SHOULD WE DO WITH HIM, BOSS?!
THWUMP
HE LET THE FERRET ESCAPE, TOO!
HEH
CALM DOWN, IDIOTS.
HEH HEH
NOW LISTEN UP.
THAT THING'S CALLED A "LUMIFERRET."
LIKE THE NAME SUGGESTS...
...IT HAS A HABIT OF COLLECTING SHINY THINGS AND TAKING THEM BACK TO ITS LAIR.
THAT'S THE KEY!
HAH!
ALL WE HAVE TO DO IS SET A TRAP...
BY: BOSS
...AND IT'LL WALK RIGHT INTO OUR CLUTCHES!
SHINY STUFF
CAGE

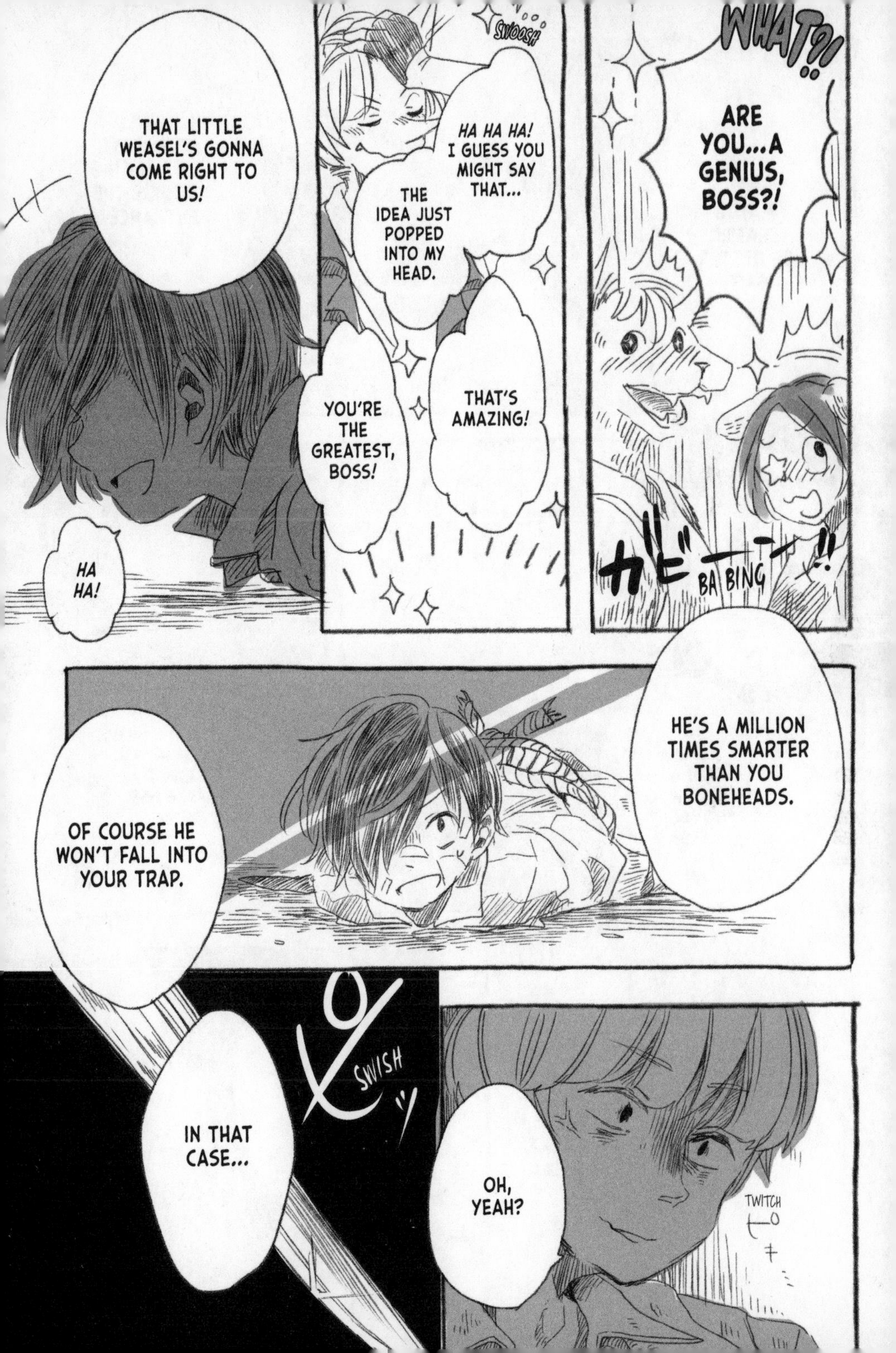
WHAT?!
ARE YOU...A GENIUS, BOSS?!
BA BING
SWOOSH
HA HA HA! I GUESS YOU MIGHT SAY THAT...
THE IDEA JUST POPPED INTO MY HEAD.
THAT'S AMAZING!
YOU'RE THE GREATEST, BOSS!
THAT LITTLE WEASEL'S GONNA COME RIGHT TO US!
HA HA!
HE'S A MILLION TIMES SMARTER THAN YOU BONEHEADS.
OF COURSE HE WON'T FALL INTO YOUR TRAP.
OH, YEAH?
TWITCH
SWISH
IN THAT CASE...

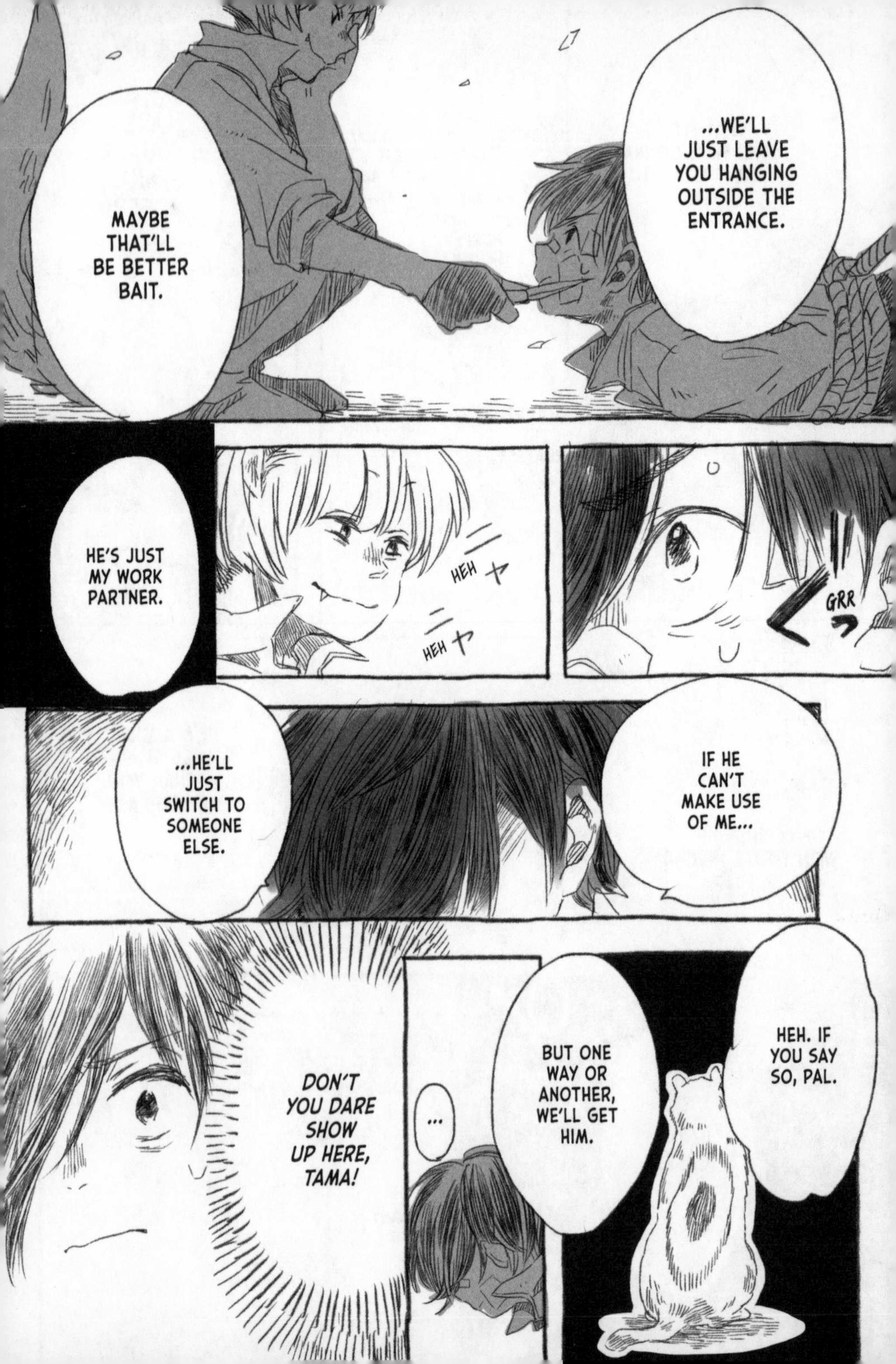
...WE'LL JUST LEAVE YOU HANGING OUTSIDE THE ENTRANCE.
MAYBE THAT'LL BE BETTER BAIT.
GRR
HE'S JUST MY WORK PARTNER.
HEH
HEH
IF HE CAN'T MAKE USE OF ME...
...HE'LL JUST SWITCH TO SOMEONE ELSE.
HEH. IF YOU SAY SO, PAL.
BUT ONE WAY OR ANOTHER, WE'LL GET HIM.
...
DON'T YOU DARE SHOW UP HERE, TAMA!

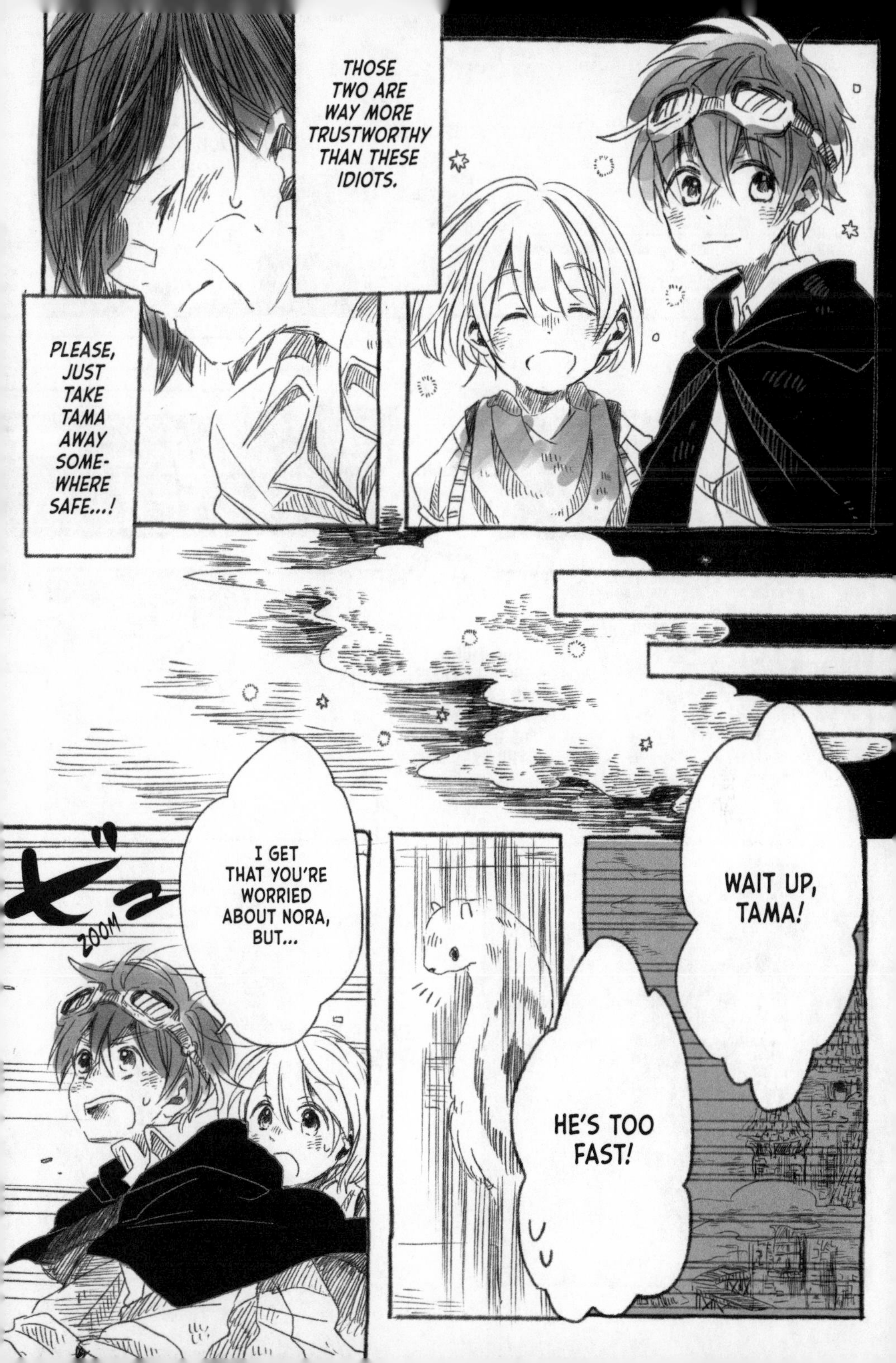
THOSE TWO ARE WAY MORE TRUSTWORTHY THAN THESE IDIOTS.
PLEASE, JUST TAKE TAMA AWAY SOME-WHERE SAFE...!
WAIT UP, TAMA!
HE'S TOO FAST!
I GET THAT YOU'RE WORRIED ABOUT NORA, BUT...
ZOOM

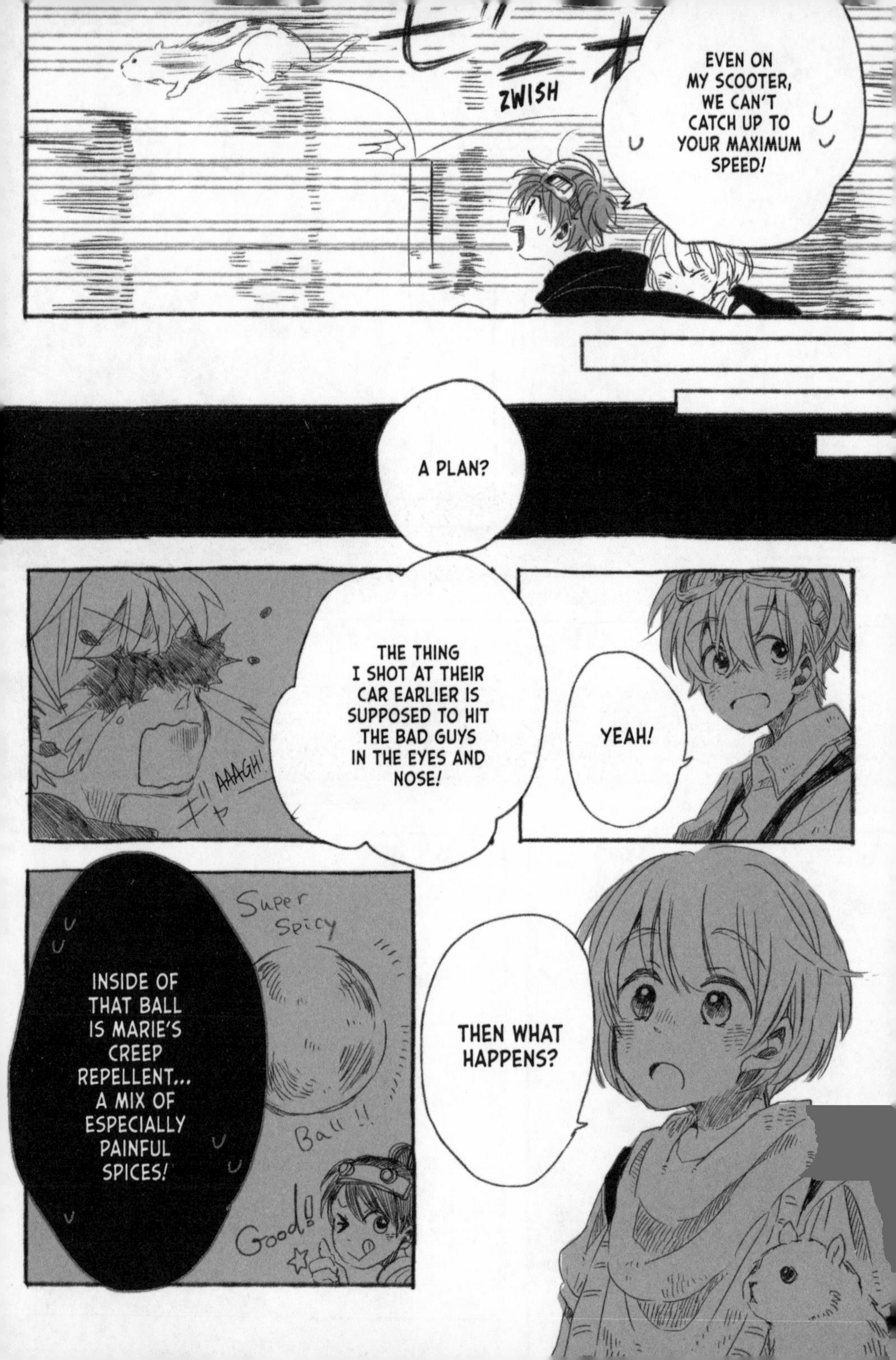
EVEN ON MY SCOOTER, WE CAN'T CATCH UP TO YOUR MAXIMUM SPEED!
ZWISH
A PLAN?
YEAH!
THE THING I SHOT AT THEIR CAR EARLIER IS SUPPOSED TO HIT THE BAD GUYS IN THE EYES AND NOSE!
AAAGH!
THEN WHAT HAPPENS?
INSIDE OF THAT BALL IS MARIE'S CREEP REPELLENT... A MIX OF ESPECIALLY PAINFUL SPICES!
Super Spicy
Ball!!
Good!

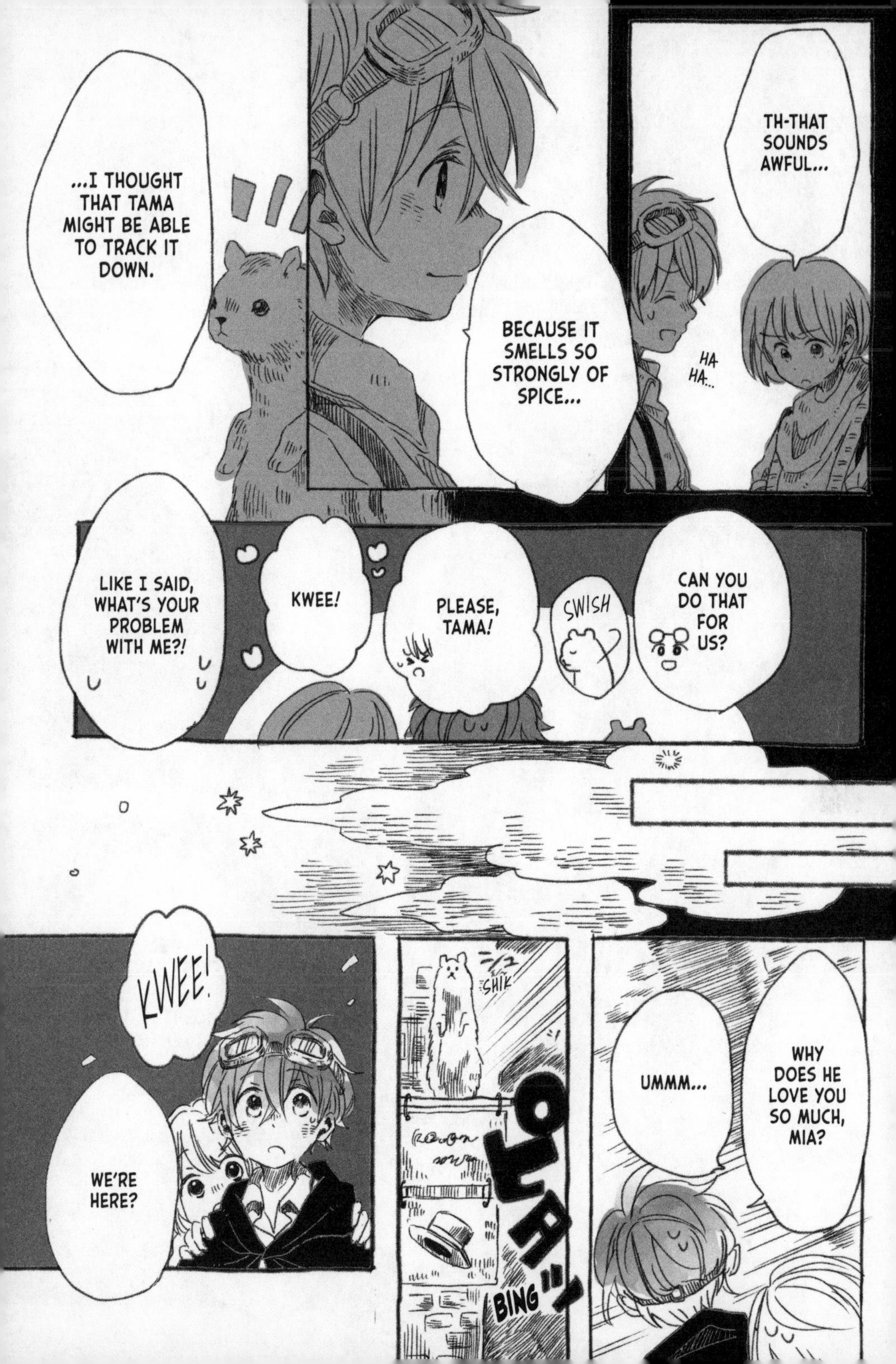
TH-THAT SOUNDS AWFUL...
HA HA...
BECAUSE IT SMELLS SO STRONGLY OF SPICE...
...I THOUGHT THAT TAMA MIGHT BE ABLE TO TRACK IT DOWN.
CAN YOU DO THAT FOR US?
SWISH
PLEASE, TAMA!
KWEE!
LIKE I SAID, WHAT'S YOUR PROBLEM WITH ME?!
WHY DOES HE LOVE YOU SO MUCH, MIA?
UMMM...
SHIK
BING!!
KWEE!
WE'RE HERE?

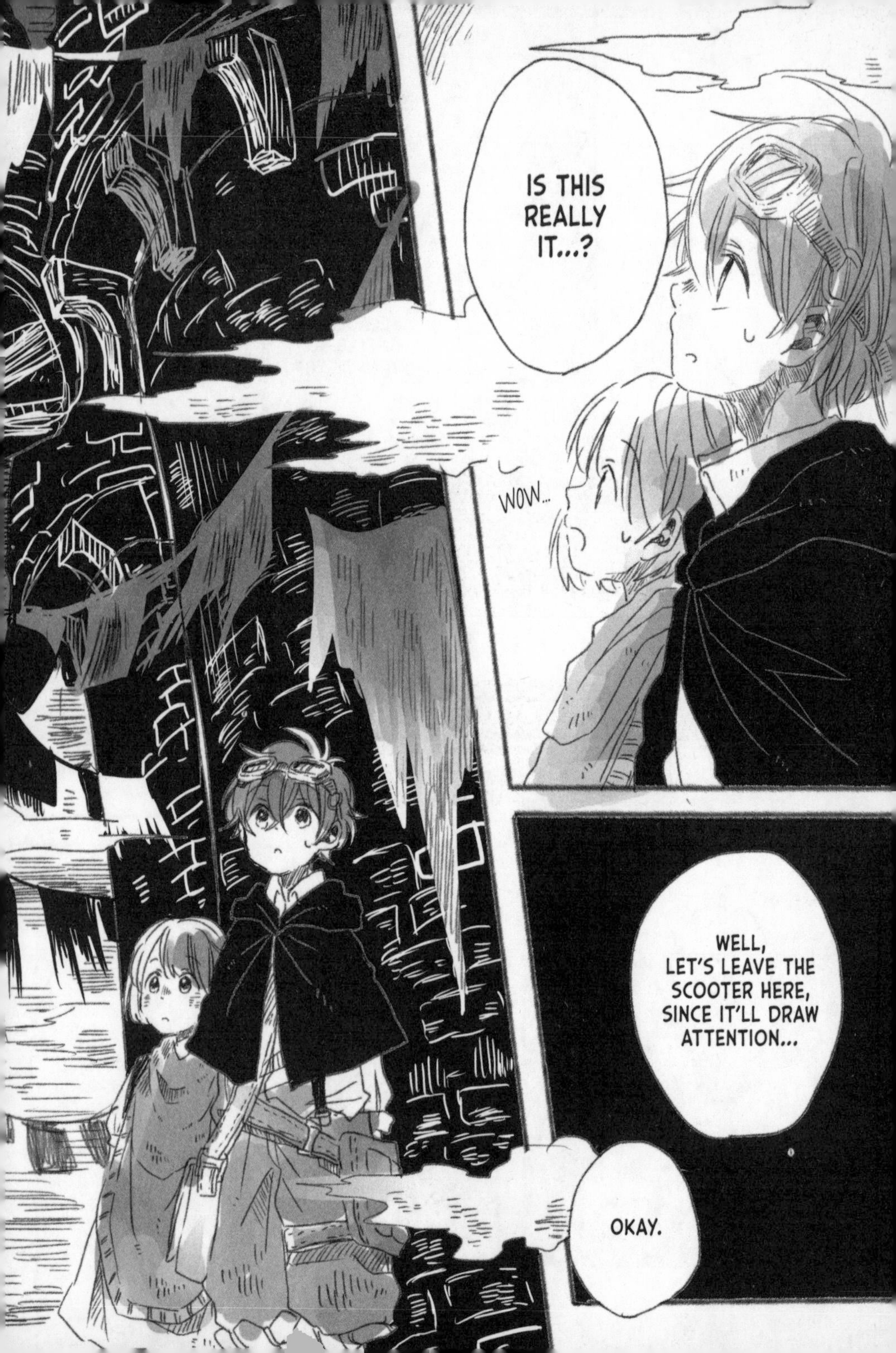
IS THIS REALLY IT...?
WOW...
WELL, LET'S LEAVE THE SCOOTER HERE, SINCE IT'LL DRAW ATTENTION...
OKAY.

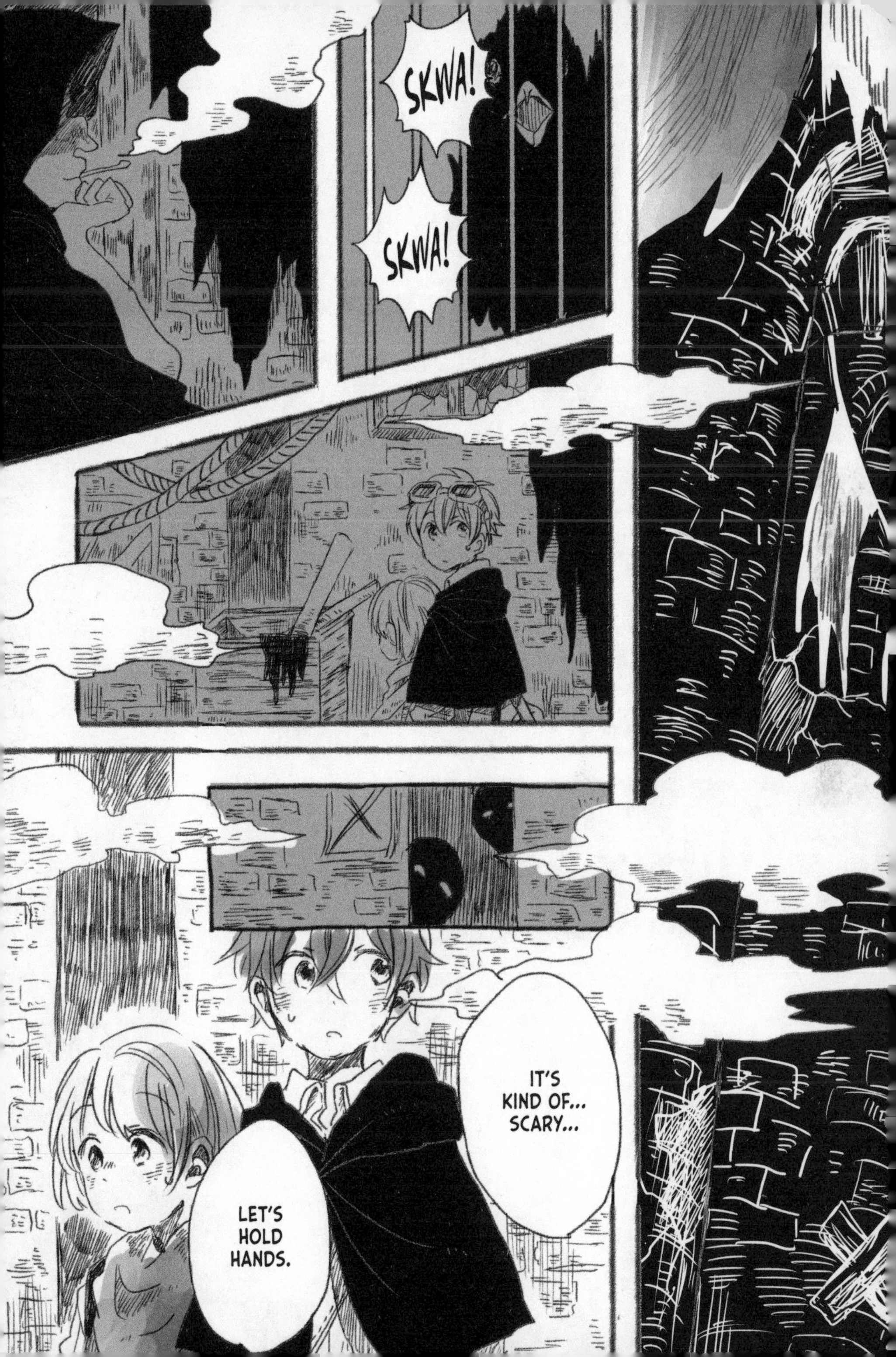
SKWA!
SKWA!
IT'S KIND OF... SCARY...
LET'S HOLD HANDS.

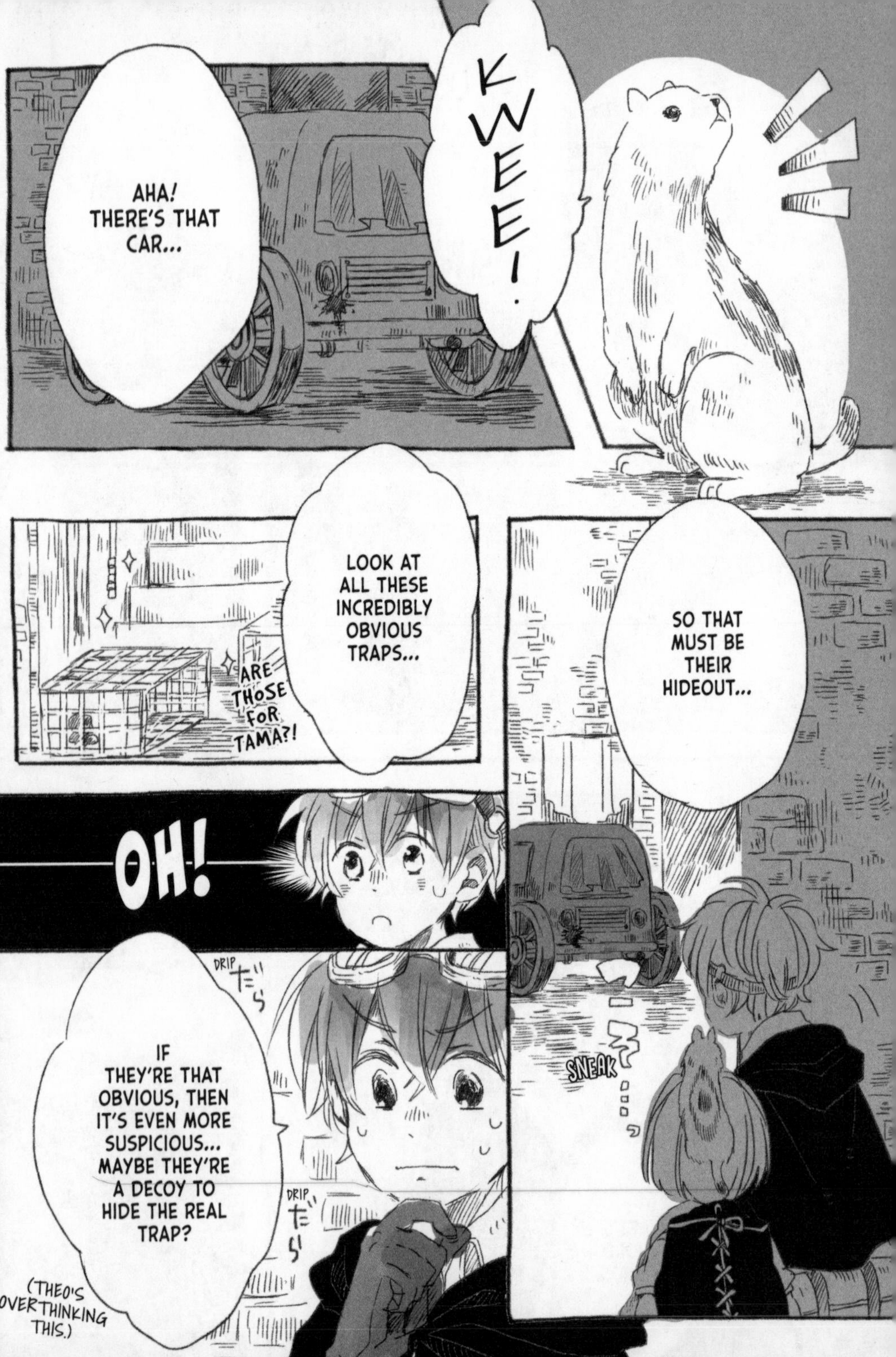
KWEE!
AHA! THERE'S THAT CAR...
SO THAT MUST BE THEIR HIDEOUT...
SNEAK
LOOK AT ALL THESE INCREDIBLY OBVIOUS TRAPS...
ARE THOSE FOR TAMA?!
OH!
DRIP
IF THEY'RE THAT OBVIOUS, THEN IT'S EVEN MORE SUSPICIOUS... MAYBE THEY'RE A DECOY TO HIDE THE REAL TRAP?
DRIP
(THEO'S OVERTHINKING THIS.)

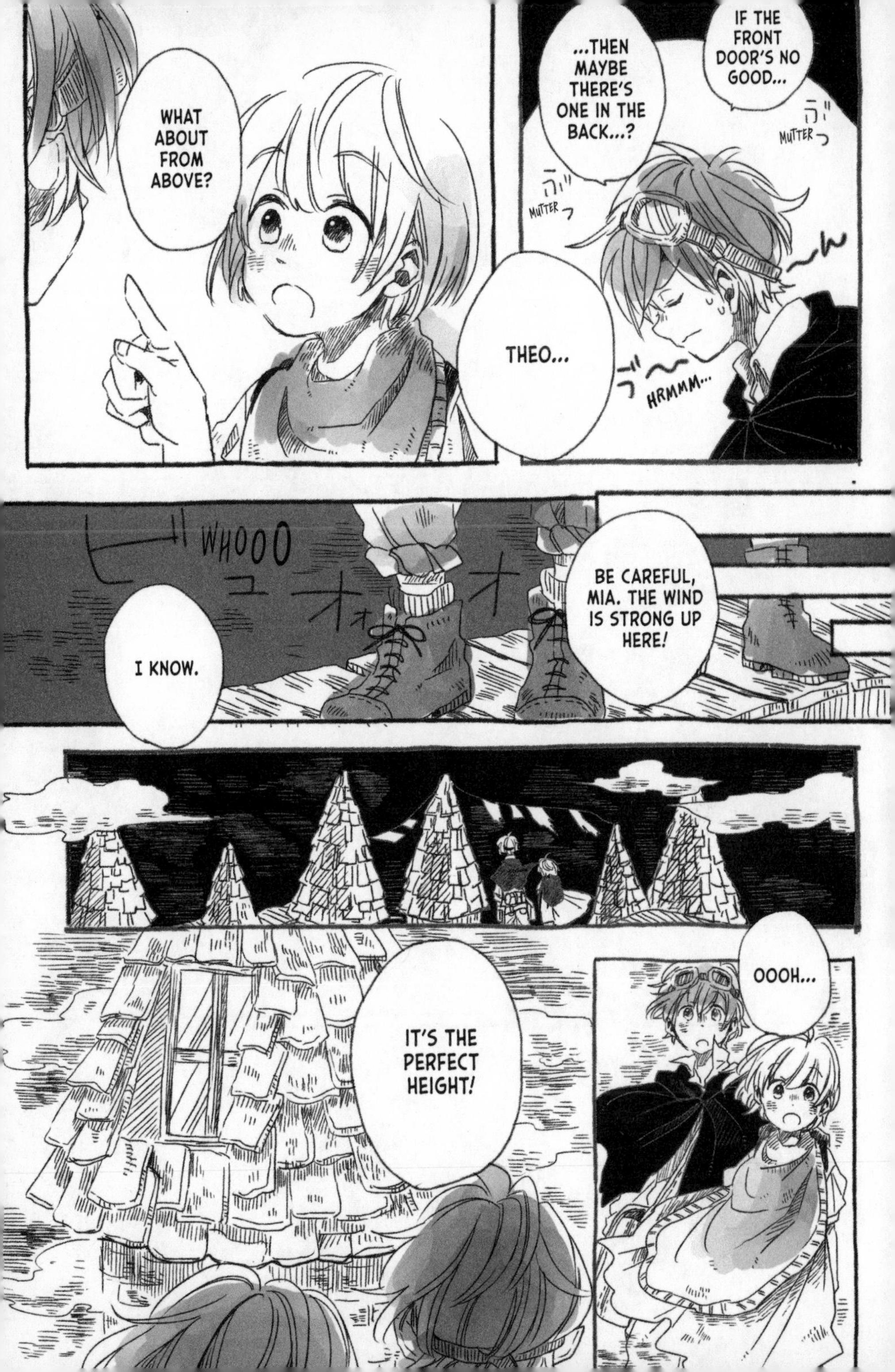
IF THE FRONT DOOR'S NO GOOD...
MUTTER
...THEN MAYBE THERE'S ONE IN THE BACK...?
MUTTER
HRMMM...
THEO...
WHAT ABOUT FROM ABOVE?
BE CAREFUL, MIA. THE WIND IS STRONG UP HERE!
WHOOO
I KNOW.
OOOH...
IT'S THE PERFECT HEIGHT!

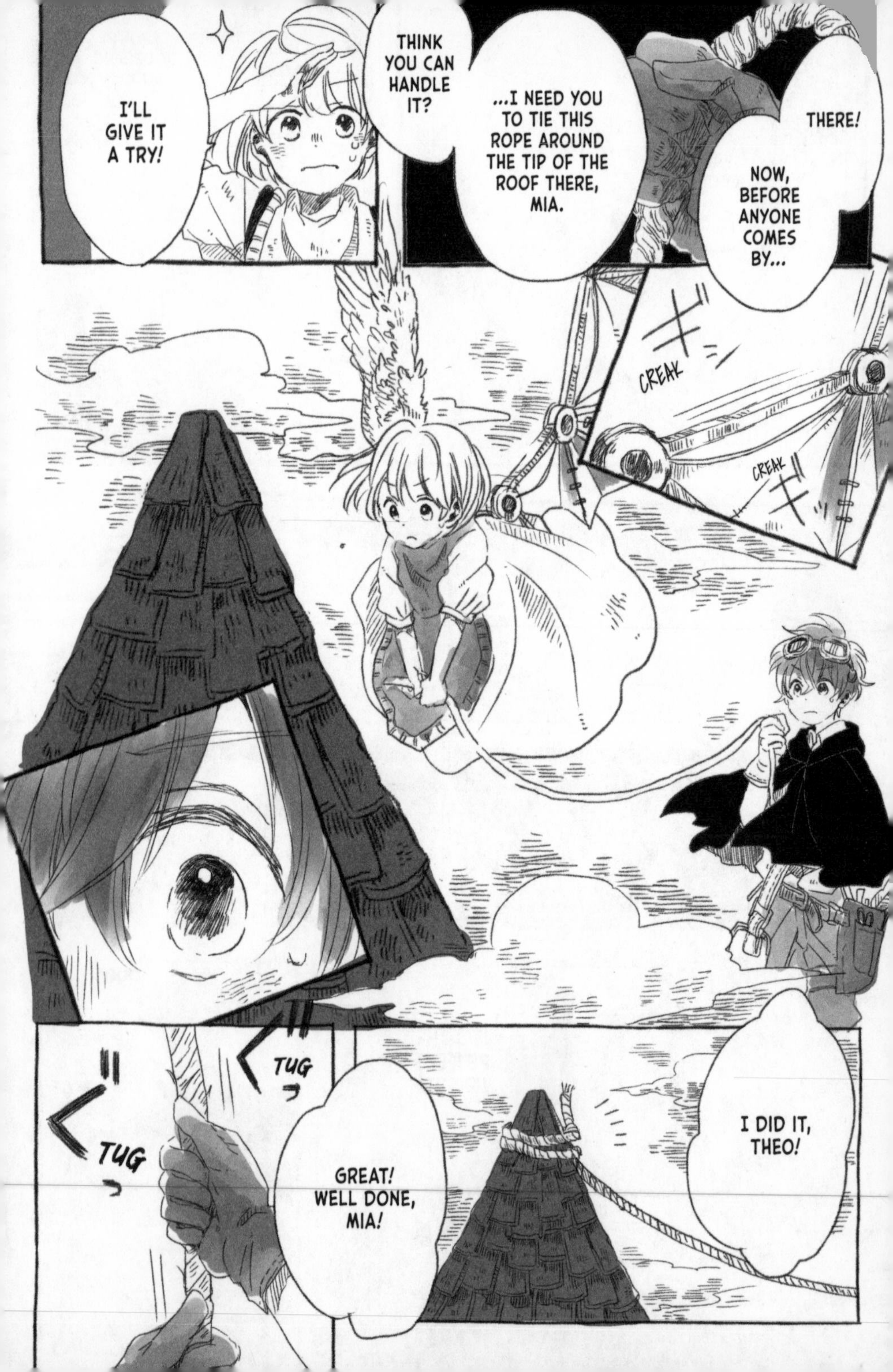
THERE!
NOW, BEFORE ANYONE COMES BY...
...I NEED YOU TO TIE THIS ROPE AROUND THE TIP OF THE ROOF THERE, MIA.
THINK YOU CAN HANDLE IT?
I'LL GIVE IT A TRY!
CREAK
CREAK
I DID IT, THEO!
GREAT! WELL DONE, MIA!
TUG
TUG

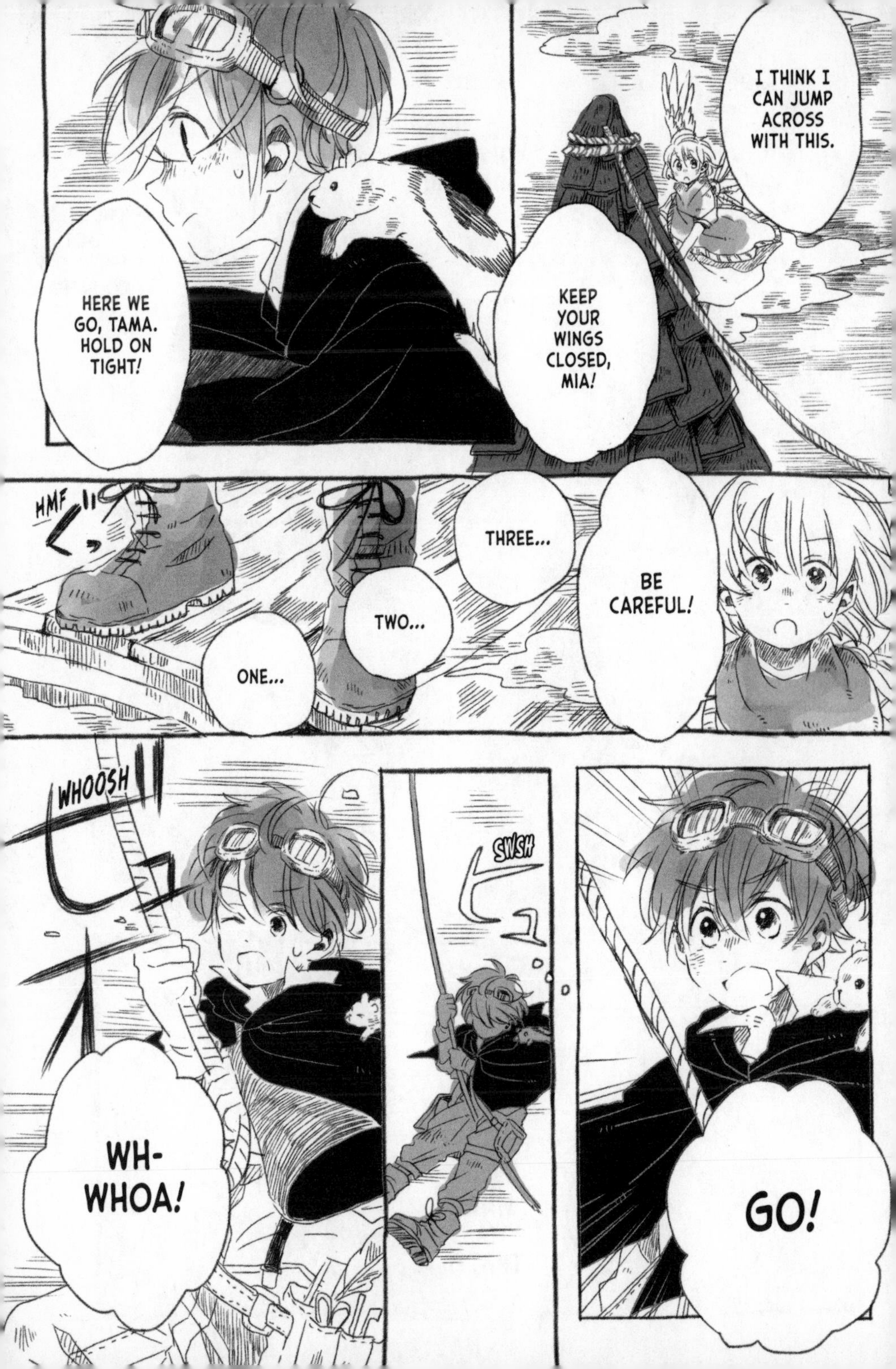

I THINK I CAN JUMP ACROSS WITH THIS.
KEEP YOUR WINGS CLOSED, MIA!
HERE WE GO, TAMA. HOLD ON TIGHT!
BE CAREFUL!
THREE...
TWO...
ONE...
HMF
GO!
SWSH
WHOOSH
WH-WHOA!

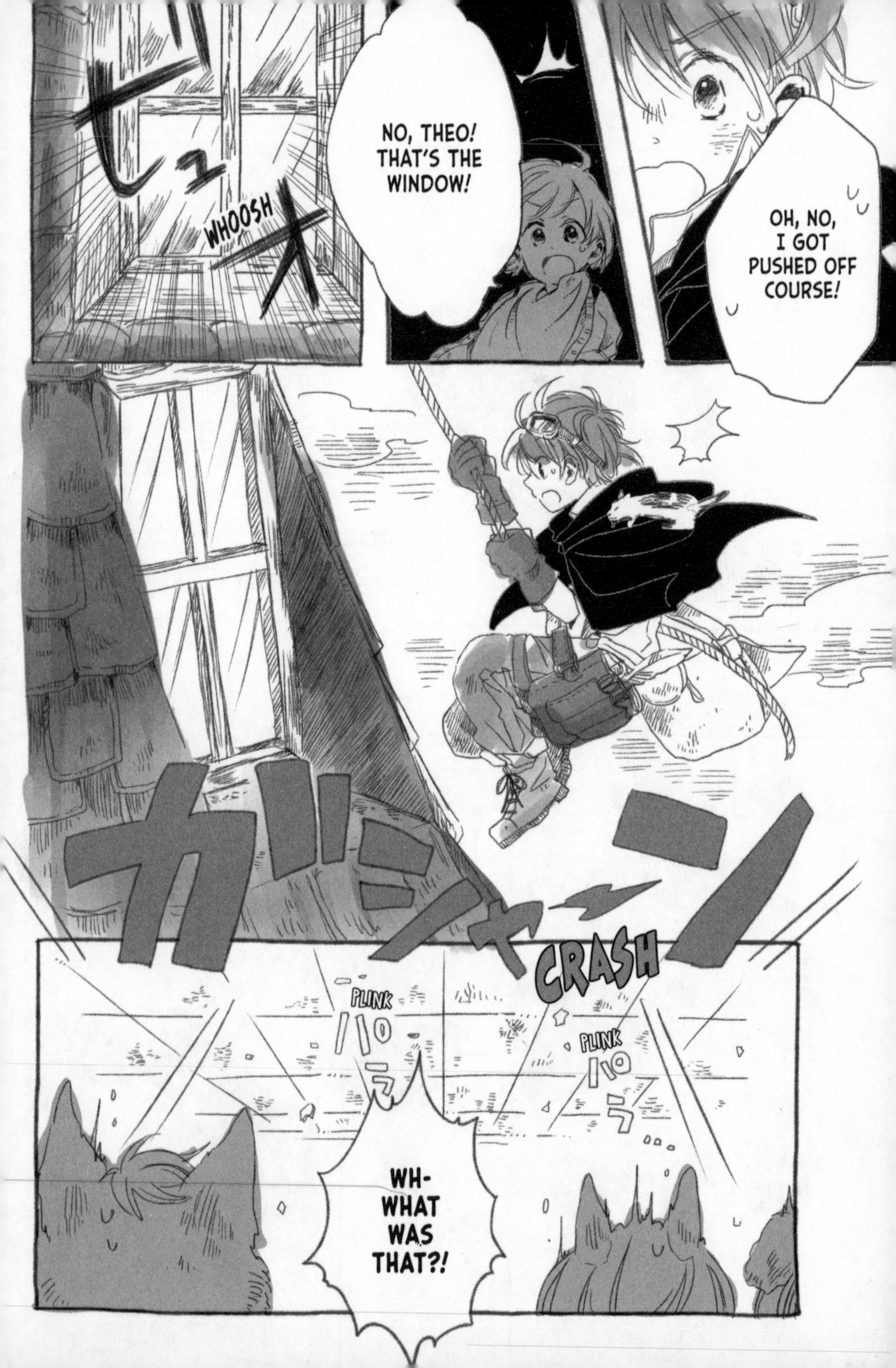
OH, NO, I GOT PUSHED OFF COURSE!
NO, THEO! THAT'S THE WINDOW!
WHOOSH
CRASH
PLINK
PLINK
WH- WHAT WAS THAT?!

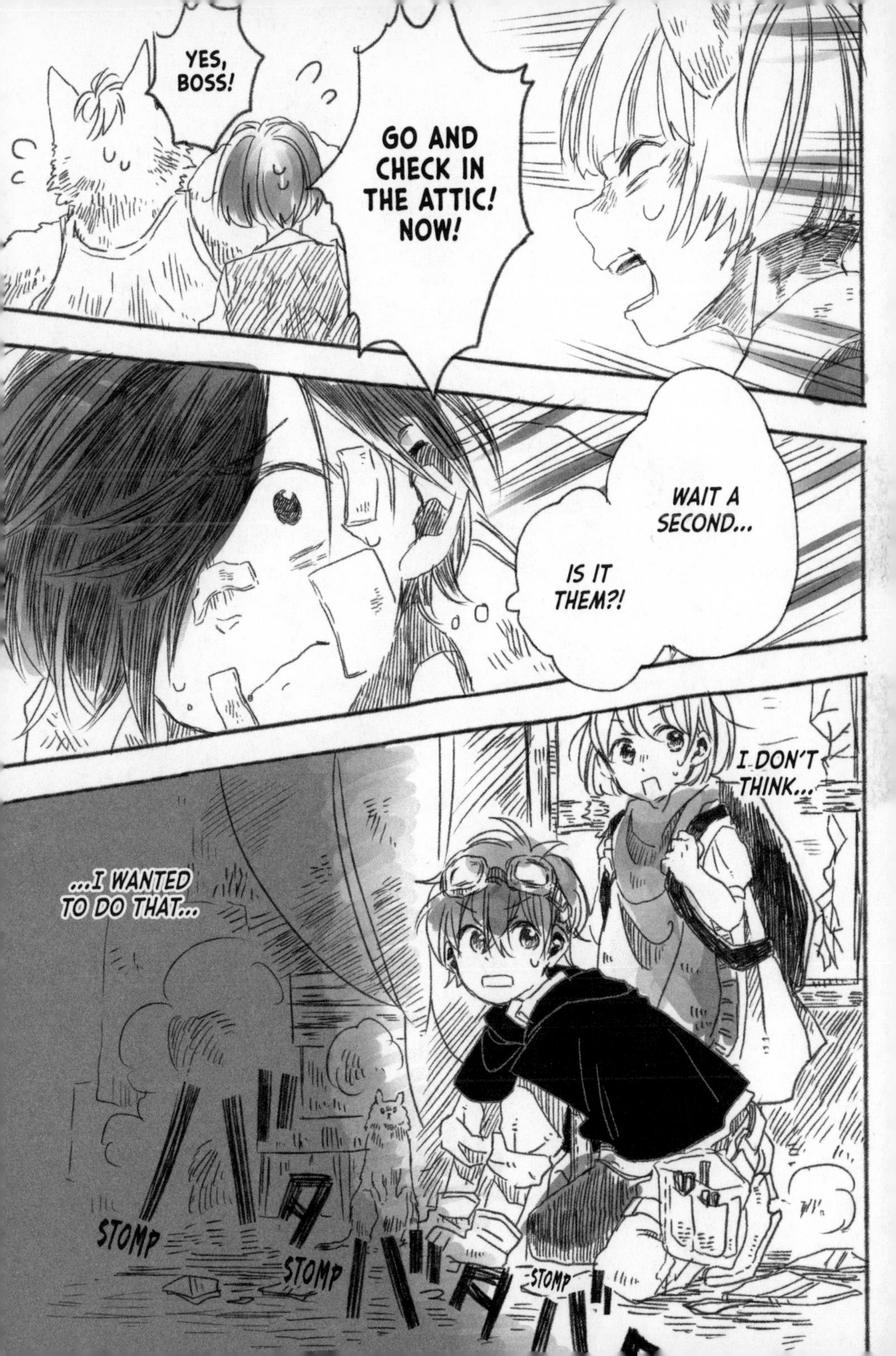
GO AND CHECK IN THE ATTIC! NOW!
YES, BOSS!
WAIT A SECOND...
IS IT THEM?!
I DON'T THINK...
...I WANTED TO DO THAT...
STOMP
STOMP
STOMP

Beyond *the* Clouds

The Girl Who Fell From the Sky

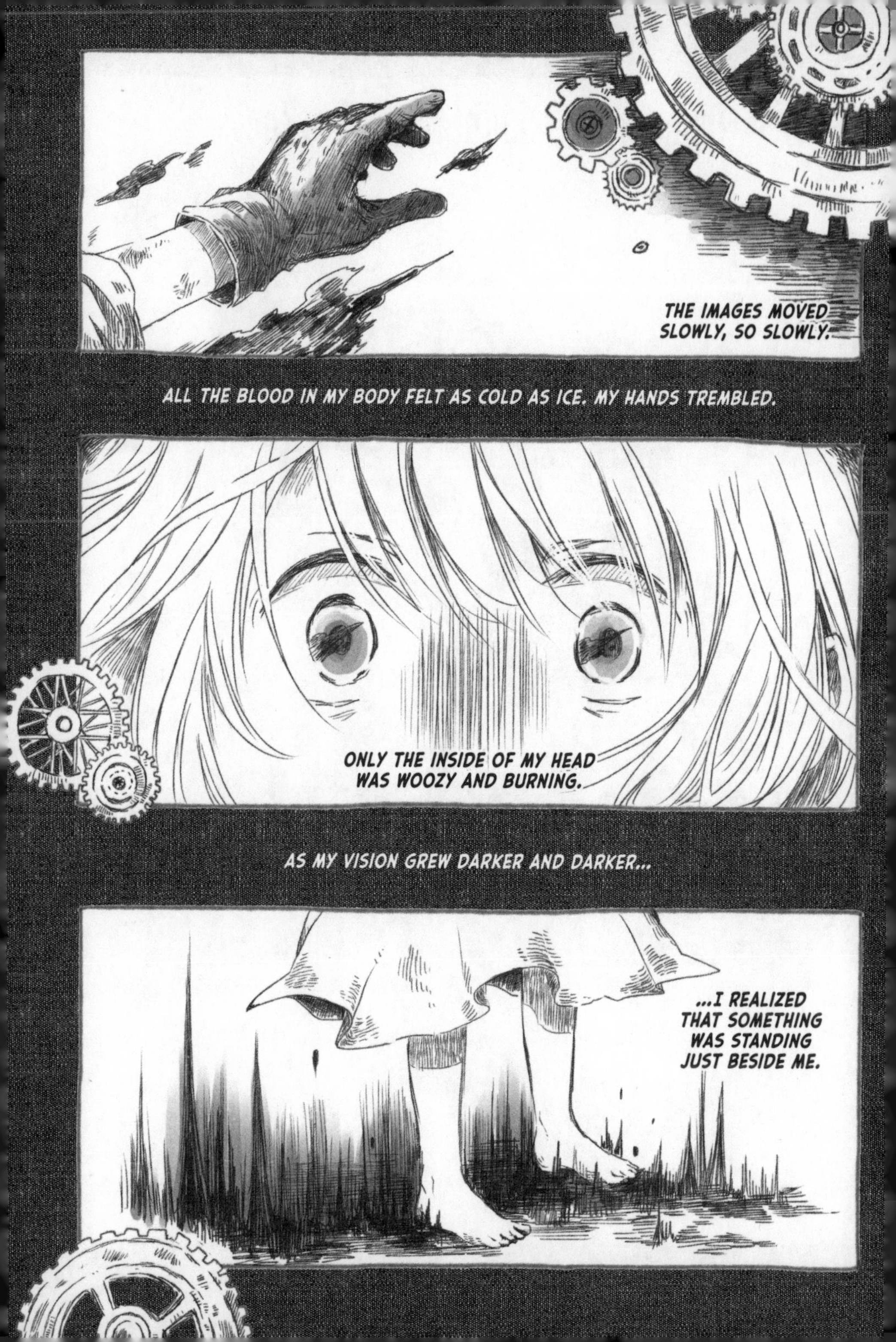
THE IMAGES MOVED SLOWLY, SO SLOWLY.
ALL THE BLOOD IN MY BODY FELT AS COLD AS ICE. MY HANDS TREMBLED.
ONLY THE INSIDE OF MY HEAD WAS WOOZY AND BURNING.
AS MY VISION GREW DARKER AND DARKER...
...I REALIZED THAT SOMETHING WAS STANDING JUST BESIDE ME.

Chapter 14: A Light in the Darkness

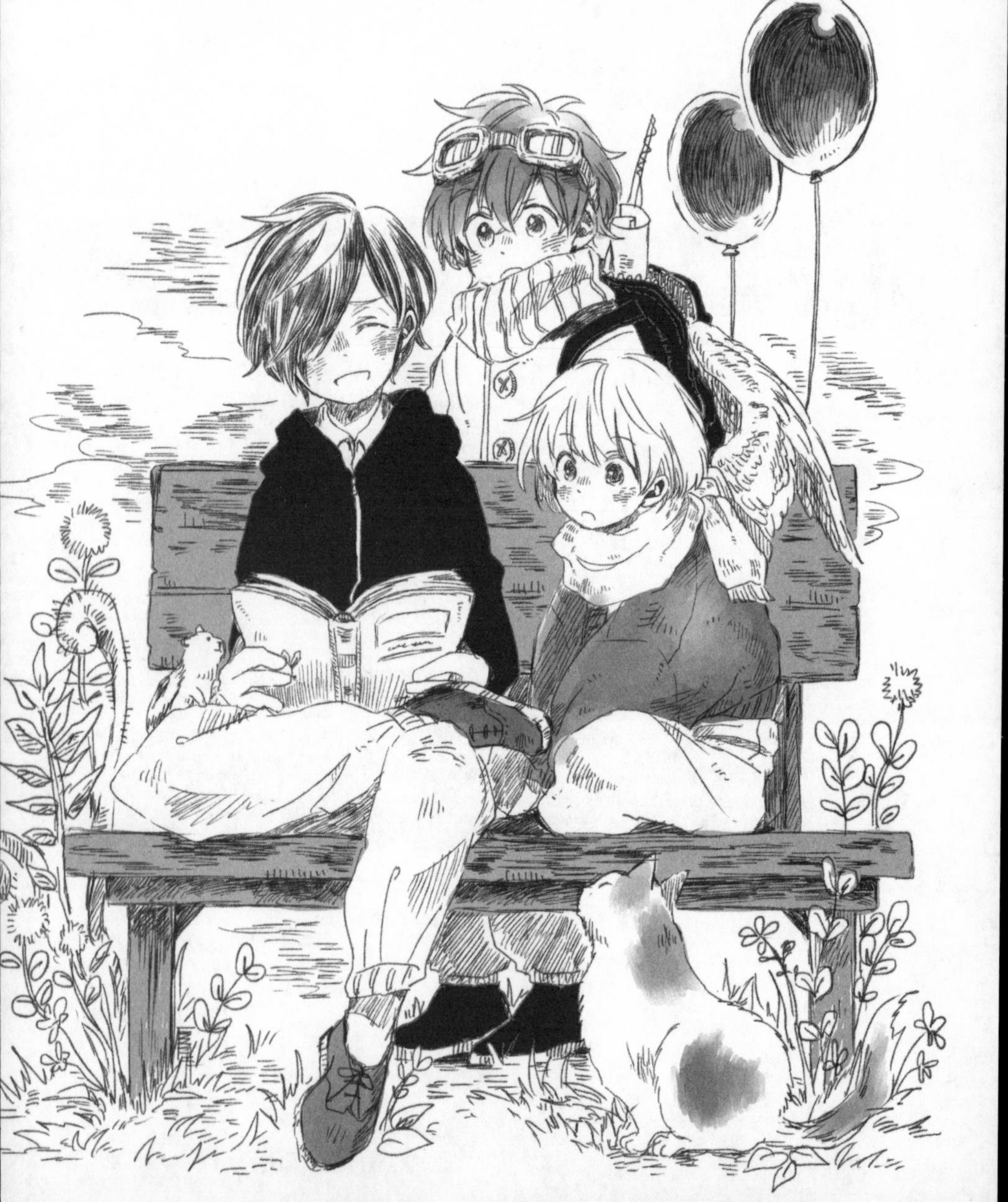

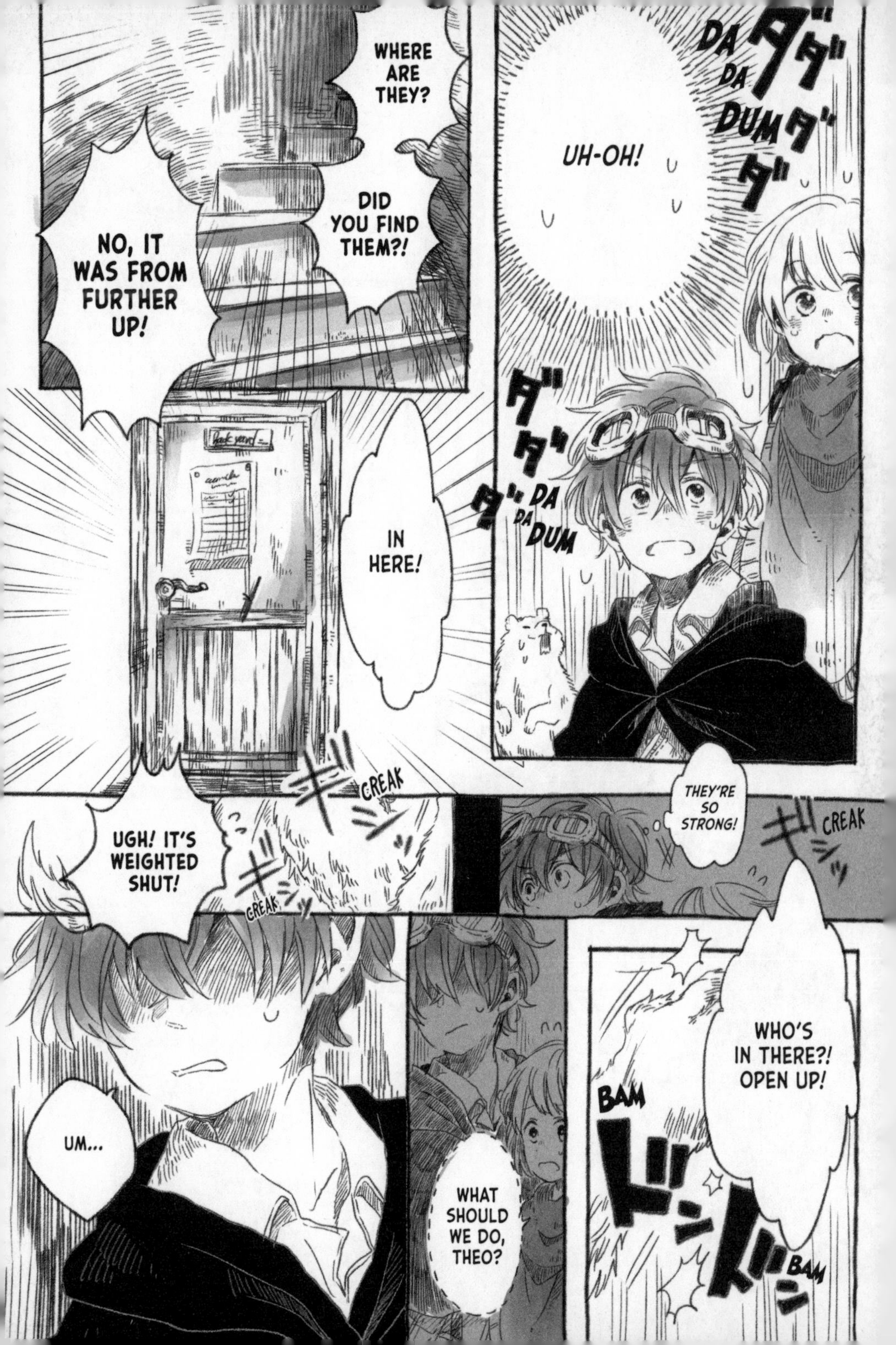
DA DA DUM
UH-OH!
DA DA DUM
WHERE ARE THEY?
DID YOU FIND THEM?!
NO, IT WAS FROM FURTHER UP!
IN HERE!
THEY'RE SO STRONG!
CREAK
UGH! IT'S WEIGHTED SHUT!
CREAK
CREAK
WHO'S IN THERE?! OPEN UP!
BAM
BAM
WHAT SHOULD WE DO, THEO?
UM...

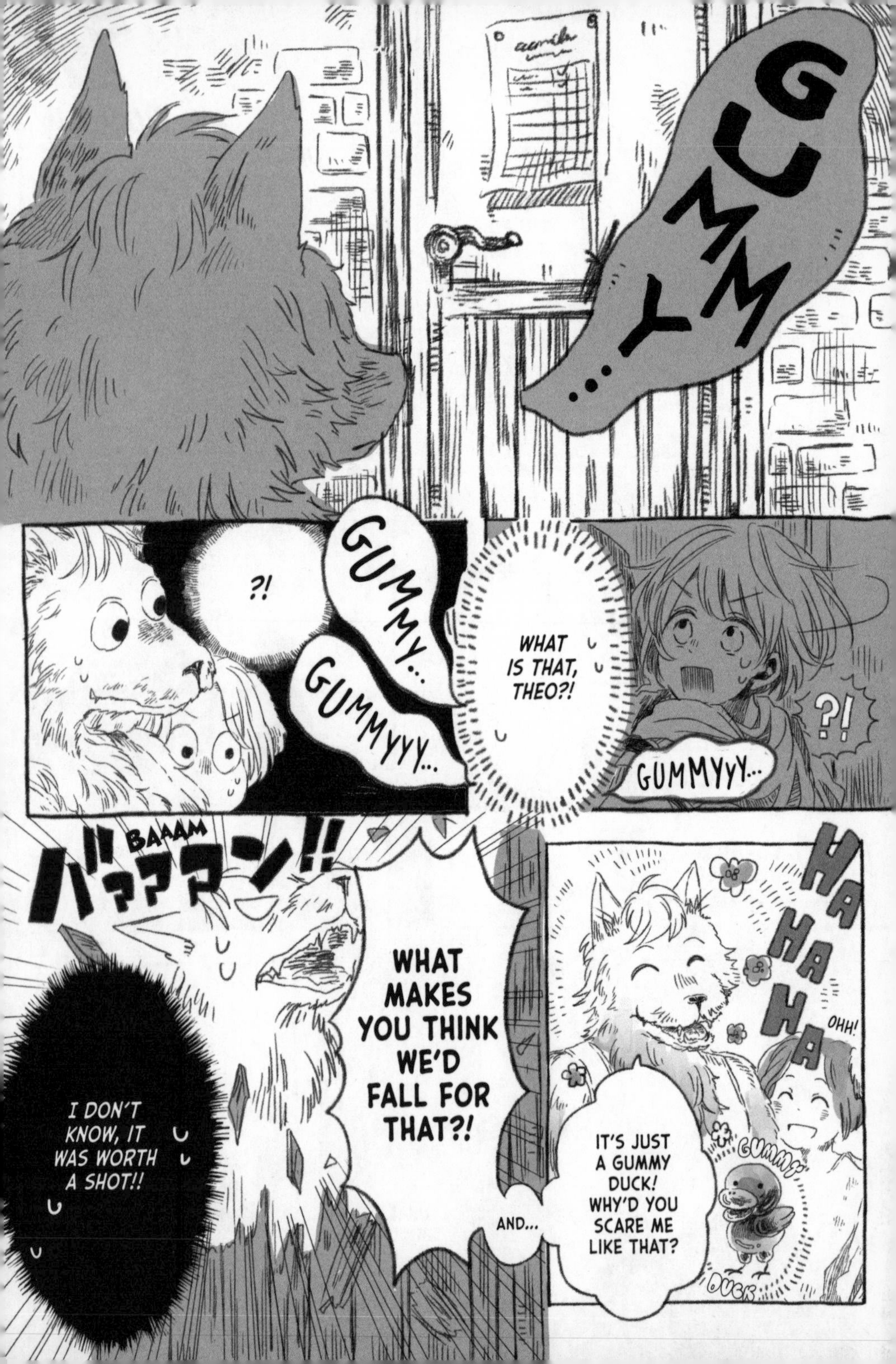
GUMMY...
?!
GUMMYyy...
WHAT IS THAT, THEO?!
GUMMY...
GUMMYyyy...
?!
HAHAHAHA
OHH!
IT'S JUST A GUMMY DUCK! WHY'D YOU SCARE ME LIKE THAT?
GUMMY DUCK
AND...
BAAAM
バァァァン!!
WHAT MAKES YOU THINK WE'D FALL FOR THAT?!
I DON'T KNOW, IT WAS WORTH A SHOT!!

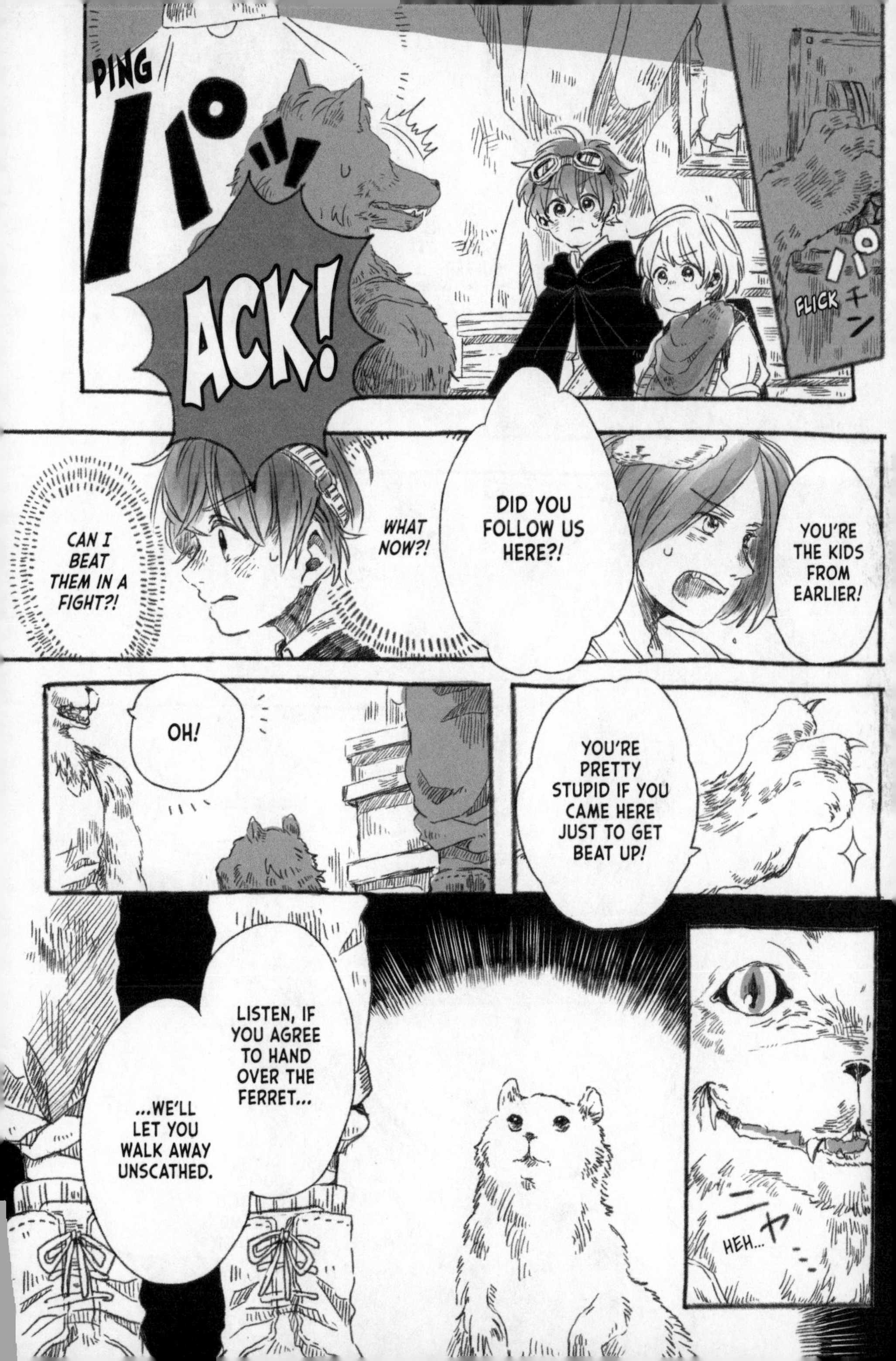
FLICK
PING
ACK!
YOU'RE THE KIDS FROM EARLIER!
DID YOU FOLLOW US HERE?!
WHAT NOW?!
CAN I BEAT THEM IN A FIGHT?!
YOU'RE PRETTY STUPID IF YOU CAME HERE JUST TO GET BEAT UP!
OH!
HEH...
LISTEN, IF YOU AGREE TO HAND OVER THE FERRET...
...WE'LL LET YOU WALK AWAY UNSCATHED.

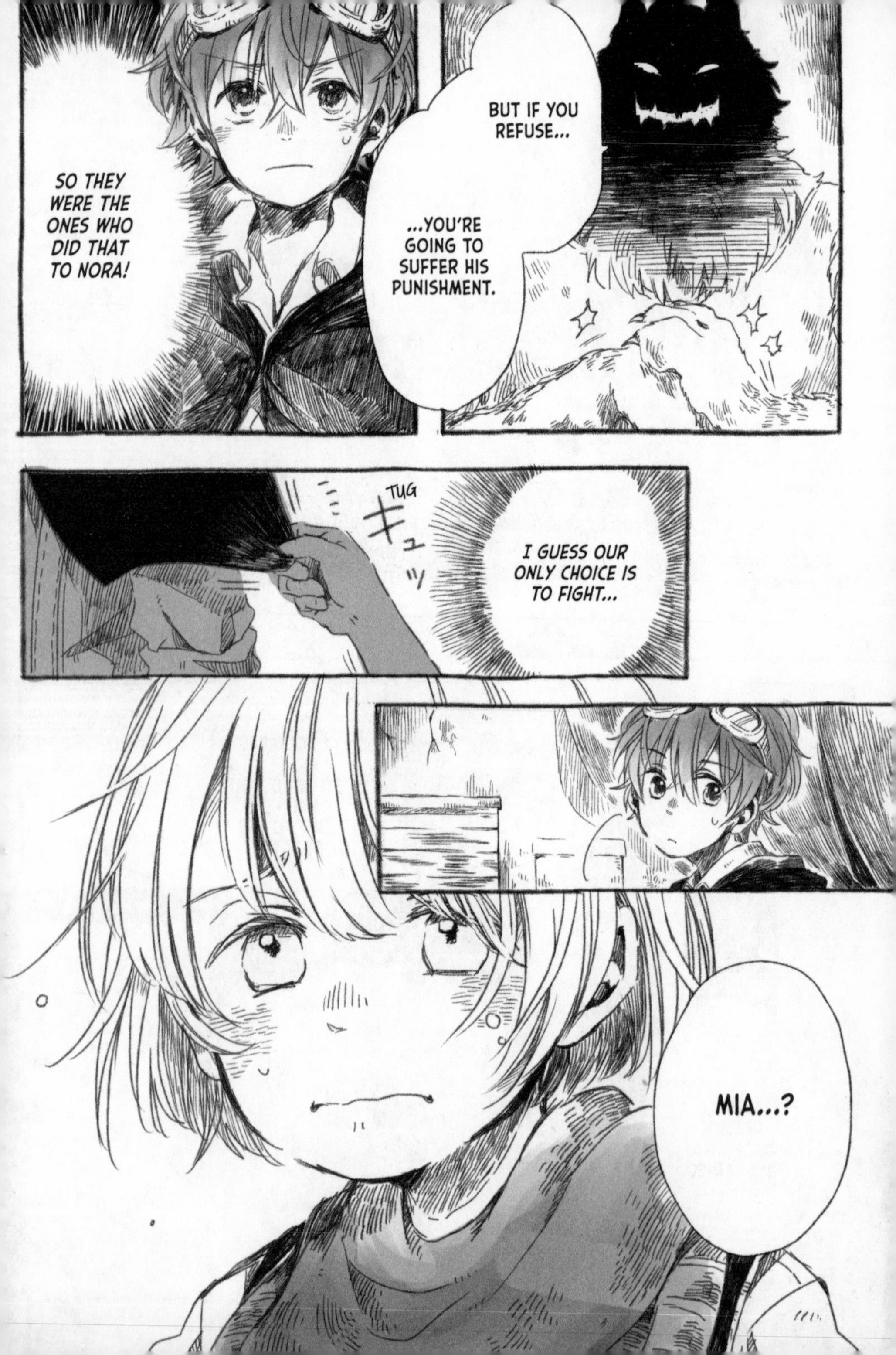
BUT IF YOU REFUSE...
...YOU'RE GOING TO SUFFER HIS PUNISHMENT.
SO THEY WERE THE ONES WHO DID THAT TO NORA!
I GUESS OUR ONLY CHOICE IS TO FIGHT...
TUG
MIA...?

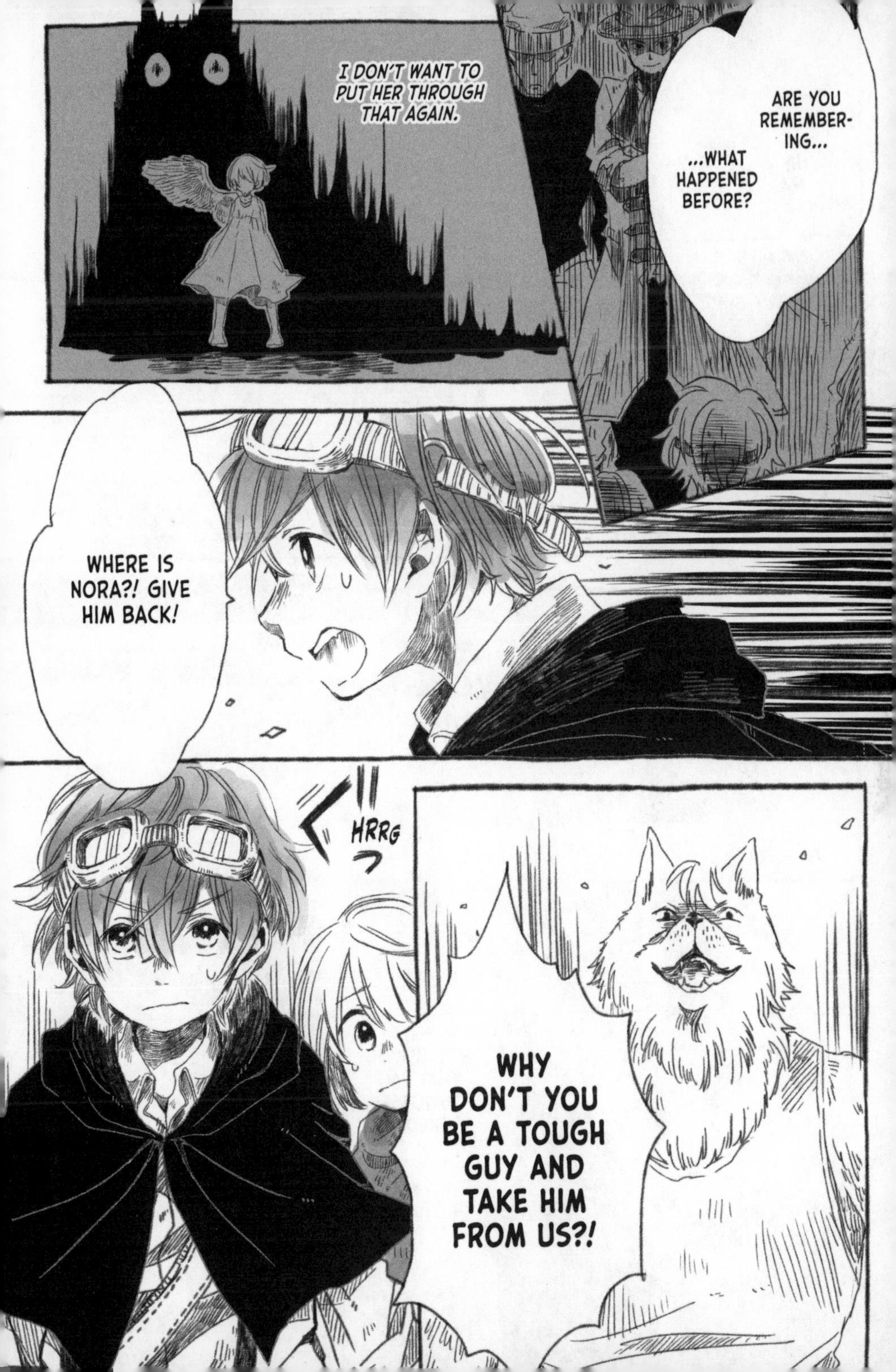
ARE YOU REMEMBERING...
...WHAT HAPPENED BEFORE?
I DON'T WANT TO PUT HER THROUGH THAT AGAIN.
WHERE IS NORA?! GIVE HIM BACK!
WHY DON'T YOU BE A TOUGH GUY AND TAKE HIM FROM US?!
HRRG

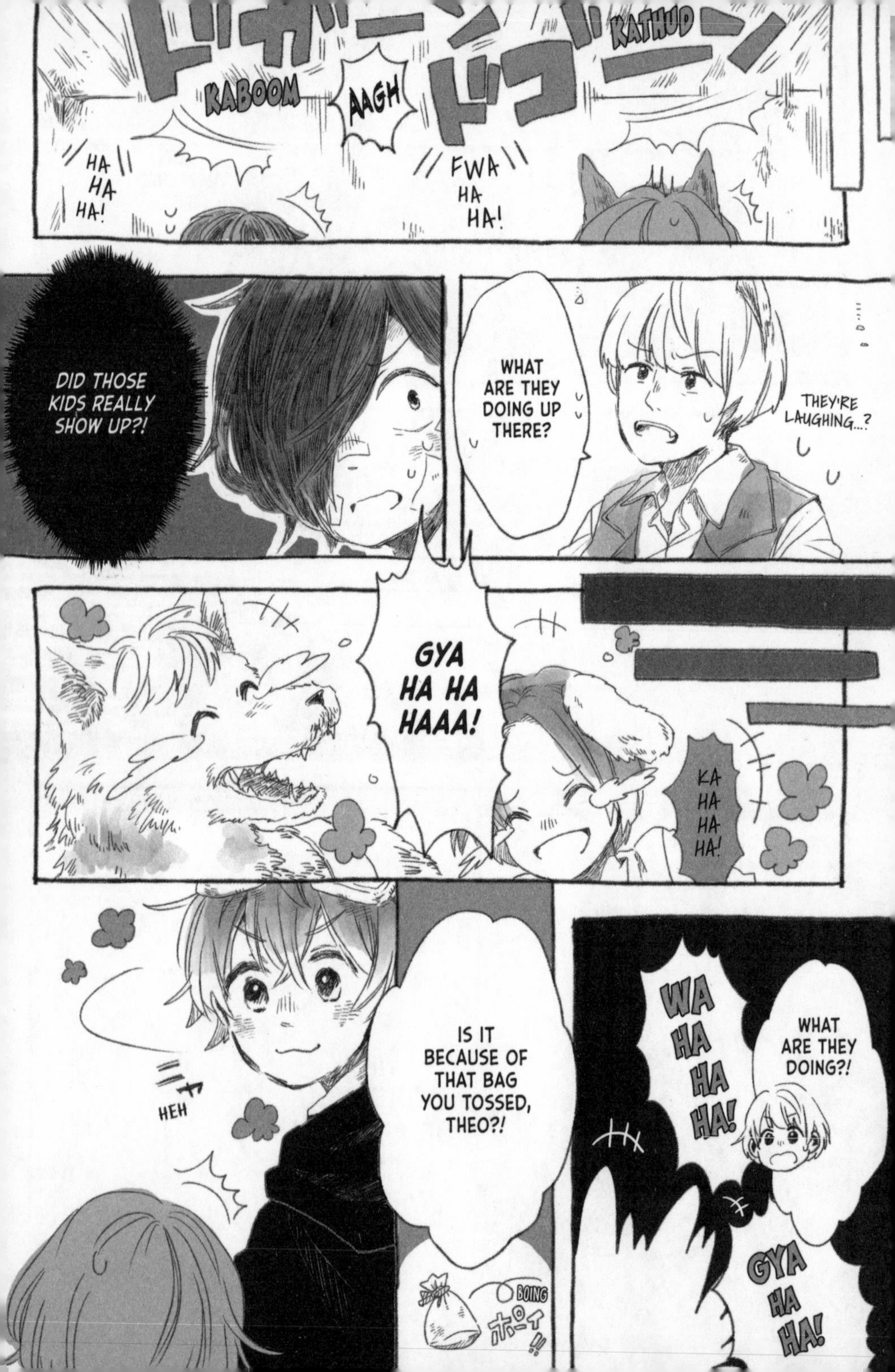

KATHUD
ドガーン
ドゴーン
FWA HA HA!
AAGH
KABOOM
HA HA HA!
WHAT ARE THEY DOING UP THERE?
THEY'RE LAUGHING...?
DID THOSE KIDS REALLY SHOW UP?!
KA HA HA HA HA!
GYA HA HA HAAA!
WHAT ARE THEY DOING?!
WA HA HA HA!
GYA HA HA!
IS IT BECAUSE OF THAT BAG YOU TOSSED, THEO?!
BOING
HEH

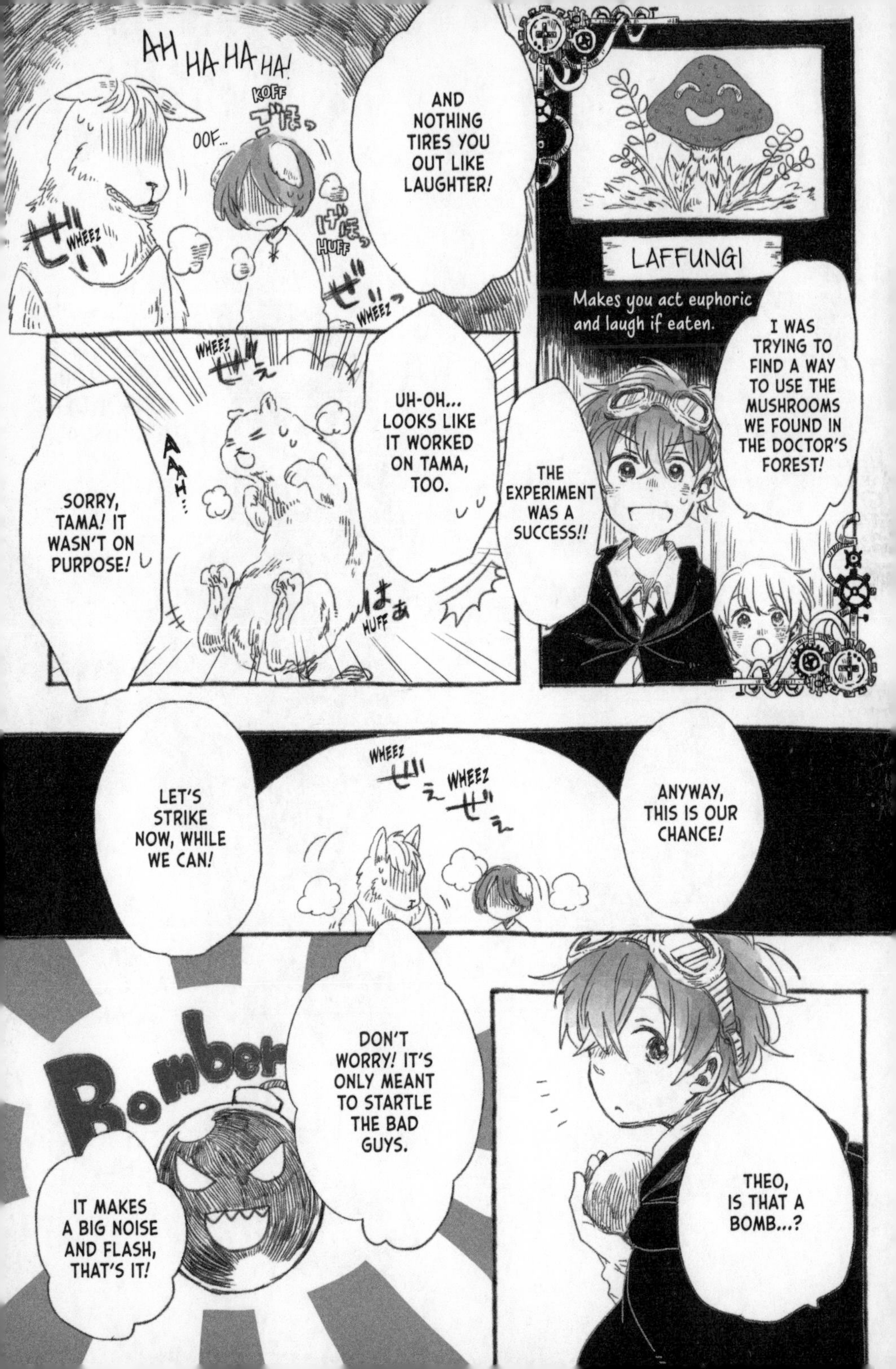
LAFFUNGI
Makes you act euphoric and laugh if eaten.
I WAS TRYING TO FIND A WAY TO USE THE MUSHROOMS WE FOUND IN THE DOCTOR'S FOREST!
THE EXPERIMENT WAS A SUCCESS!!
AH HA HA HA!
AND NOTHING TIRES YOU OUT LIKE LAUGHTER!
KOFF
OOF...
HUFF
WHEEZ
WHEEZ
UH-OH... LOOKS LIKE IT WORKED ON TAMA, TOO.
WHEEZ
SORRY, TAMA! IT WASN'T ON PURPOSE!
AAAH...
HUFF
ANYWAY, THIS IS OUR CHANCE!
WHEEZ
WHEEZ
LET'S STRIKE NOW, WHILE WE CAN!
THEO, IS THAT A BOMB...?
DON'T WORRY! IT'S ONLY MEANT TO STARTLE THE BAD GUYS.
Bomber
IT MAKES A BIG NOISE AND FLASH, THAT'S IT!

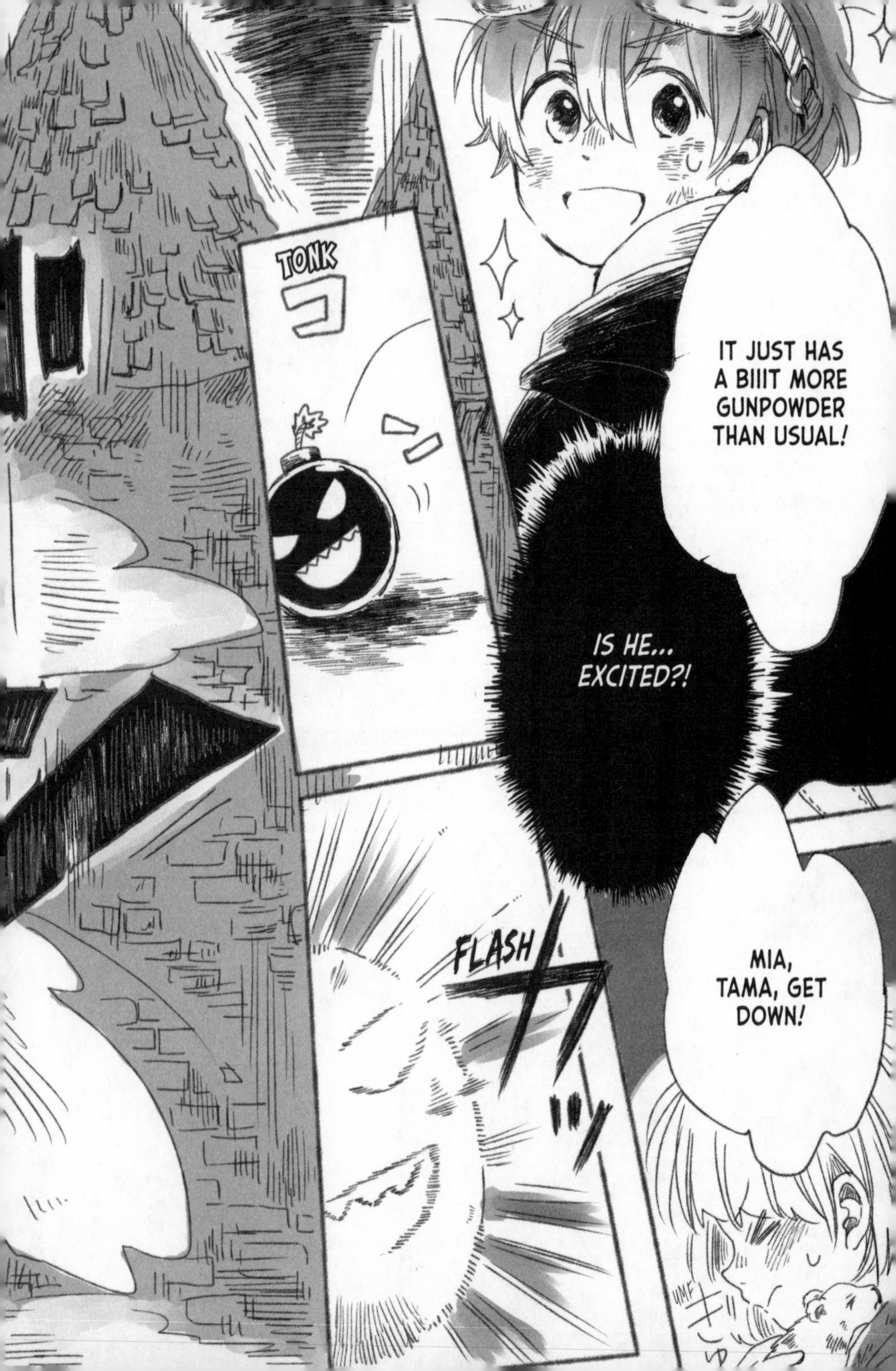
IT JUST HAS A BIIIT MORE GUNPOWDER THAN USUAL!
IS HE... EXCITED?!
TONK
MIA, TAMA, GET DOWN!
UMF
FLASH

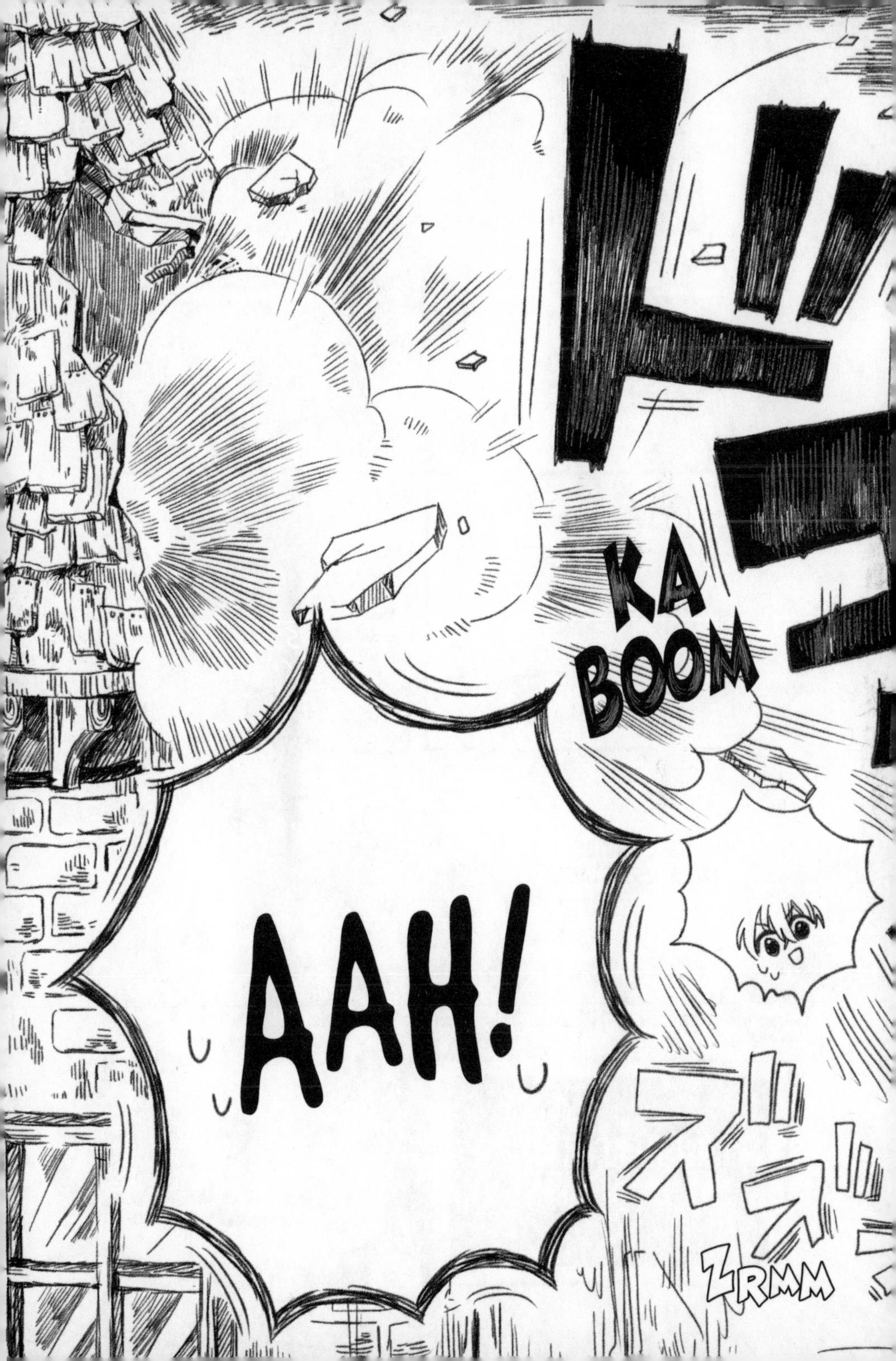
KA BOOM
AAH!
ZRMM

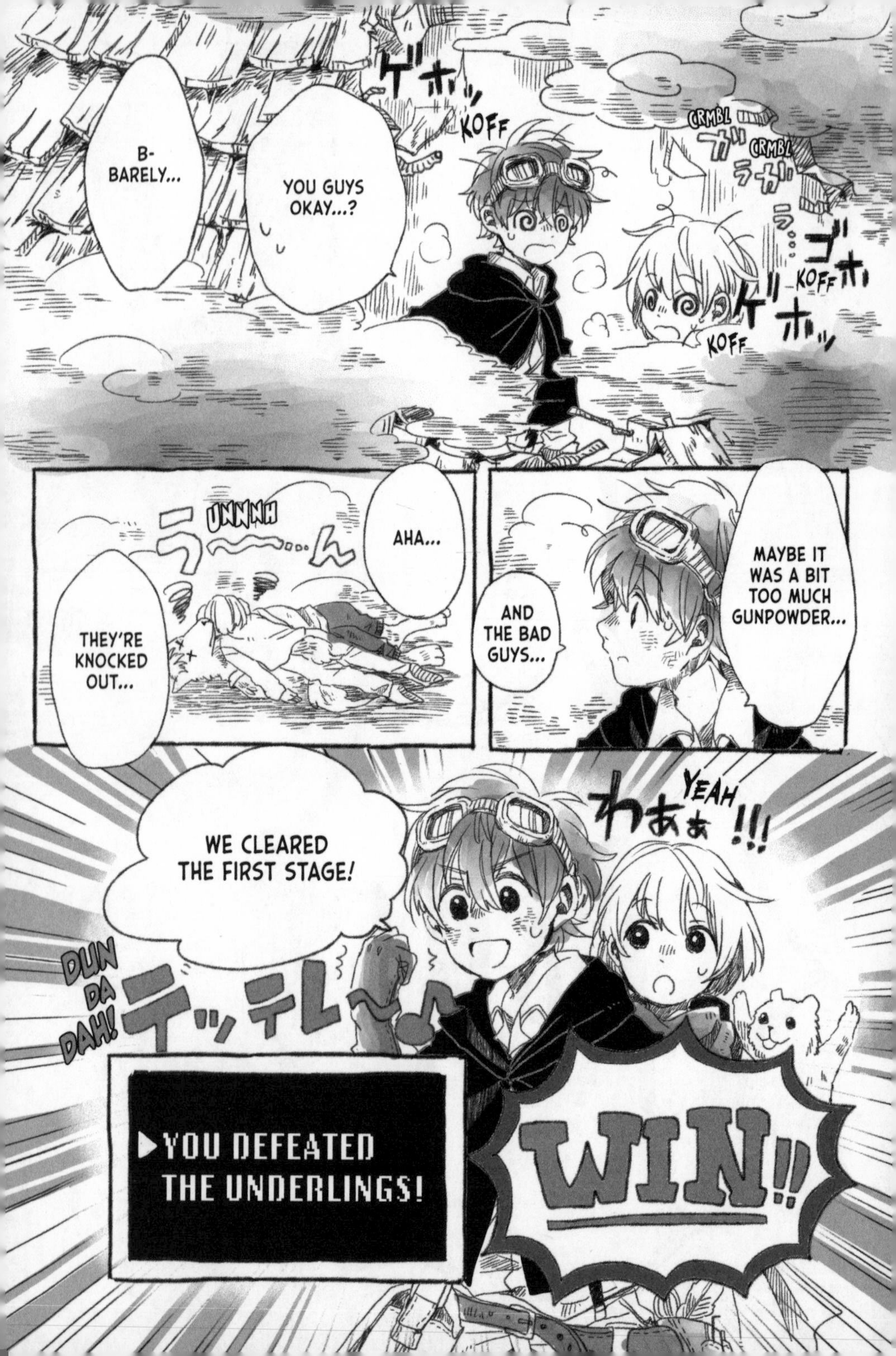
CRMBL
CRMBL
KOFF
KOFF
KOFF
YOU GUYS OKAY...?
B- BARELY...
MAYBE IT WAS A BIT TOO MUCH GUNPOWDER...
AND THE BAD GUYS...
AHA...
UNNNH
THEY'RE KNOCKED OUT...
YEAH
わあぁ!!!
WE CLEARED THE FIRST STAGE!
DUN DA DAH!
WIN!!
▶YOU DEFEATED THE UNDERLINGS!

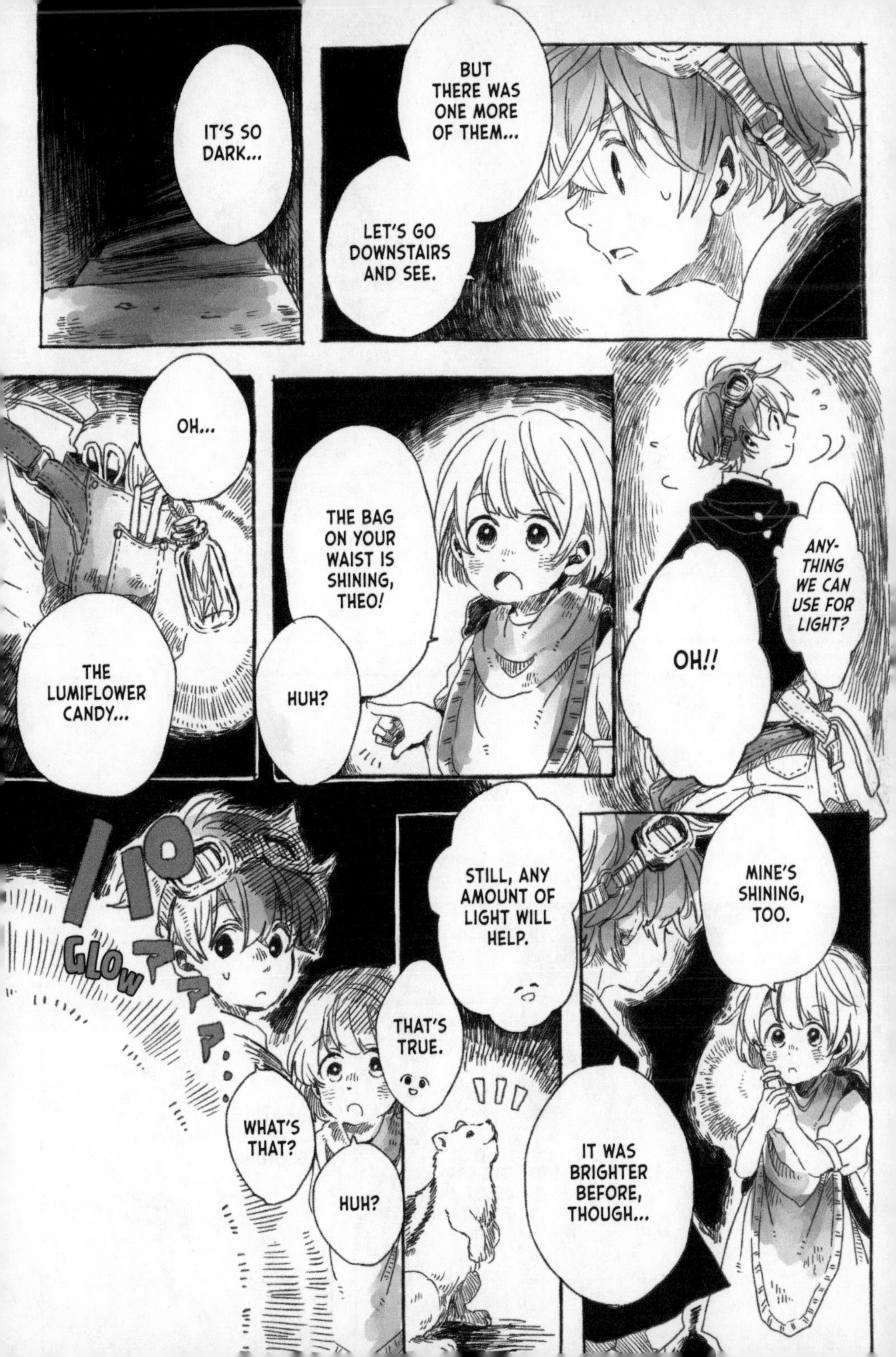
BUT THERE WAS ONE MORE OF THEM...
LET'S GO DOWNSTAIRS AND SEE.
IT'S SO DARK...
ANY-THING WE CAN USE FOR LIGHT?
OH!!
THE BAG ON YOUR WAIST IS SHINING, THEO!
HUH?
OH...
THE LUMIFLOWER CANDY...
MINE'S SHINING, TOO.
IT WAS BRIGHTER BEFORE, THOUGH...
STILL, ANY AMOUNT OF LIGHT WILL HELP.
THAT'S TRUE.
GLOW
WHAT'S THAT?
HUH?

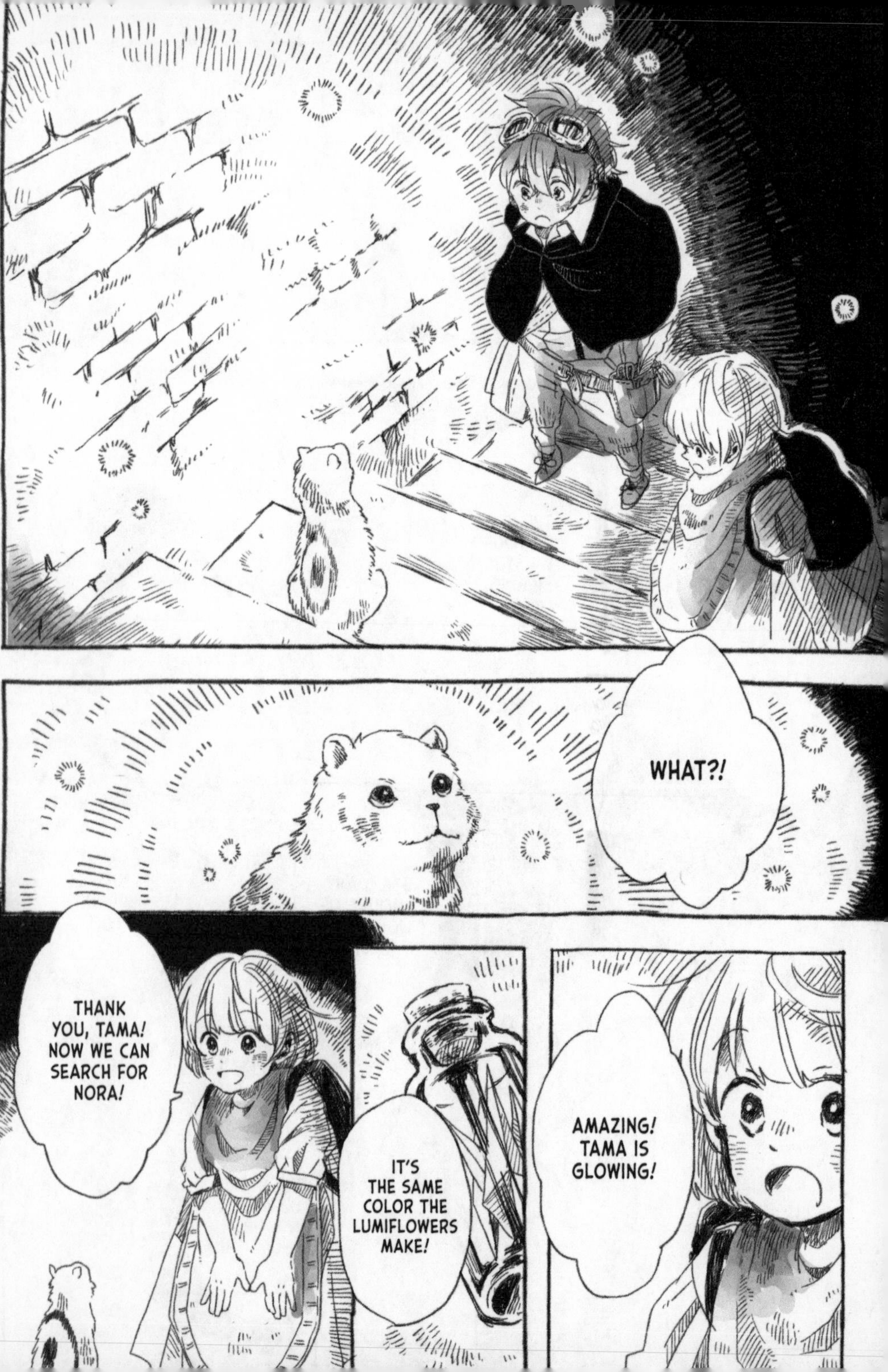
WHAT?!
AMAZING! TAMA IS GLOWING!
IT'S THE SAME COLOR THE LUMIFLOWERS MAKE!
THANK YOU, TAMA! NOW WE CAN SEARCH FOR NORA!

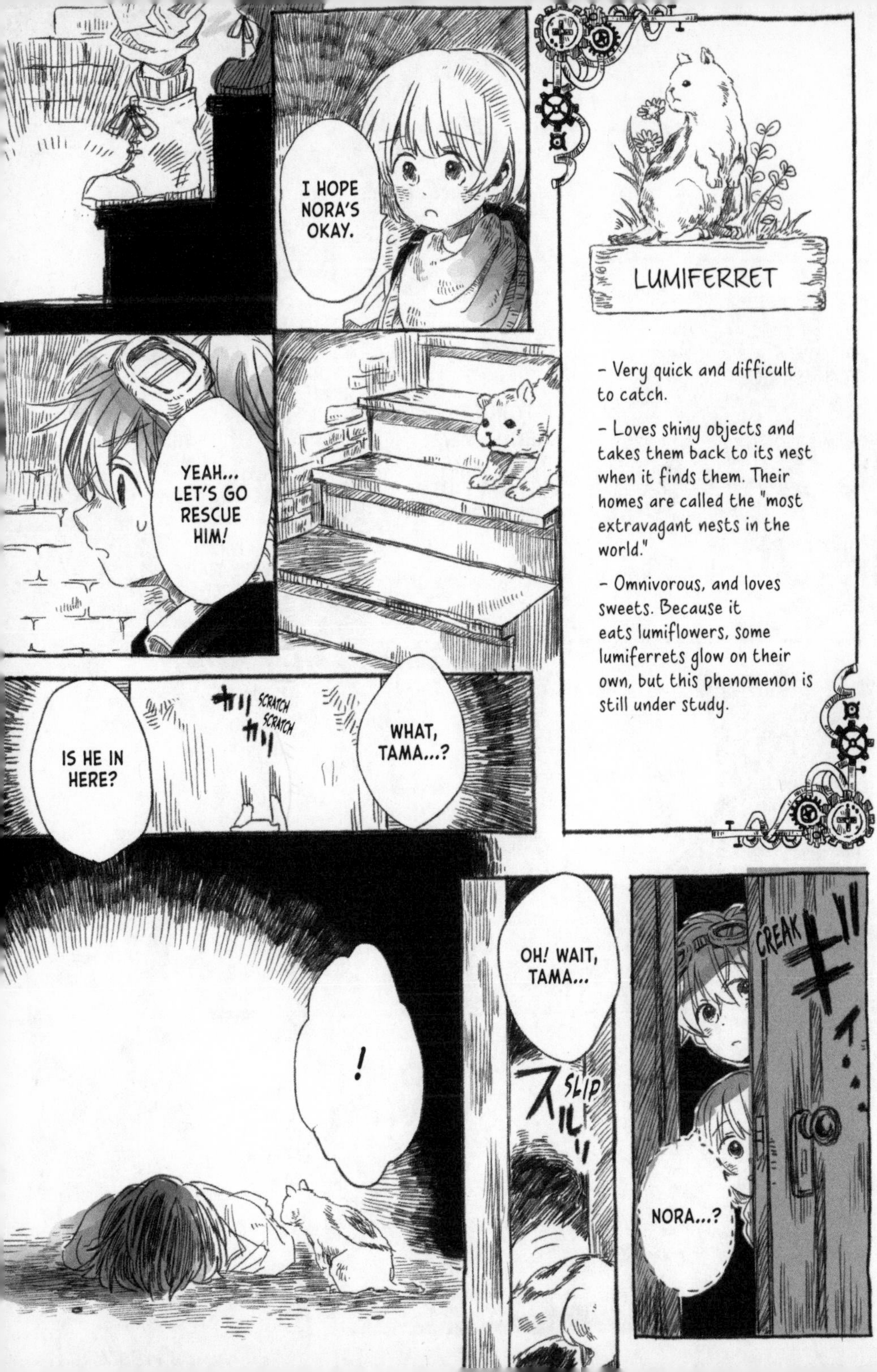
LUMIFERRET
- Very quick and difficult to catch.
- Loves shiny objects and takes them back to its nest when it finds them. Their homes are called the "most extravagant nests in the world."
- Omnivorous, and loves sweets. Because it eats lumiflowers, some lumiferrets glow on their own, but this phenomenon is still under study.
I HOPE NORA'S OKAY.
YEAH... LET'S GO RESCUE HIM!
WHAT, TAMA...?
SCRATCH SCRATCH
IS HE IN HERE?
CREAK
NORA...?
OH! WAIT, TAMA...
SLIP
!

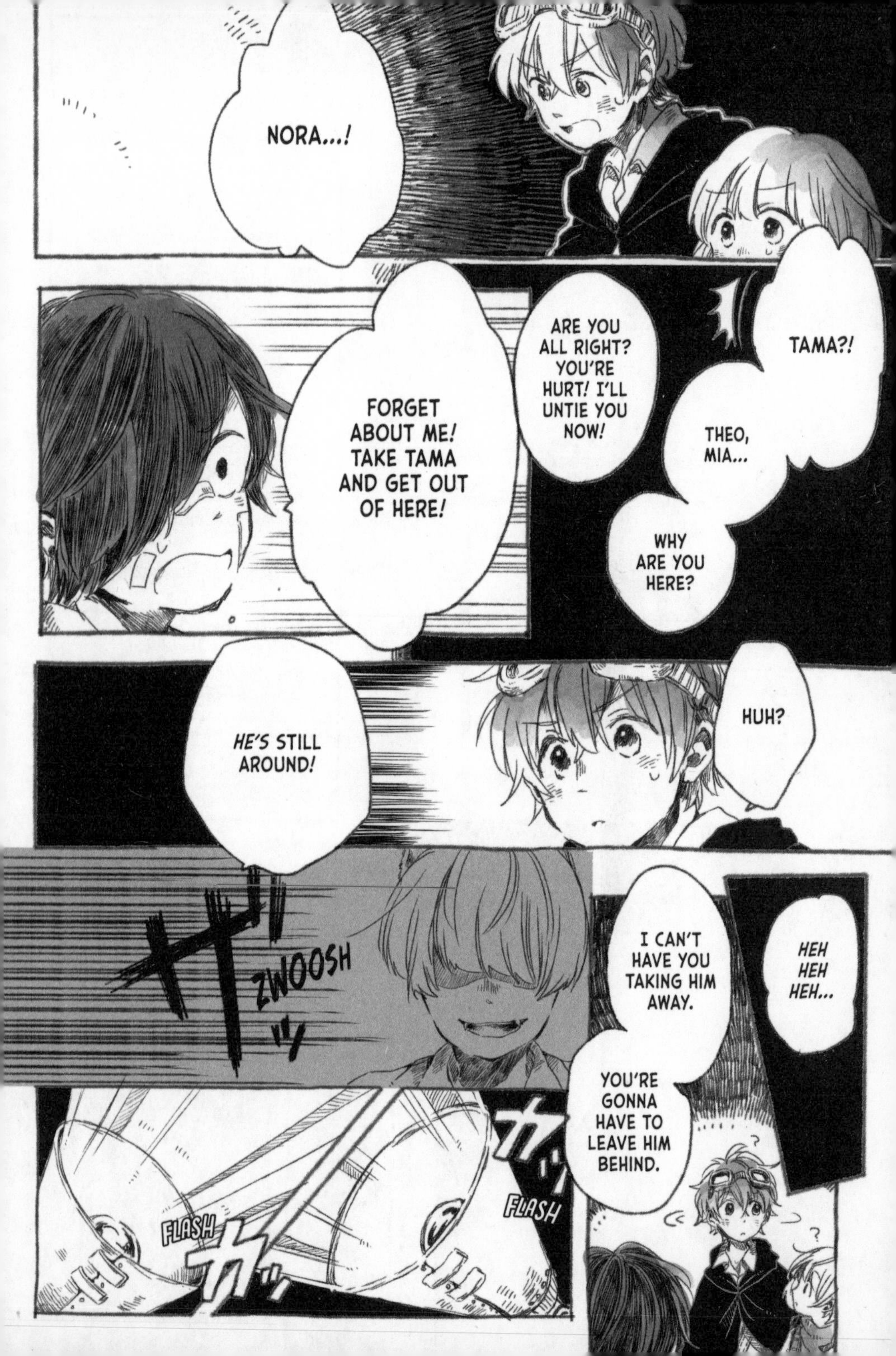
NORA...!
TAMA?!
THEO, MIA...
WHY ARE YOU HERE?
ARE YOU ALL RIGHT? YOU'RE HURT! I'LL UNTIE YOU NOW!
FORGET ABOUT ME! TAKE TAMA AND GET OUT OF HERE!
HUH?
HE'S STILL AROUND!
HEH HEH HEH...
I CAN'T HAVE YOU TAKING HIM AWAY.
YOU'RE GONNA HAVE TO LEAVE HIM BEHIND.
ZWOOSH
FLASH
FLASH

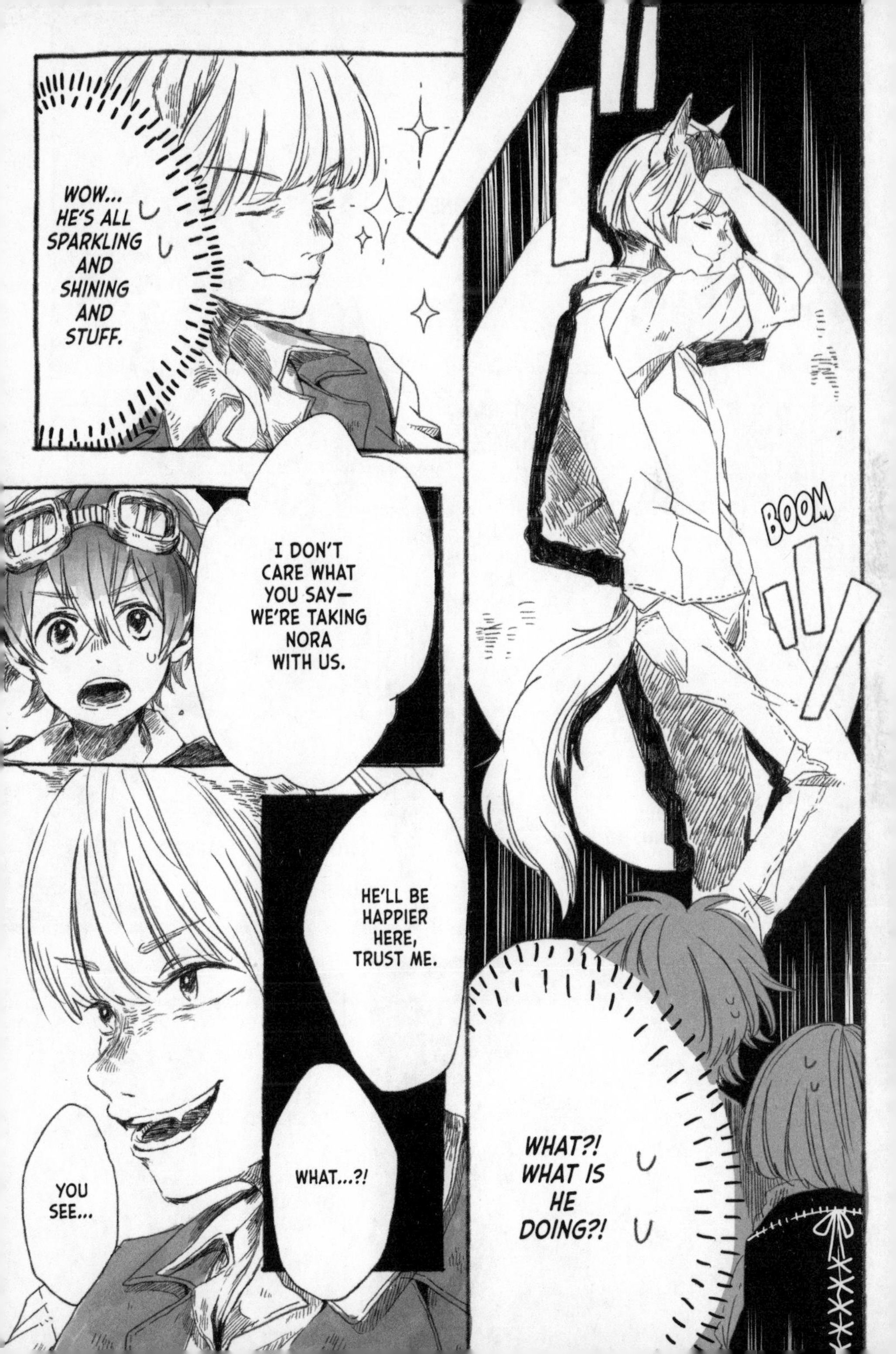

BOOM
WHAT?! WHAT IS HE DOING?!
WOW... HE'S ALL SPARKLING AND SHINING AND STUFF.
I DON'T CARE WHAT YOU SAY— WE'RE TAKING NORA WITH US.
HE'LL BE HAPPIER HERE, TRUST ME.
WHAT...?!
YOU SEE...

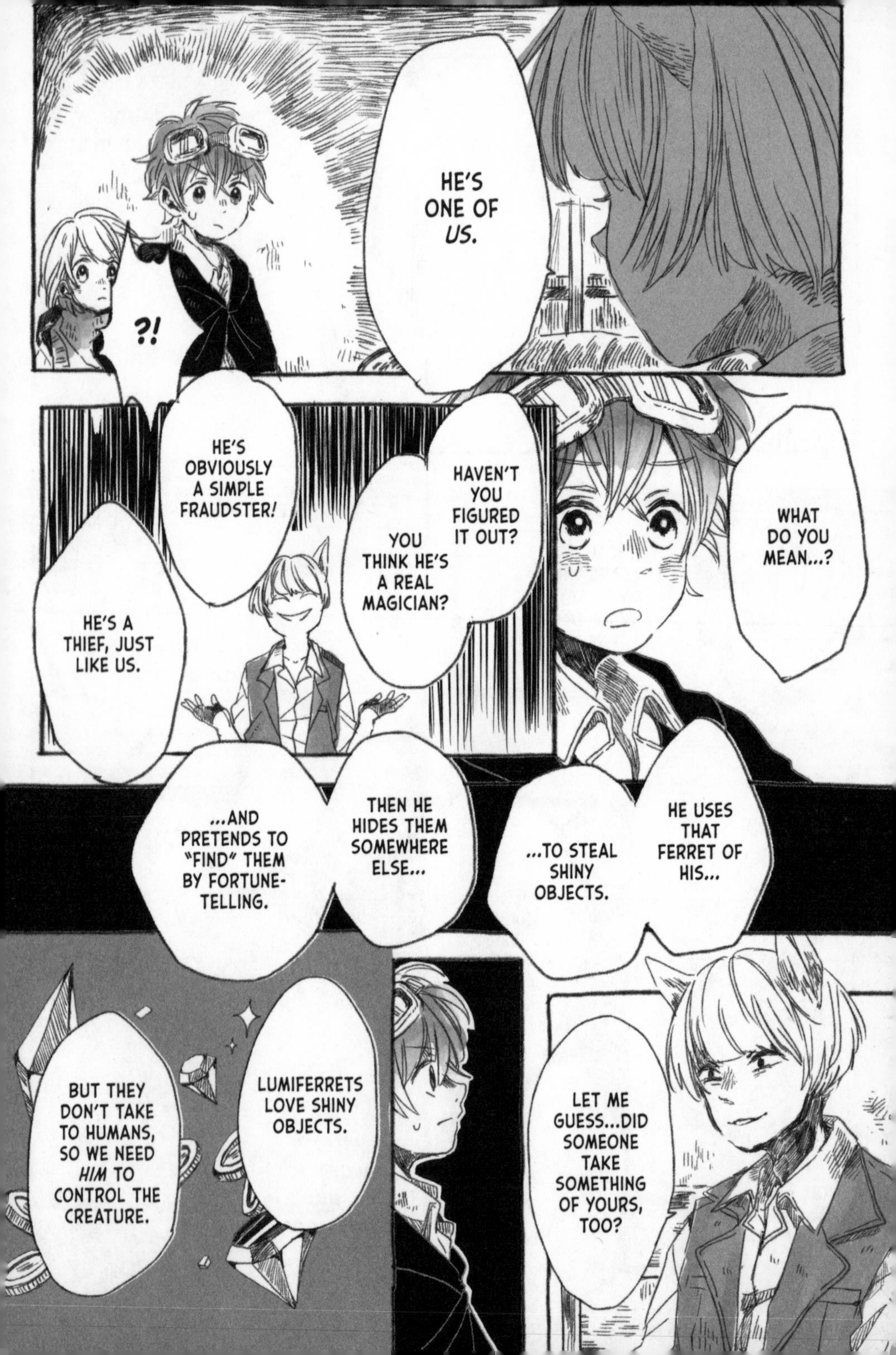
HE'S ONE OF *US.*
?!
WHAT DO YOU MEAN...?
HAVEN'T YOU FIGURED IT OUT?
YOU THINK HE'S A REAL MAGICIAN?
HE'S OBVIOUSLY A SIMPLE FRAUDSTER!
HE'S A THIEF, JUST LIKE US.
HE USES THAT FERRET OF HIS...
...TO STEAL SHINY OBJECTS.
THEN HE HIDES THEM SOMEWHERE ELSE...
...AND PRETENDS TO "FIND" THEM BY FORTUNE-TELLING.
LET ME GUESS...DID SOMEONE TAKE SOMETHING OF YOURS, TOO?
LUMIFERRETS LOVE SHINY OBJECTS.
BUT THEY DON'T TAKE TO HUMANS, SO WE NEED *HIM* TO CONTROL THE CREATURE.

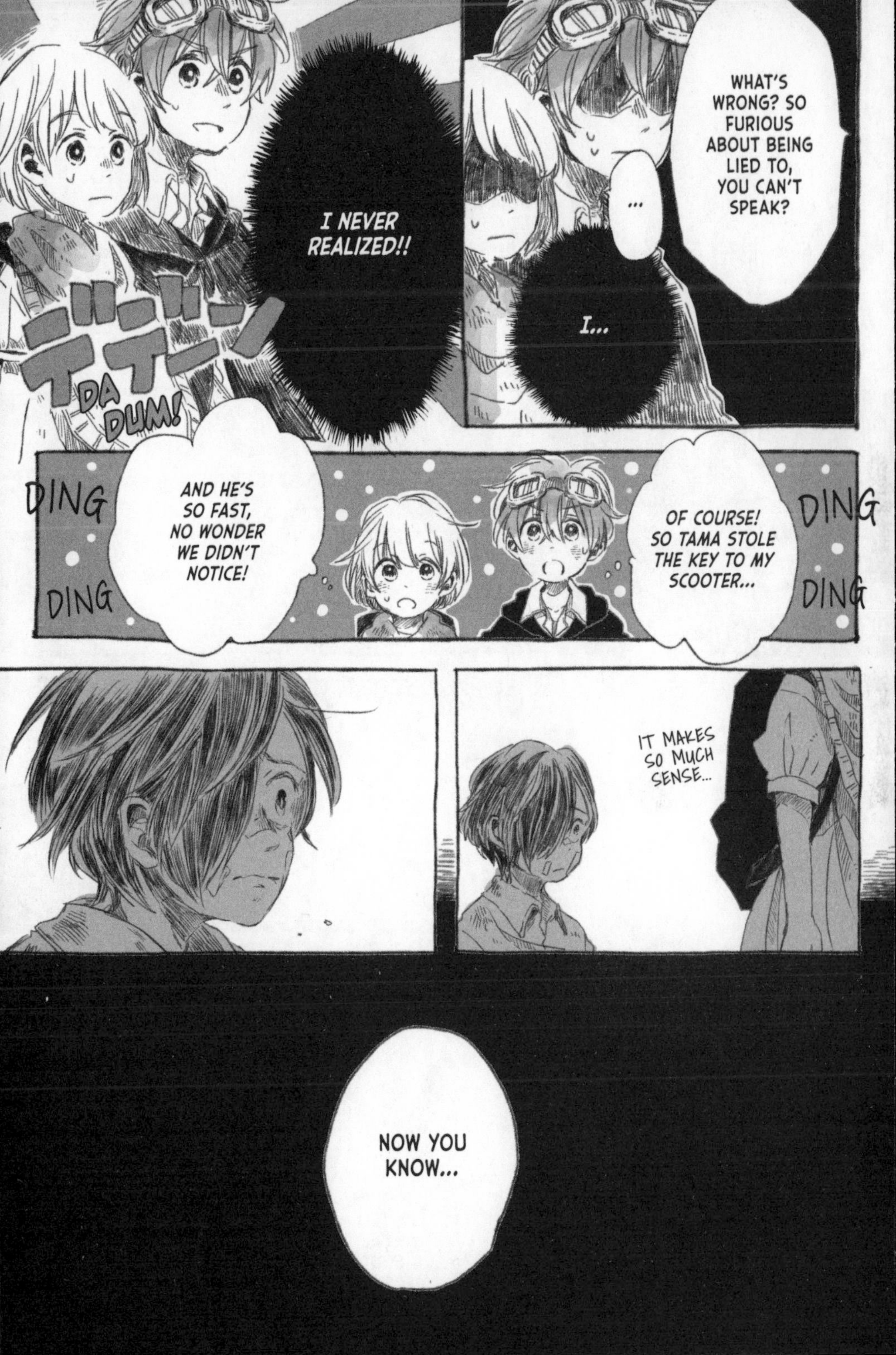
WHAT'S WRONG? SO FURIOUS ABOUT BEING LIED TO, YOU CAN'T SPEAK?
...
I...
I NEVER REALIZED!!
DA DUM!
DING
DING
OF COURSE! SO TAMA STOLE THE KEY TO MY SCOOTER...
AND HE'S SO FAST, NO WONDER WE DIDN'T NOTICE!
DING
DING
IT MAKES SO MUCH SENSE...
NOW YOU KNOW...

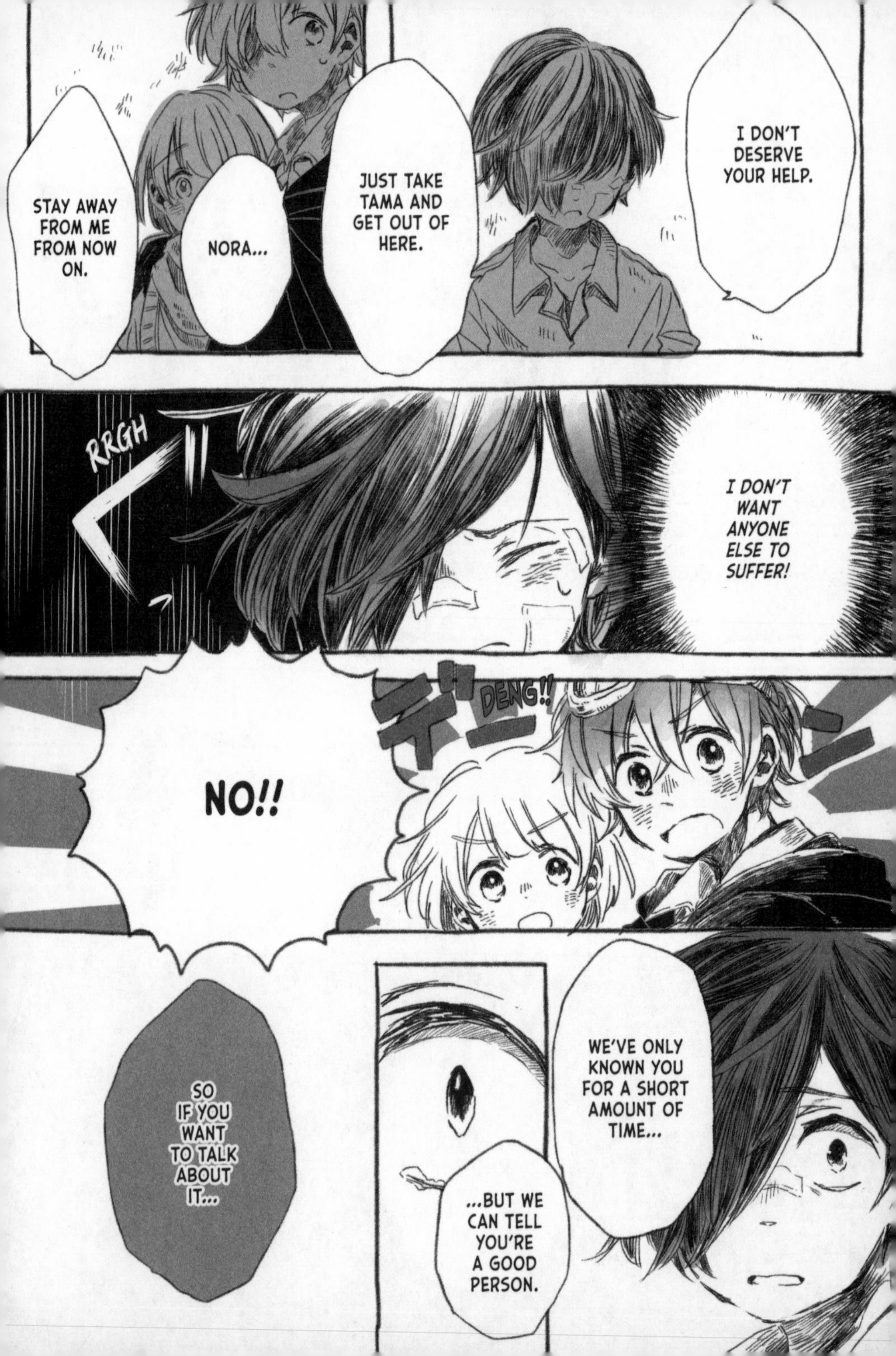
I DON'T DESERVE YOUR HELP.
JUST TAKE TAMA AND GET OUT OF HERE.
NORA...
STAY AWAY FROM ME FROM NOW ON.
I DON'T WANT ANYONE ELSE TO SUFFER!
RRGH
DENG!!
NO!!
WE'VE ONLY KNOWN YOU FOR A SHORT AMOUNT OF TIME...
...BUT WE CAN TELL YOU'RE A GOOD PERSON.
SO IF YOU WANT TO TALK ABOUT IT...

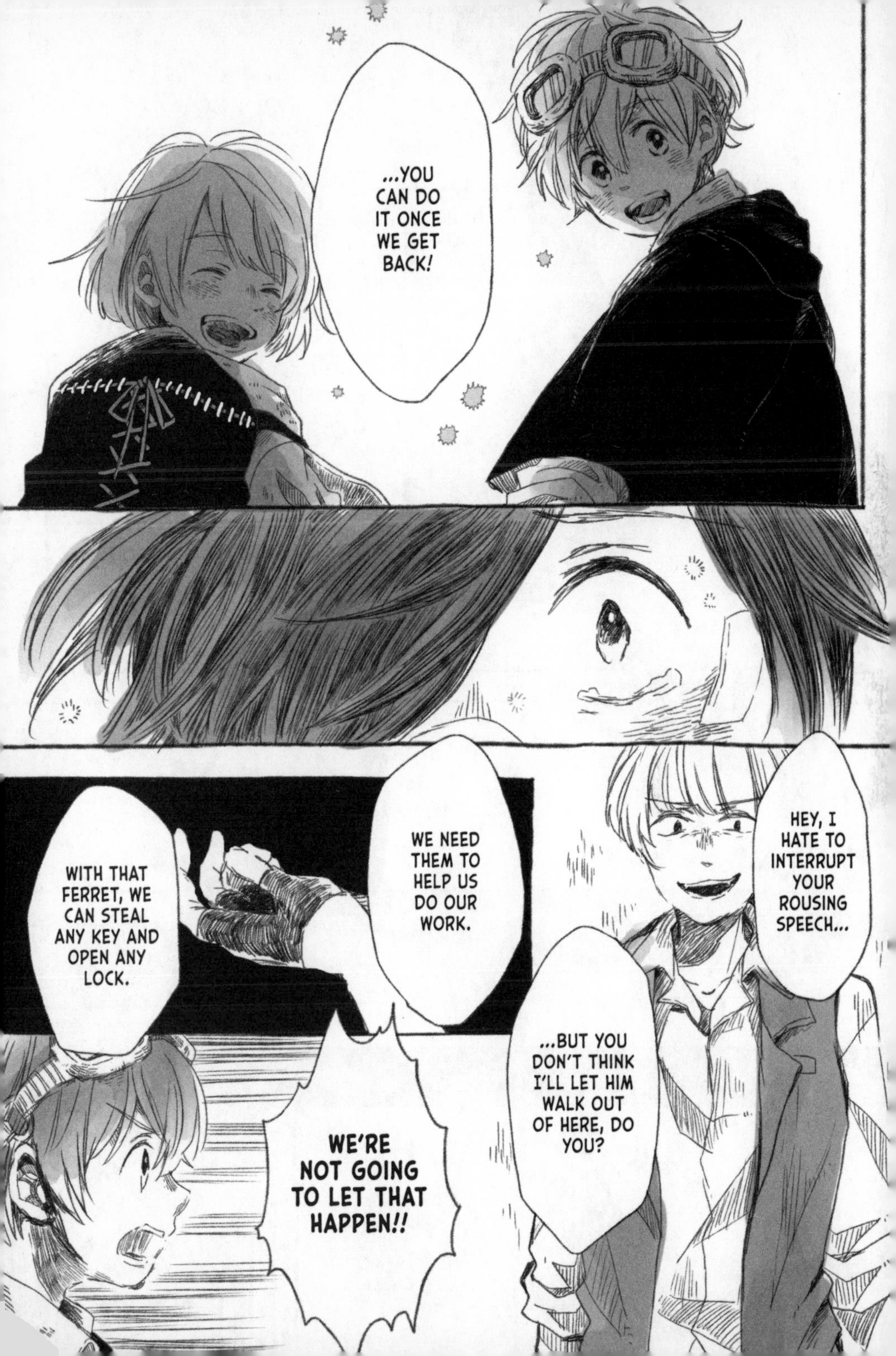

...YOU CAN DO IT ONCE WE GET BACK!
HEY, I HATE TO INTERRUPT YOUR ROUSING SPEECH...
...BUT YOU DON'T THINK I'LL LET HIM WALK OUT OF HERE, DO YOU?
WE NEED THEM TO HELP US DO OUR WORK.
WITH THAT FERRET, WE CAN STEAL ANY KEY AND OPEN ANY LOCK.
WE'RE NOT GOING TO LET THAT HAPPEN!!

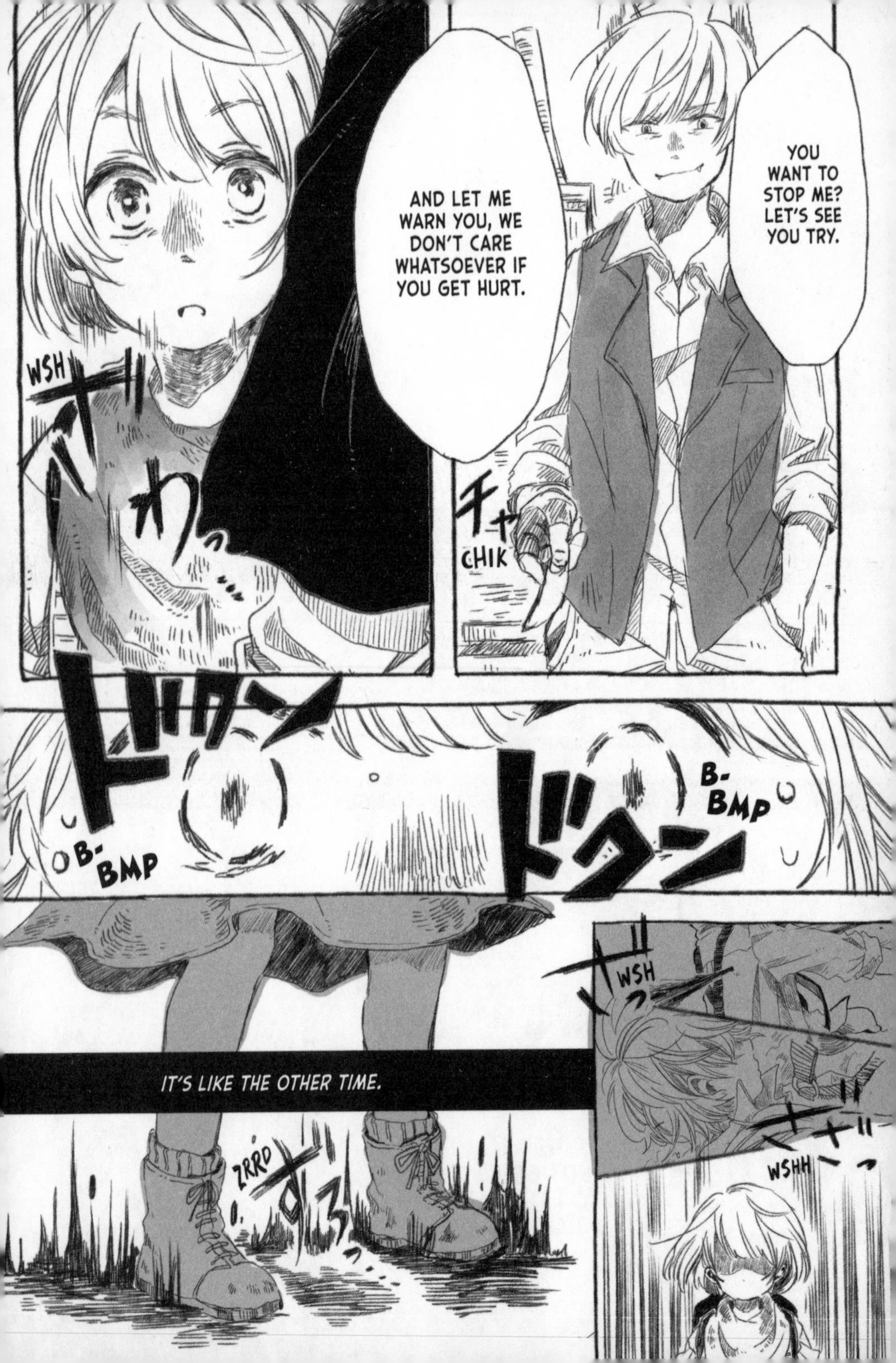
YOU WANT TO STOP ME? LET'S SEE YOU TRY.
AND LET ME WARN YOU, WE DON'T CARE WHATSOEVER IF YOU GET HURT.
CHIK
WSH
B-BMP
B-BMP
WSH
WSHH
IT'S LIKE THE OTHER TIME.
ZRRD

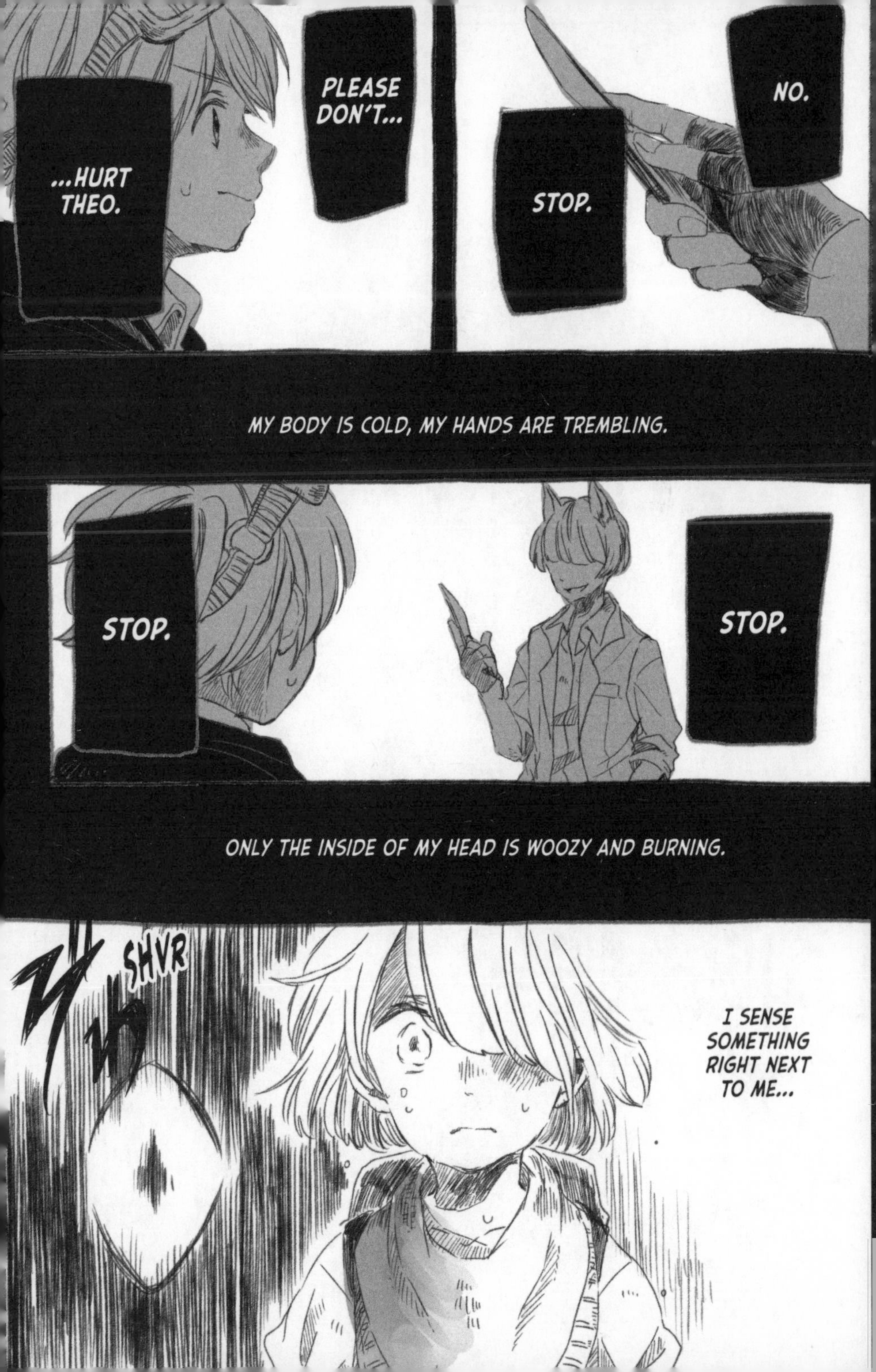
NO.
STOP.
PLEASE DON'T...
...HURT THEO.
MY BODY IS COLD, MY HANDS ARE TREMBLING.
STOP.
STOP.
ONLY THE INSIDE OF MY HEAD IS WOOZY AND BURNING.
I SENSE SOMETHING RIGHT NEXT TO ME...
SHVR

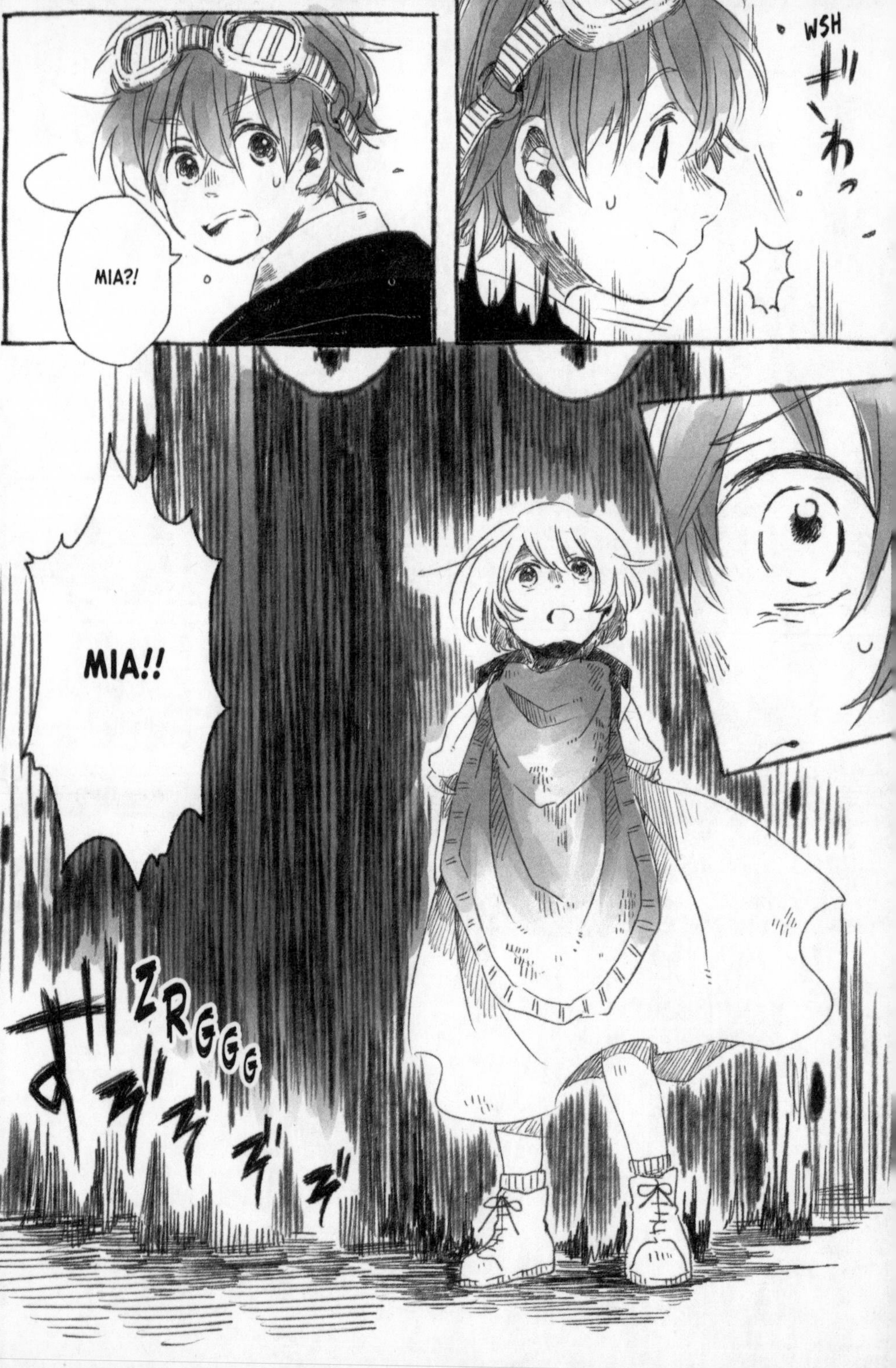
WSH
ざわっ
MIA?!
MIA!!
ZRGGG
ずずずずず

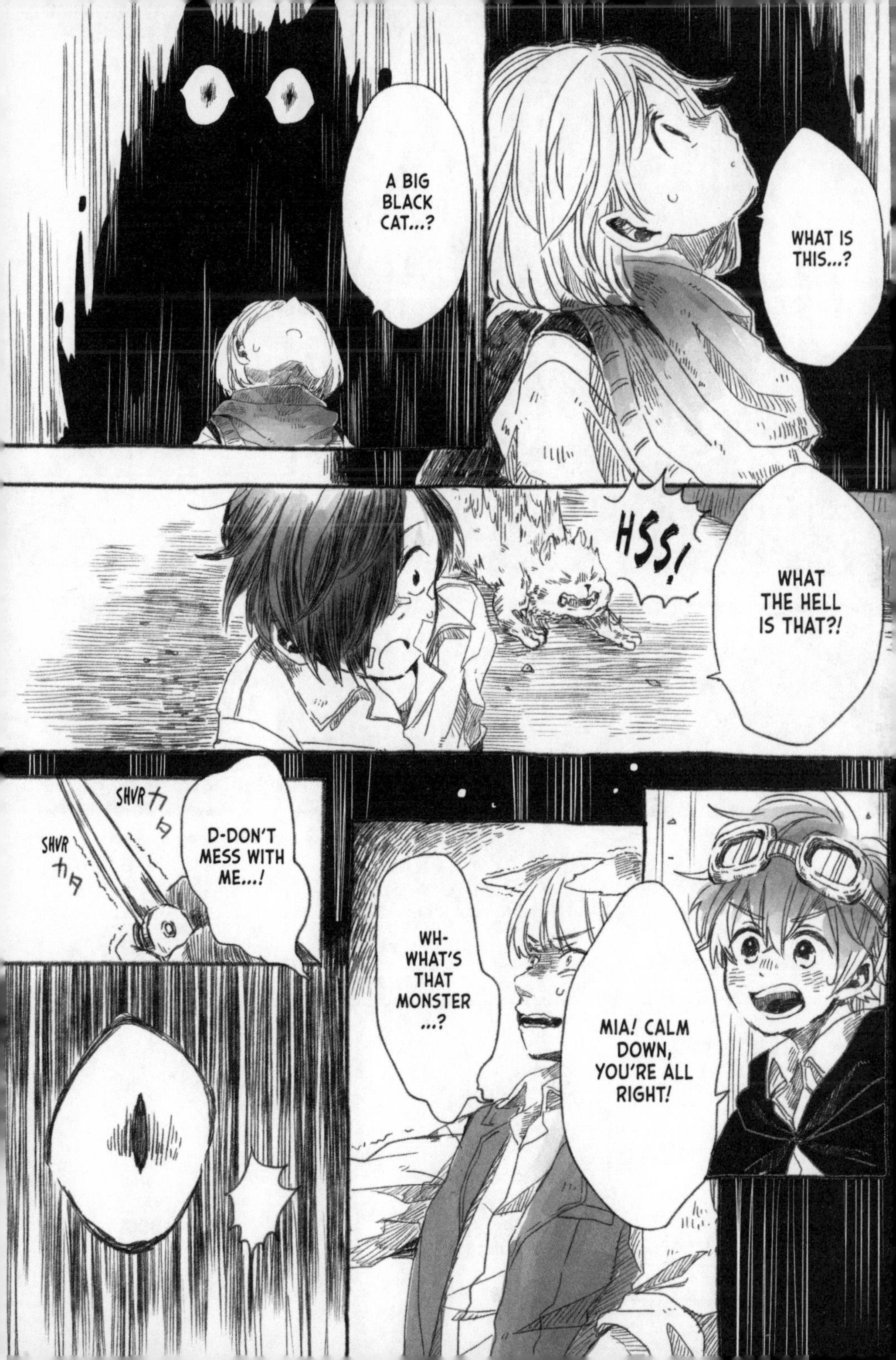
WHAT IS THIS...?
A BIG BLACK CAT...?
WHAT THE HELL IS THAT?!
HSS!
MIA! CALM DOWN, YOU'RE ALL RIGHT!
WH-WHAT'S THAT MONSTER ...?
SHVR カタ
D-DON'T MESS WITH ME...!
SHVR カタ

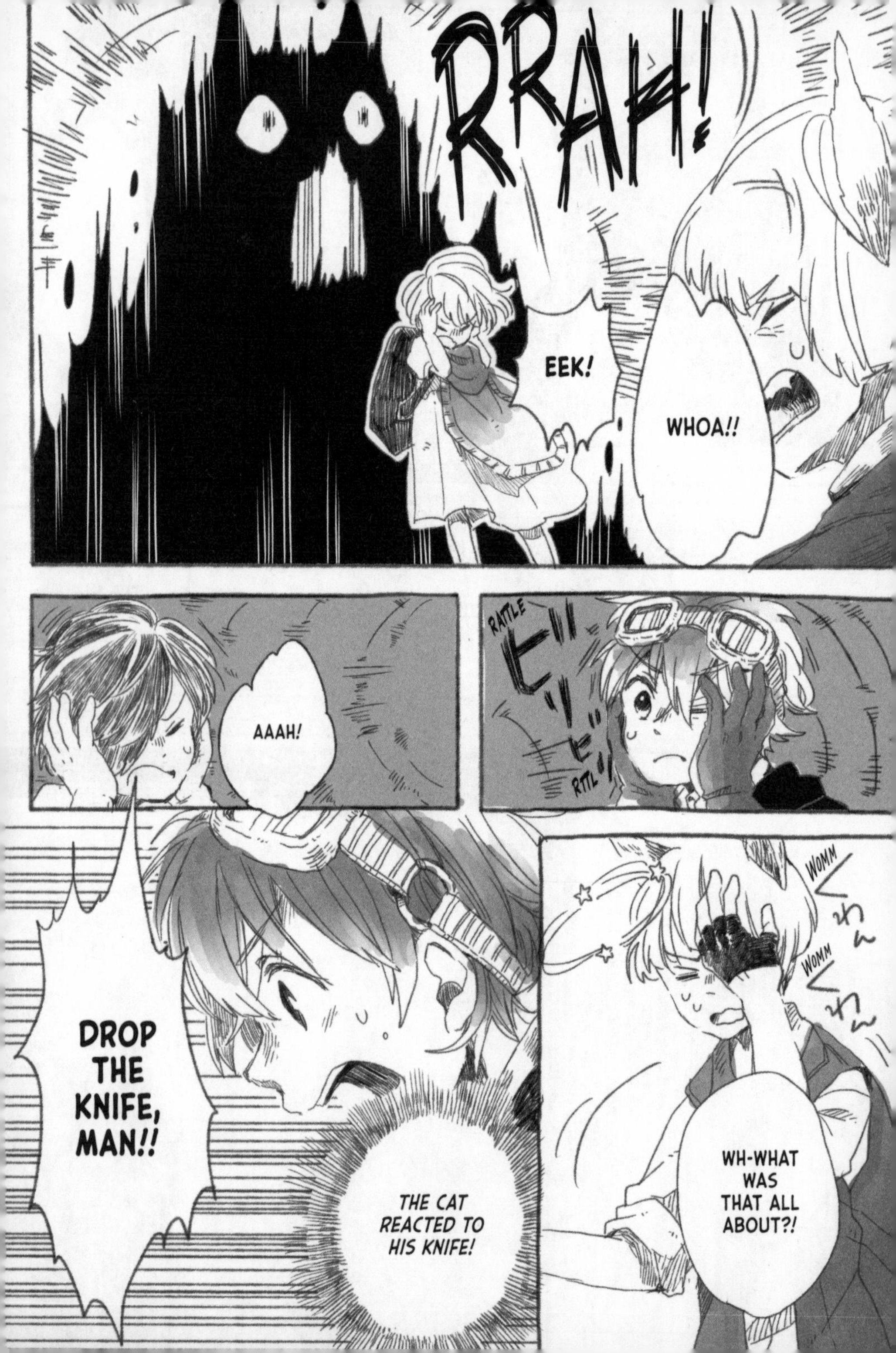
RRAH!
WHOA!!
EEK!
RATTLE
RTTL
AAAH!
WOMM
WOMM
WH-WHAT WAS THAT ALL ABOUT?!
THE CAT REACTED TO HIS KNIFE!
DROP THE KNIFE, MAN!!

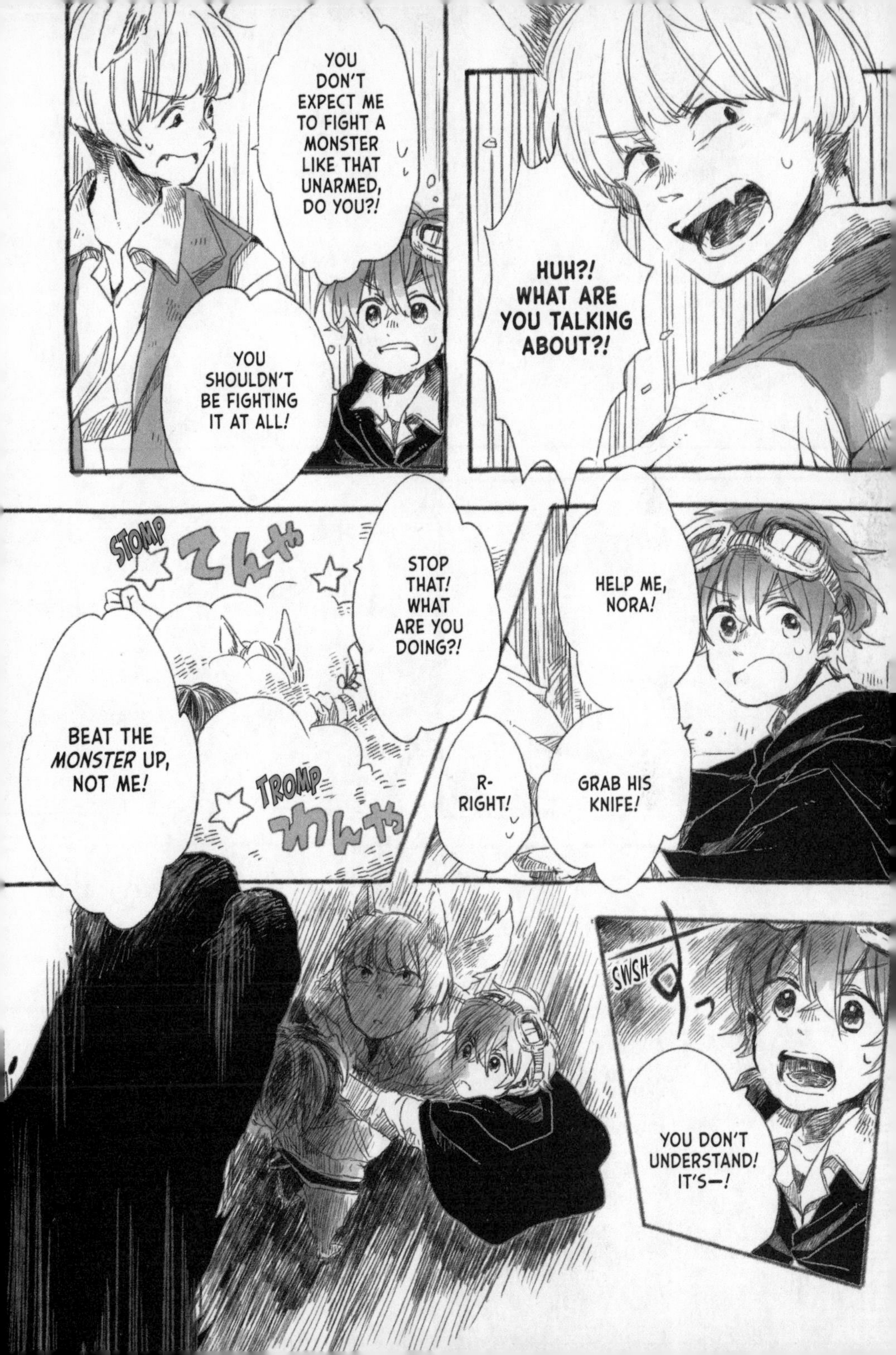
HUH?! WHAT ARE YOU TALKING ABOUT?!
YOU DON'T EXPECT ME TO FIGHT A MONSTER LIKE THAT UNARMED, DO YOU?!
YOU SHOULDN'T BE FIGHTING IT AT ALL!
HELP ME, NORA!
GRAB HIS KNIFE!
R-RIGHT!
STOMP
てんや
STOP THAT! WHAT ARE YOU DOING?!
BEAT THE *MONSTER* UP, NOT ME!
TROMP
わんや
SWSH
YOU DON'T UNDERSTAND! IT'S—!

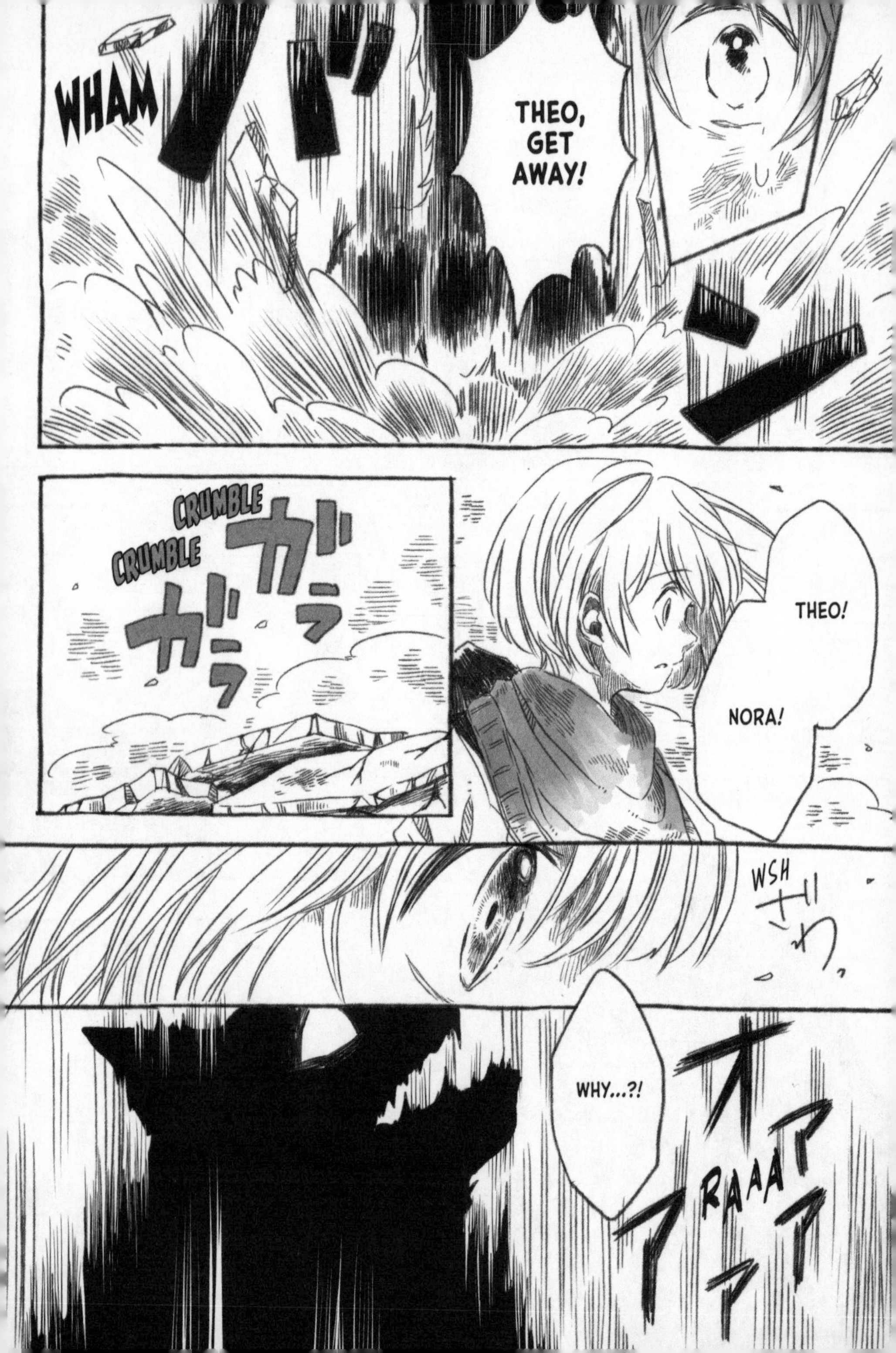
THEO, GET AWAY!
WHAM
THEO!
NORA!
CRUMBLE
ガラ
CRUMBLE
ガラ
WSH
ざわ
WHY...?!
RAAA

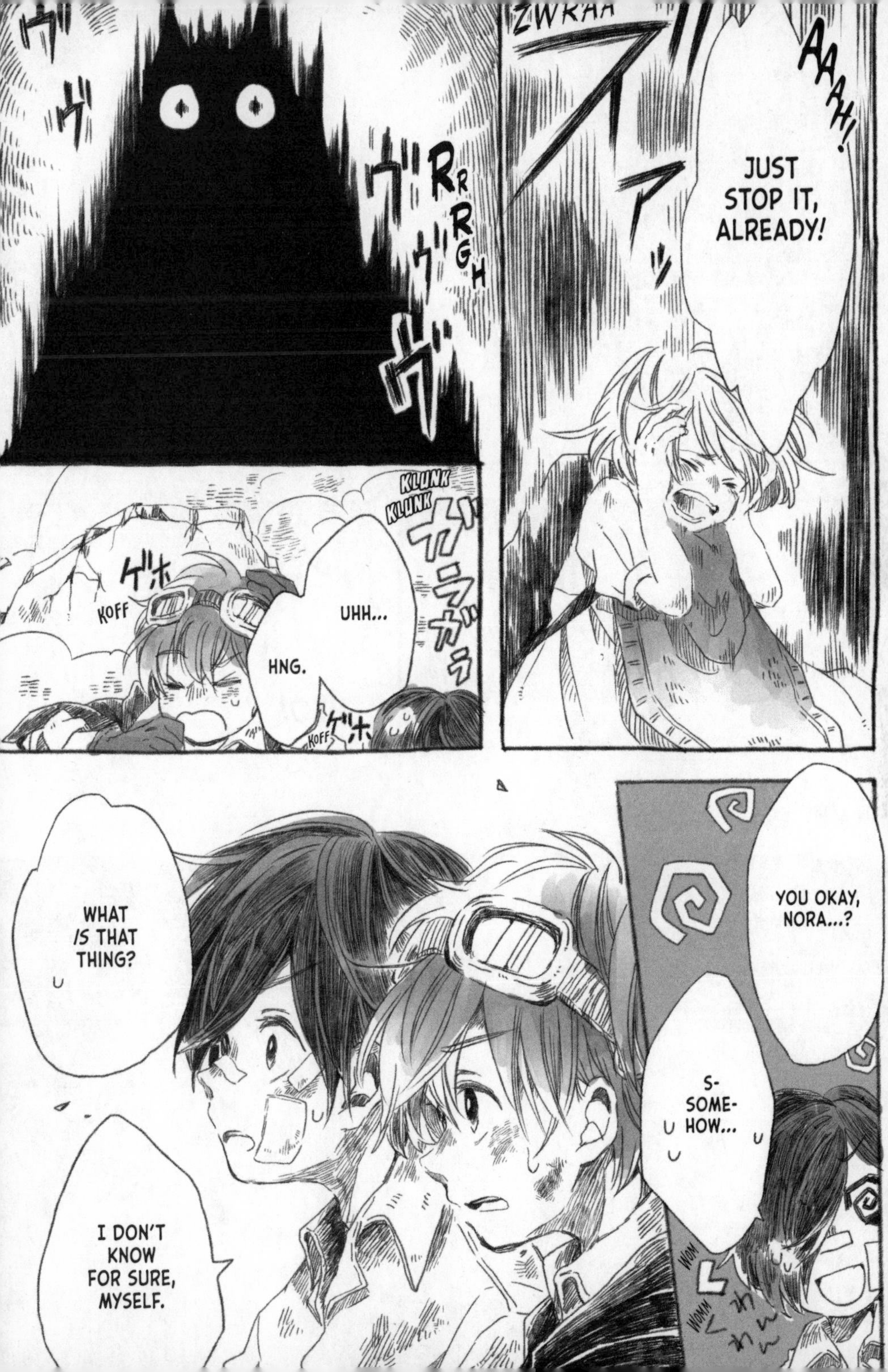
ZWRAA
AAAAH!
JUST STOP IT, ALREADY!
RRRGH
KLUNK KLUNK
UHH...
HNG.
KOFF
KOFF
YOU OKAY, NORA...?
S-SOMEHOW...
WOM
WOMM
WHAT IS THAT THING?
I DON'T KNOW FOR SURE, MYSELF.

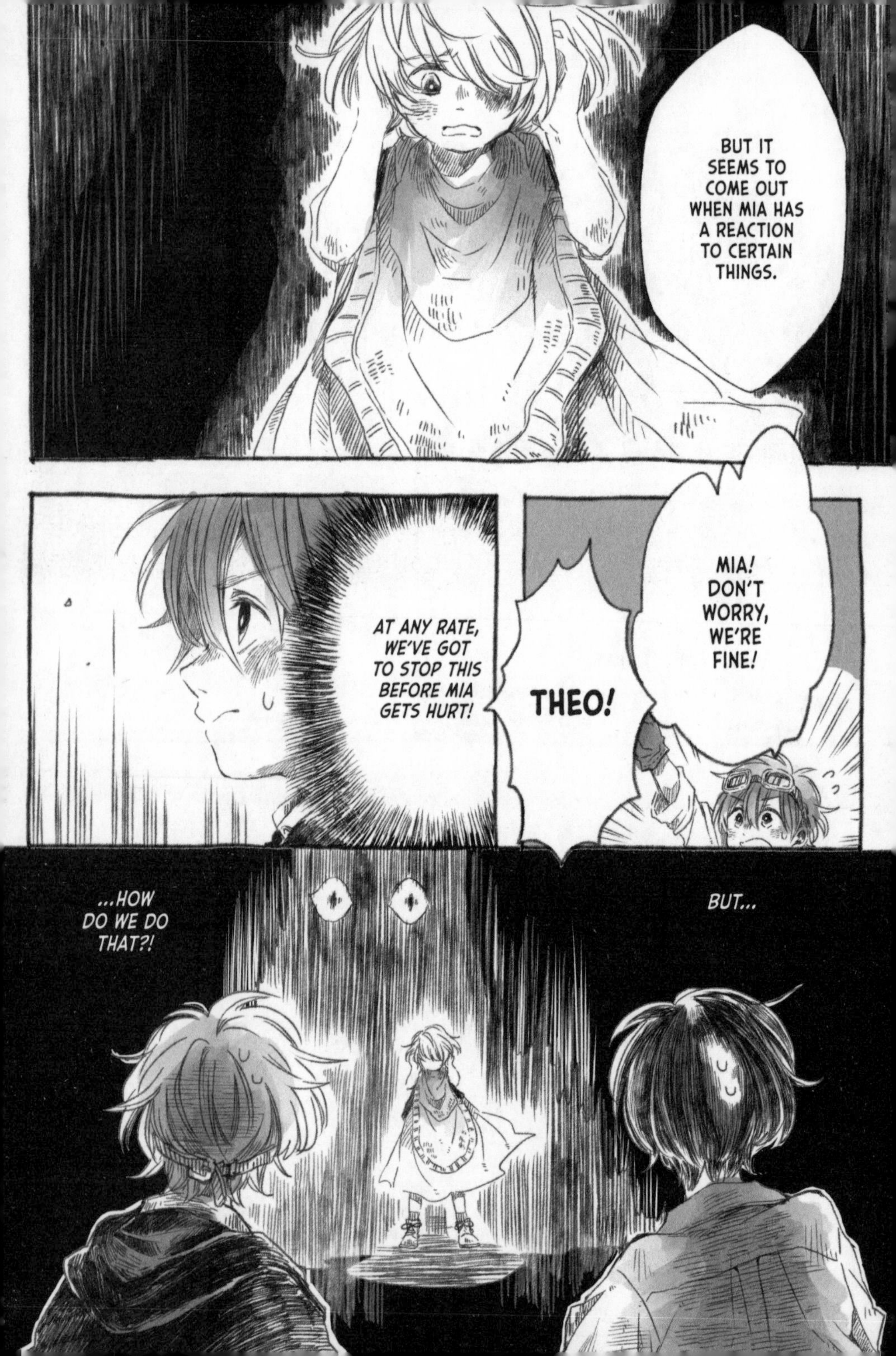
BUT IT SEEMS TO COME OUT WHEN MIA HAS A REACTION TO CERTAIN THINGS.
MIA! DON'T WORRY, WE'RE FINE!
THEO!
AT ANY RATE, WE'VE GOT TO STOP THIS BEFORE MIA GETS HURT!
BUT...
...HOW DO WE DO THAT?!

Chapter 15: Dynamic Duo

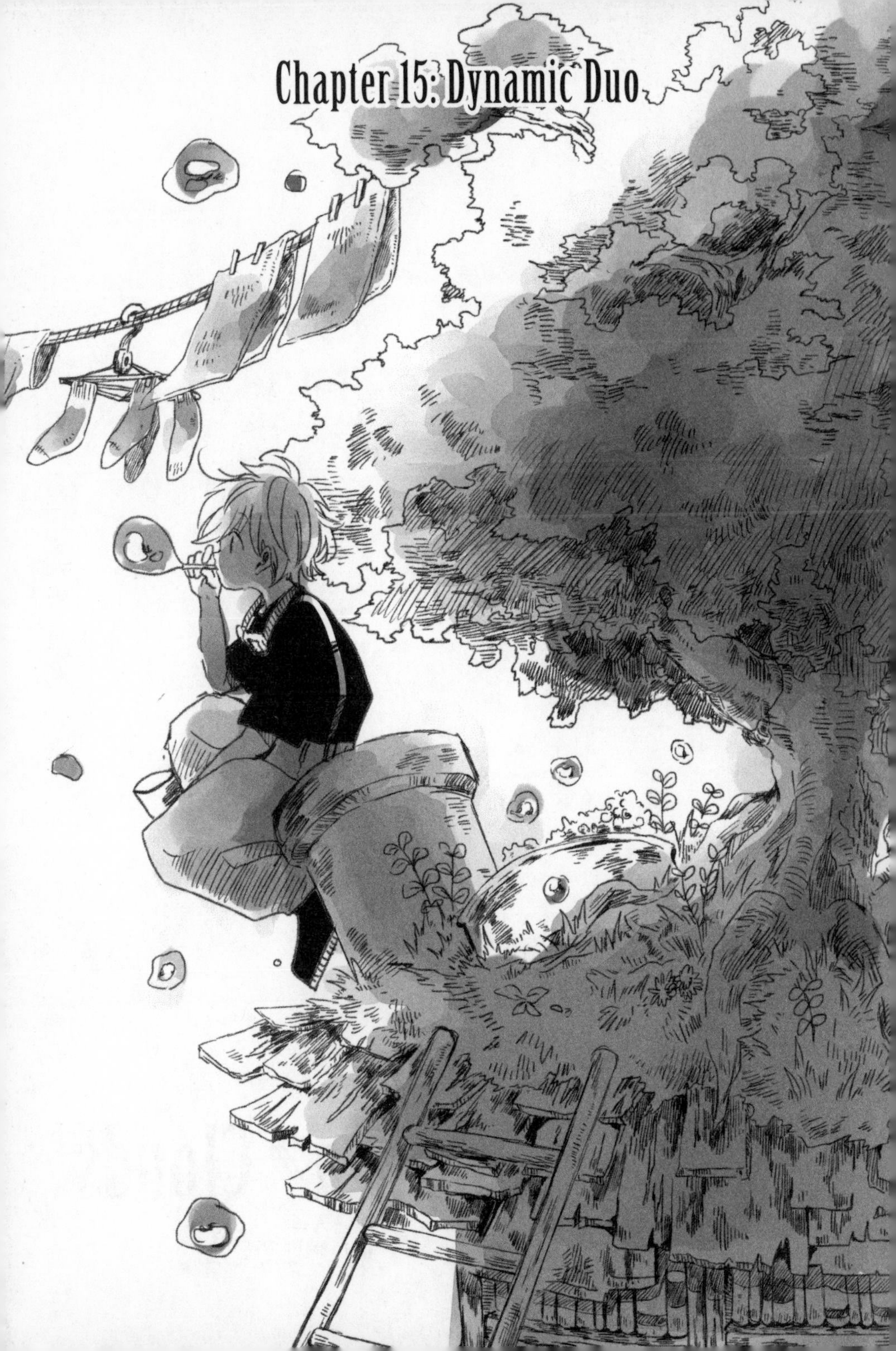

Beyond *the* Clouds

The Girl Who Fell From the Sky

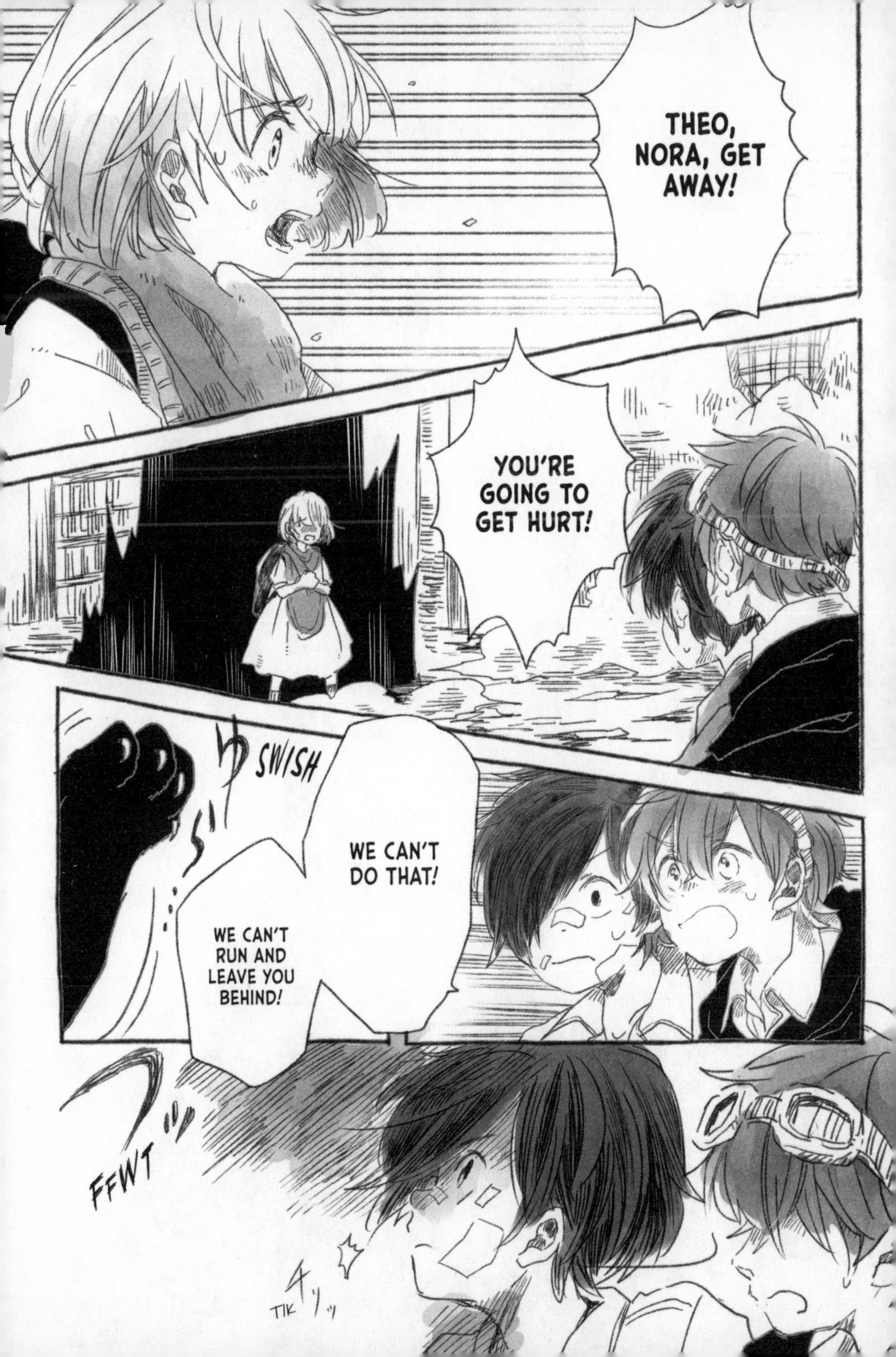
THEO, NORA, GET AWAY!
YOU'RE GOING TO GET HURT!
WE CAN'T DO THAT!
WE CAN'T RUN AND LEAVE YOU BEHIND!
SWISH
FFWT
TIK

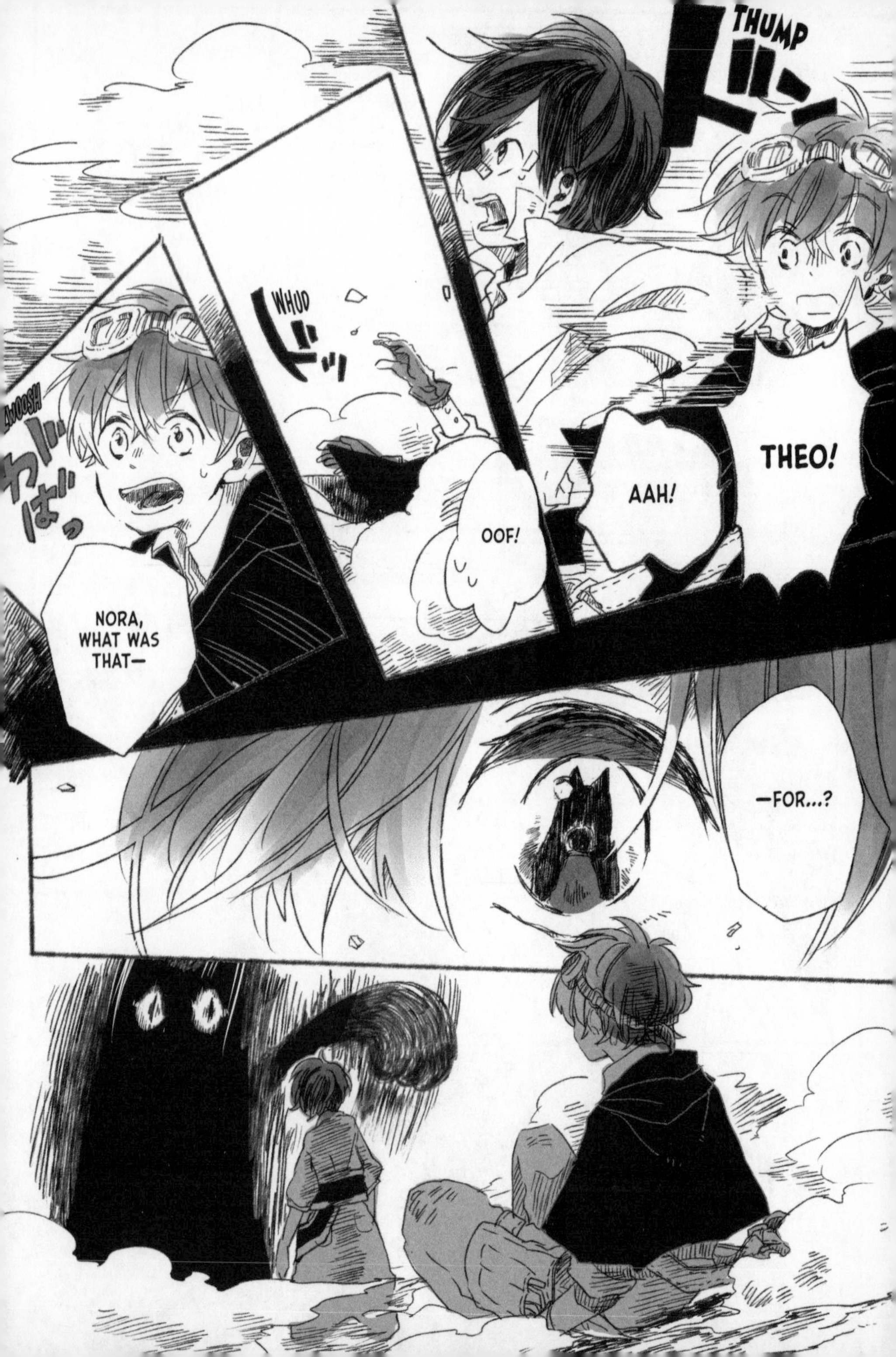
THUMP
THEO!
AAH!
WHUD
OOF!
WHOOSH
NORA, WHAT WAS THAT—
—FOR...?

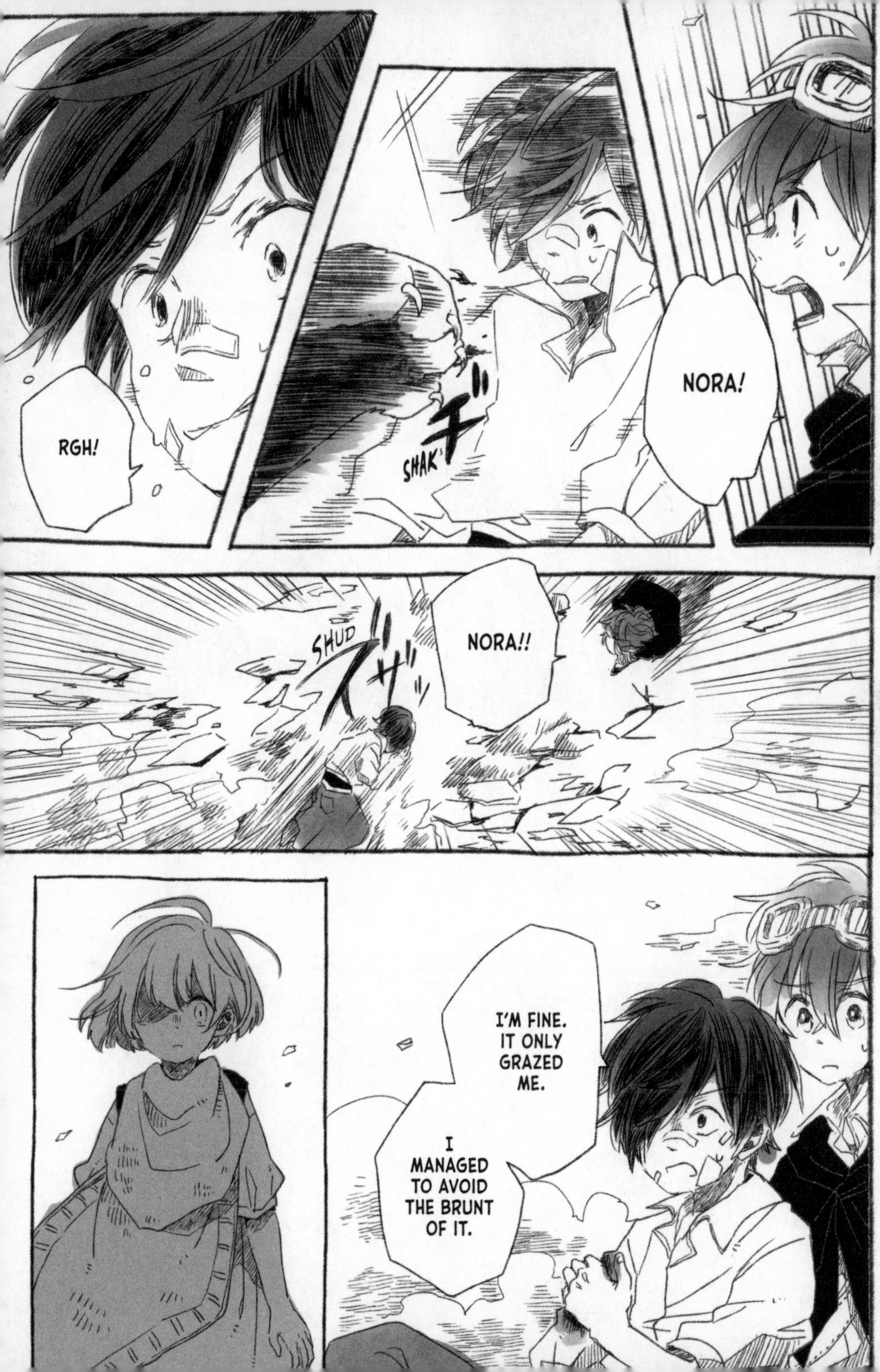
NORA!
SHAK
RGH!
NORA!!
SHUD
I'M FINE. IT ONLY GRAZED ME.
I MANAGED TO AVOID THE BRUNT OF IT.

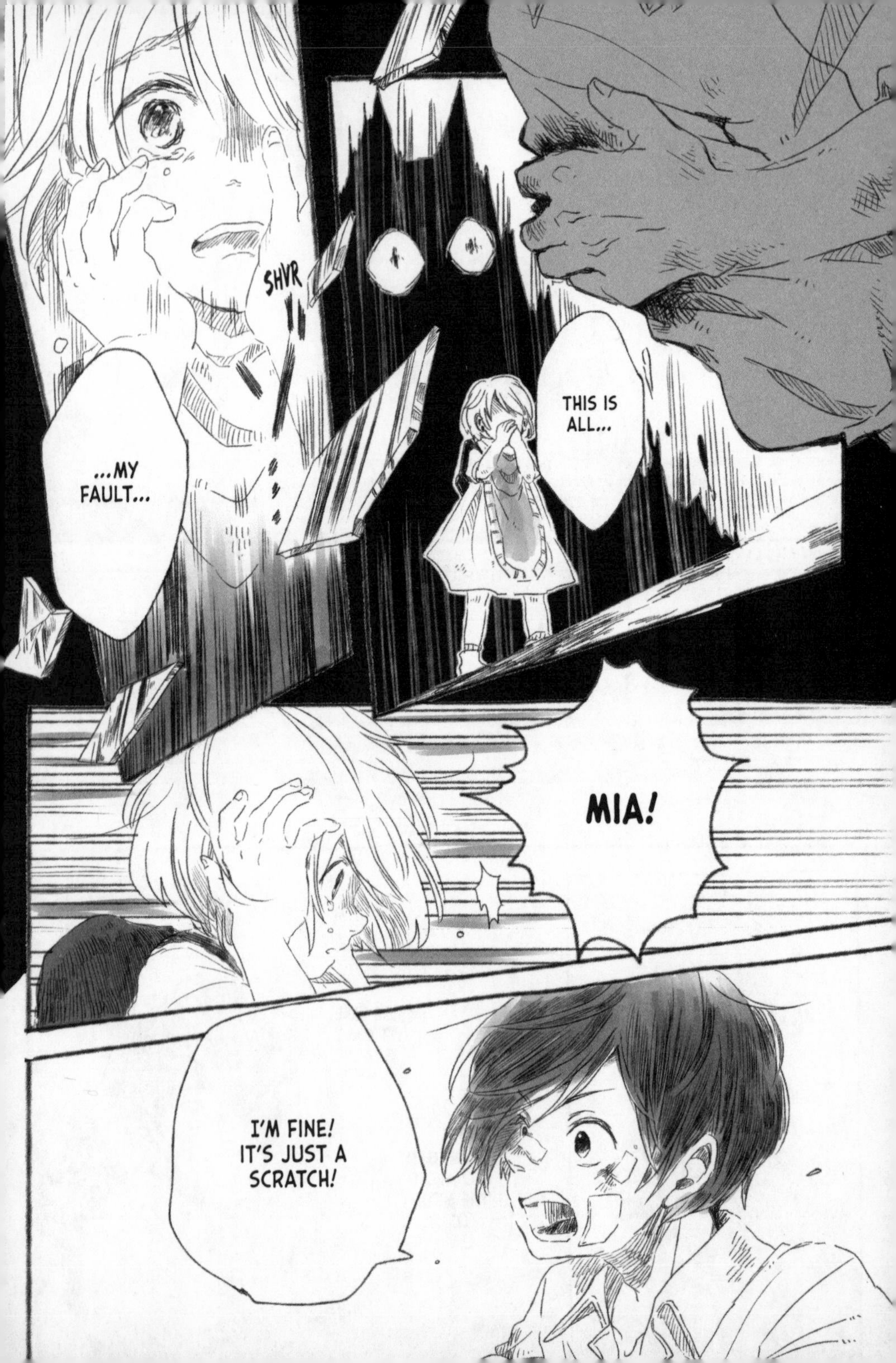
THIS IS ALL...
SHVR
...MY FAULT...
MIA!
I'M FINE! IT'S JUST A SCRATCH!

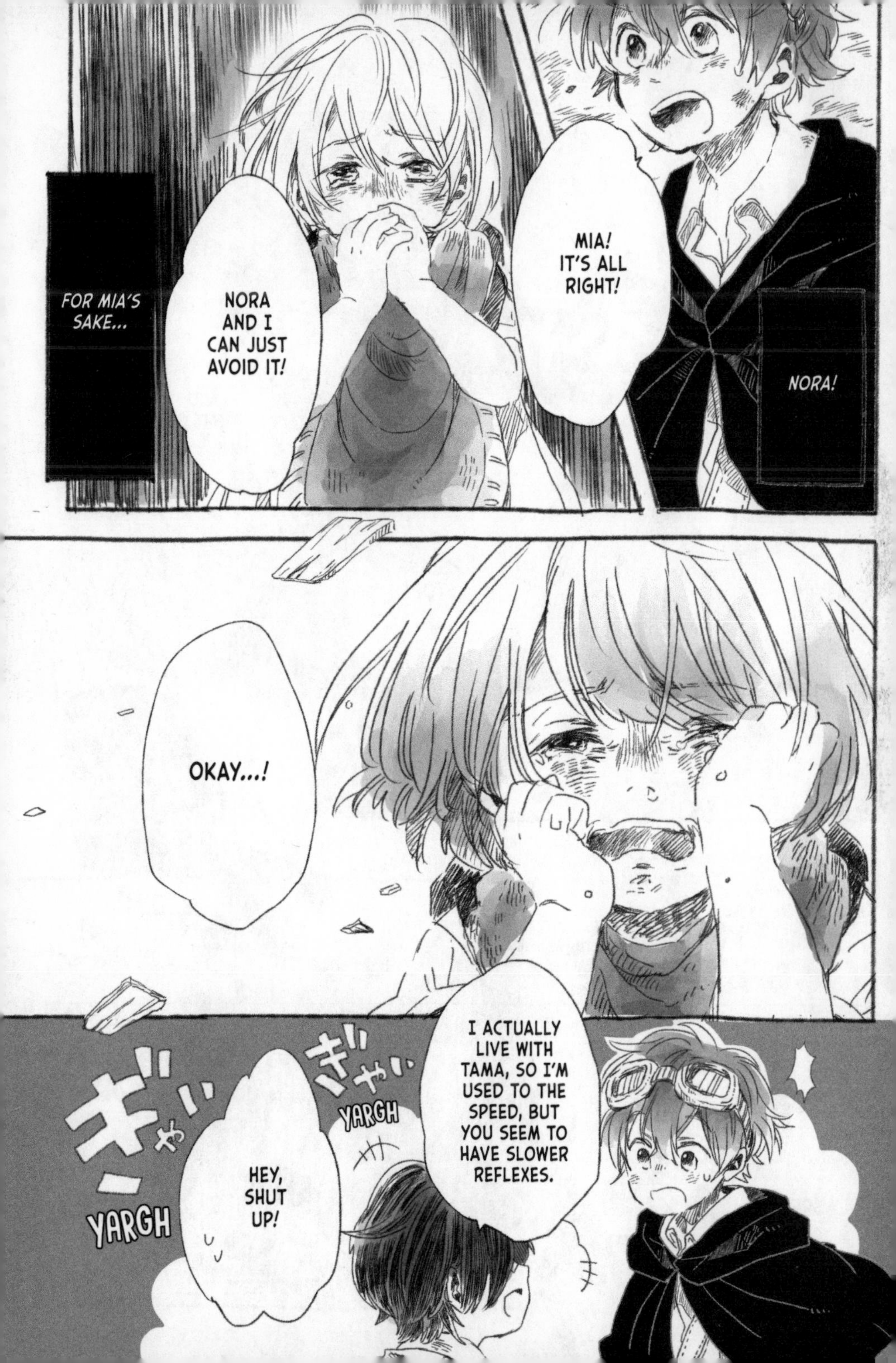
MIA! IT'S ALL RIGHT!
NORA!
NORA AND I CAN JUST AVOID IT!
FOR MIA'S SAKE...
OKAY...!
I ACTUALLY LIVE WITH TAMA, SO I'M USED TO THE SPEED, BUT YOU SEEM TO HAVE SLOWER REFLEXES.
YARGH
HEY, SHUT UP!
YARGH

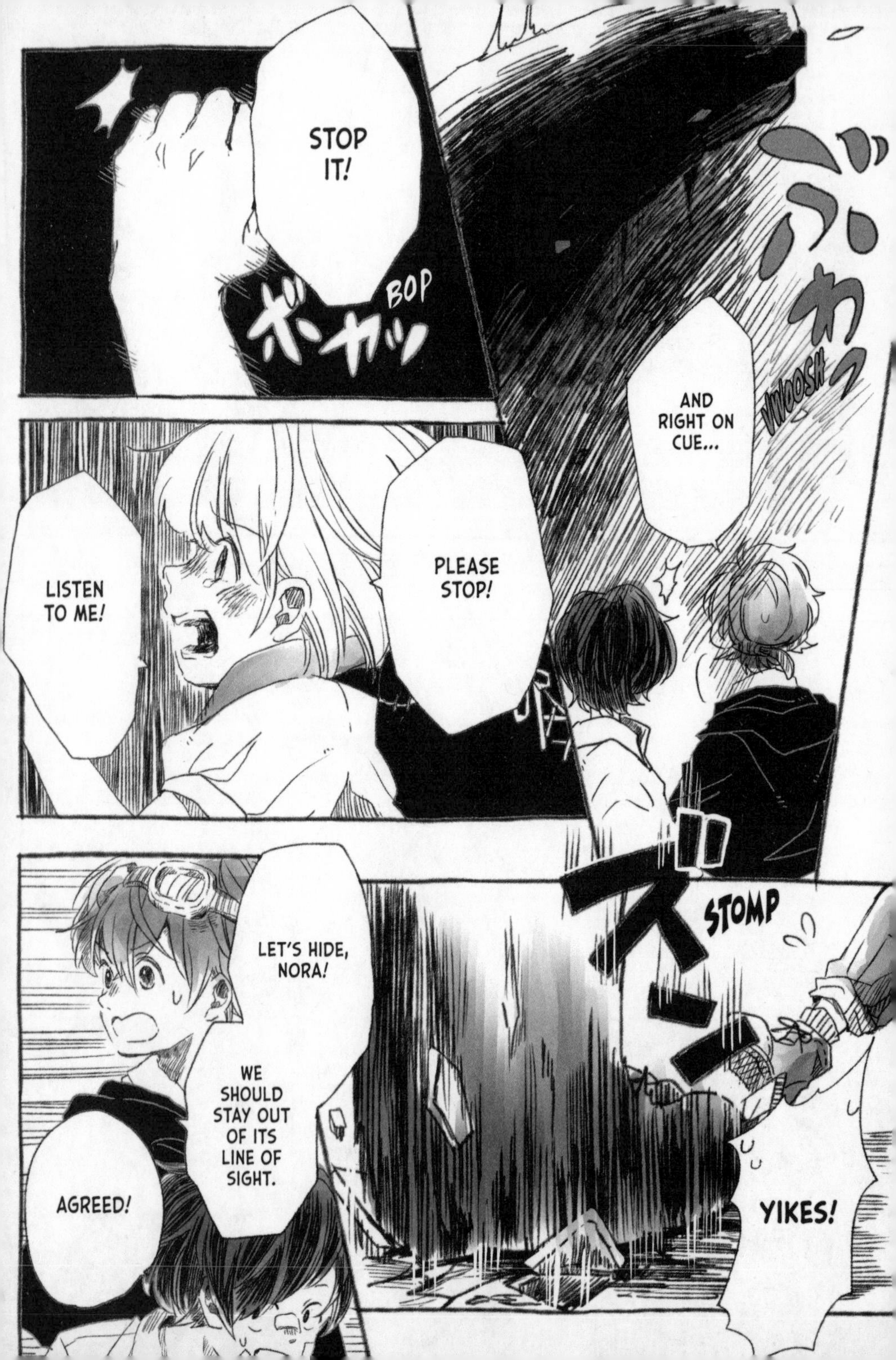
ぶわっ
VWOOSH
AND RIGHT ON CUE...
STOP IT!
BOP
ボカッ
PLEASE STOP!
LISTEN TO ME!
STOMP
YIKES!
LET'S HIDE, NORA!
WE SHOULD STAY OUT OF ITS LINE OF SIGHT.
AGREED!

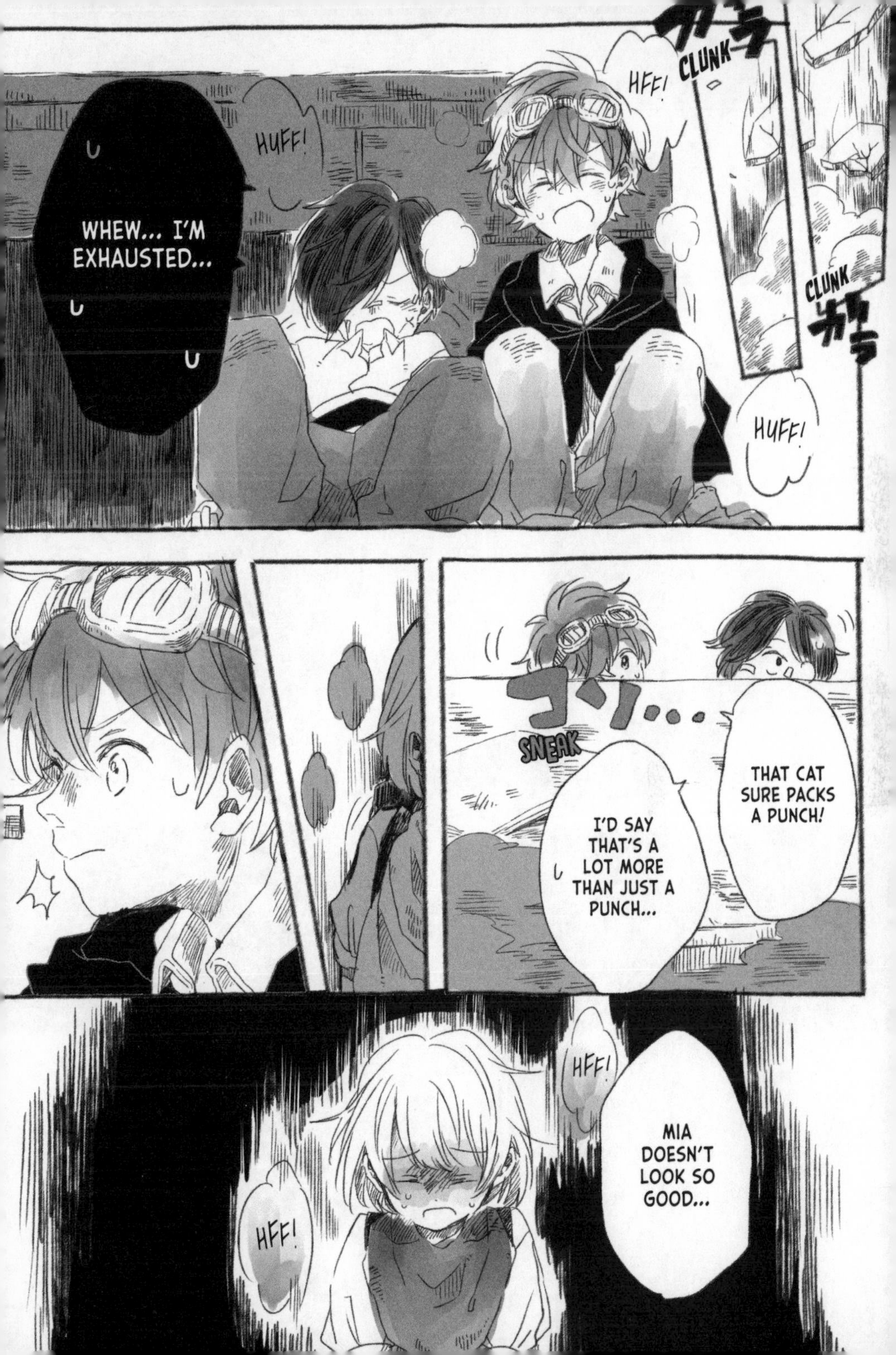
CLUNK
HFF!
CLUNK
HUFF!
HUFF!
WHEW... I'M EXHAUSTED...
SNEAK
THAT CAT SURE PACKS A PUNCH!
I'D SAY THAT'S A LOT MORE THAN JUST A PUNCH...
HFF!
MIA DOESN'T LOOK SO GOOD...
HFF!

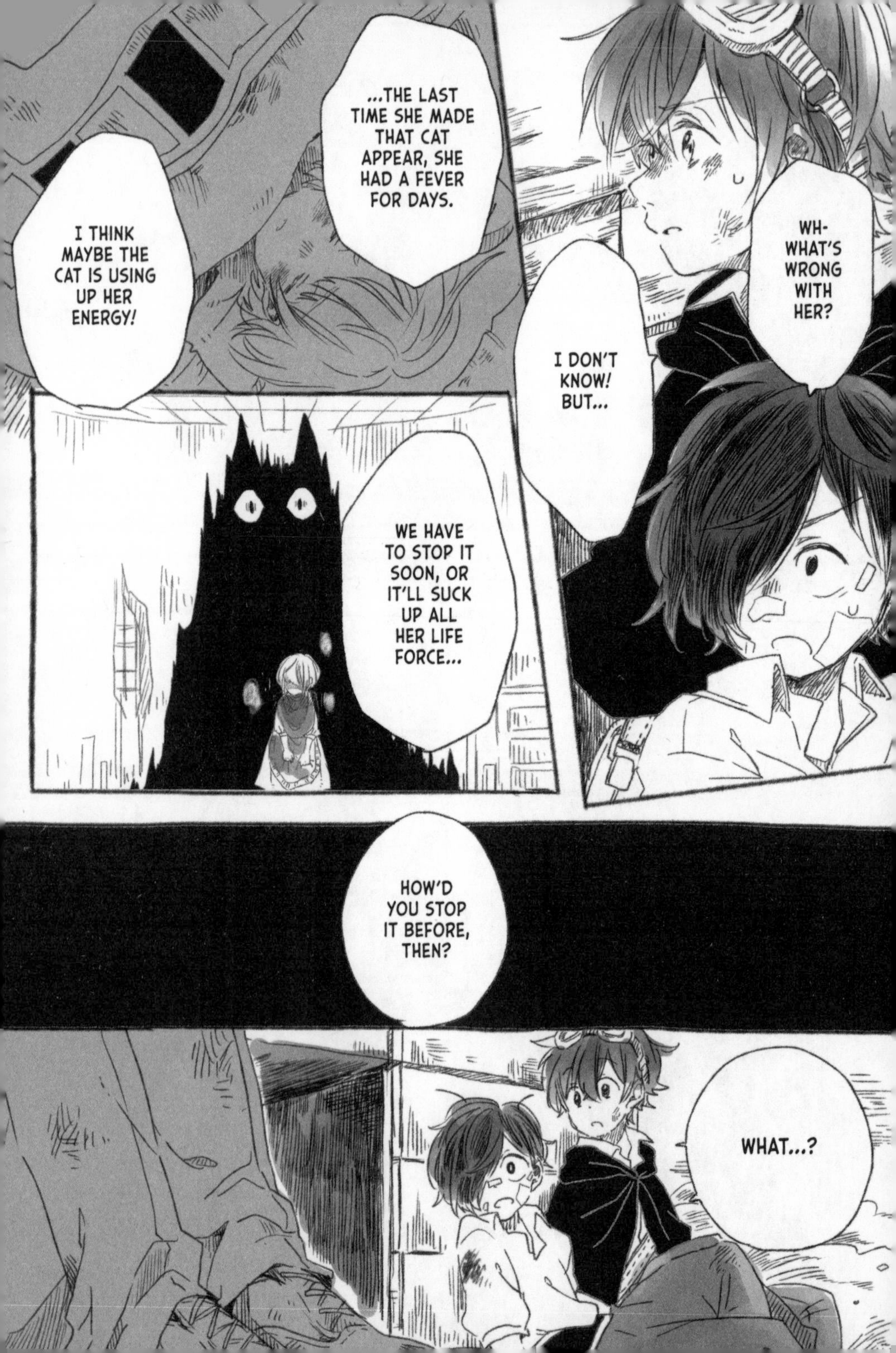
WH- WHAT'S WRONG WITH HER?
I DON'T KNOW! BUT...
...THE LAST TIME SHE MADE THAT CAT APPEAR, SHE HAD A FEVER FOR DAYS.
I THINK MAYBE THE CAT IS USING UP HER ENERGY!
WE HAVE TO STOP IT SOON, OR IT'LL SUCK UP ALL HER LIFE FORCE...
HOW'D YOU STOP IT BEFORE, THEN?
WHAT...?

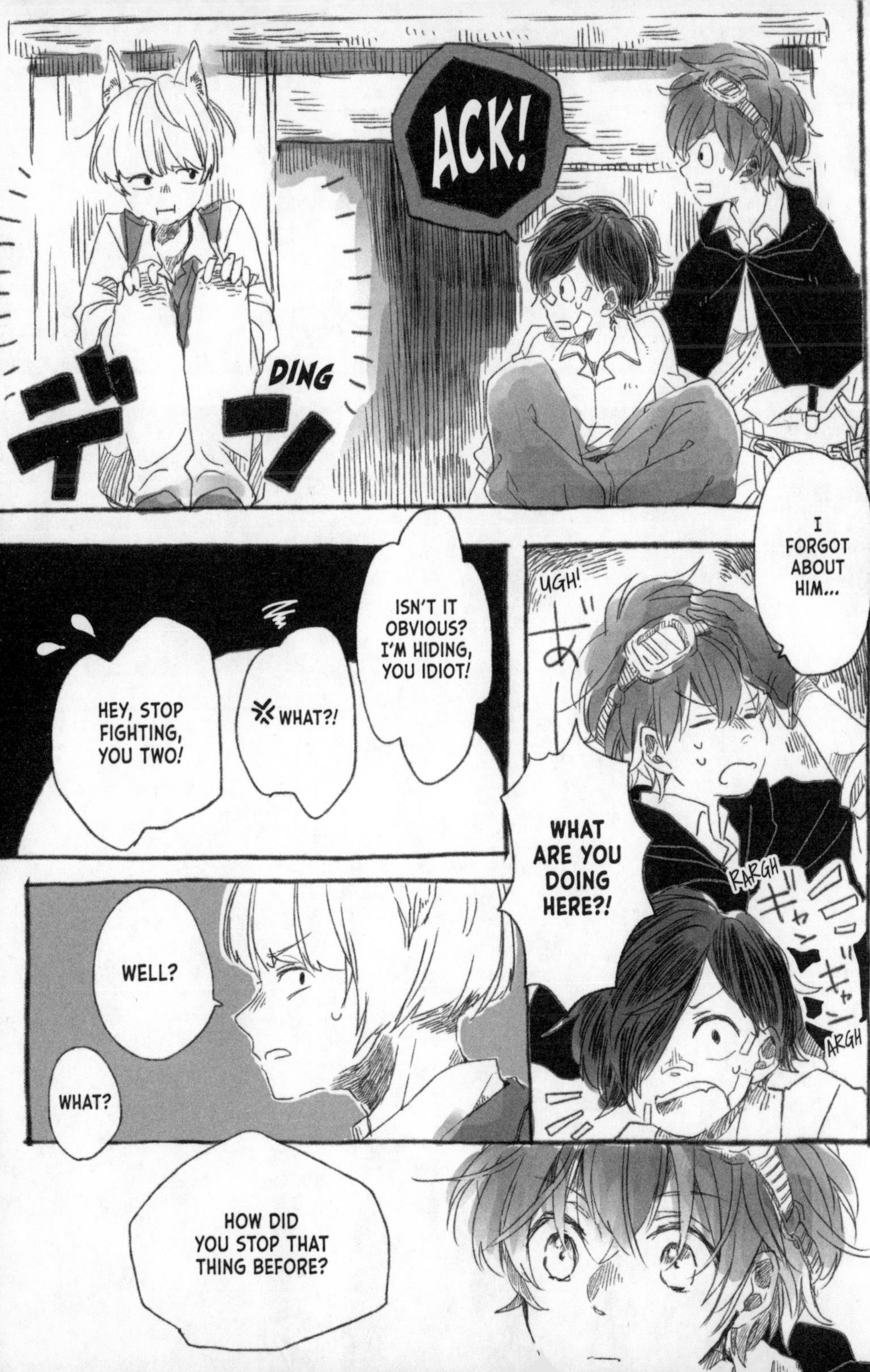
ACK!
DING
I FORGOT ABOUT HIM...
UGH!
WHAT ARE YOU DOING HERE?!
ISN'T IT OBVIOUS? I'M HIDING, YOU IDIOT!
WHAT?!
HEY, STOP FIGHTING, YOU TWO!
RARGH
ARGH
WELL?
WHAT?
HOW DID YOU STOP THAT THING BEFORE?

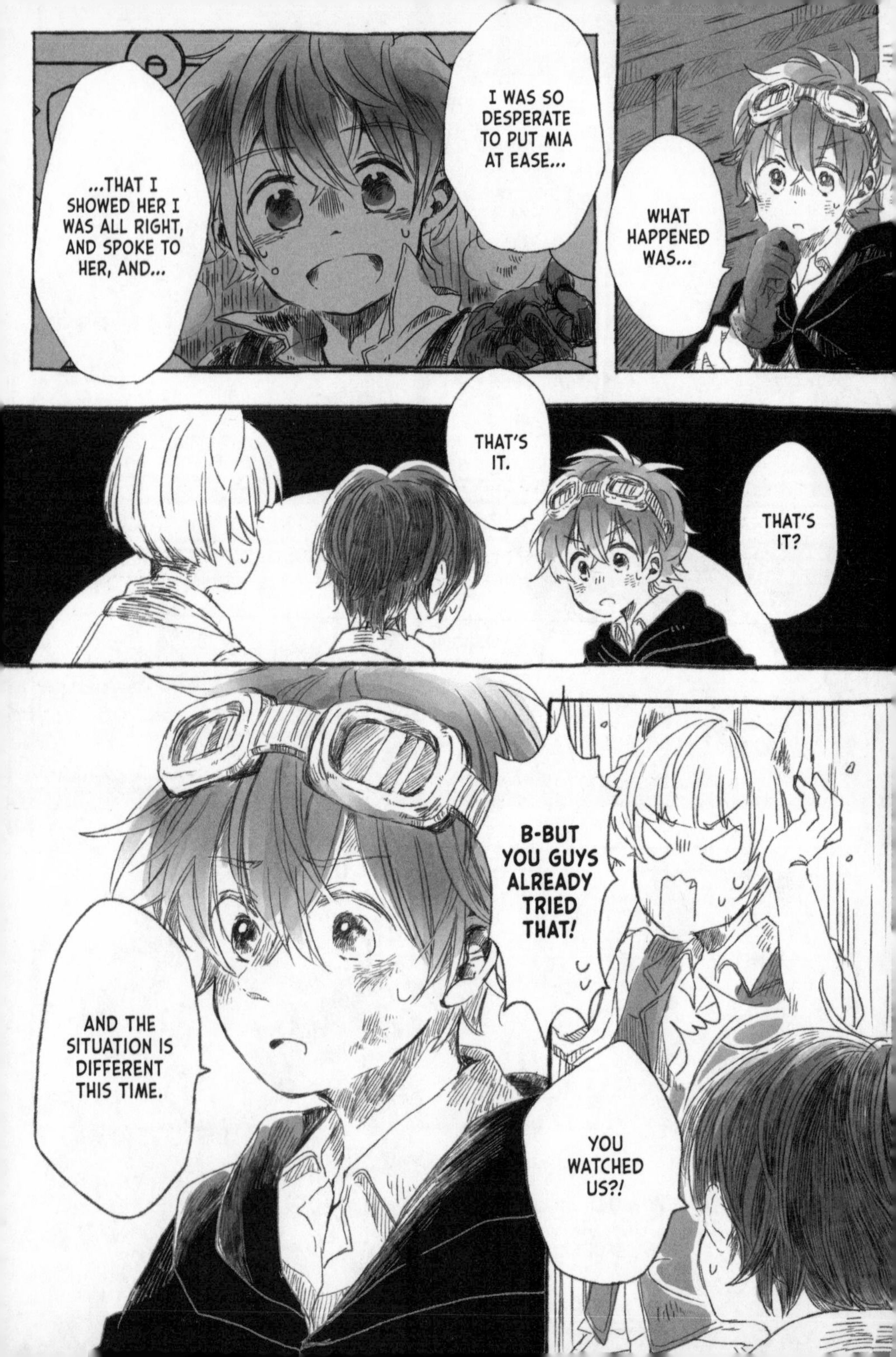
WHAT HAPPENED WAS...
I WAS SO DESPERATE TO PUT MIA AT EASE...
...THAT I SHOWED HER I WAS ALL RIGHT, AND SPOKE TO HER, AND...
THAT'S IT.
THAT'S IT?
B-BUT YOU GUYS ALREADY TRIED THAT!
AND THE SITUATION IS DIFFERENT THIS TIME.
YOU WATCHED US?!

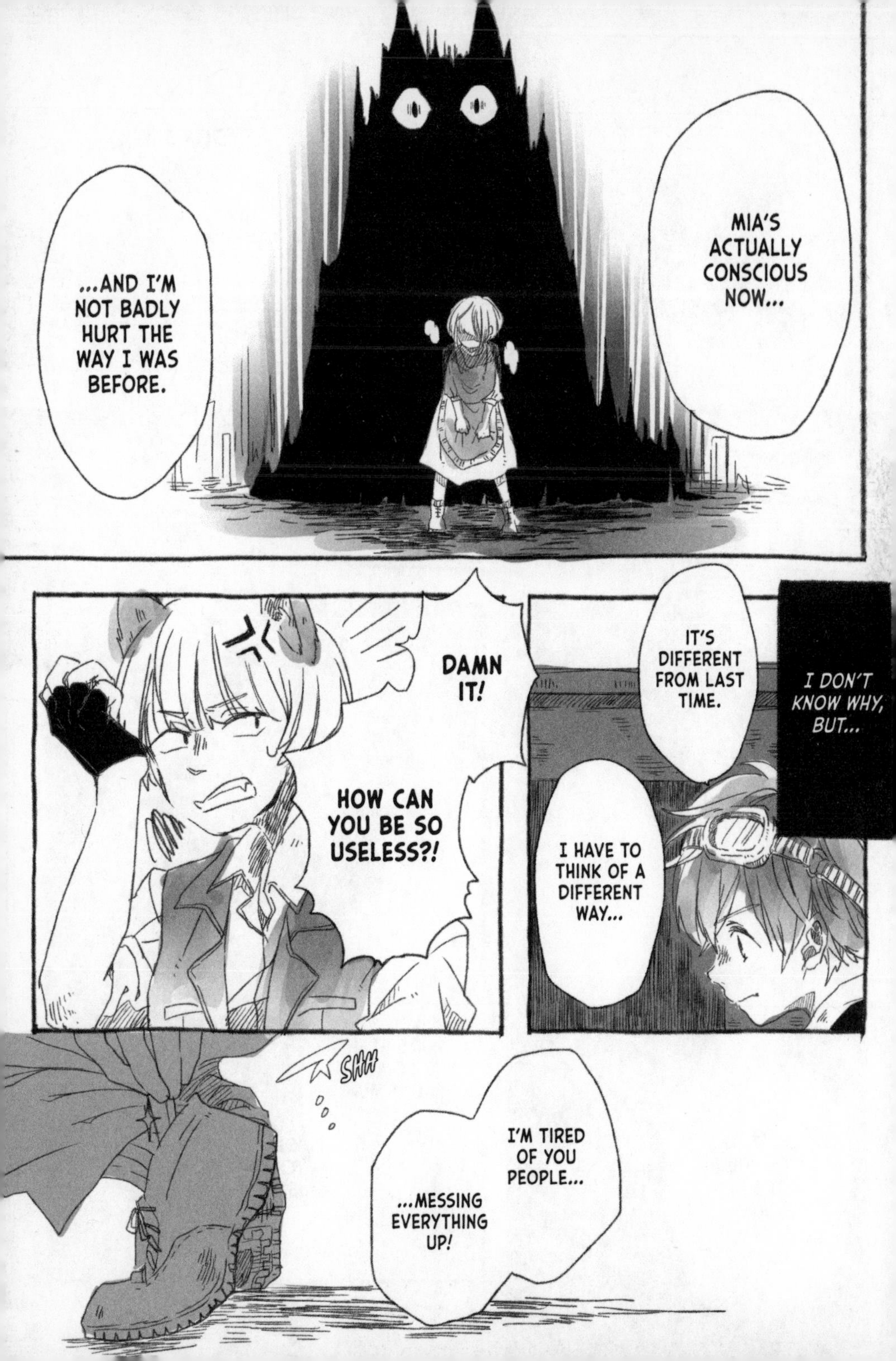
MIA'S ACTUALLY CONSCIOUS NOW...
...AND I'M NOT BADLY HURT THE WAY I WAS BEFORE.
I DON'T KNOW WHY, BUT...
IT'S DIFFERENT FROM LAST TIME.
I HAVE TO THINK OF A DIFFERENT WAY...
DAMN IT!
HOW CAN YOU BE SO USELESS?!
SHH
I'M TIRED OF YOU PEOPLE...
...MESSING EVERYTHING UP!

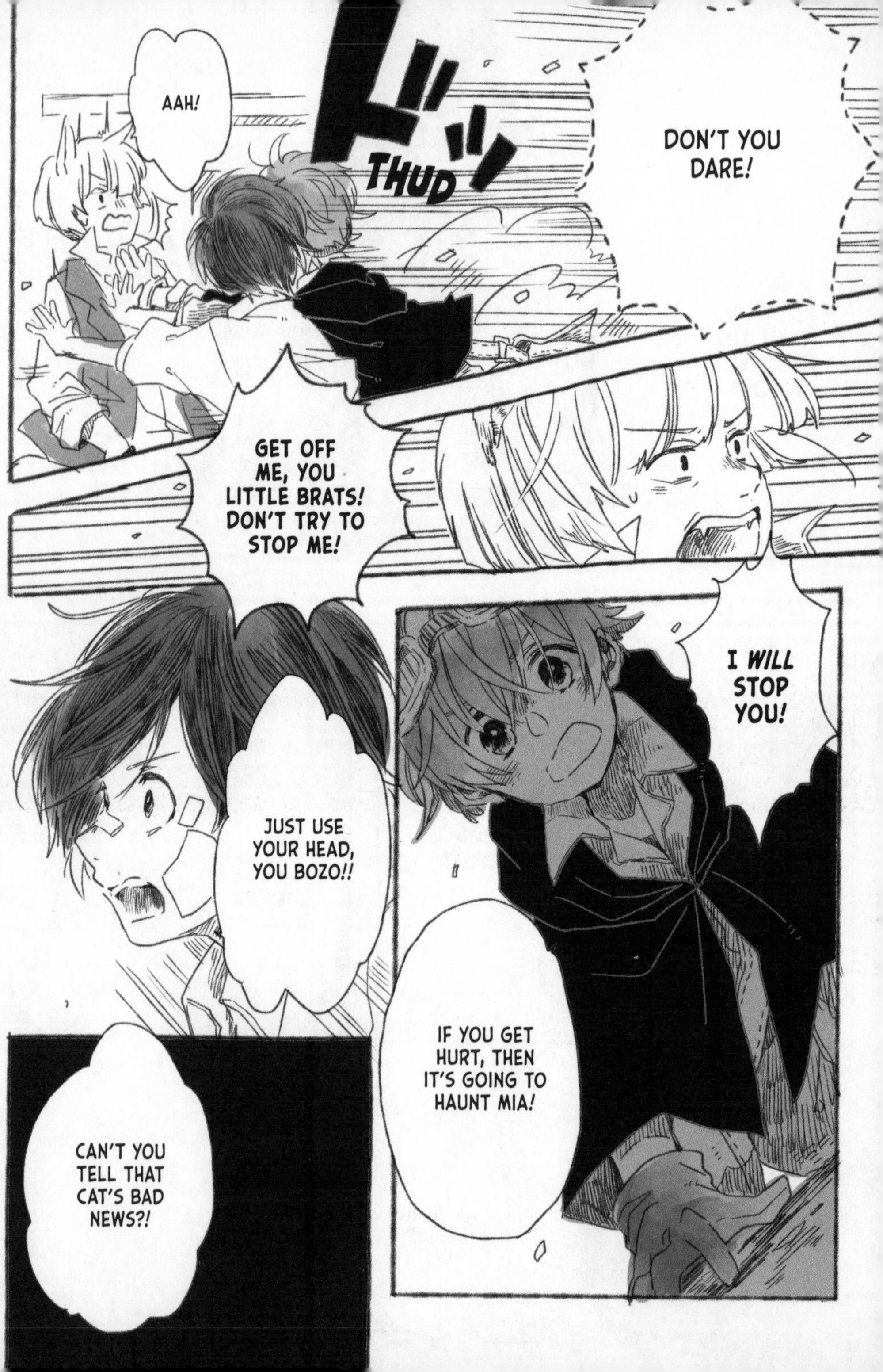
DON'T YOU DARE!
THUD
AAH!
GET OFF ME, YOU LITTLE BRATS! DON'T TRY TO STOP ME!
I *WILL* STOP YOU!
IF YOU GET HURT, THEN IT'S GOING TO HAUNT MIA!
JUST USE YOUR HEAD, YOU BOZO!!
CAN'T YOU TELL THAT CAT'S BAD NEWS?!

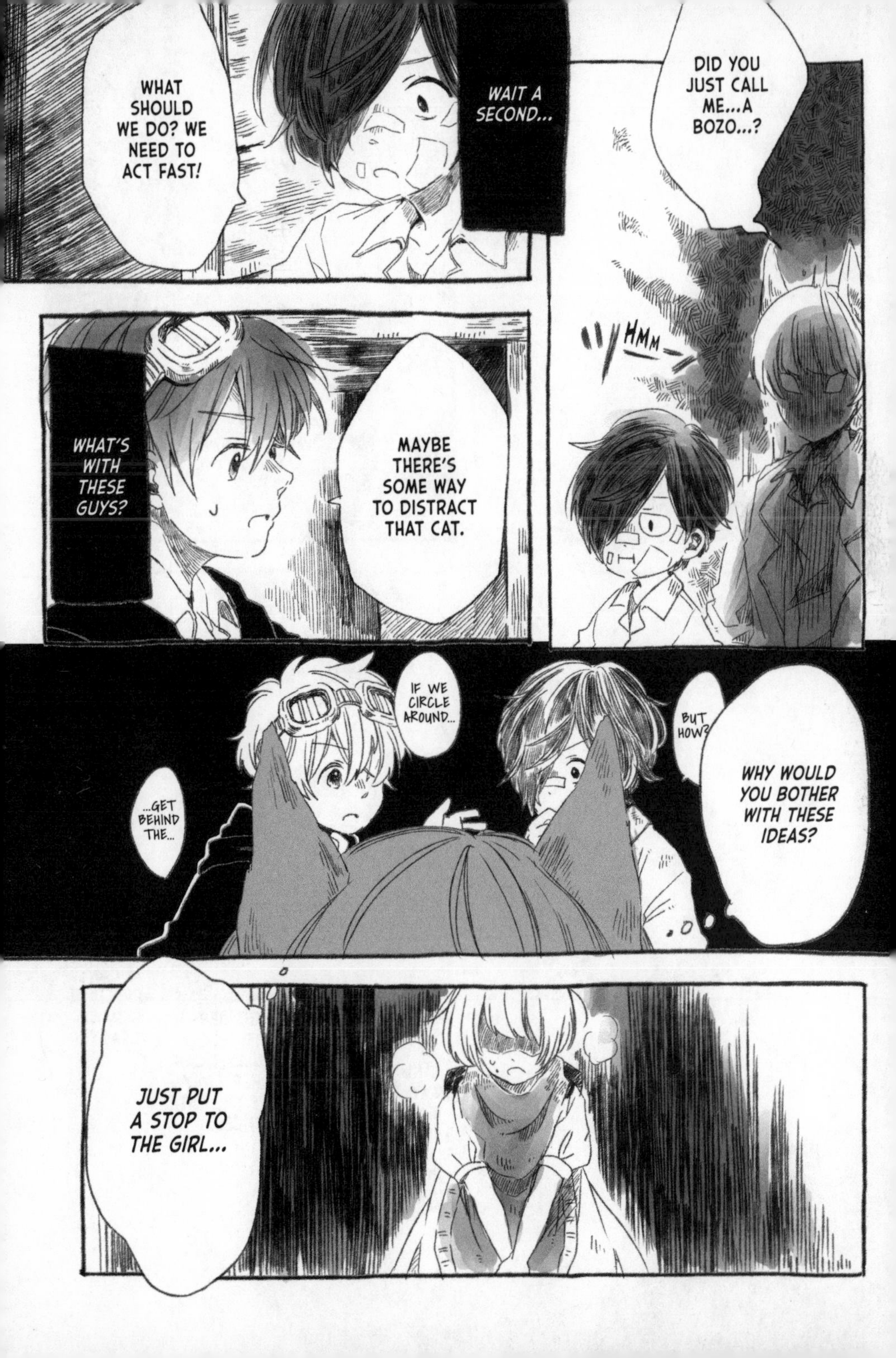
DID YOU JUST CALL ME...A BOZO...?
HMM
WAIT A SECOND...
WHAT SHOULD WE DO? WE NEED TO ACT FAST!
MAYBE THERE'S SOME WAY TO DISTRACT THAT CAT.
WHAT'S WITH THESE GUYS?
WHY WOULD YOU BOTHER WITH THESE IDEAS?
BUT HOW?
IF WE CIRCLE AROUND...
...GET BEHIND THE...
JUST PUT A STOP TO THE GIRL...

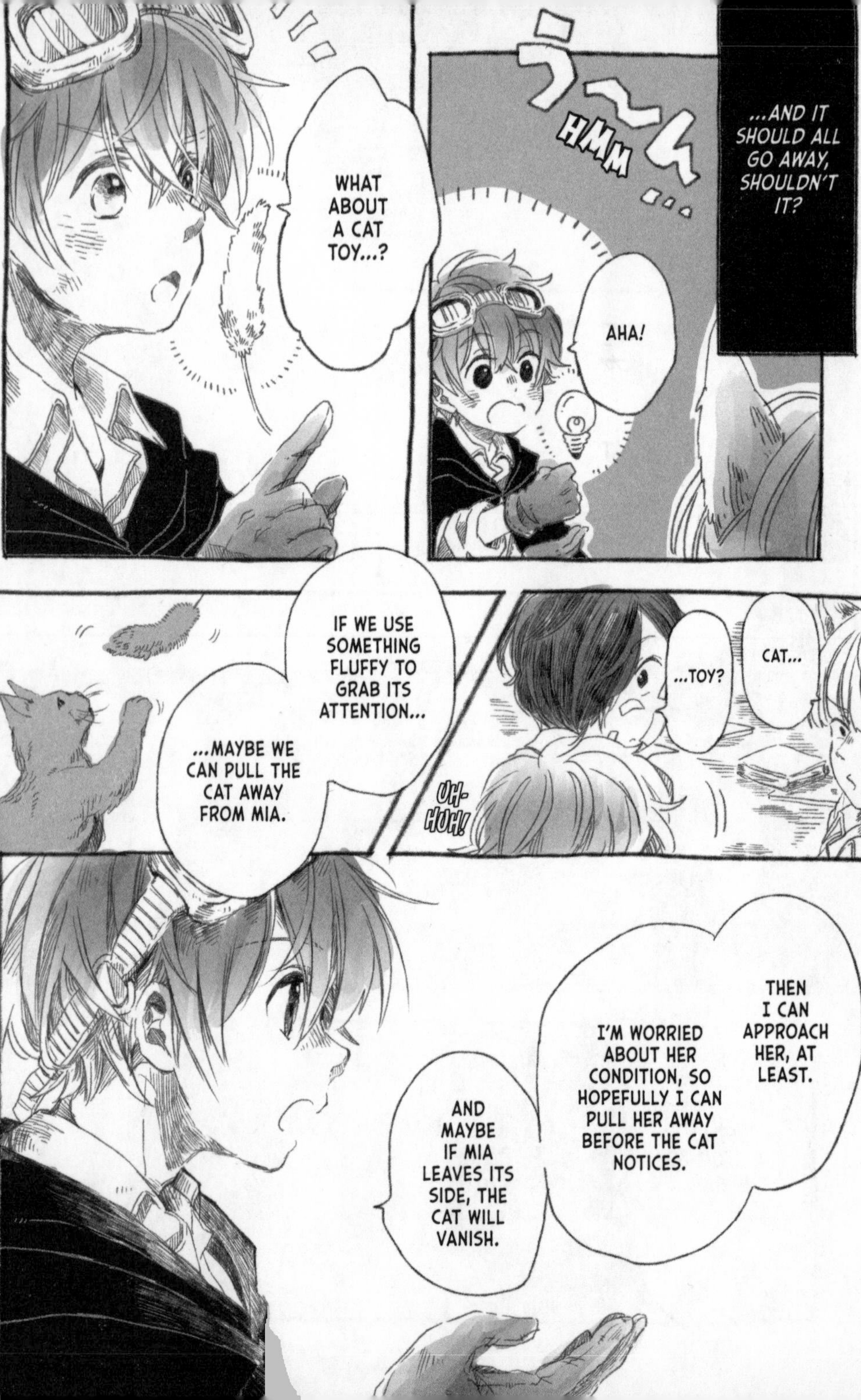
...AND IT SHOULD ALL GO AWAY, SHOULDN'T IT?
うーん
HMM
AHA!
WHAT ABOUT A CAT TOY...?
CAT...
...TOY?
UH-HUH!
IF WE USE SOMETHING FLUFFY TO GRAB ITS ATTENTION...
...MAYBE WE CAN PULL THE CAT AWAY FROM MIA.
THEN I CAN APPROACH HER, AT LEAST.
I'M WORRIED ABOUT HER CONDITION, SO HOPEFULLY I CAN PULL HER AWAY BEFORE THE CAT NOTICES.
AND MAYBE IF MIA LEAVES ITS SIDE, THE CAT WILL VANISH.

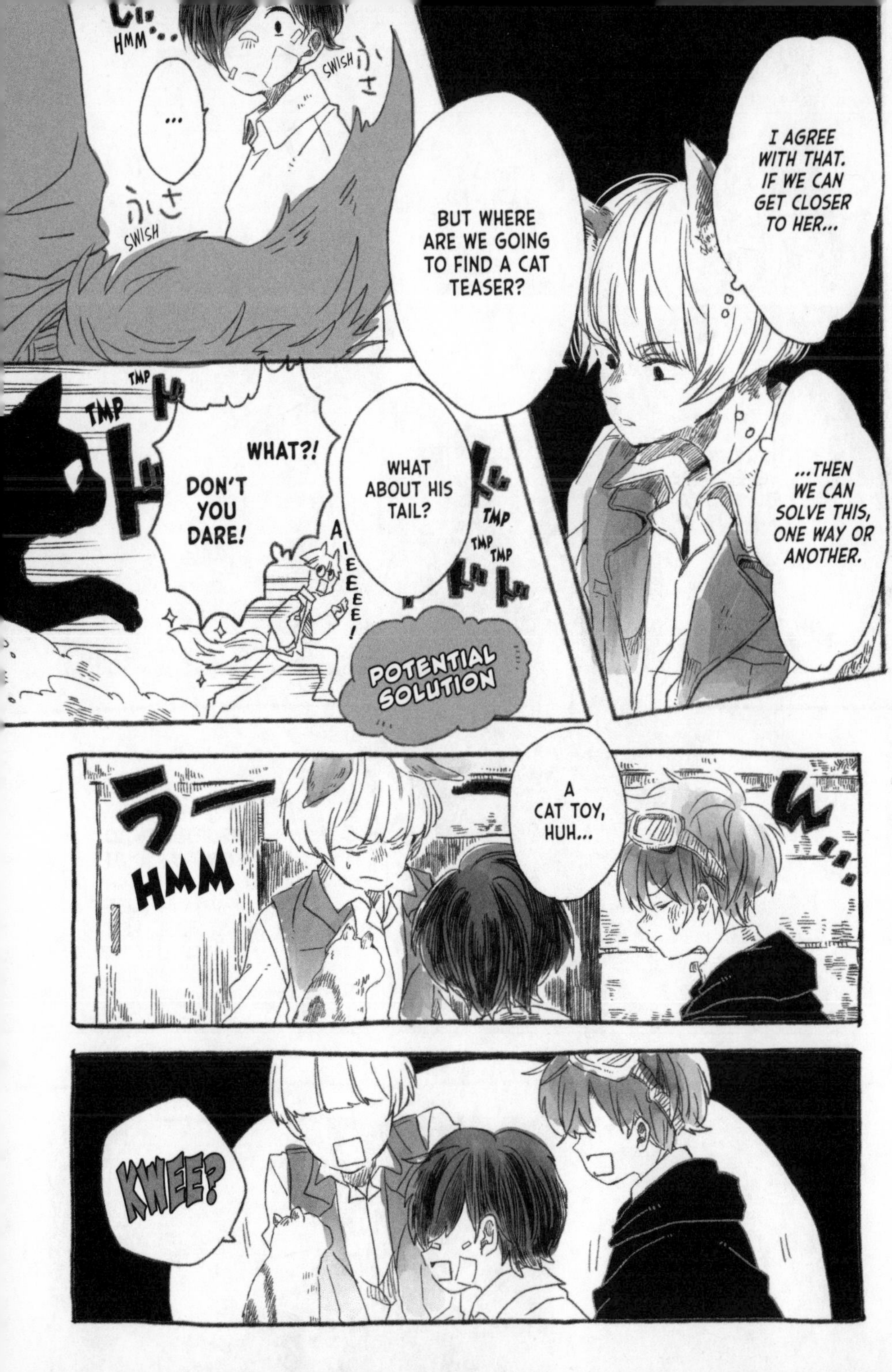
BUT WHERE ARE WE GOING TO FIND A CAT TEASER?
I AGREE WITH THAT. IF WE CAN GET CLOSER TO HER...
...THEN WE CAN SOLVE THIS, ONE WAY OR ANOTHER.
HMM...
...
SWISH
SWISH
WHAT ABOUT HIS TAIL?
TMP TMP TMP
WHAT?!
DON'T YOU DARE!
TMP TMP
AIEEEEE!
POTENTIAL SOLUTION
A CAT TOY, HUH...
HMM
KWEE?

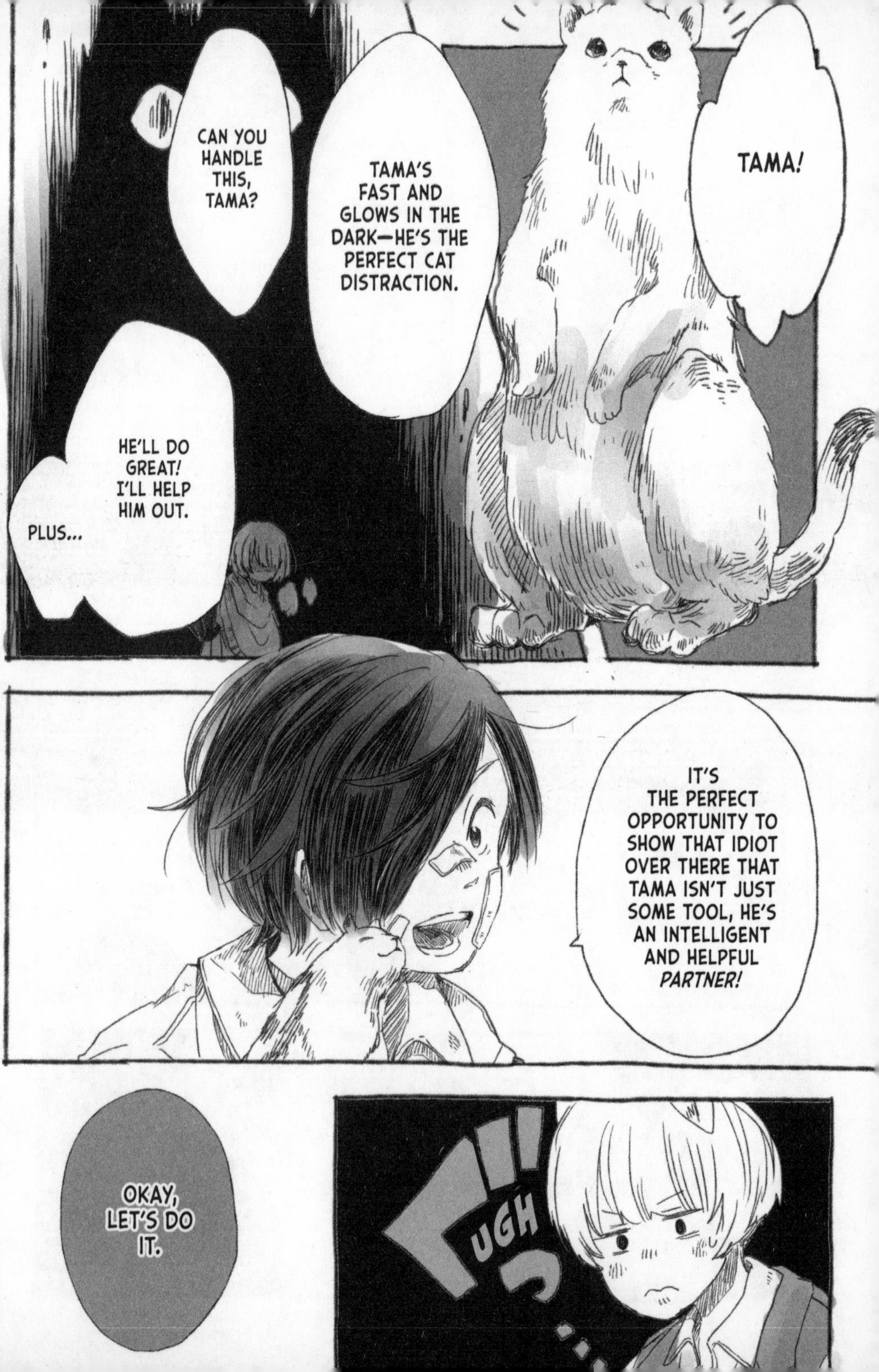
TAMA!
TAMA'S FAST AND GLOWS IN THE DARK—HE'S THE PERFECT CAT DISTRACTION.
CAN YOU HANDLE THIS, TAMA?
HE'LL DO GREAT! I'LL HELP HIM OUT.
PLUS...
IT'S THE PERFECT OPPORTUNITY TO SHOW THAT IDIOT OVER THERE THAT TAMA ISN'T JUST SOME TOOL, HE'S AN INTELLIGENT AND HELPFUL *PARTNER!*
UGH
OKAY, LET'S DO IT.

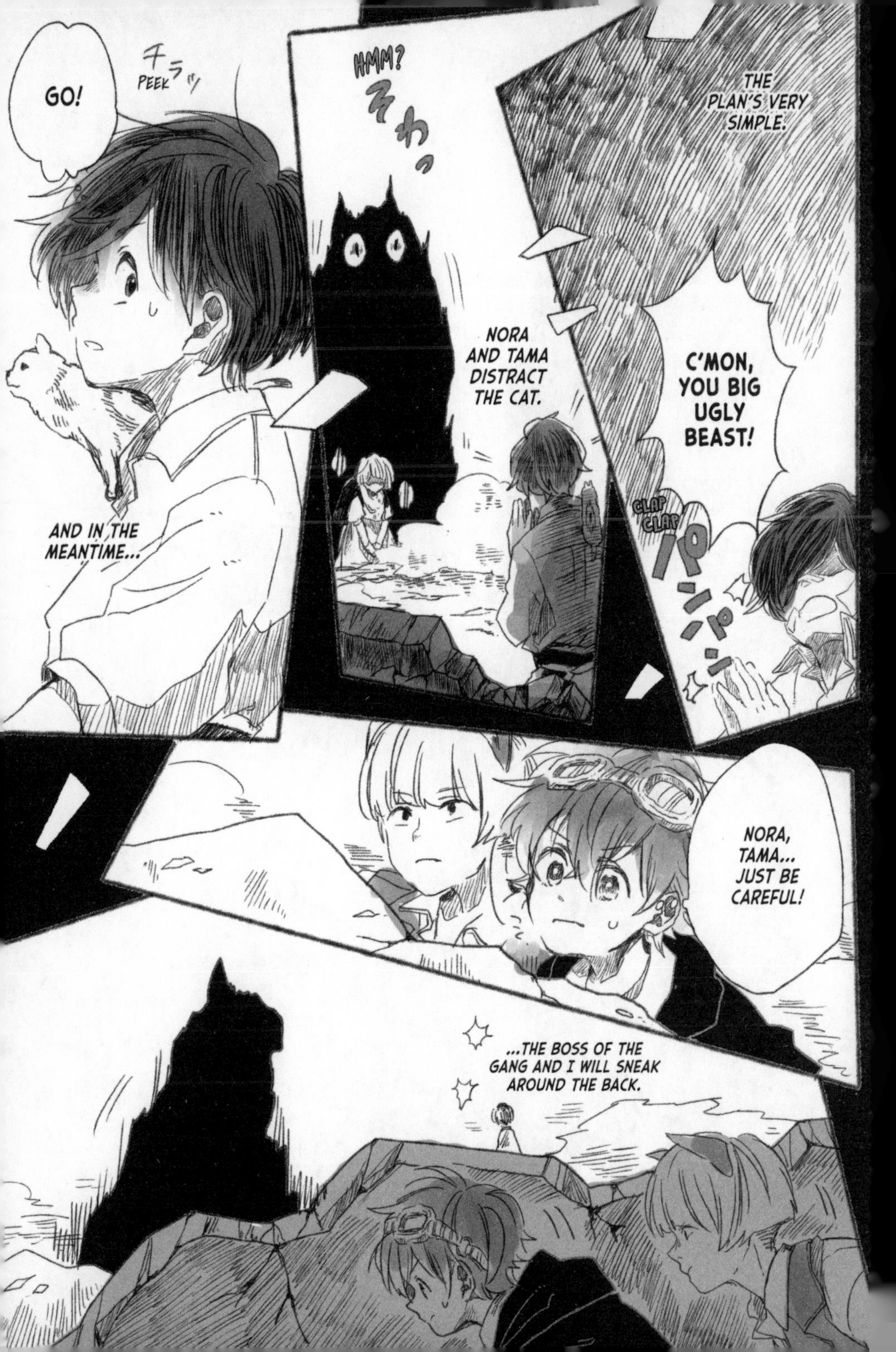
THE PLAN'S VERY SIMPLE.
C'MON, YOU BIG UGLY BEAST!
CLAP CLAP
パンパン
HMM?
ぞわっ
NORA AND TAMA DISTRACT THE CAT.
GO!
PEEK
チラッ
AND IN THE MEANTIME...
NORA, TAMA... JUST BE CAREFUL!
...THE BOSS OF THE GANG AND I WILL SNEAK AROUND THE BACK.

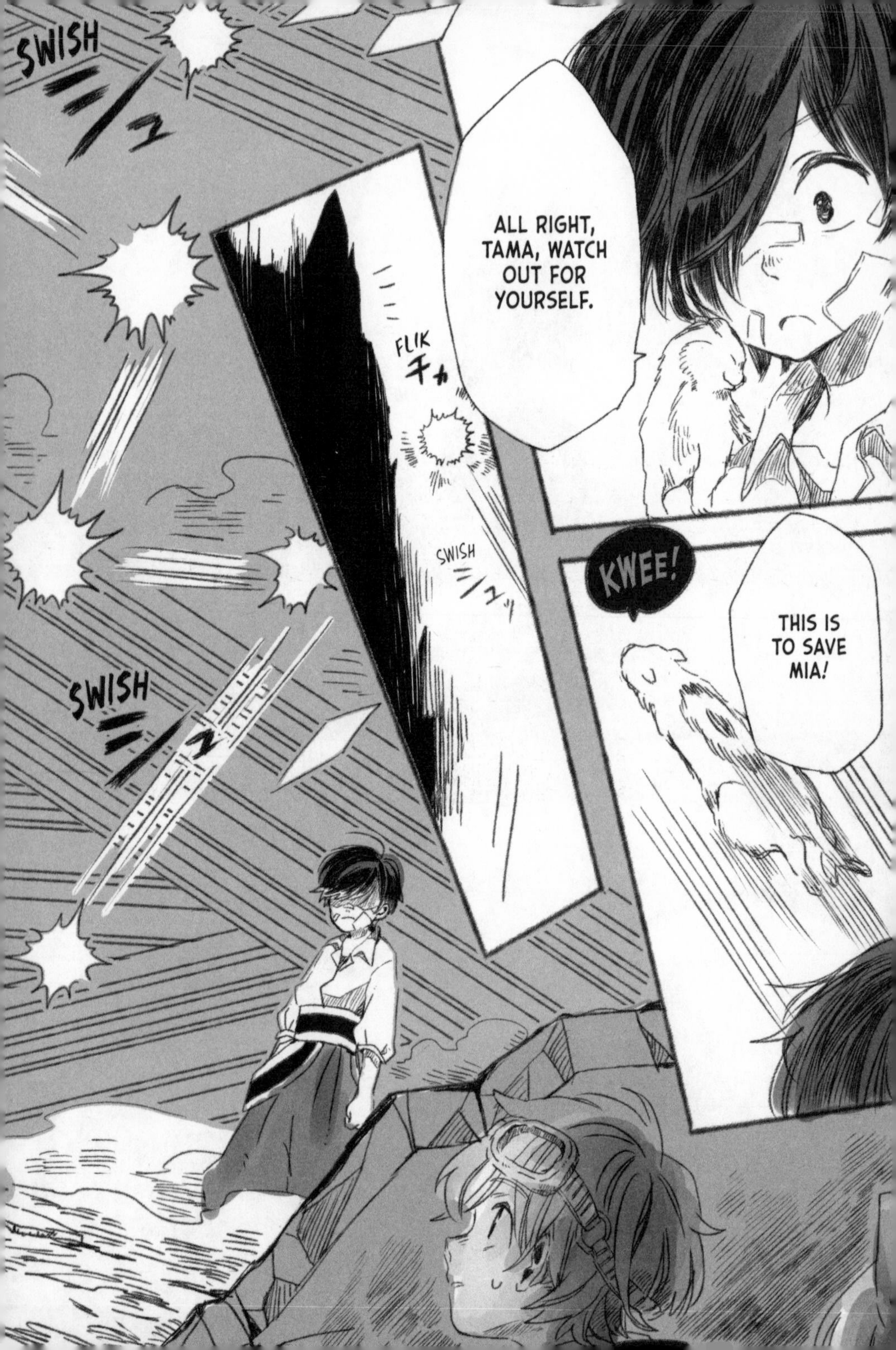
ALL RIGHT, TAMA, WATCH OUT FOR YOURSELF.
KWEE!
THIS IS TO SAVE MIA!
FLIK
SWISH
SWISH
SWISH

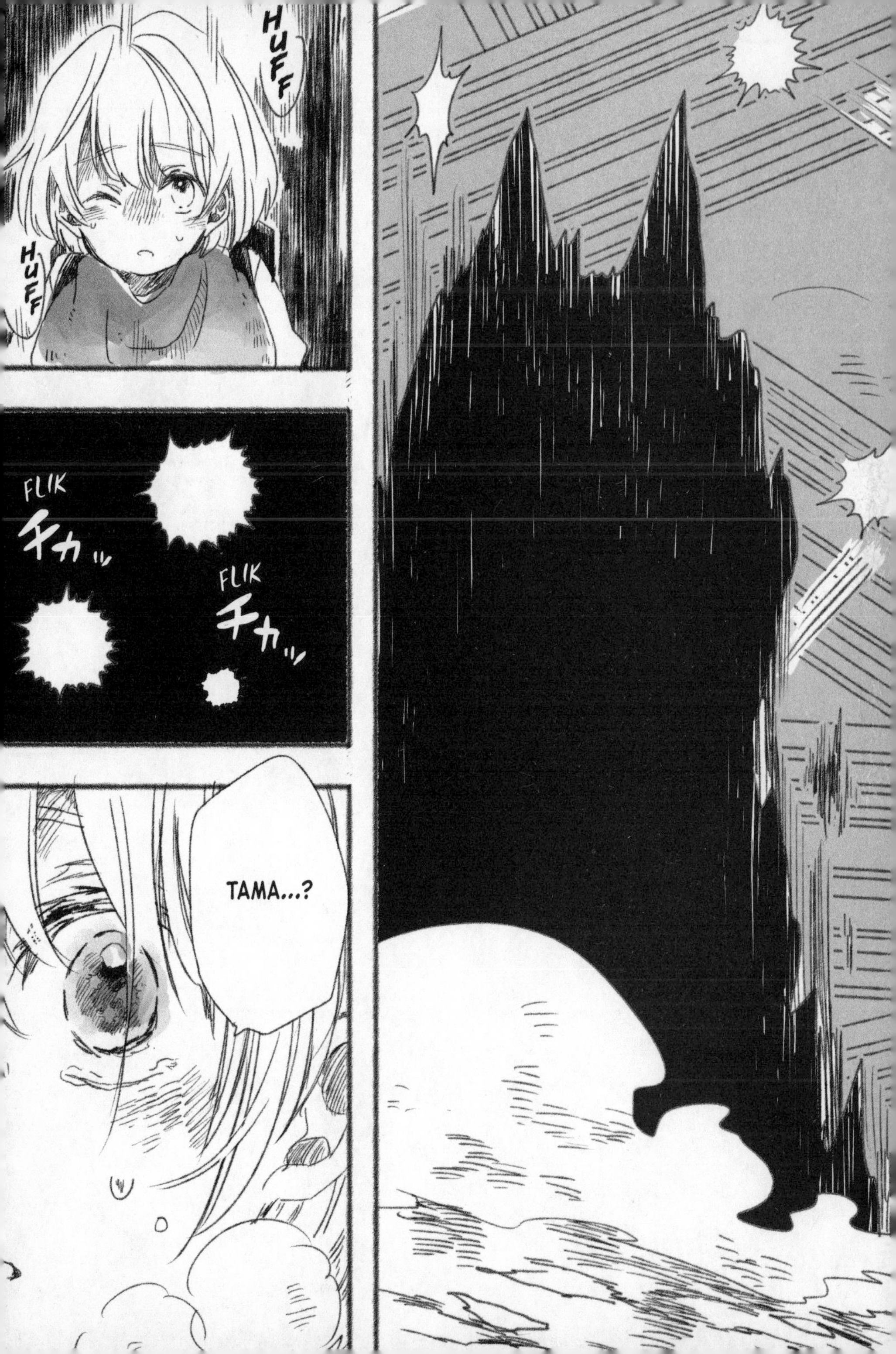
HUFF
HUFF
FLIK
チカッ
FLIK
チカッ
TAMA...?

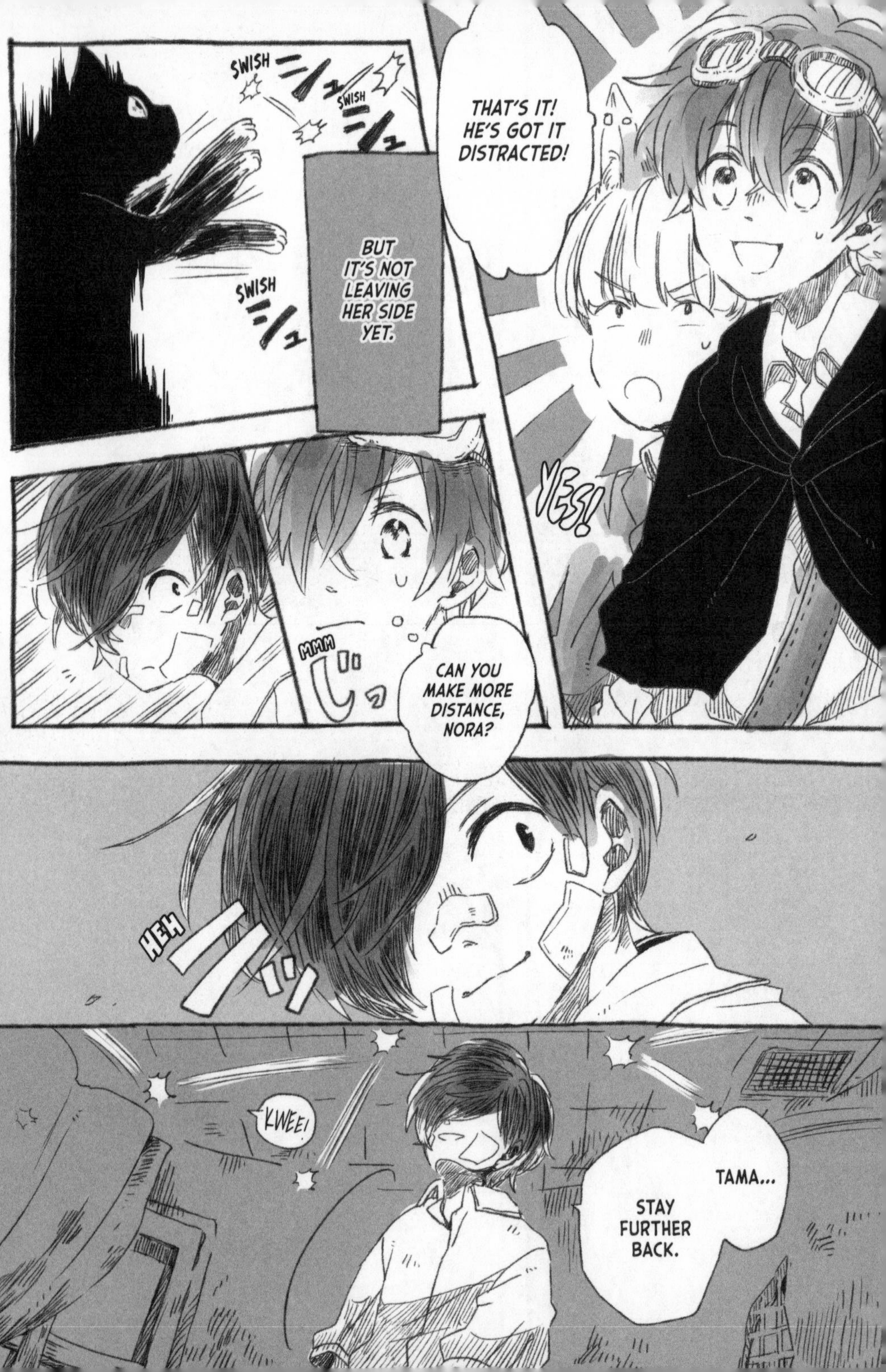
THAT'S IT! HE'S GOT IT DISTRACTED!
YES!
SWISH
SWISH
BUT IT'S NOT LEAVING HER SIDE YET.
SWISH
MMM
CAN YOU MAKE MORE DISTANCE, NORA?
HEH
TAMA...
STAY FURTHER BACK.
KWEE!

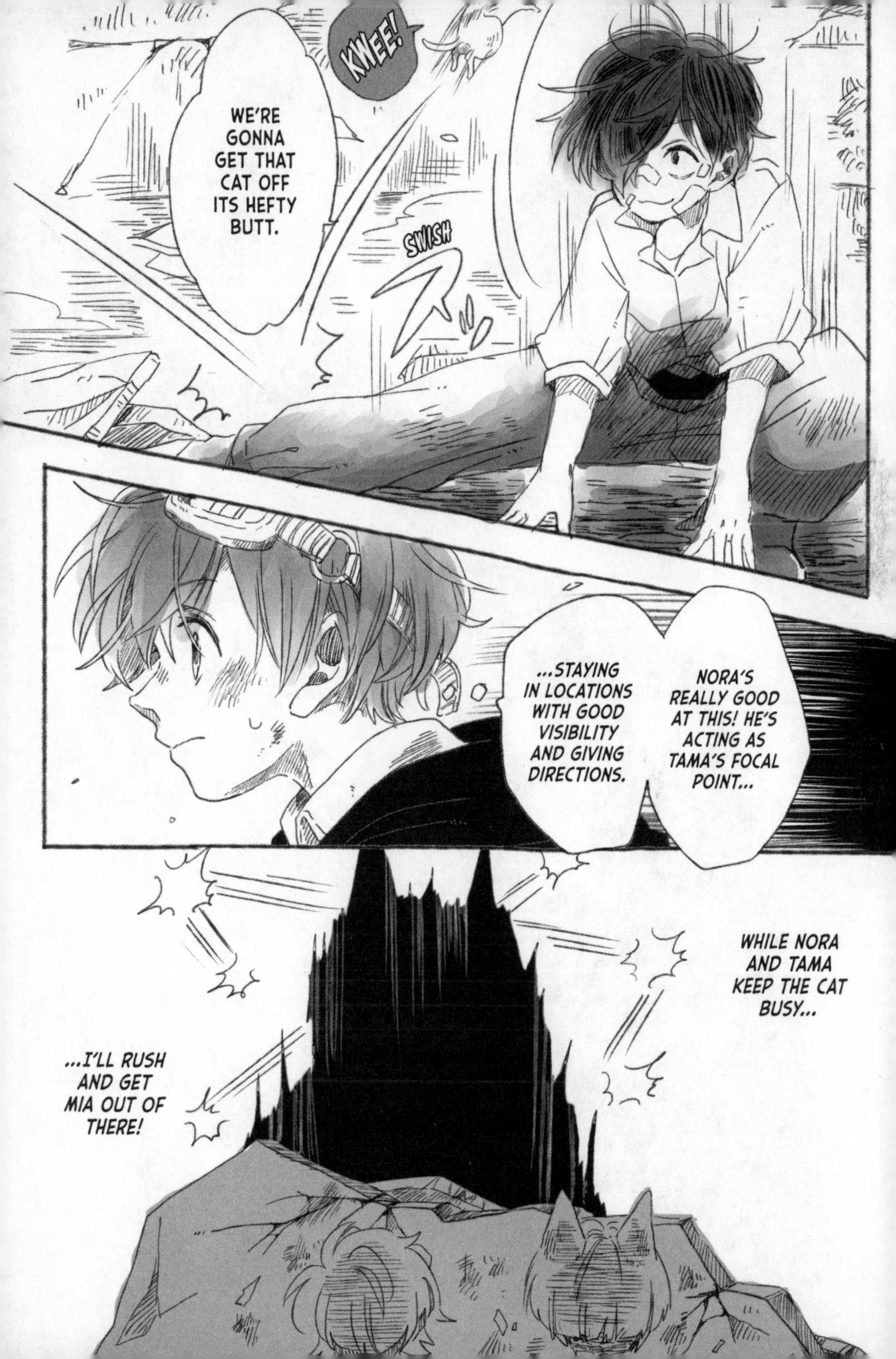
KWEE!
WE'RE GONNA GET THAT CAT OFF ITS HEFTY BUTT.
SWISH
NORA'S REALLY GOOD AT THIS! HE'S ACTING AS TAMA'S FOCAL POINT...
...STAYING IN LOCATIONS WITH GOOD VISIBILITY AND GIVING DIRECTIONS.
WHILE NORA AND TAMA KEEP THE CAT BUSY...
...I'LL RUSH AND GET MIA OUT OF THERE!

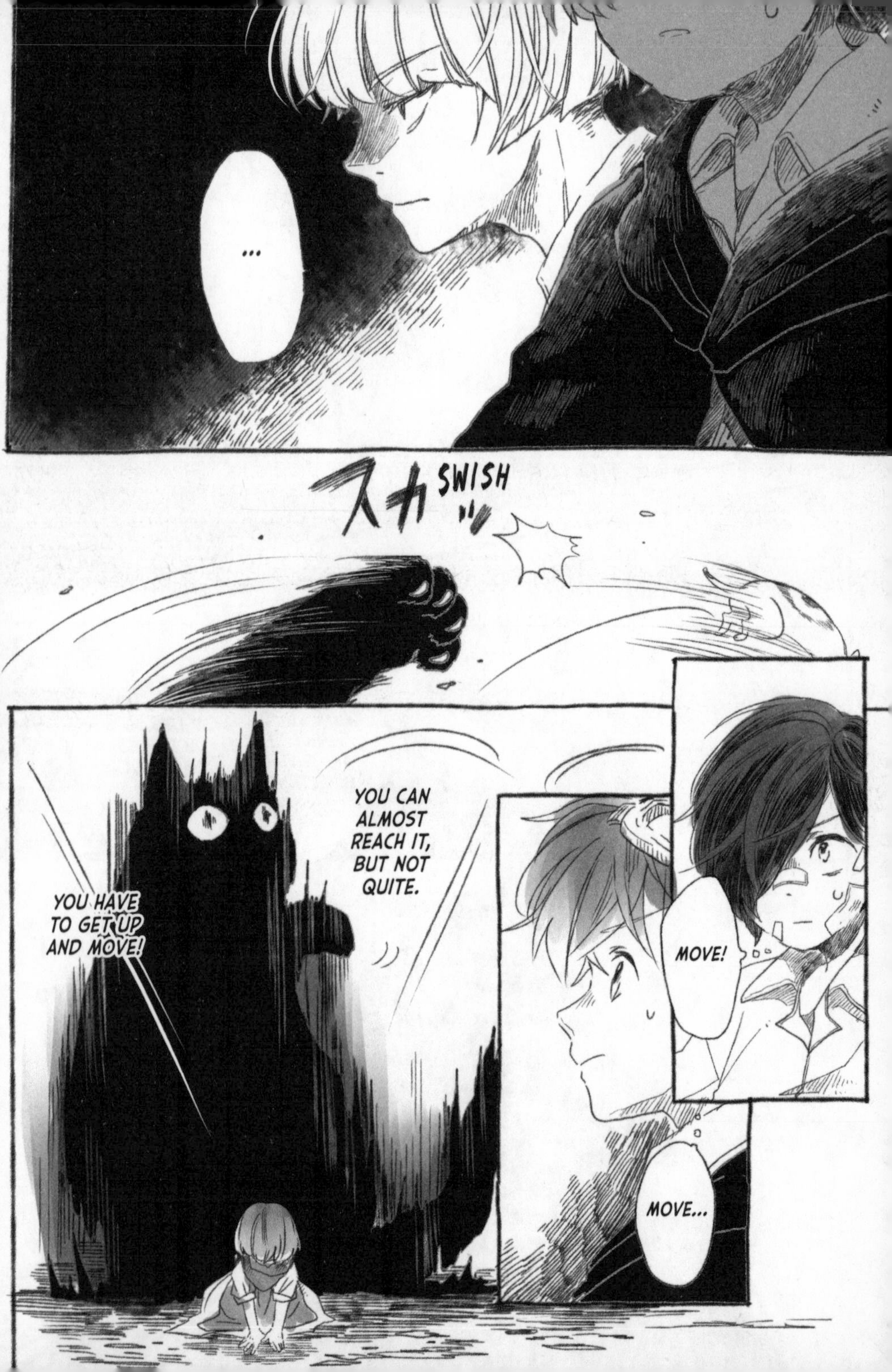
...
スカッ
SWISH
MOVE!
MOVE...
YOU CAN ALMOST REACH IT, BUT NOT QUITE.
YOU HAVE TO GET UP AND MOVE!

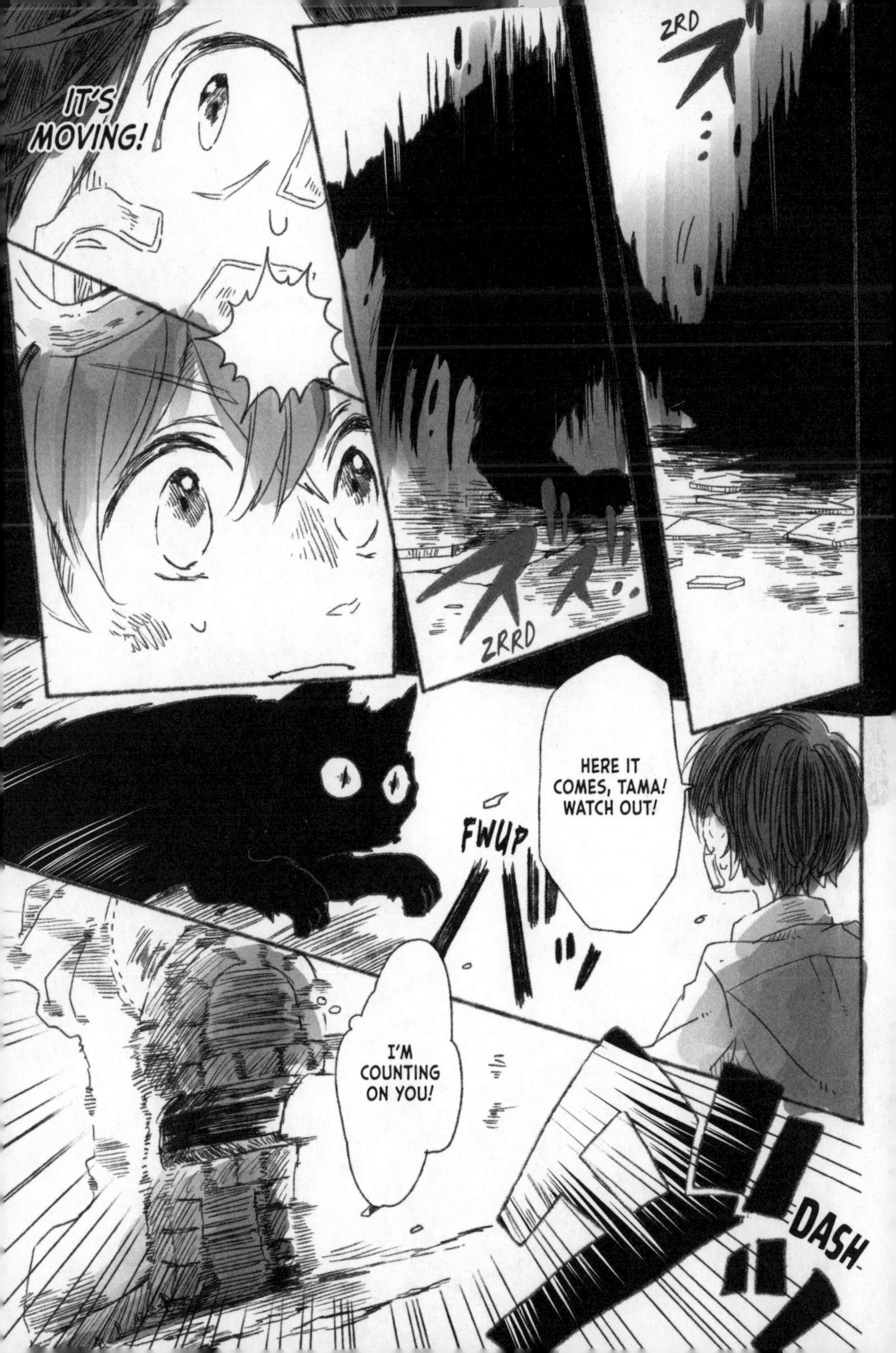
ZRD
ZRRD
IT'S MOVING!
HERE IT COMES, TAMA! WATCH OUT!
FWUP
I'M COUNTING ON YOU!
DASH

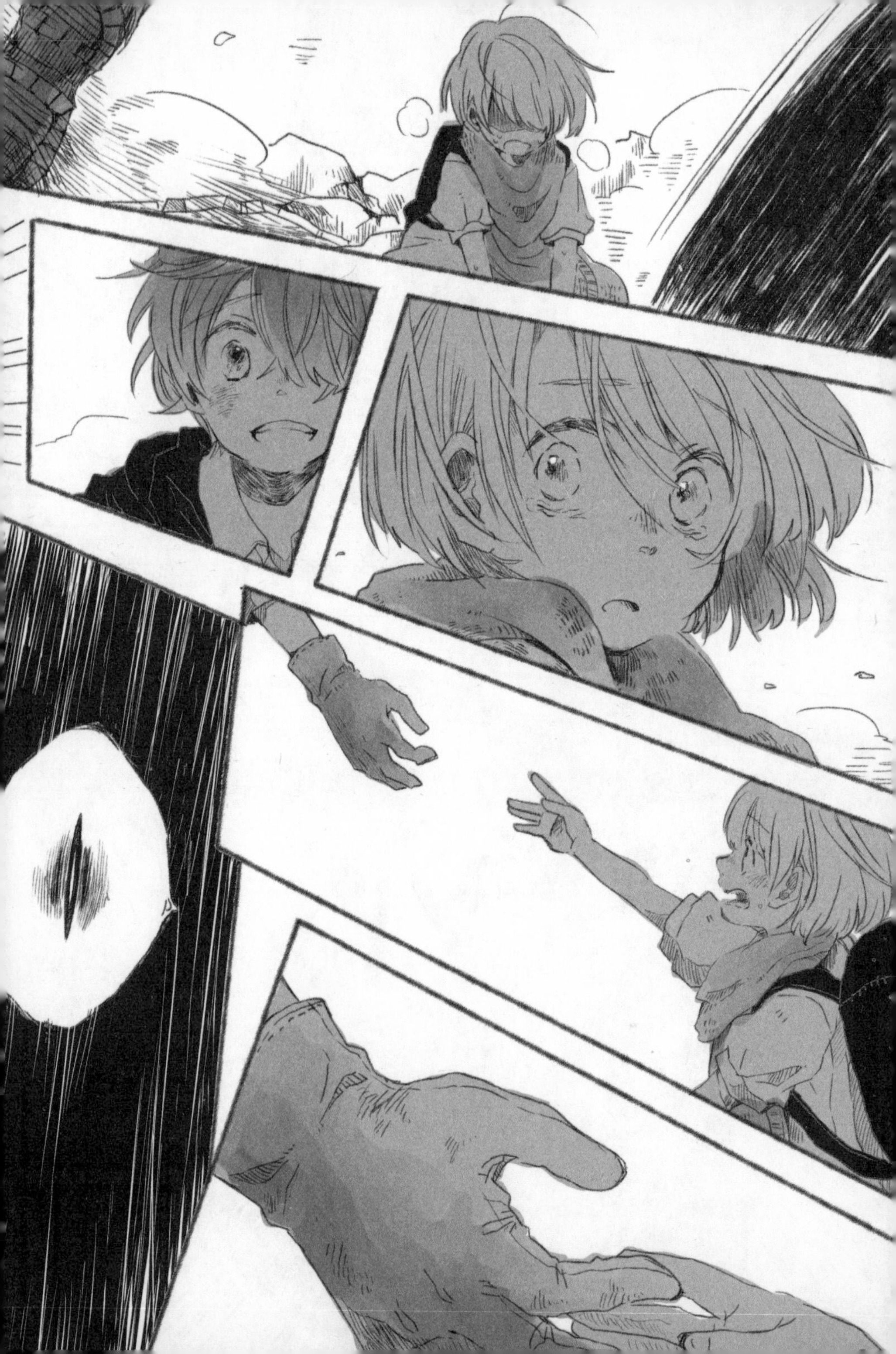

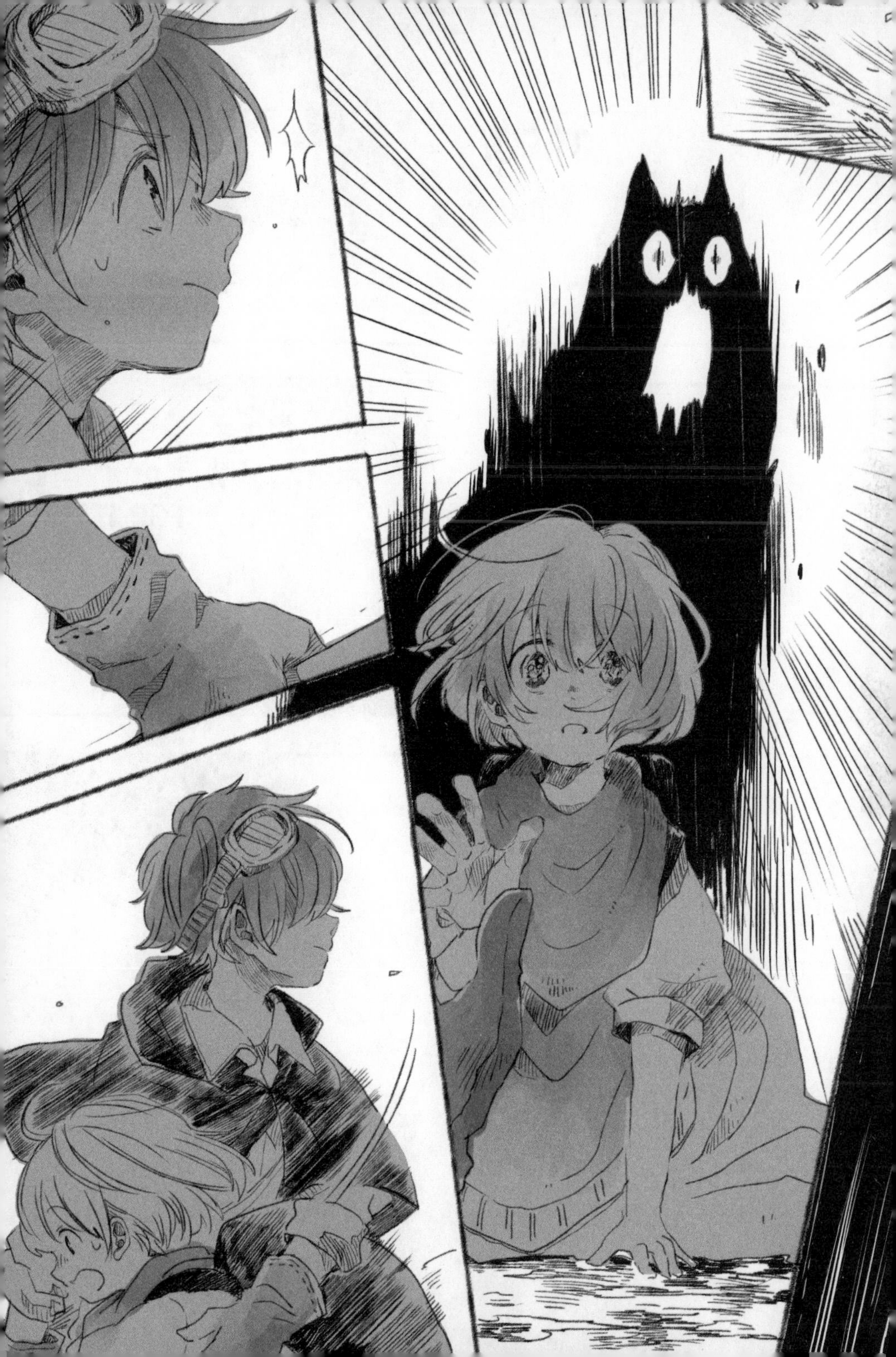

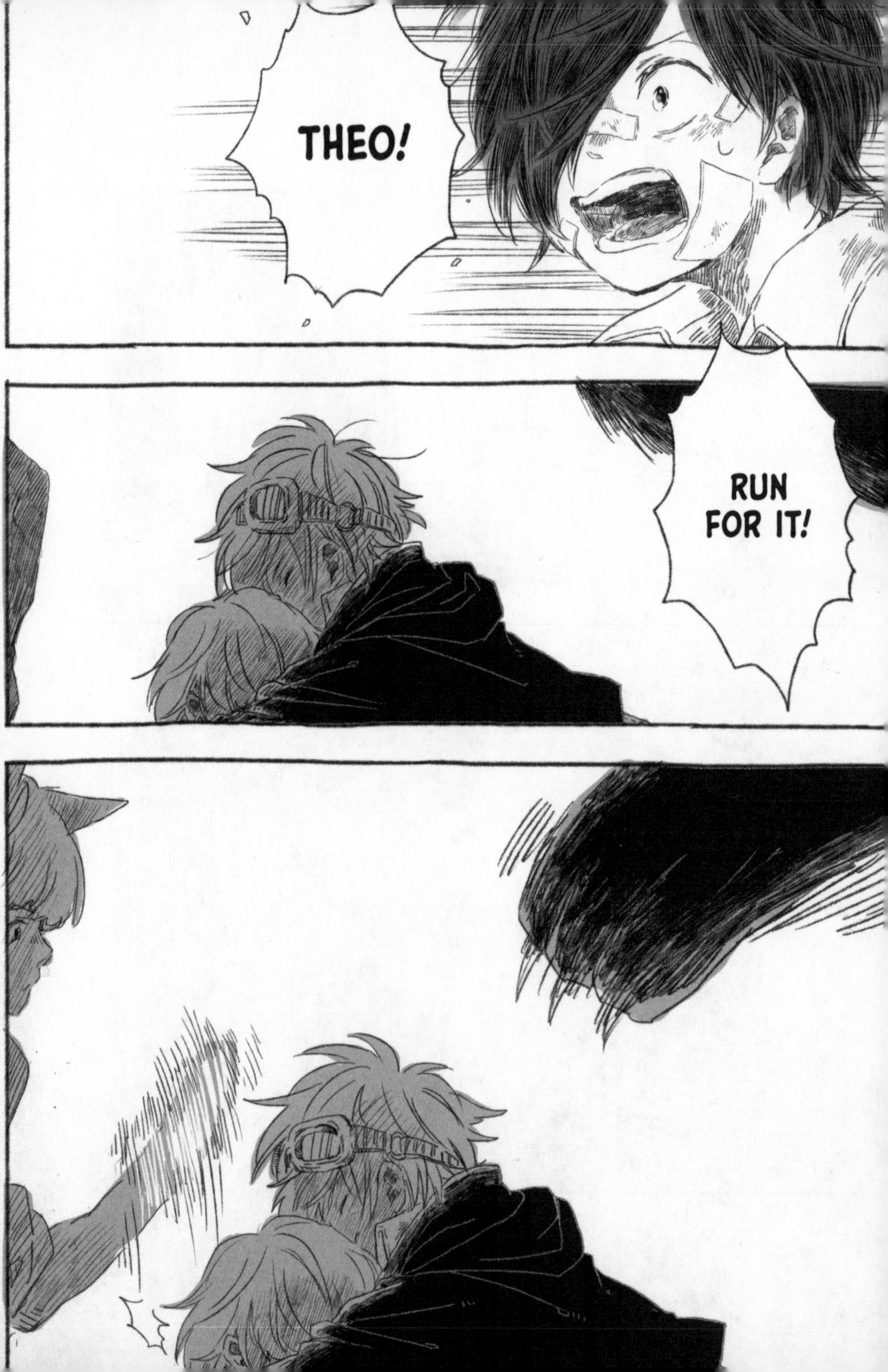
THEO!
RUN FOR IT!

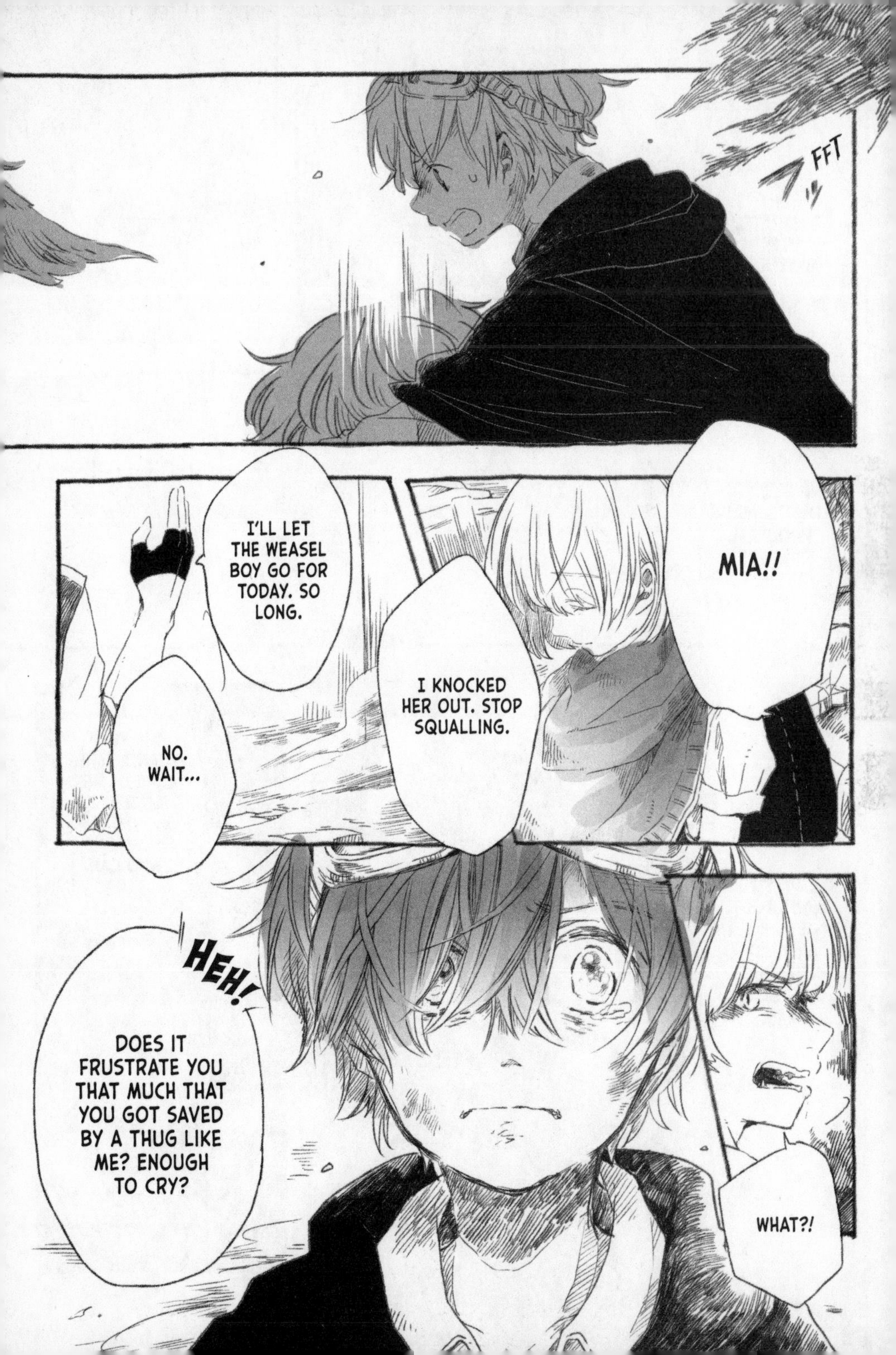
FFT
MIA!!
I KNOCKED HER OUT. STOP SQUALLING.
I'LL LET THE WEASEL BOY GO FOR TODAY. SO LONG.
NO. WAIT...
WHAT?!
HEH!
DOES IT FRUSTRATE YOU THAT MUCH THAT YOU GOT SAVED BY A THUG LIKE ME? ENOUGH TO CRY?

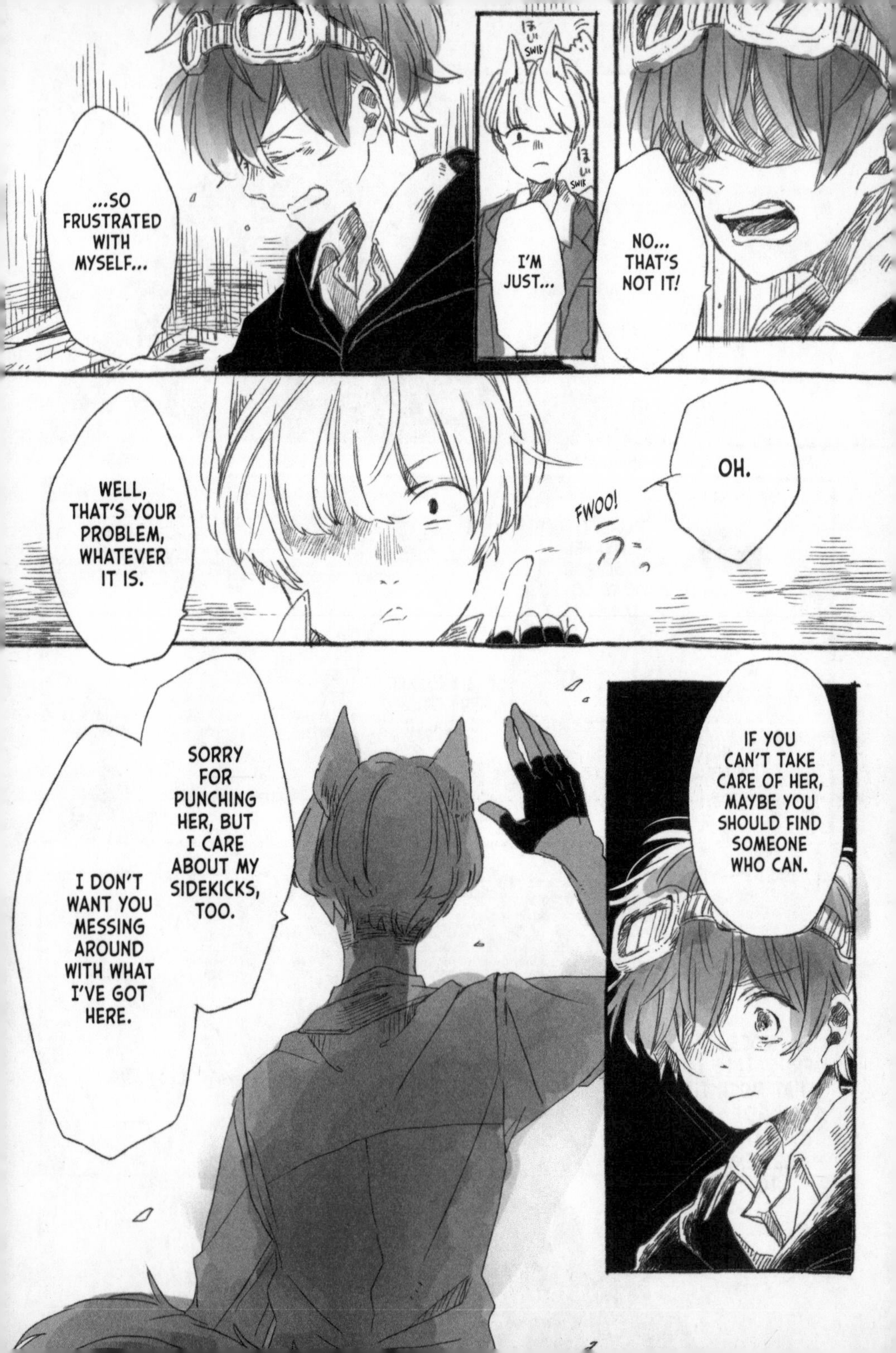
NO... THAT'S NOT IT!
SWIK
SWIK
I'M JUST...
...SO FRUSTRATED WITH MYSELF...
OH.
FWOO!
WELL, THAT'S YOUR PROBLEM, WHATEVER IT IS.
IF YOU CAN'T TAKE CARE OF HER, MAYBE YOU SHOULD FIND SOMEONE WHO CAN.
SORRY FOR PUNCHING HER, BUT I CARE ABOUT MY SIDEKICKS, TOO.
I DON'T WANT YOU MESSING AROUND WITH WHAT I'VE GOT HERE.

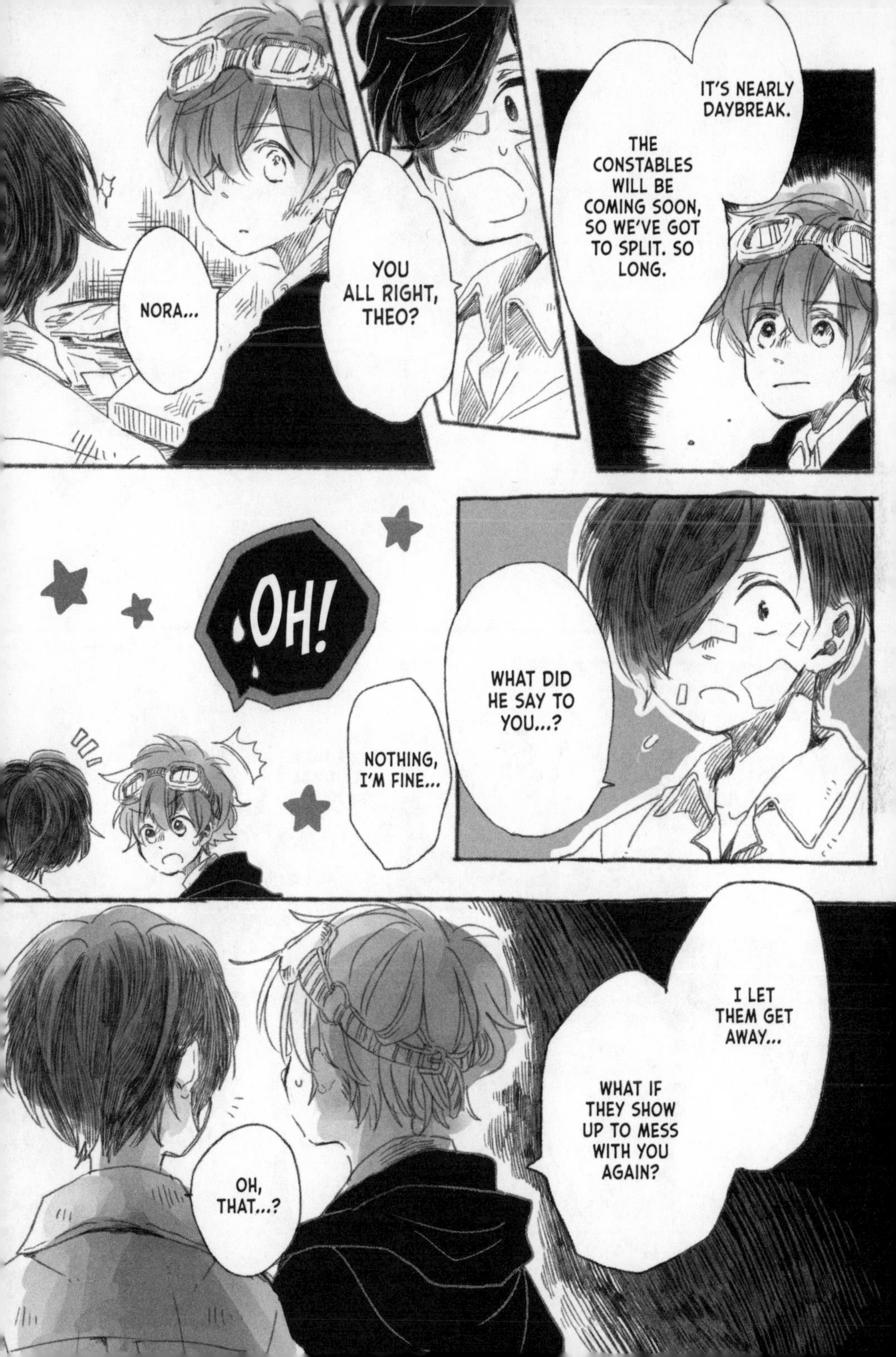
IT'S NEARLY DAYBREAK.
THE CONSTABLES WILL BE COMING SOON, SO WE'VE GOT TO SPLIT. SO LONG.
YOU ALL RIGHT, THEO?
NORA...
WHAT DID HE SAY TO YOU...?
OH!
NOTHING, I'M FINE...
I LET THEM GET AWAY...
WHAT IF THEY SHOW UP TO MESS WITH YOU AGAIN?
OH, THAT...?

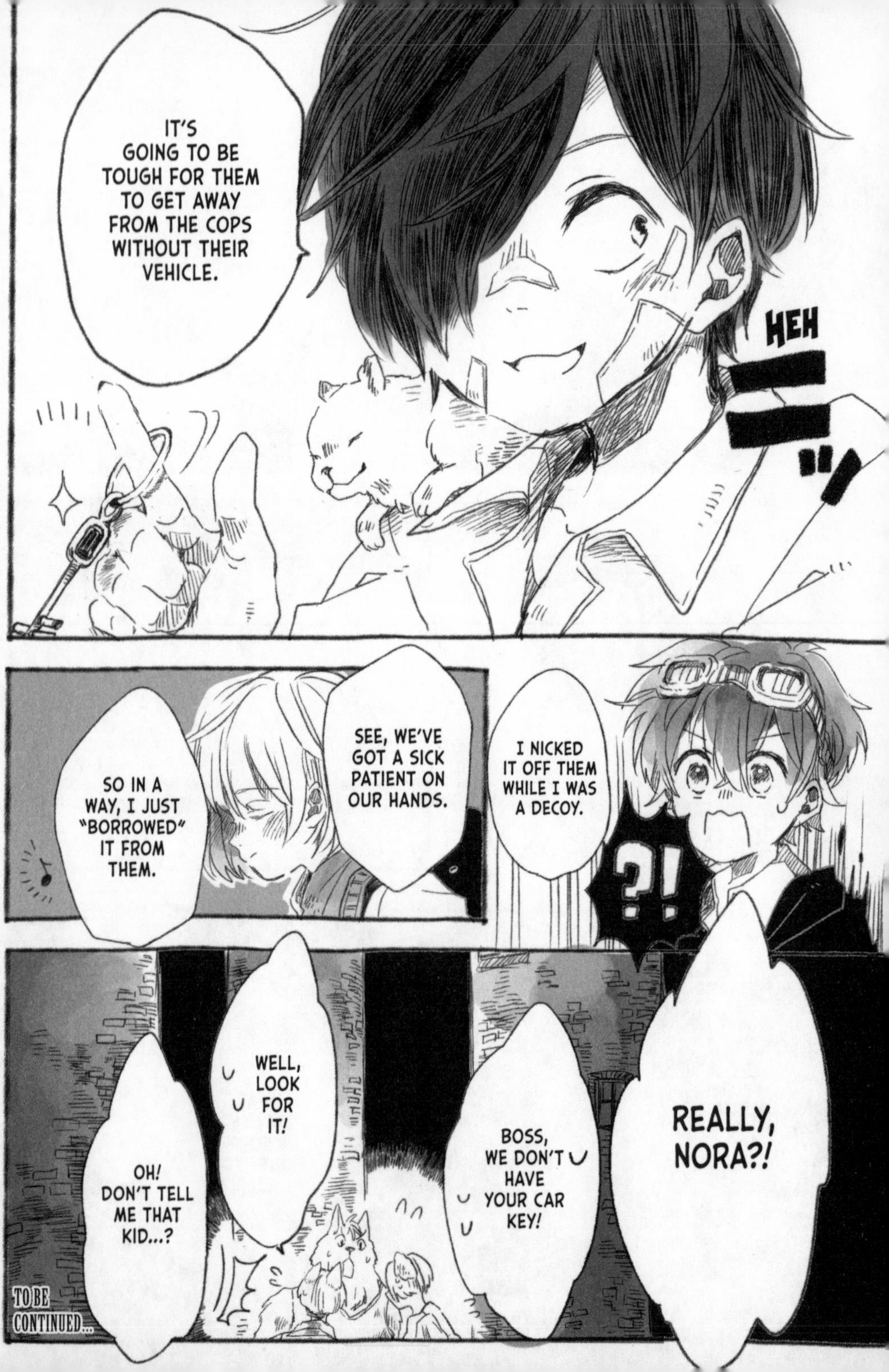
HEH
IT'S GOING TO BE TOUGH FOR THEM TO GET AWAY FROM THE COPS WITHOUT THEIR VEHICLE.
?!
I NICKED IT OFF THEM WHILE I WAS A DECOY.
SEE, WE'VE GOT A SICK PATIENT ON OUR HANDS.
SO IN A WAY, I JUST "BORROWED" IT FROM THEM.
REALLY, NORA?!
BOSS, WE DON'T HAVE YOUR CAR KEY!
WELL, LOOK FOR IT!
OH! DON'T TELL ME THAT KID...?
TO BE CONTINUED...

Beyond *the* Clouds

The Girl Who Fell From the Sky

Beyond the Clouds started as a self-published series created by Nicke known as *The Yellow Town*. Here are the first two chapters as originally presented!

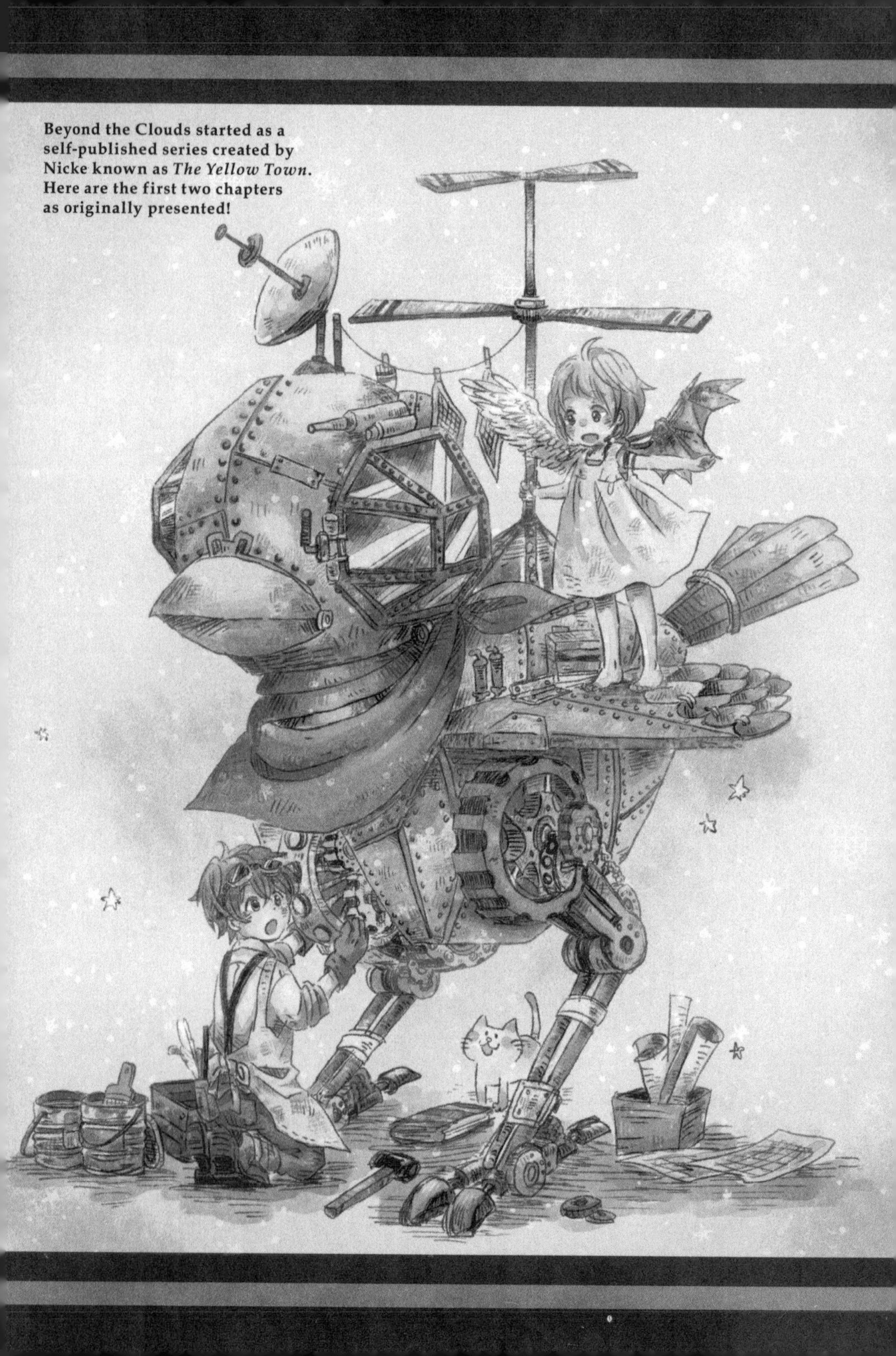

Here is my very first original manga...

I love reading about adventures and fantastical worlds, but in real life, there's no escape from the daily grind. So I'm happy for Theo that he gets to pursue his quest around the world...and a little jealous, too!

I remember the first time I ever talked about this project. It was one evening while over at a friend's house. I said that I really wanted to draw a manga about this theme...

When I actually sold my first copy at an event, I was so happy that I cried tears of joy!

I never could have imagined that this little story I developed all on my own in my room would have the opportunity to touch people all over the world.

"BEYOND THE CLOUDS"

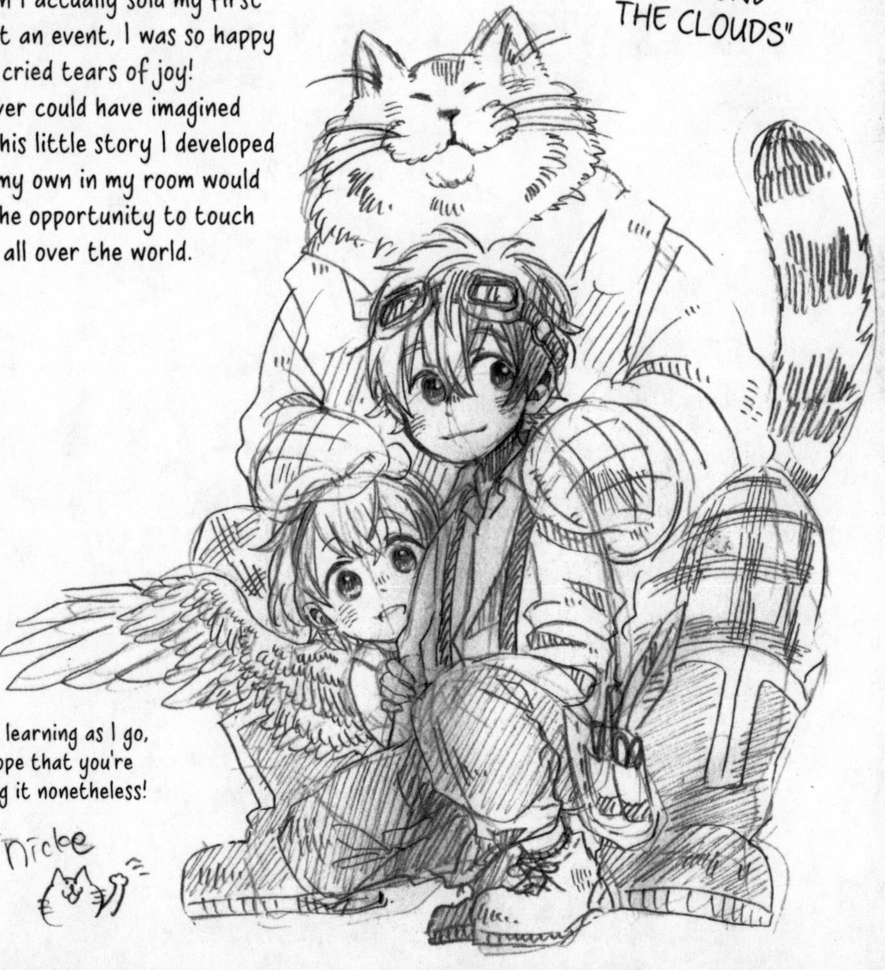

I'm still learning as I go, but I hope that you're enjoying it nonetheless!

nicke

SINCE I WAS SMALL, I'VE LOVED TO READ FANTASTICAL STORIES.

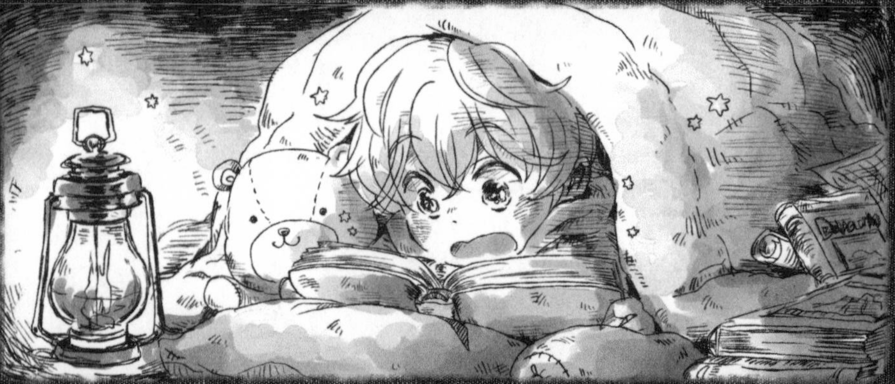

DRAGONS THAT HATE VEGETABLES. FISH THAT FLY IN THE SKY.
CAVES THAT GLITTER WITH LIGHT.
WORLDS FULL OF THINGS I'D NEVER SEEN BEFORE.

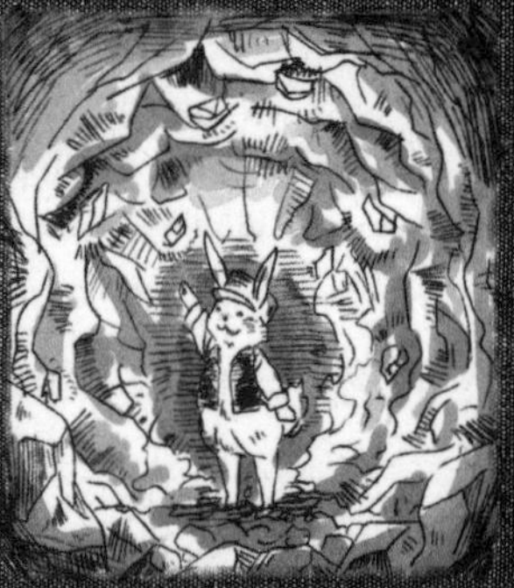

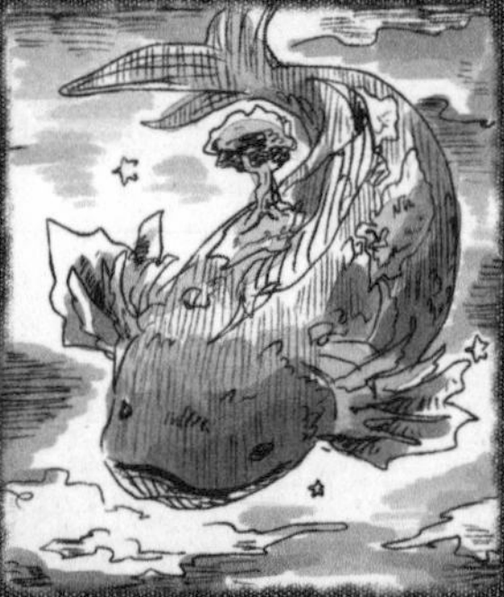

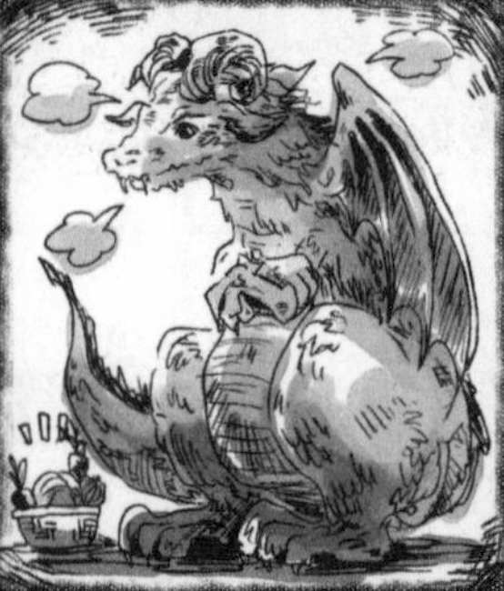

MY FAVORITE OF ALL WAS A STORY ABOUT A SAILOR
WHO TOOK A BOAT ALL OVER THE WORLD.

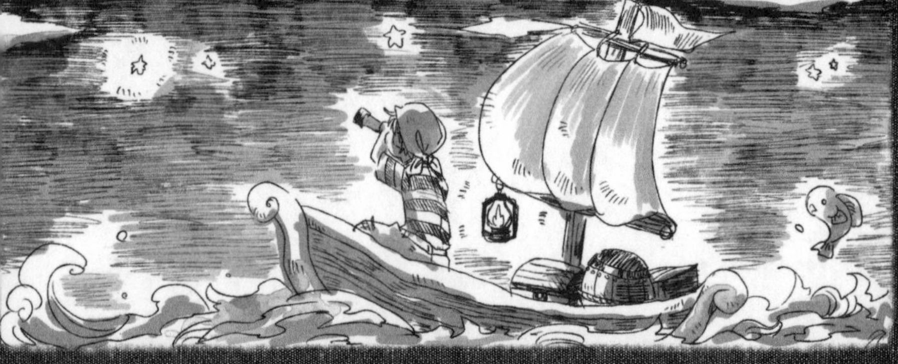

I ADMIRED THE WAY HE USED THE STARS TO NAVIGATE.

I ENVISIONED INVISIBLE STARS AROUND ME.

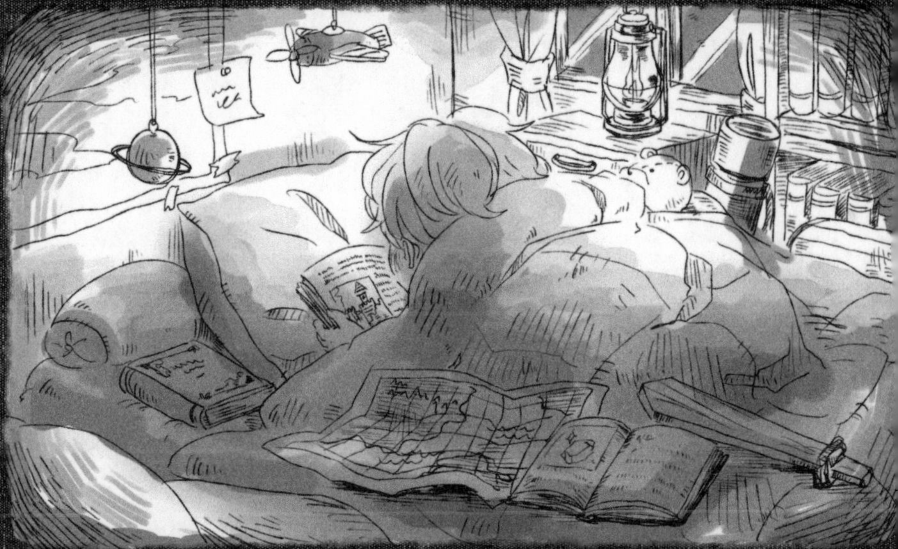

I COULDN'T WAIT TO GROW UP AND GO ON REAL ADVENTURES OF MY OWN, SEEING STRANGE CREATURES AND SEARCHING FOR LOST TREASURES.

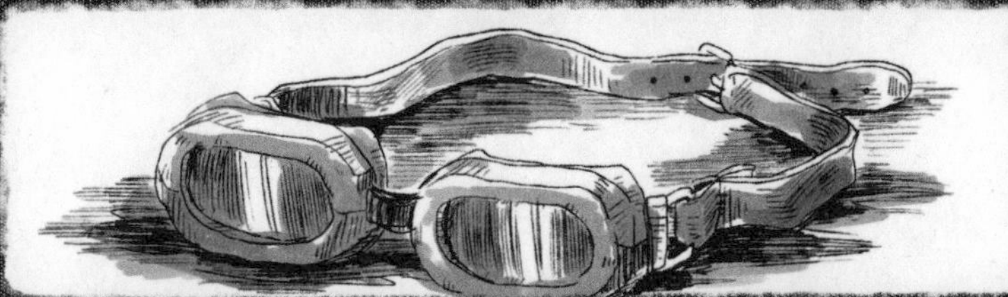

BUT ABOUT THE ONLY THING THAT ACTUALLY CHANGED...

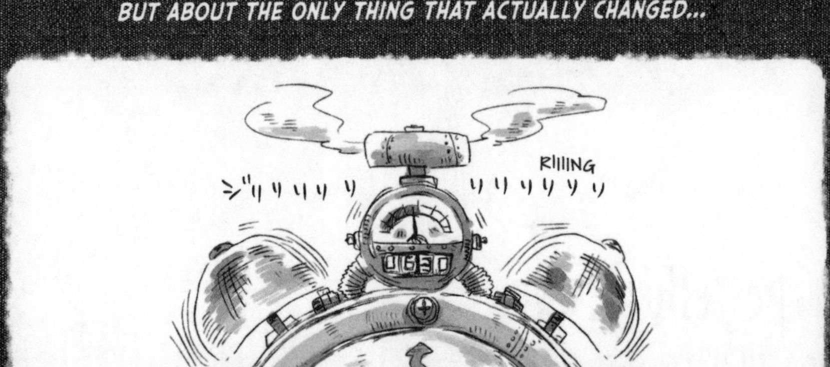
ジリリリリリ
RIIIING
リリリリリリ
0630

WAS THAT I HAD READ SO MANY BOOKS, MY EYESIGHT WENT BAD

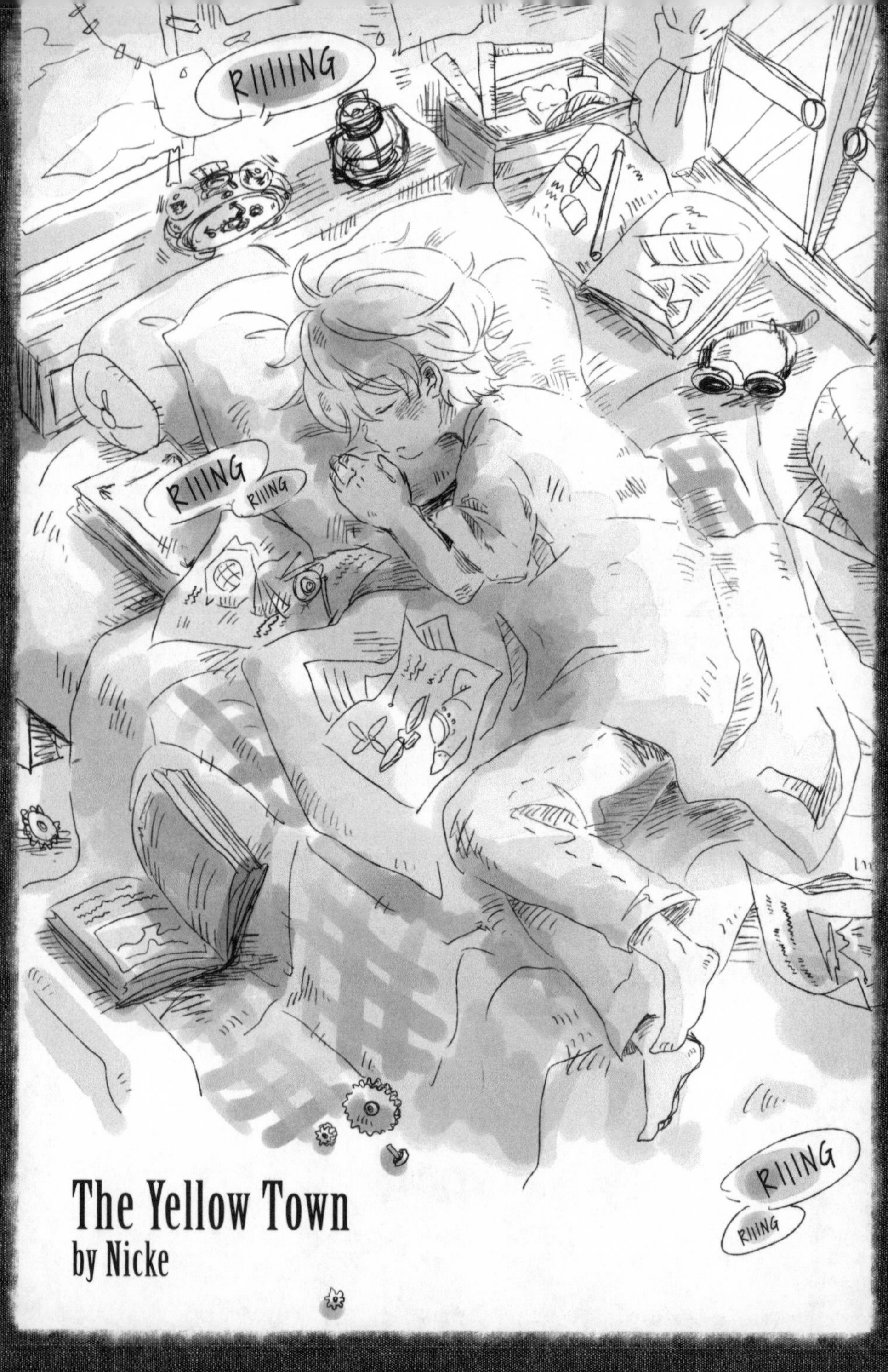
RIIIIING
RIIING
RIIING
RIIING
RIIING

The Yellow Town
by Nicke

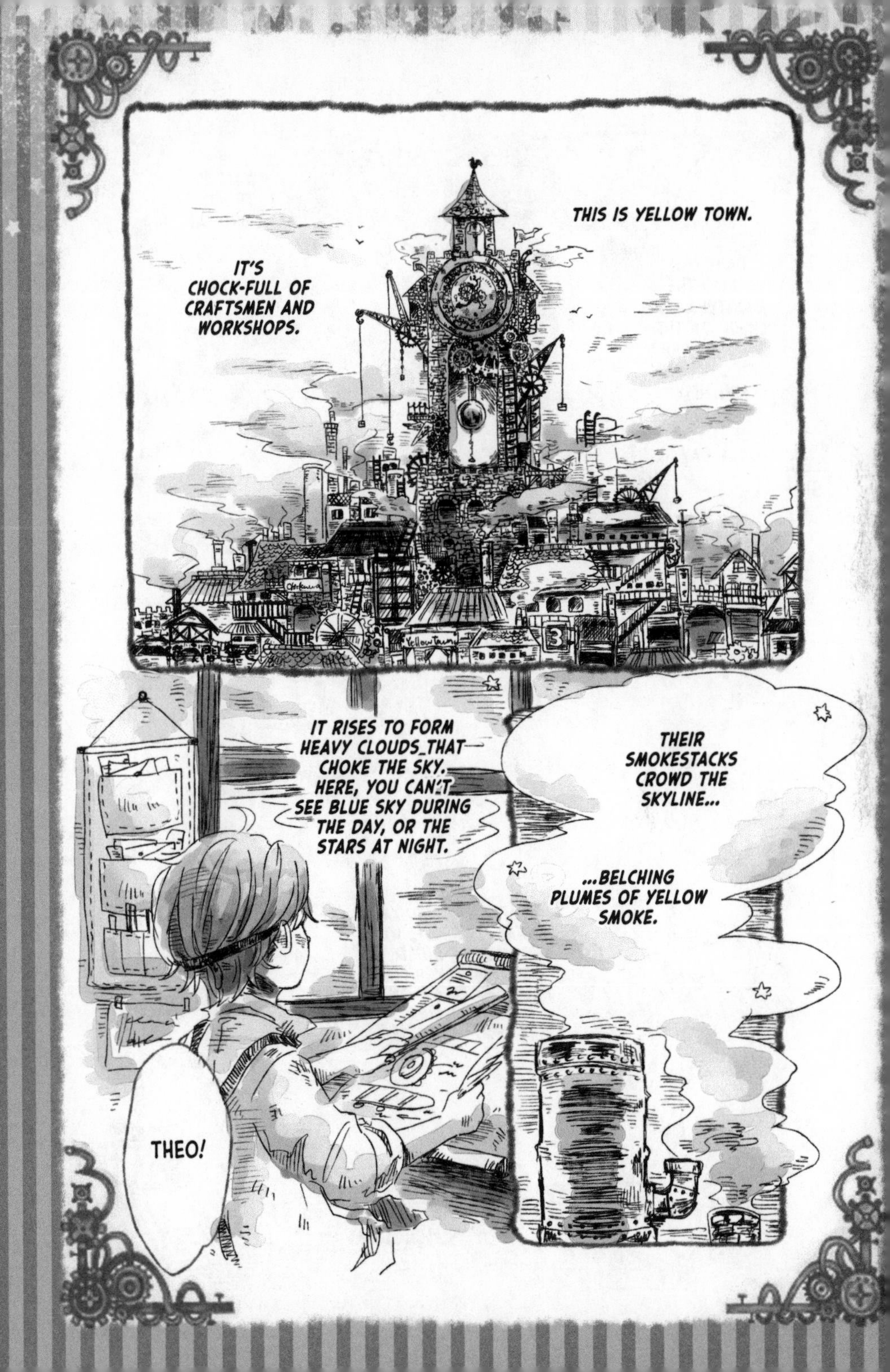
THIS IS YELLOW TOWN.
IT'S CHOCK-FULL OF CRAFTSMEN AND WORKSHOPS.
THEIR SMOKESTACKS CROWD THE SKYLINE...
...BELCHING PLUMES OF YELLOW SMOKE.
IT RISES TO FORM HEAVY CLOUDS THAT CHOKE THE SKY. HERE, YOU CAN'T SEE BLUE SKY DURING THE DAY, OR THE STARS AT NIGHT.
THEO!

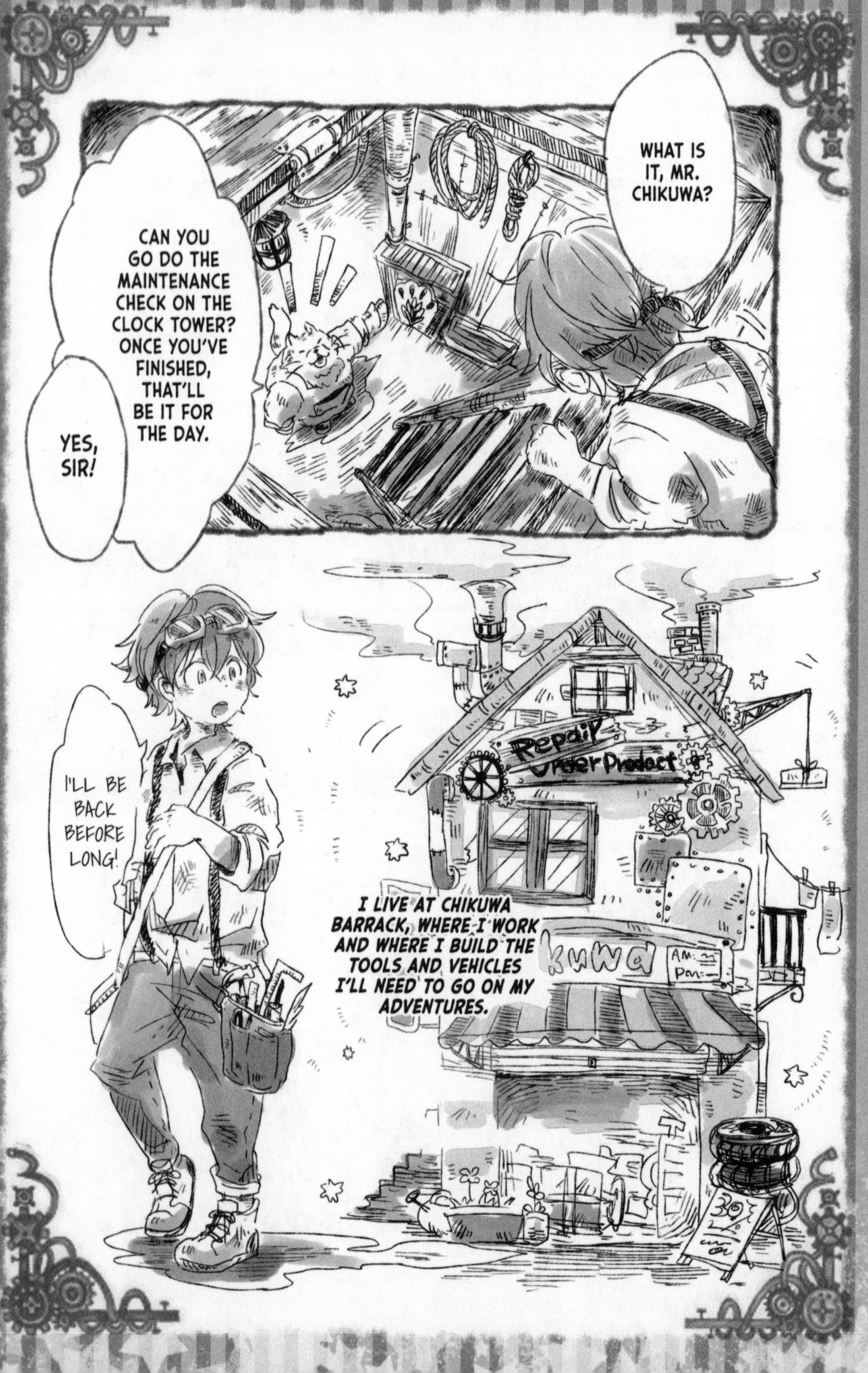
WHAT IS IT, MR. CHIKUWA?
CAN YOU GO DO THE MAINTENANCE CHECK ON THE CLOCK TOWER? ONCE YOU'VE FINISHED, THAT'LL BE IT FOR THE DAY.
YES, SIR!
I LIVE AT CHIKUWA BARRACK, WHERE I WORK AND WHERE I BUILD THE TOOLS AND VEHICLES I'LL NEED TO GO ON MY ADVENTURES.
I'LL BE BACK BEFORE LONG!

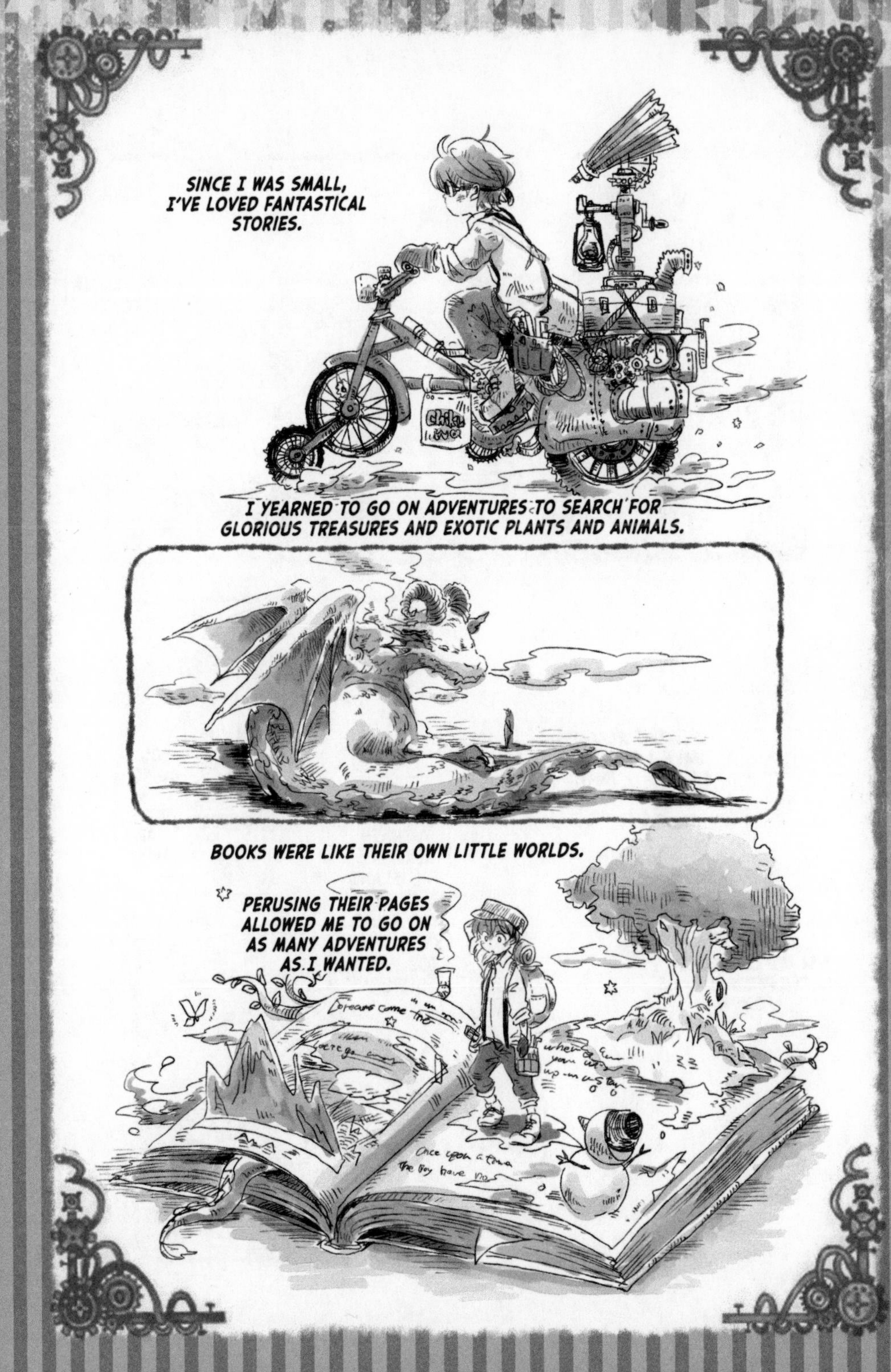
SINCE I WAS SMALL, I'VE LOVED FANTASTICAL STORIES.
I YEARNED TO GO ON ADVENTURES TO SEARCH FOR GLORIOUS TREASURES AND EXOTIC PLANTS AND ANIMALS.
BOOKS WERE LIKE THEIR OWN LITTLE WORLDS.
PERUSING THEIR PAGES ALLOWED ME TO GO ON AS MANY ADVENTURES AS I WANTED.

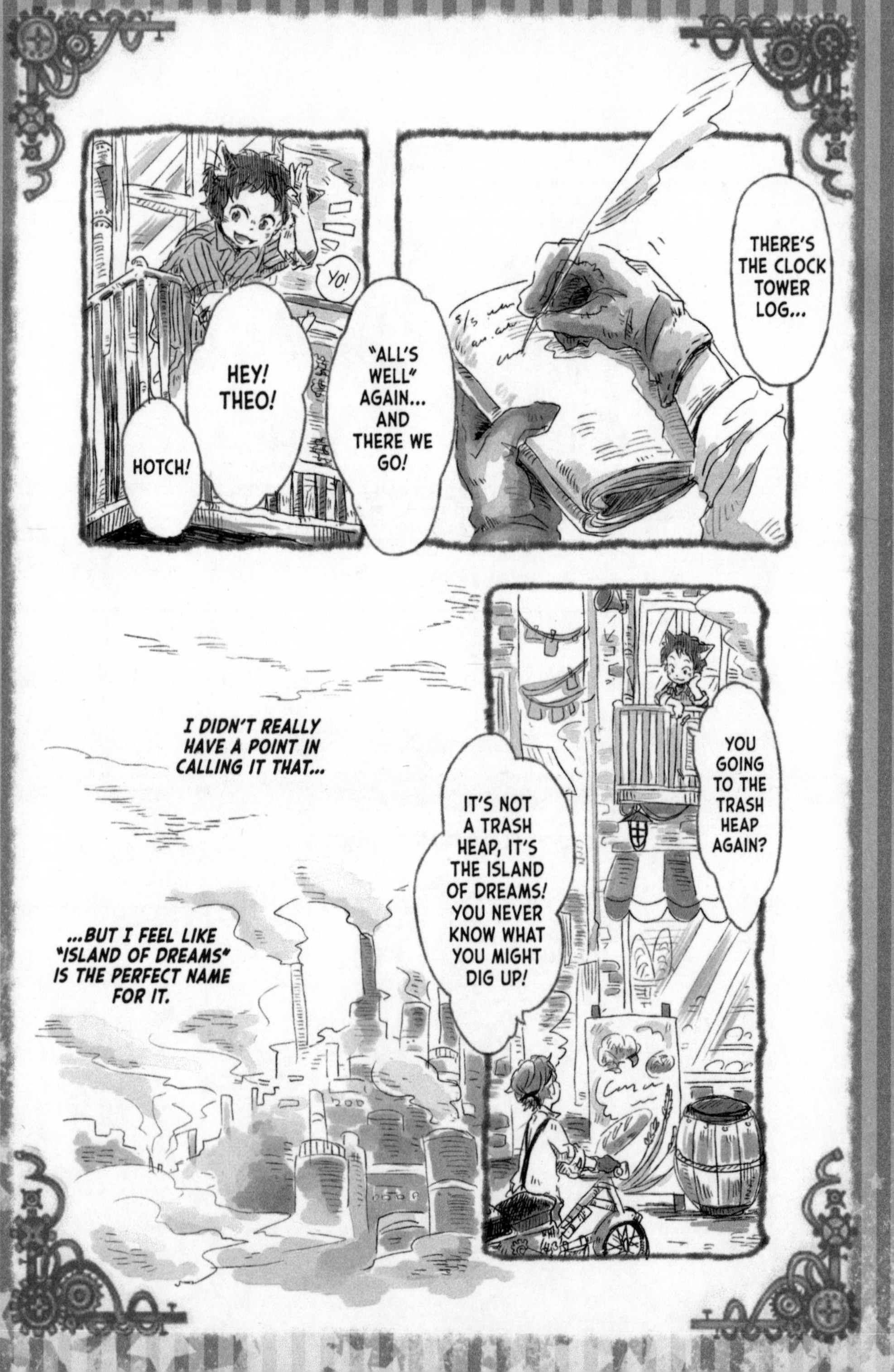
THERE'S THE CLOCK TOWER LOG...
"ALL'S WELL" AGAIN... AND THERE WE GO!
YO!
HEY! THEO!
HOTCH!
YOU GOING TO THE TRASH HEAP AGAIN?
IT'S NOT A TRASH HEAP, IT'S THE ISLAND OF DREAMS! YOU NEVER KNOW WHAT YOU MIGHT DIG UP!
I DIDN'T REALLY HAVE A POINT IN CALLING IT THAT...
...BUT I FEEL LIKE "ISLAND OF DREAMS" IS THE PERFECT NAME FOR IT.

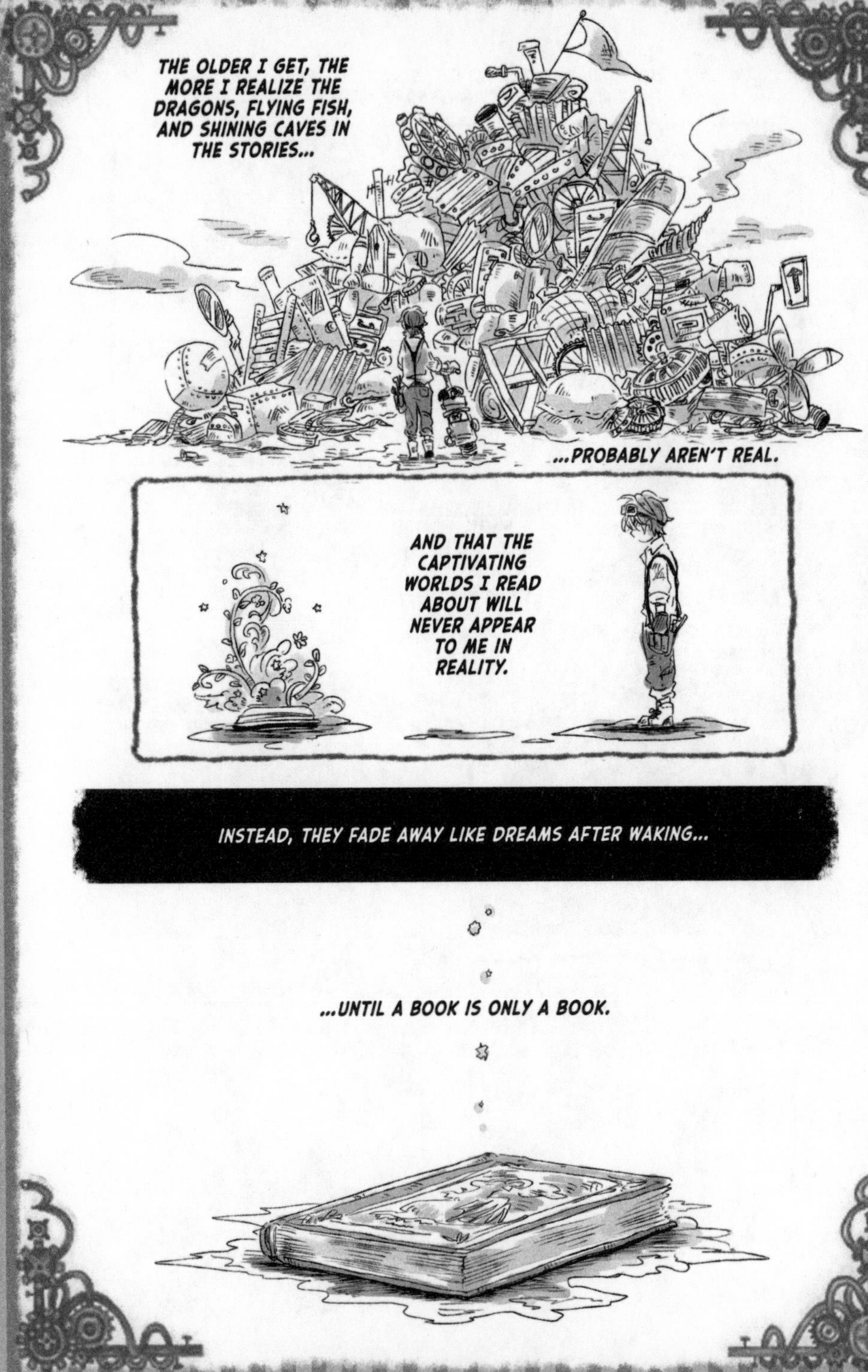
THE OLDER I GET, THE MORE I REALIZE THE DRAGONS, FLYING FISH, AND SHINING CAVES IN THE STORIES...
...PROBABLY AREN'T REAL.
AND THAT THE CAPTIVATING WORLDS I READ ABOUT WILL NEVER APPEAR TO ME IN REALITY.
INSTEAD, THEY FADE AWAY LIKE DREAMS AFTER WAKING...
...UNTIL A BOOK IS ONLY A BOOK.

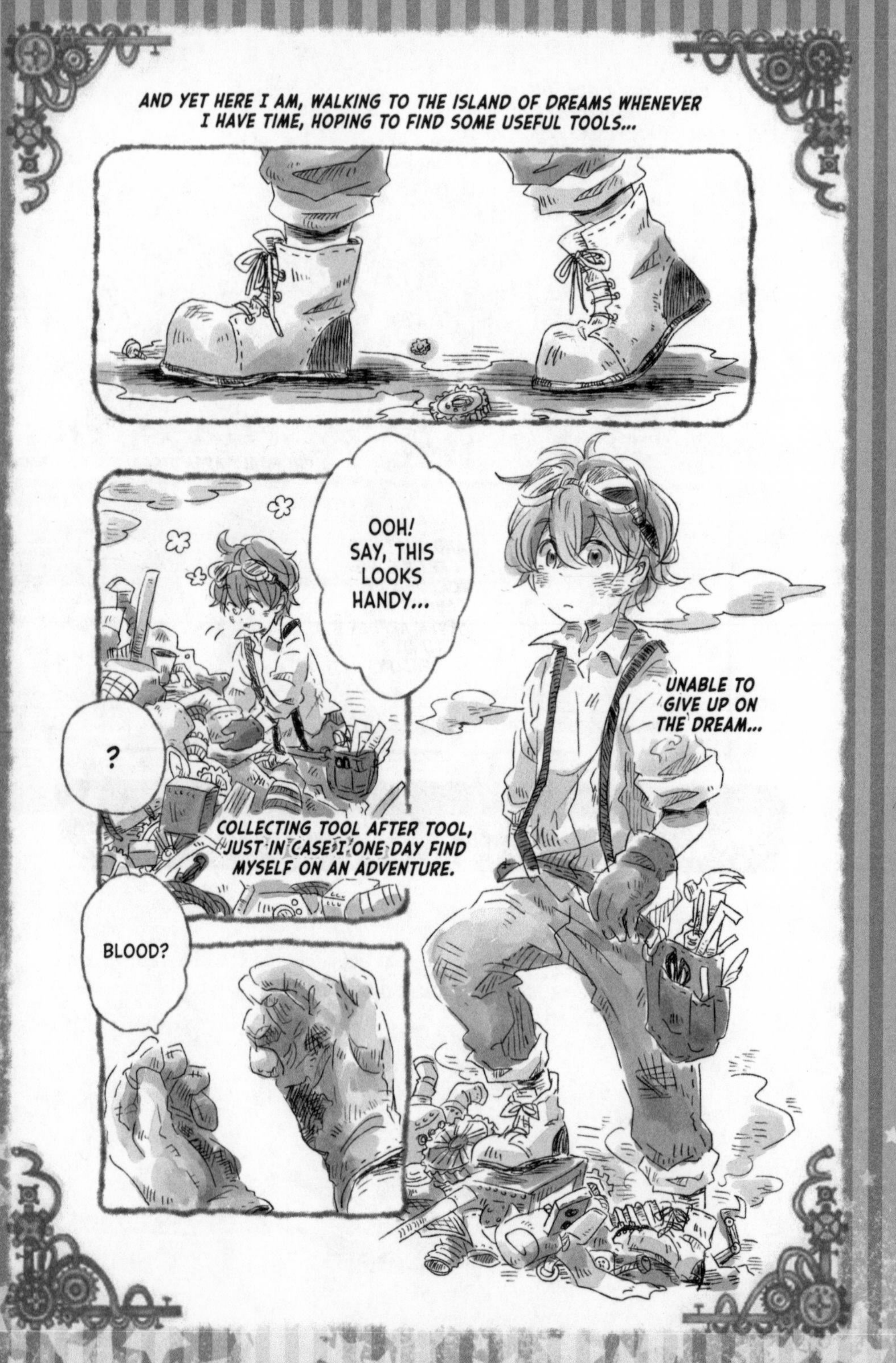
AND YET HERE I AM, WALKING TO THE ISLAND OF DREAMS WHENEVER I HAVE TIME, HOPING TO FIND SOME USEFUL TOOLS...
UNABLE TO GIVE UP ON THE DREAM...
OOH! SAY, THIS LOOKS HANDY...
?
COLLECTING TOOL AFTER TOOL, JUST IN CASE I ONE DAY FIND MYSELF ON AN ADVENTURE.
BLOOD?

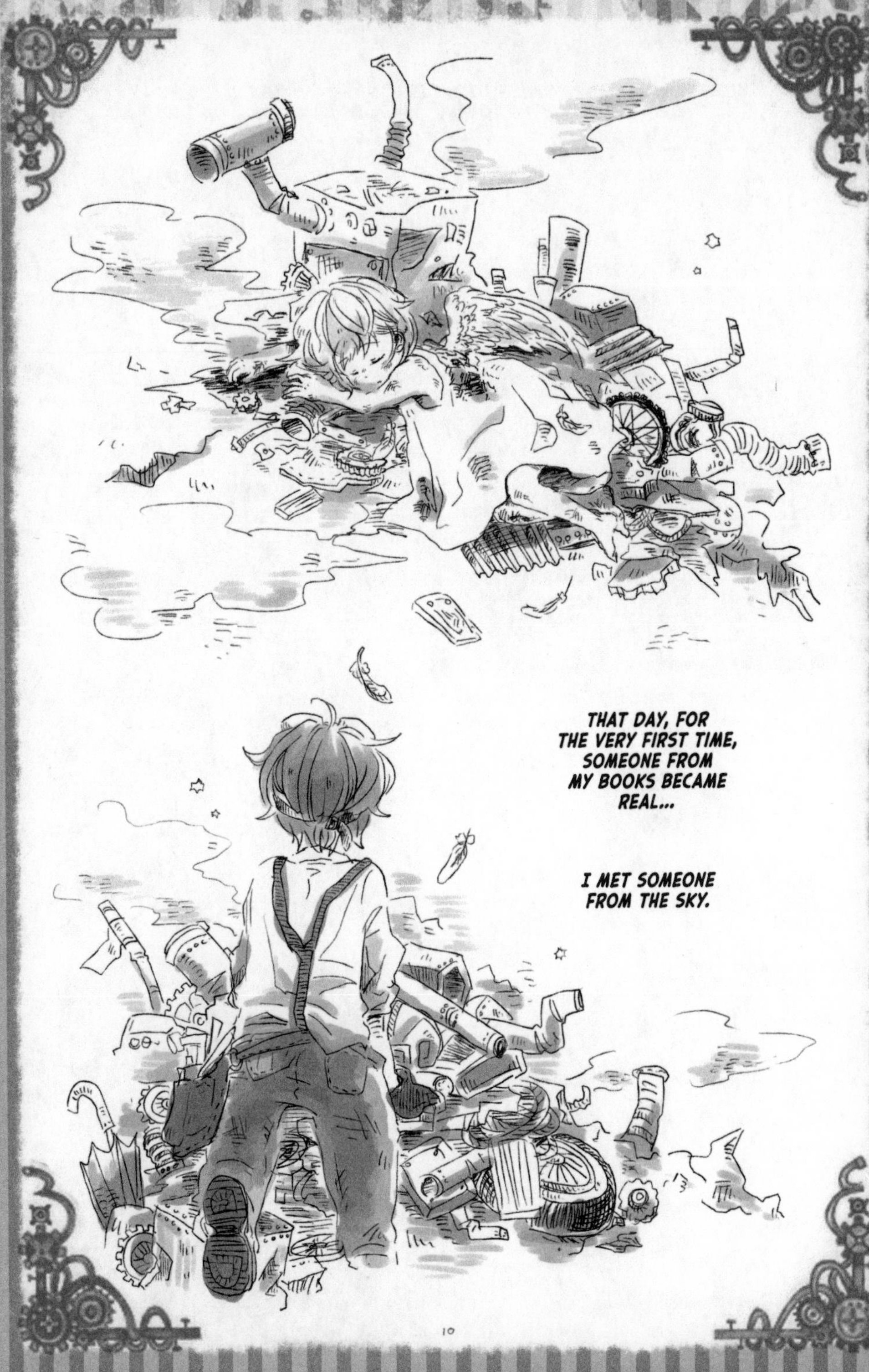
THAT DAY, FOR THE VERY FIRST TIME, SOMEONE FROM MY BOOKS BECAME REAL...
I MET SOMEONE FROM THE SKY.

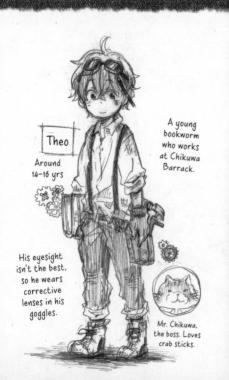

The Yellow Town

Theo
A young bookworm who works at Chikuwa Barrack.
Around 14–16 yrs
His eyesight isn't the best, so he wears corrective lenses in his goggles.
Mr. Chikuwa, the boss. Loves crab sticks.

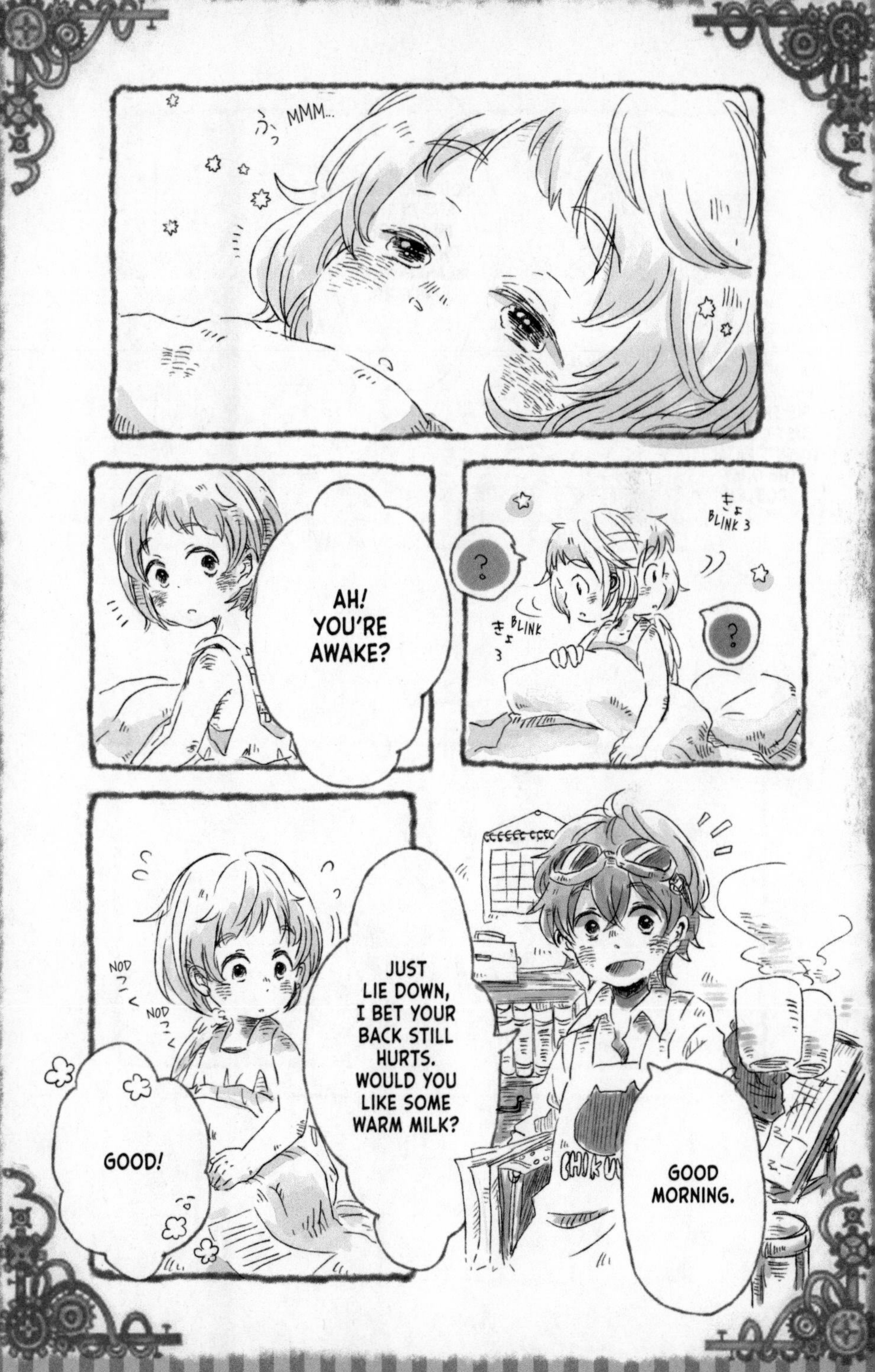
ふっ MMM...
きょ BLINK 3
?
?
きょ BLINK 3
AH! YOU'RE AWAKE?
GOOD MORNING.
JUST LIE DOWN, I BET YOUR BACK STILL HURTS. WOULD YOU LIKE SOME WARM MILK?
NOD
NOD
GOOD!

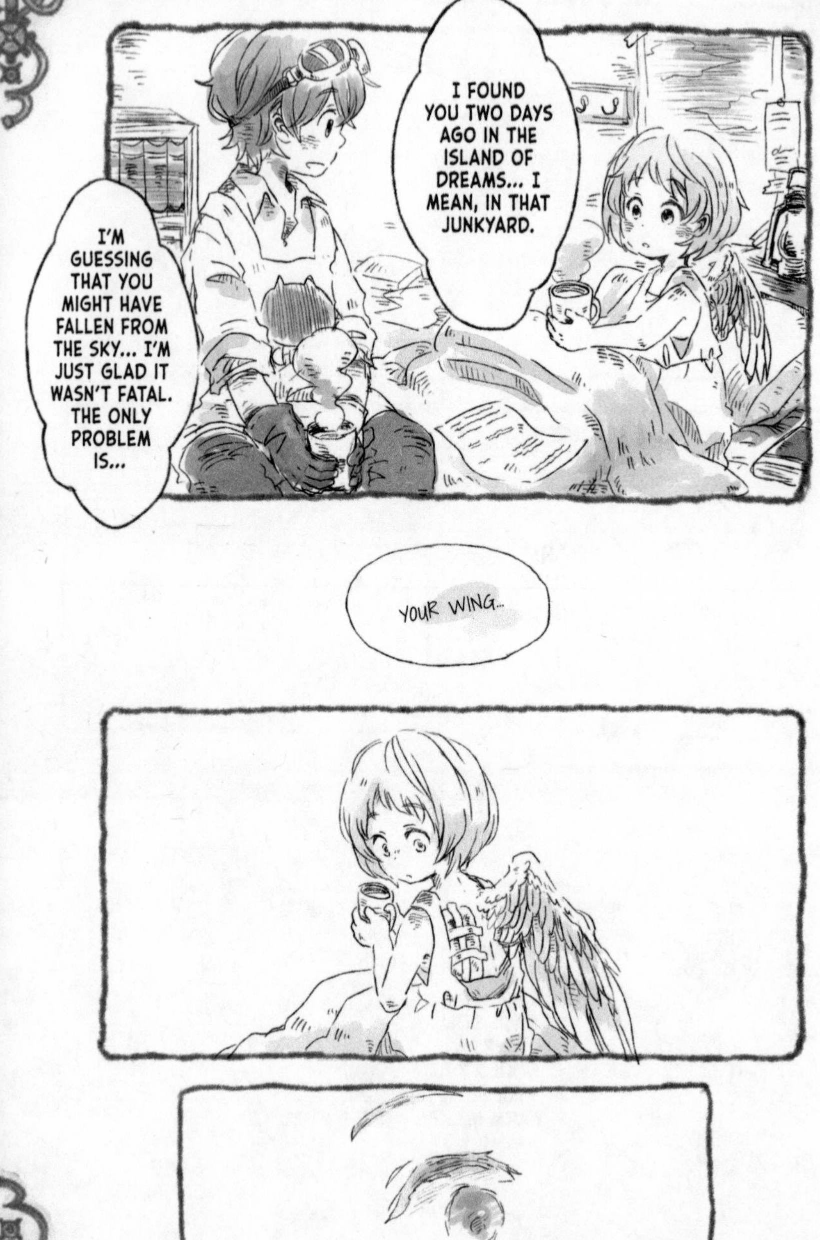
I FOUND YOU TWO DAYS AGO IN THE ISLAND OF DREAMS... I MEAN, IN THAT JUNKYARD.
I'M GUESSING THAT YOU MIGHT HAVE FALLEN FROM THE SKY... I'M JUST GLAD IT WASN'T FATAL. THE ONLY PROBLEM IS...
YOUR WING...

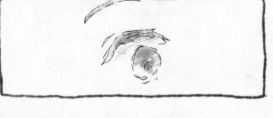

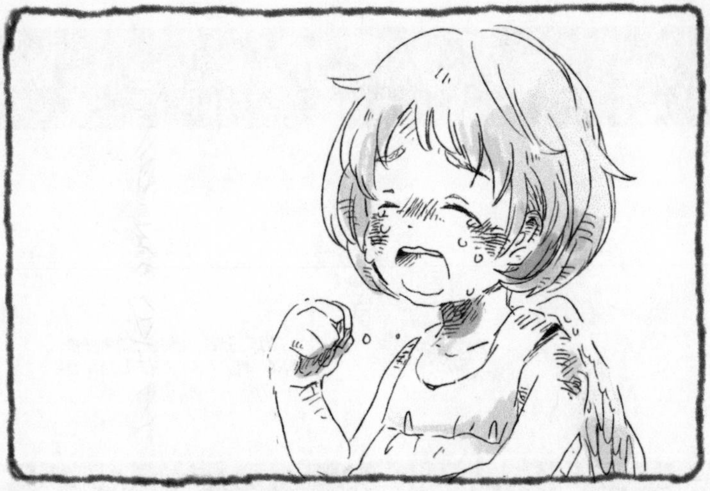

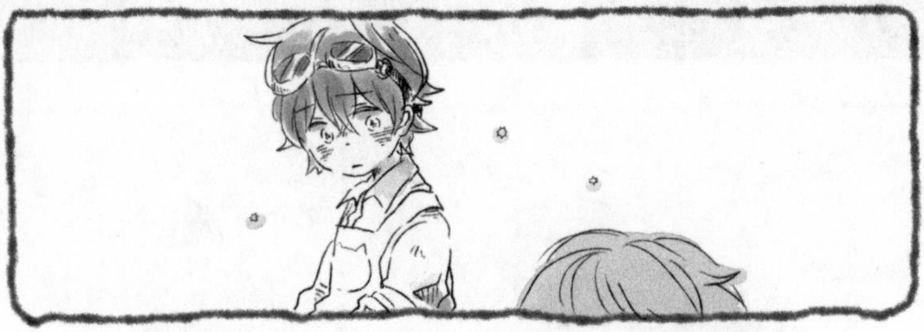

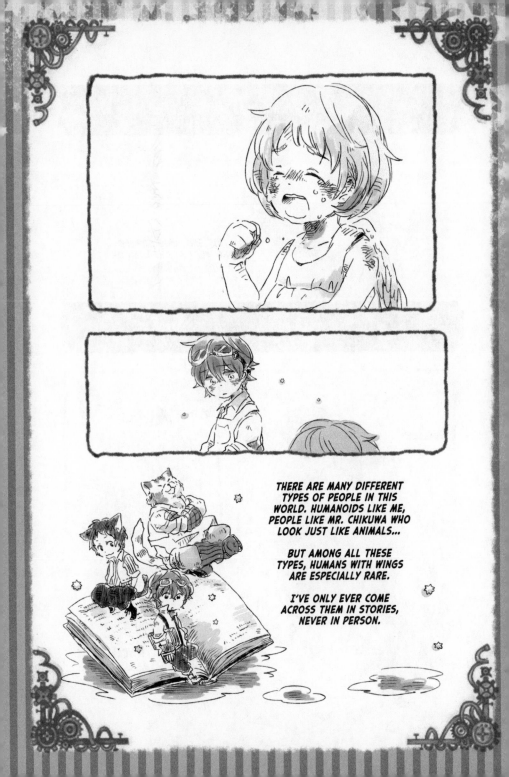

THERE ARE MANY DIFFERENT TYPES OF PEOPLE IN THIS WORLD. HUMANOIDS LIKE ME, PEOPLE LIKE MR. CHIKUWA WHO LOOK JUST LIKE ANIMALS...

BUT AMONG ALL THESE TYPES, HUMANS WITH WINGS ARE ESPECIALLY RARE.

I'VE ONLY EVER COME ACROSS THEM IN STORIES, NEVER IN PERSON.

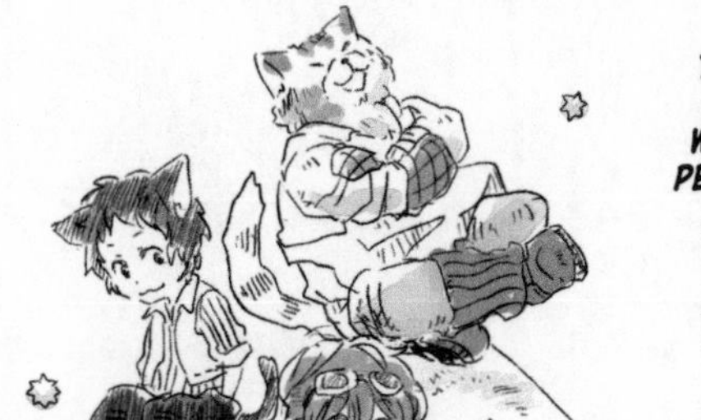

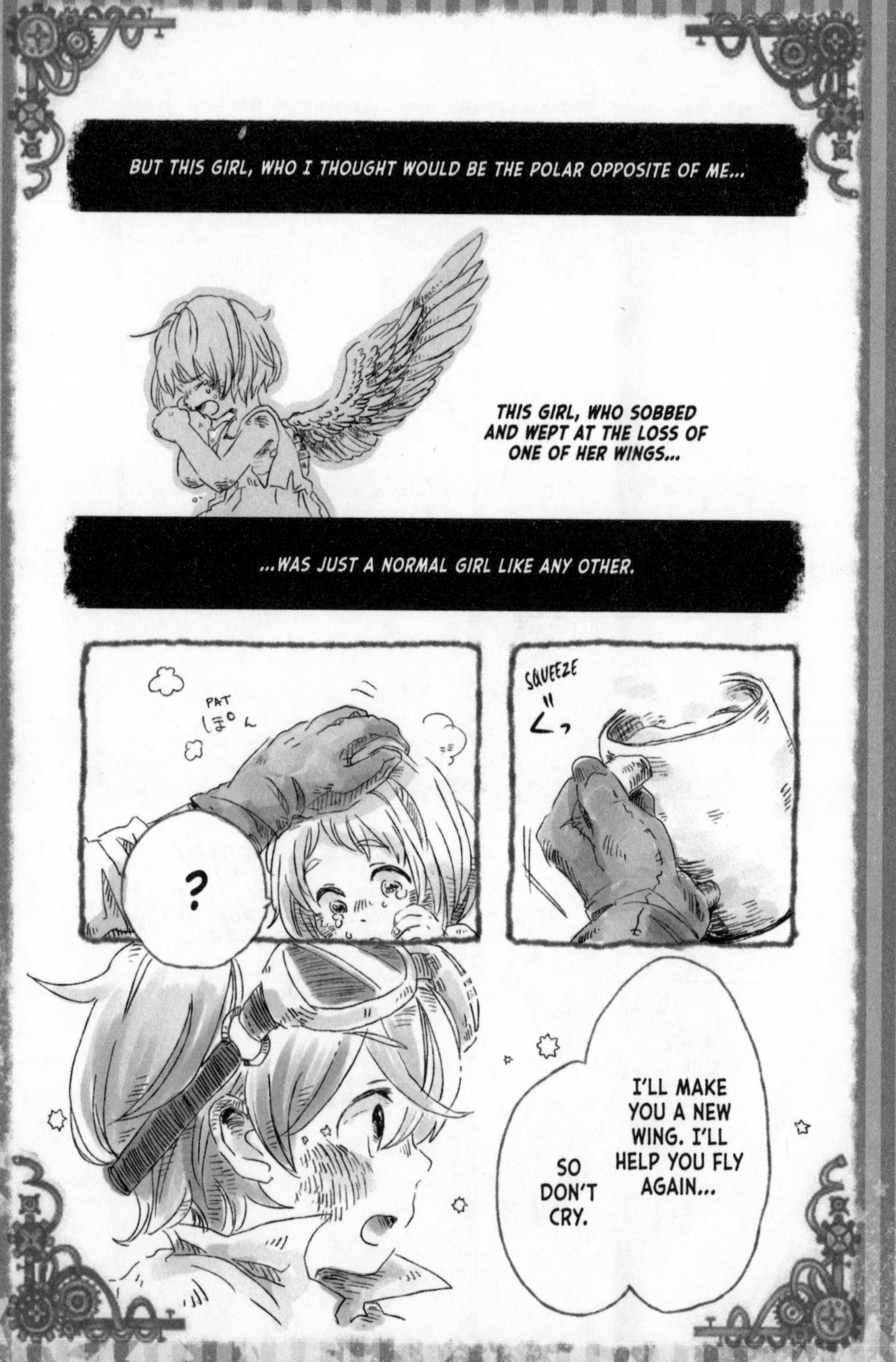
BUT THIS GIRL, WHO I THOUGHT WOULD BE THE POLAR OPPOSITE OF ME...
THIS GIRL, WHO SOBBED AND WEPT AT THE LOSS OF ONE OF HER WINGS...
...WAS JUST A NORMAL GIRL LIKE ANY OTHER.
SQUEEZE
ぐっ
PAT
ぽん
?
I'LL MAKE YOU A NEW WING. I'LL HELP YOU FLY AGAIN...
SO DON'T CRY.

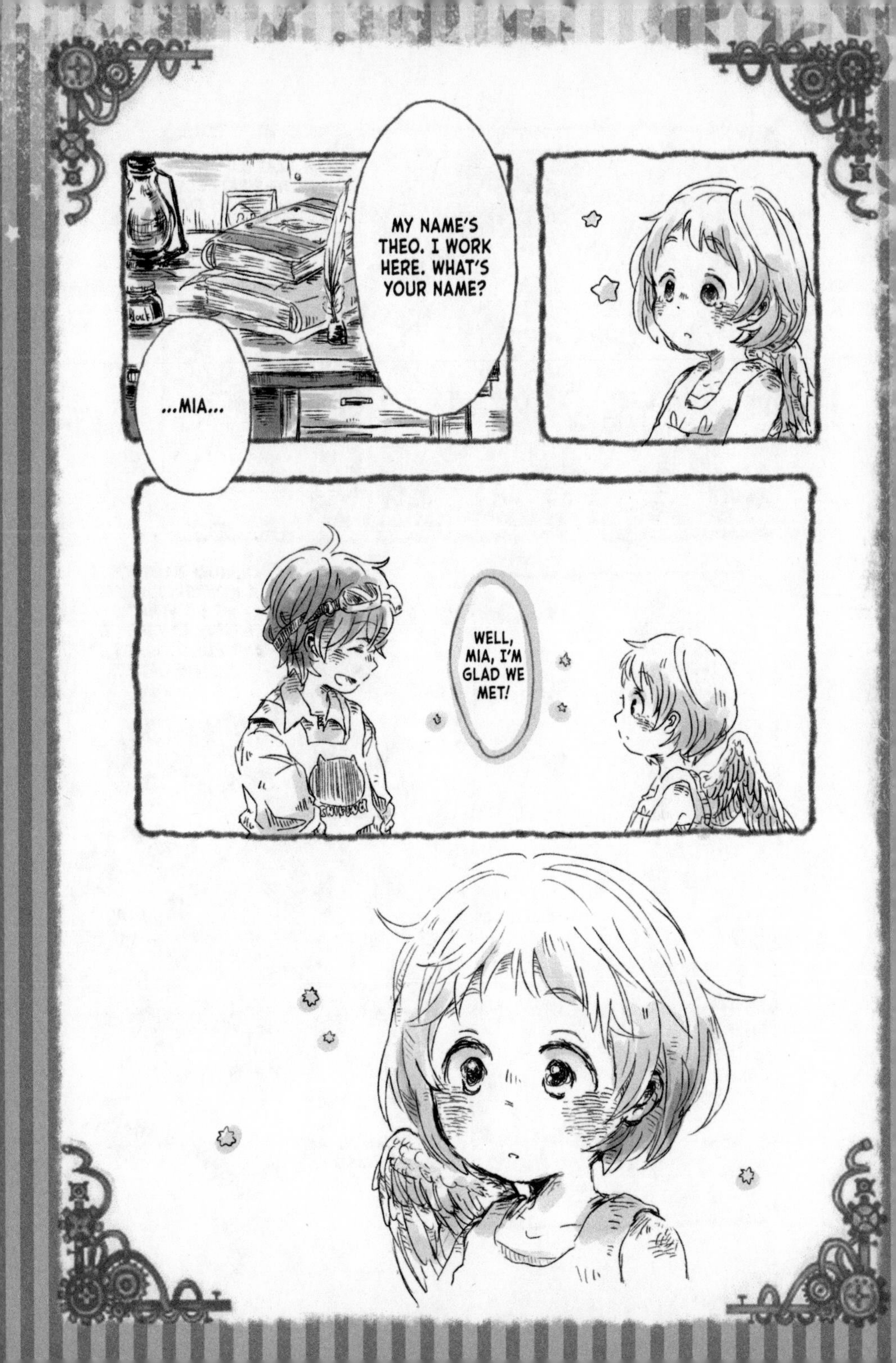
MY NAME'S THEO. I WORK HERE. WHAT'S YOUR NAME?
...MIA...
WELL, MIA, I'M GLAD WE MET!

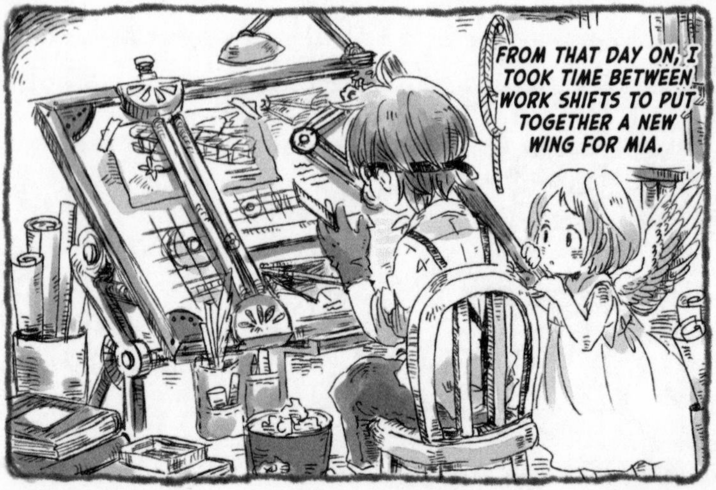
FROM THAT DAY ON, I TOOK TIME BETWEEN WORK SHIFTS TO PUT TOGETHER A NEW WING FOR MIA.
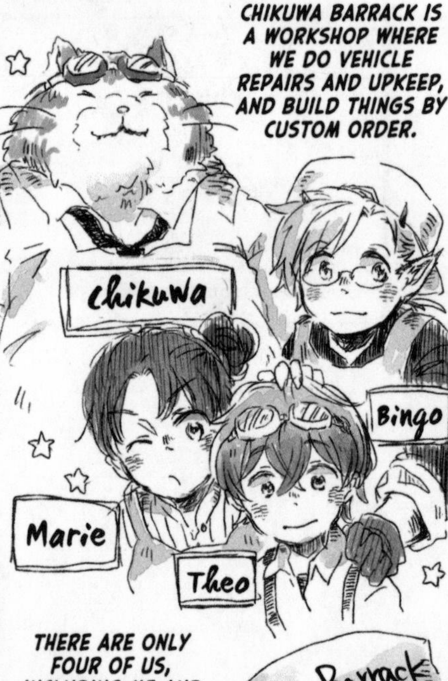
CHIKUWA BARRACK IS A WORKSHOP WHERE WE DO VEHICLE REPAIRS AND UPKEEP, AND BUILD THINGS BY CUSTOM ORDER.
Chikuwa
Bingo
Marie
Theo
THERE ARE ONLY FOUR OF US, INCLUDING ME AND THE BOSS, SO IT'S PRETTY BUSY.
ChikuwaBarrack
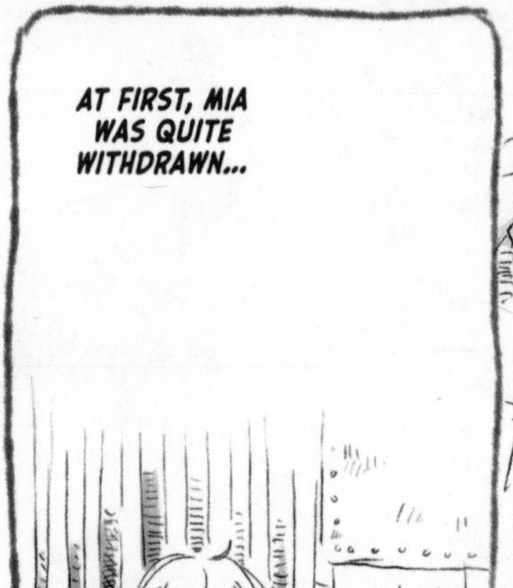
AT FIRST, MIA WAS QUITE WITHDRAWN...

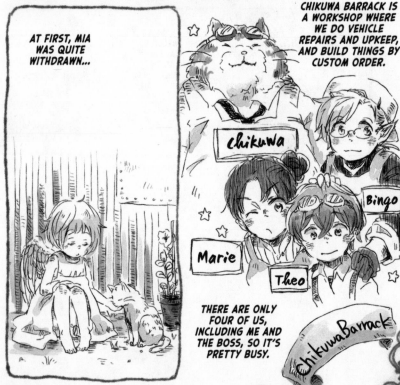

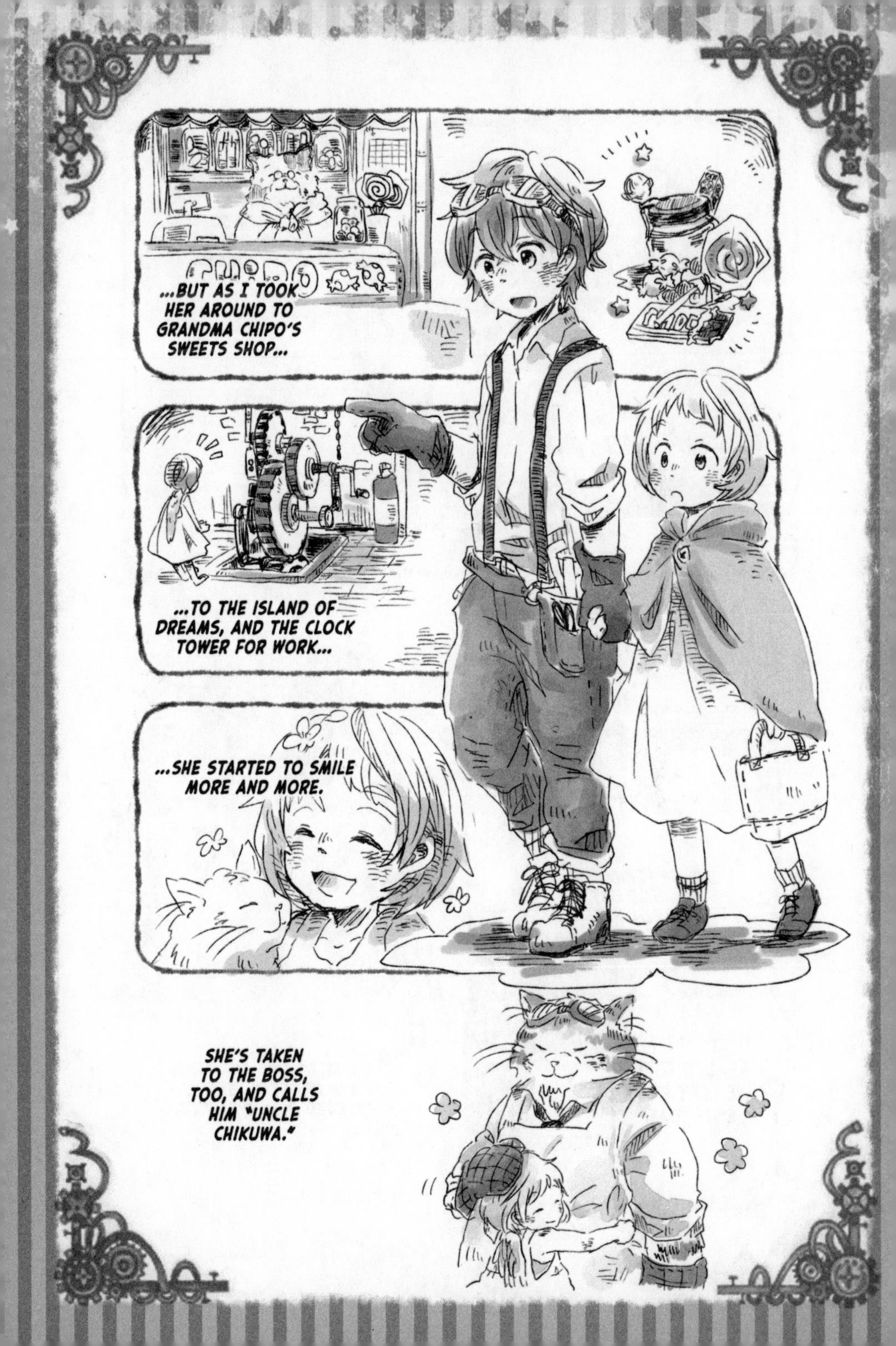
...BUT AS I TOOK HER AROUND TO GRANDMA CHIPO'S SWEETS SHOP...
...TO THE ISLAND OF DREAMS, AND THE CLOCK TOWER FOR WORK...
...SHE STARTED TO SMILE MORE AND MORE.
SHE'S TAKEN TO THE BOSS, TOO, AND CALLS HIM "UNCLE CHIKUWA."

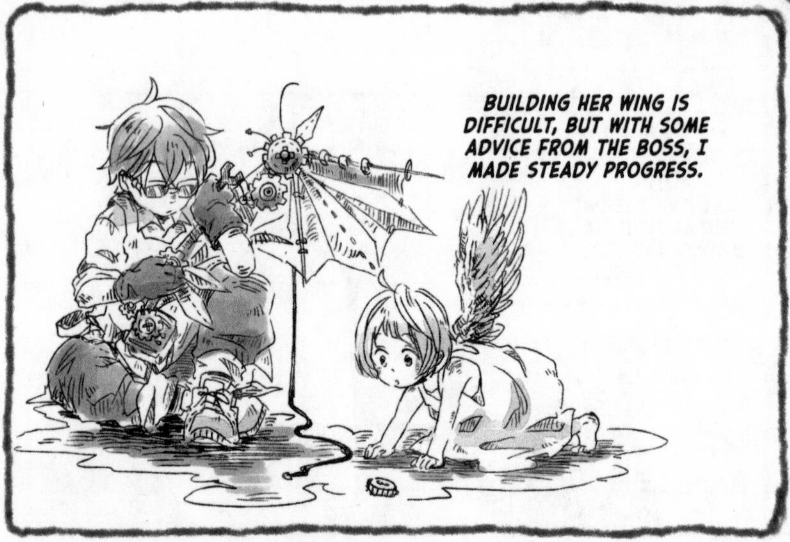
BUILDING HER WING IS DIFFICULT, BUT WITH SOME ADVICE FROM THE BOSS, I MADE STEADY PROGRESS.

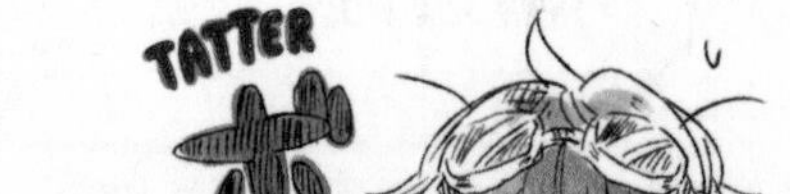
TATTER
ボロ
WE TRIED THIS AND THAT, AND IT OFTEN LEFT US COVERED IN MUD AND OIL.

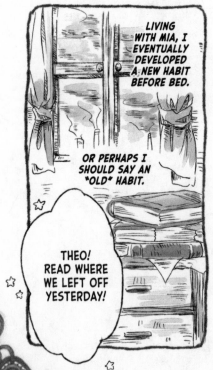

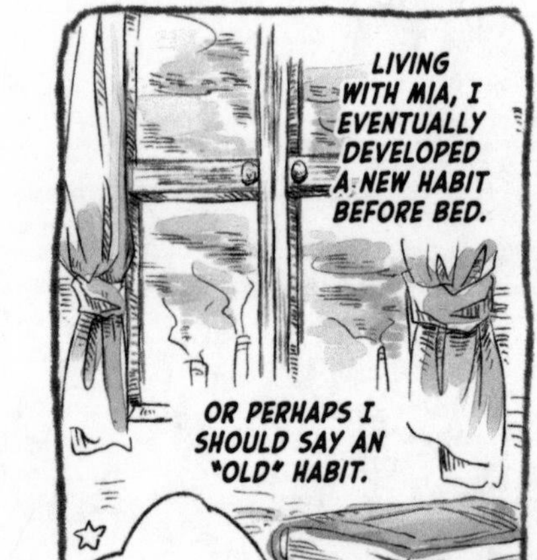
LIVING WITH MIA, I EVENTUALLY DEVELOPED A NEW HABIT BEFORE BED.
OR PERHAPS I SHOULD SAY AN *OLD* HABIT.
THEO! READ WHERE WE LEFT OFF YESTERDAY!

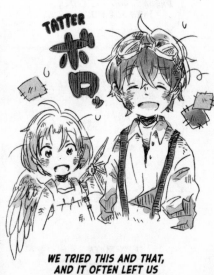

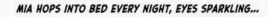

MIA HOPS INTO BED EVERY NIGHT, EYES SPARKLING...

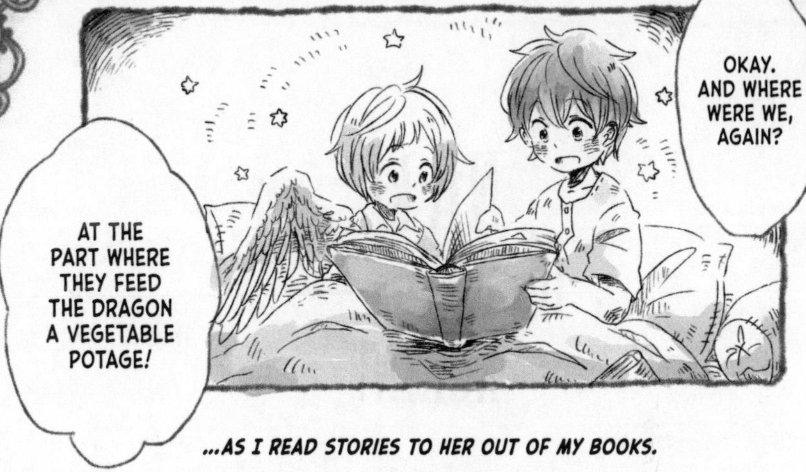
OKAY. AND WHERE WERE WE, AGAIN?
AT THE PART WHERE THEY FEED THE DRAGON A VEGETABLE POTAGE!

...AS I READ STORIES TO HER OUT OF MY BOOKS.

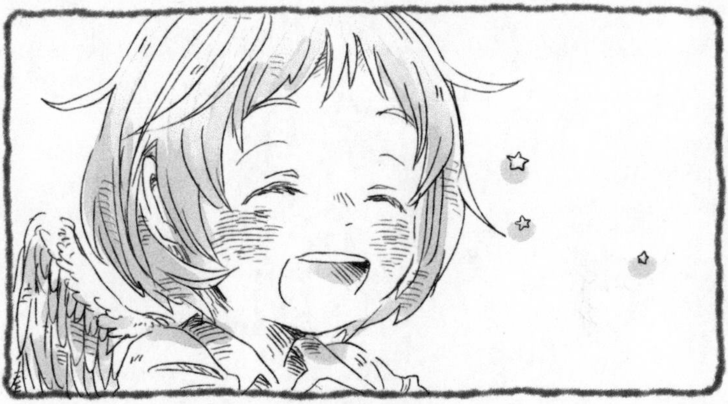

SOMETHING ABOUT THAT INNOCENCE OF HERS...

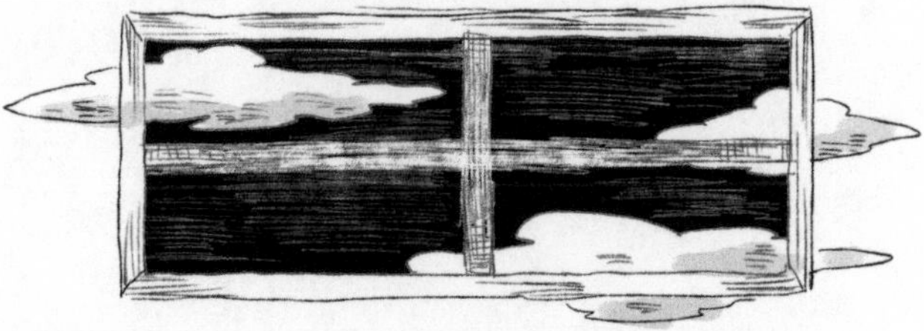

...MAKES ME VERY JEALOUS.

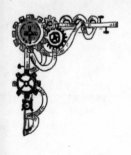

Nicke
in France—
AGAIN!

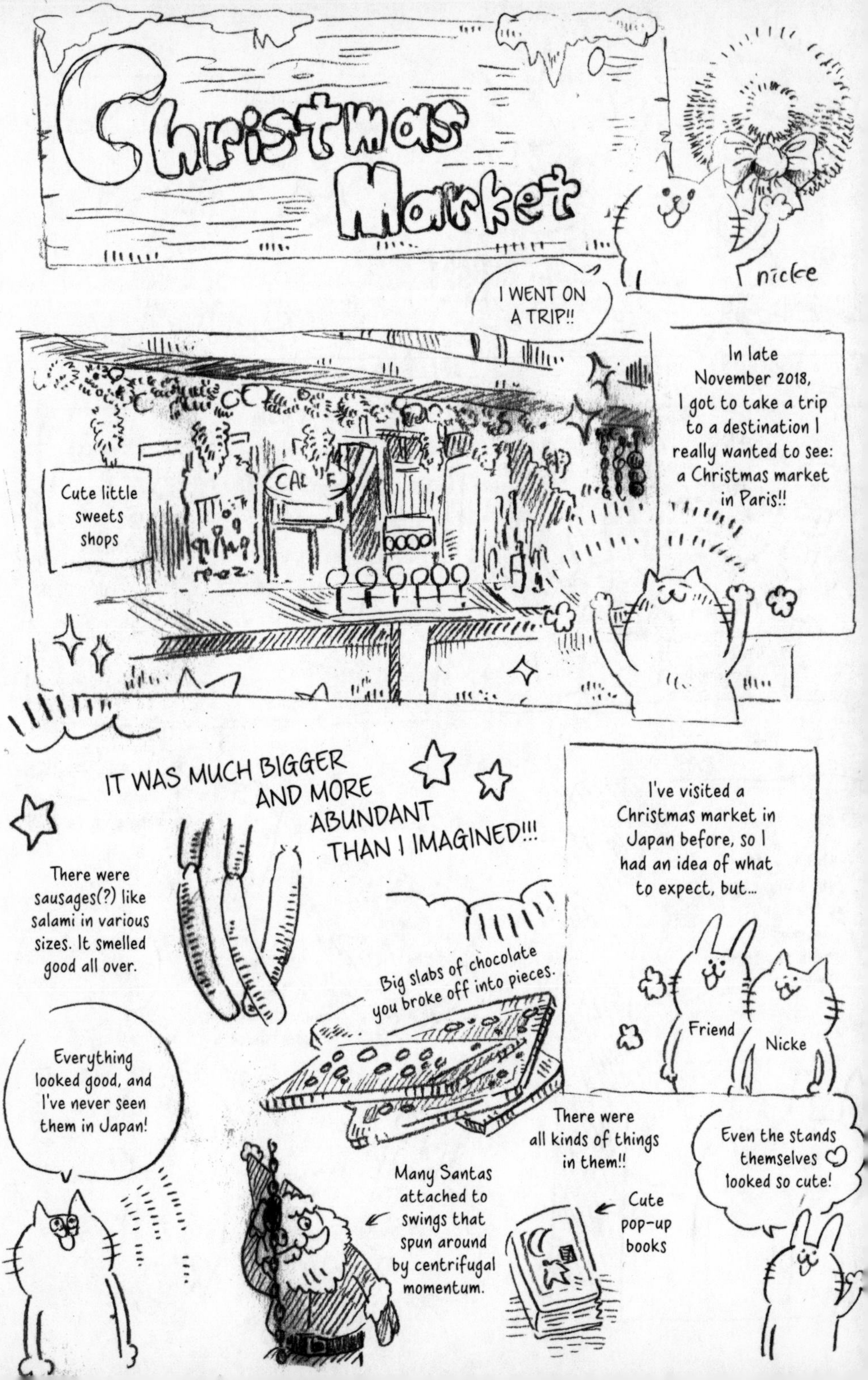
Christmas Market
nicke
I WENT ON A TRIP!!
In late November 2018, I got to take a trip to a destination I really wanted to see: a Christmas market in Paris!!
Cute little sweets shops
CAFE
I've visited a Christmas market in Japan before, so I had an idea of what to expect, but...
Friend
Nicke
IT WAS MUCH BIGGER AND MORE ABUNDANT THAN I IMAGINED!!!
Big slabs of chocolate you broke off into pieces.
There were sausages(?) like salami in various sizes. It smelled good all over.
Even the stands themselves looked so cute!
There were all kinds of things in them!!
Cute pop-up books
Many Santas attached to swings that spun around by centrifugal momentum.
Everything looked good, and I've never seen them in Japan!

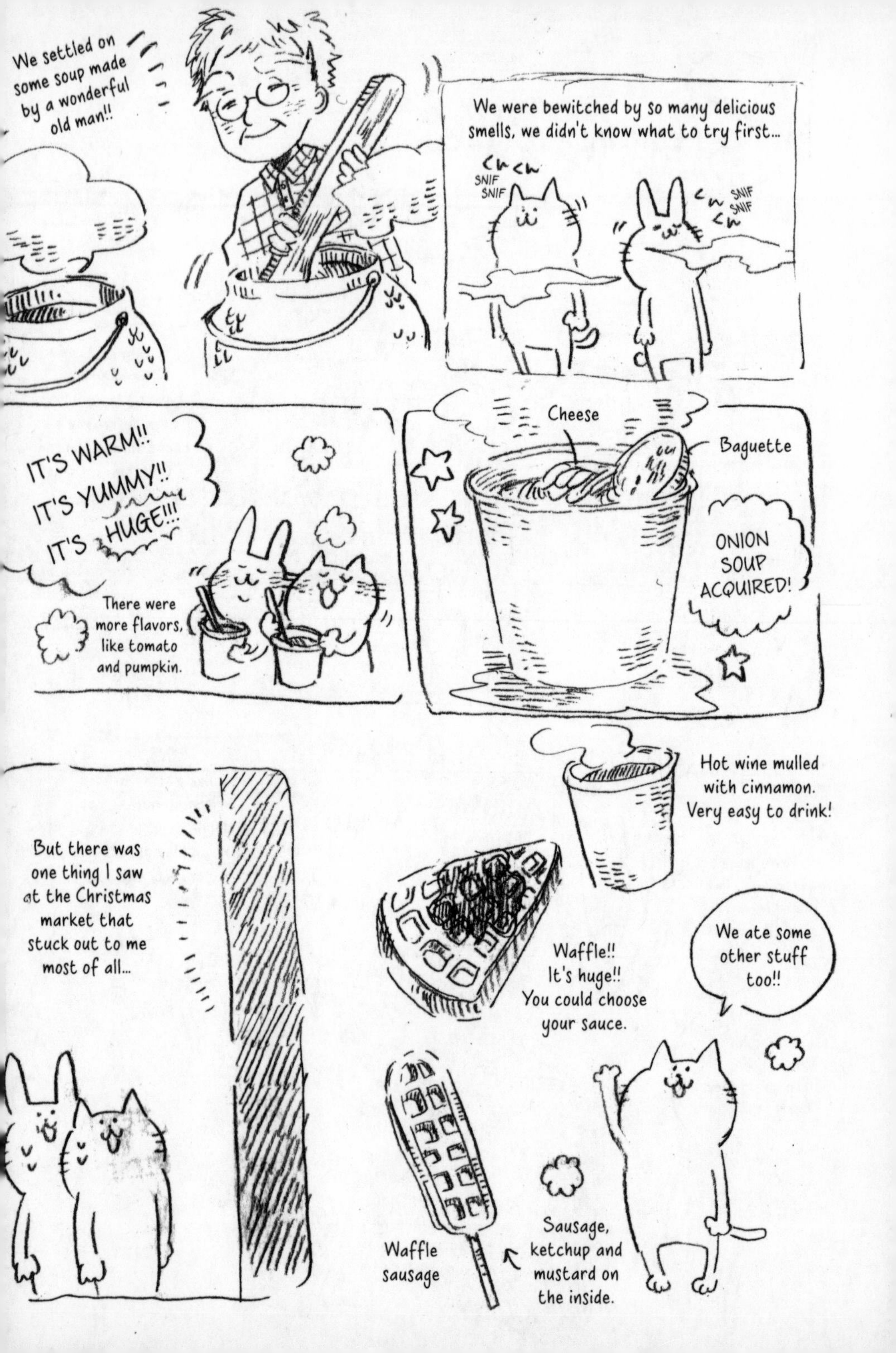

We were bewitched by so many delicious smells, we didn't know what to try first...
くんくん
SNIF SNIF
くんくん
SNIF SNIF
We settled on some soup made by a wonderful old man!!
Cheese
Baguette
ONION SOUP ACQUIRED!
IT'S WARM!!
IT'S YUMMY!!
IT'S HUGE!!!
There were more flavors, like tomato and pumpkin.
Hot wine mulled with cinnamon. Very easy to drink!
We ate some other stuff too!!
Waffle!! It's huge!! You could choose your sauce.
Sausage, ketchup and mustard on the inside.
Waffle sausage
But there was one thing I saw at the Christmas market that stuck out to me most of all...

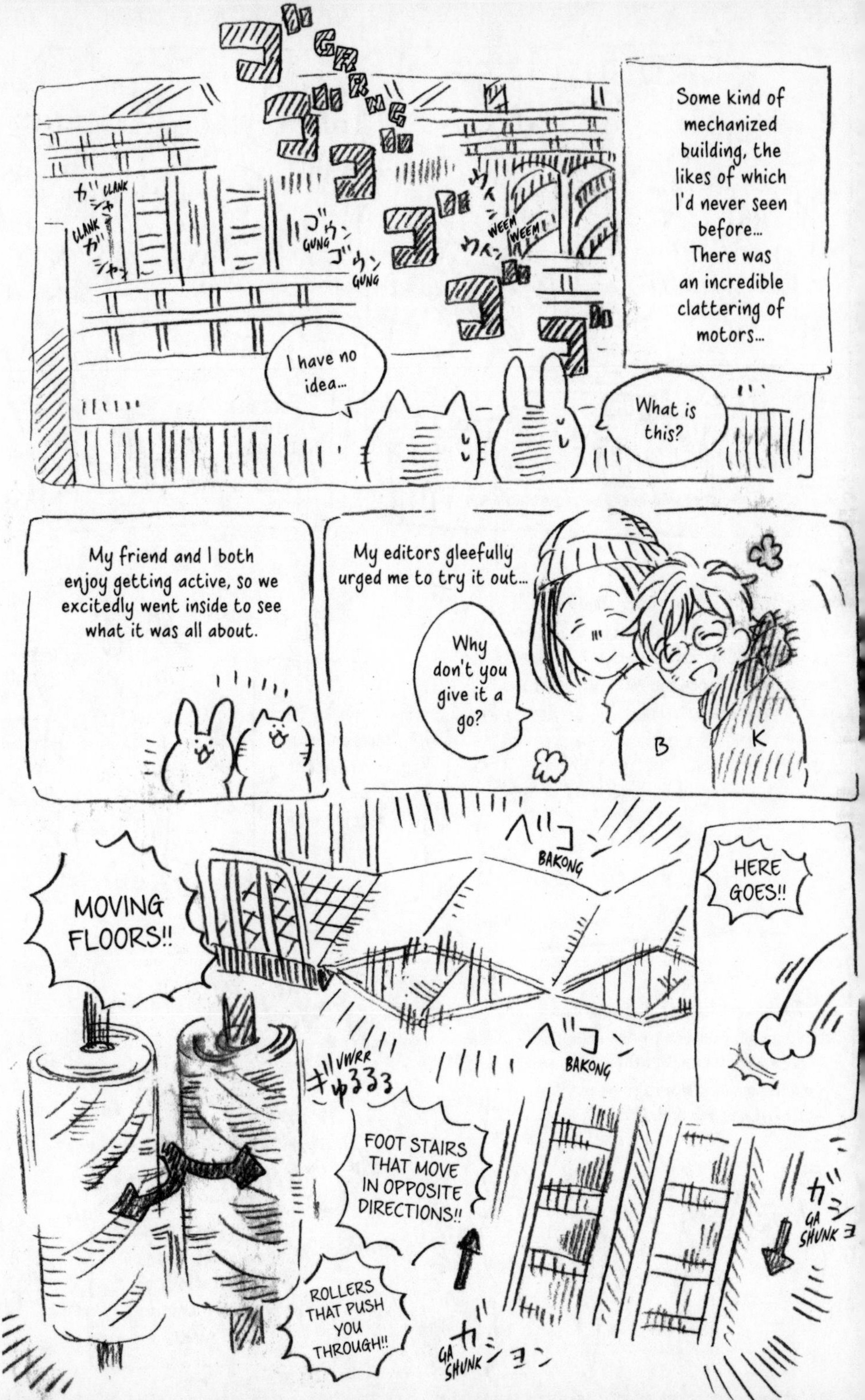

Some kind of mechanized building, the likes of which I'd never seen before... There was an incredible clattering of motors...
GRRNG
CLANK
CLANK
GUNG
GUNG
WEEM
WEEM
What is this?
I have no idea...
My editors gleefully urged me to try it out...
Why don't you give it a go?
B
K
My friend and I both enjoy getting active, so we excitedly went inside to see what it was all about.
HERE GOES!!
BAKONG
MOVING FLOORS!!
BAKONG
VWRR
FOOT STAIRS THAT MOVE IN OPPOSITE DIRECTIONS!!
GA SHUNK
ROLLERS THAT PUSH YOU THROUGH!!
GA SHUNK

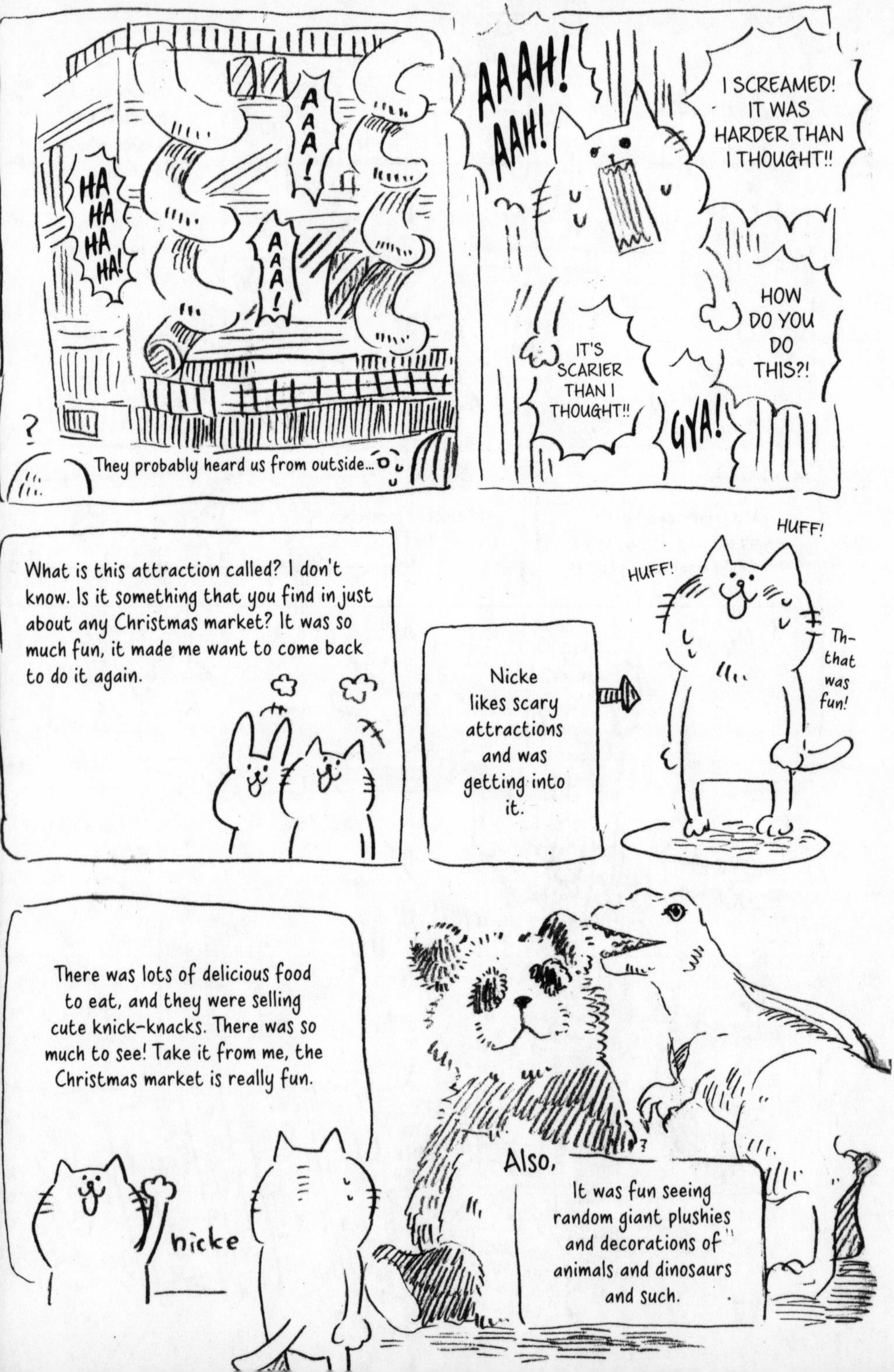
AAAH! AAH!
I SCREAMED! IT WAS HARDER THAN I THOUGHT!!
HOW DO YOU DO THIS?!
IT'S SCARIER THAN I THOUGHT!!
GYA!
AAA!
AAA!
HA HA HA HA!
?
They probably heard us from outside...
HUFF!
HUFF!
Th-that was fun!
Nicke likes scary attractions and was getting into it.
What is this attraction called? I don't know. Is it something that you find in just about any Christmas market? It was so much fun, it made me want to come back to do it again.
Also,
It was fun seeing random giant plushies and decorations of animals and dinosaurs and such.
There was lots of delicious food to eat, and they were selling cute knick-knacks. There was so much to see! Take it from me, the Christmas market is really fun.
nicke

Theo's Notebook

Oり×な...

A sphere I got from a deer I saved in the

forest. It's translucent and sparkles

if you hold it up to your eye. Its colors

shift between green and yellow. It's

lighter than it seems. Given that the deer gave it to me,

I think it might be some kind of plant.

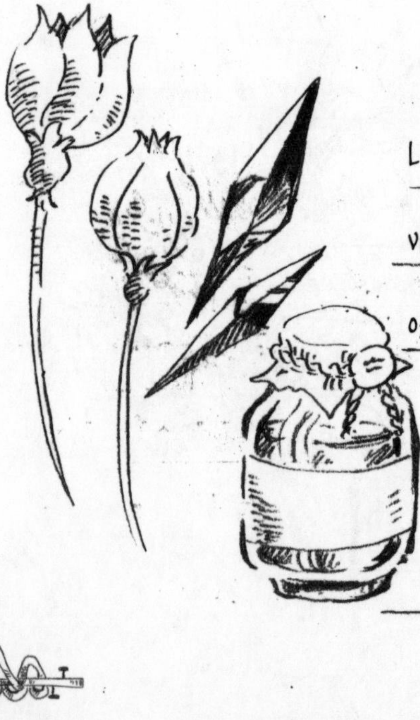

Oりな...

Lumiflowers, the special export of Doug's

village. They have five large, sheer petals

of a light pink color. The nectar inside

of the flower glows orange in dark

places. The village makes candy and

cakes out of the nectar to sell.

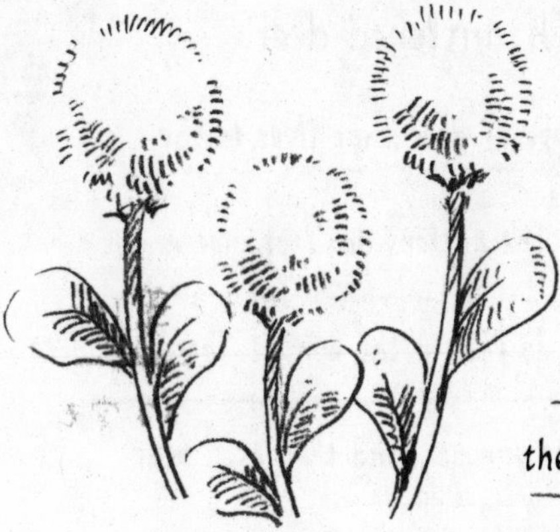

Plants that Nitch and Satch called "fluffgrass." Much of it was growing in the sage's forest. Apparently the tufts they wear around their necks were made of these. Nitch says that when the fluffy part wears down, they go and pick some more to make their mufflers.

A Karatope specialty called "makkuri." A light yellow translucent outer layer of bread that is wrapped around all sorts of ingredients. It's famous for mimicking the tall, thin buildings of the town. Mia really likes the ones with sweet boiled fruit inside.

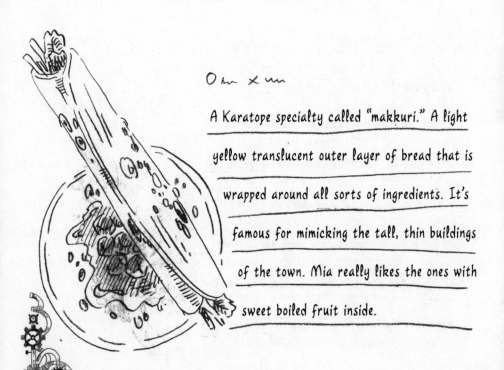

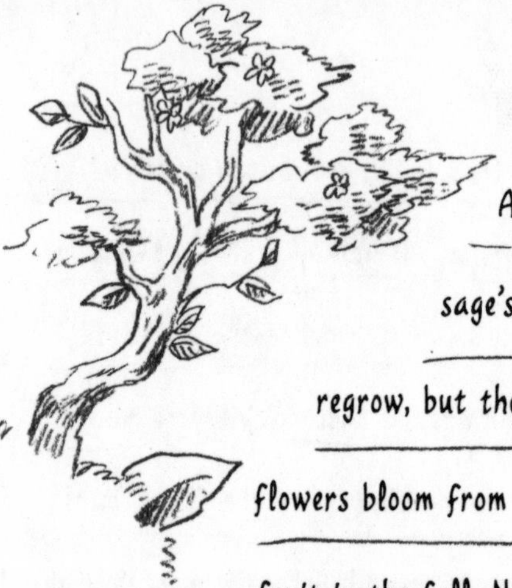

Branch-antlered deer

A rare type of deer that lives in the sage's forest. The antlers don't change and regrow, but the leaves do fall in the winter. The flowers bloom from spring to summer, and they even bear fruit in the fall. Nitch and Satch say that both males and females grow antlers, and the type of flower varies by individual.

Wugmort

The plant that is the basis for the medicine Doctor gave us. It grows along the waterside. It can be found just about anywhere and is widely used for medicine, but it only keeps for a short time. Doctor mixed it with other herbs to create a more powerful and long-lasting medicine.

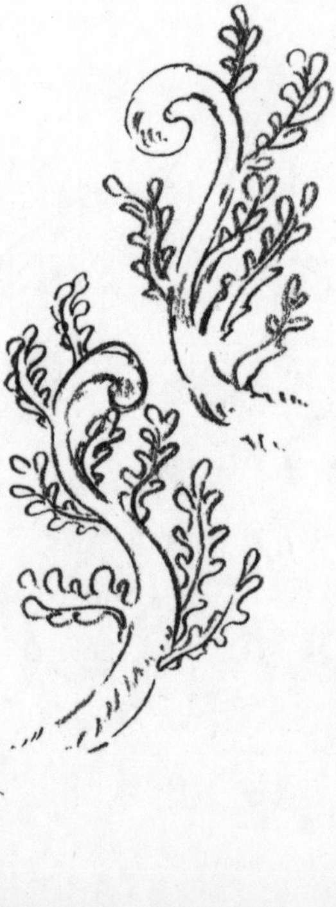

Beyond *the* Clouds

The Girl Who Fell From the Sky

A Kodansha Comics Trade Paperback Original
Beyond the Clouds 3 copyright © 2019 Nicke / Ki-oon
English translation copyright © 2020 Nicke / Ki-oon

All rights reserved.

Published in the United States by Kodansha Comics, an imprint of Kodansha USA Publishing, LLC, New York.

Publication rights for this English edition arranged with AC Media Ltd. through Tuttle-Mori Agency, Inc., Tokyo.

First published in France in 2019 by Ki-oon, an imprint of AC Media Ltd.

ISBN 978-1-63236-980-2

Printed in the United States of America.

www.kodanshacomics.com

9 8 7 6 5 4 3 2 1
Translation: Stephen Paul
Lettering: Abigail Blackman
Editing: Megan Ling
Kodansha Comics edition cover design by Phil Balsman

Publisher: Kiichiro Sugawara

Director of publishing services: Ben Applegate
Associate director of operations: Stephen Pakula
Publishing services managing editor: Noelle Webster
Assistant production manager: Emi Lotto, Angela Zurlo